Dear Customer,

Thank you for your purchase from Mometrix! We consider it an honor and a privilege that you have purchased our product and we want to ensure your satisfaction.

As part of our ongoing effort to meet the needs of test takers, we have developed a set of Study Skills Videos that we would like to give you for FREE. These videos cover our *best practices* for getting ready for your exam, from how to use our study materials to how to best prepare for the day of the test.

All that we ask is that you email us with feedback that would describe your experience so far with our product. Good, bad, or indifferent, we want to know what you think!

To get your FREE Study Skills Videos, you can use the **QR code** below, or send us an **email** at studyvideos@mometrix.com with *FREE VIDEOS* in the subject line and the following information in the body of the email:

- The name of the product you purchased.
- Your product rating on a scale of 1-5, with 5 being the highest rating.
- Your feedback. It can be long, short, or anything in between. We just want to know your impressions and experience so far with our product. (Good feedback might include how our study material met your needs and ways we might be able to make it even better. You could highlight features that you found helpful or features that you think we should add.)

If you have any questions or concerns, please don't hesitate to contact me directly.

Thanks again!

Sincerely,

Jay Willis
Vice President
jay.willis@mometrix.com
1-800-673-8175

PMP

Exam Prep 2024-2025

2 Full-Length Practice Tests

Project Management Professional Certification Secrets Study Guide with Detailed Answer Explanations

PMBOK 7th Edition

Written and edited by Mometrix Test Preparation

Printed in the United States of America

This paper meets the requirements of ANSI/NISO Z39.48-1992 (Permanence of Paper).

Paperback
ISBN 13: 978-1-5167-2513-7
ISBN 10: 1-5167-2513-1

Dear Future Exam Success Story

First of all, **THANK YOU** for purchasing Mometrix study materials!

Second, congratulations! You are one of the few determined test-takers who are committed to doing whatever it takes to excel on your exam. **You have come to the right place.** We developed these study materials with one goal in mind: to deliver you the information you need in a format that's concise and easy to use.

In addition to optimizing your guide for the content of the test, we've outlined our recommended steps for breaking down the preparation process into small, attainable goals so you can make sure you stay on track.

We've also analyzed the entire test-taking process, identifying the most common pitfalls and showing how you can overcome them and be ready for any curveball the test throws you.

Standardized testing is one of the biggest obstacles on your road to success, which only increases the importance of doing well in the high-pressure, high-stakes environment of test day. Your results on this test could have a significant impact on your future, and this guide provides the information and practical advice to help you achieve your full potential on test day.

Your success is our success

We would love to hear from you! If you would like to share the story of your exam success or if you have any questions or comments in regard to our products, please contact us at **800-673-8175** or **support@mometrix.com**.

Thanks again for your business and we wish you continued success!

Sincerely,
The Mometrix Test Preparation Team

Need more help? Check out our flashcards at:
http://mometrixflashcards.com/PMP

Written and edited by the Mometrix Exam Secrets Test Prep Team
Printed in the United States of America

Table of Contents

Introduction

Thank you for purchasing this resource! You have made the choice to prepare yourself for a test that could have a huge impact on your future, and this guide is designed to help you be fully ready for test day. Obviously, it's important to have a solid understanding of the test material, but you also need to be prepared for the unique environment and stressors of the test, so that you can perform to the best of your abilities.

For this purpose, the first section that appears in this guide is the **Secret Keys**. We've devoted countless hours to meticulously researching what works and what doesn't, and we've boiled down our findings to the five most impactful steps you can take to improve your performance on the test. We start at the beginning with study planning and move through the preparation process, all the way to the testing strategies that will help you get the most out of what you know when you're finally sitting in front of the test.

We recommend that you start preparing for your test as far in advance as possible. However, if you've bought this guide as a last-minute study resource and only have a few days before your test, we recommend that you skip over the first two Secret Keys since they address a long-term study plan.

If you struggle with **test anxiety**, we strongly encourage you to check out our recommendations for how you can overcome it. Test anxiety is a formidable foe, but it can be beaten, and we want to make sure you have the tools you need to defeat it.

Secret Key #1 – Plan Big, Study Small

There's a lot riding on your performance. If you want to ace this test, you're going to need to keep your skills sharp and the material fresh in your mind. You need a plan that lets you review everything you need to know while still fitting in your schedule. We'll break this strategy down into three categories.

Information Organization

Start with the information you already have: the official test outline. From this, you can make a complete list of all the concepts you need to cover before the test. Organize these concepts into groups that can be studied together, and create a list of any related vocabulary you need to learn so you can brush up on any difficult terms. You'll want to keep this vocabulary list handy once you actually start studying since you may need to add to it along the way.

Time Management

Once you have your set of study concepts, decide how to spread them out over the time you have left before the test. Break your study plan into small, clear goals so you have a manageable task for each day and know exactly what you're doing. Then just focus on one small step at a time. When you manage your time this way, you don't need to spend hours at a time studying. Studying a small block of content for a short period each day helps you retain information better and avoid stressing over how much you have left to do. You can relax knowing that you have a plan to cover everything in time. In order for this strategy to be effective though, you have to start studying early and stick to your schedule. Avoid the exhaustion and futility that comes from last-minute cramming!

Study Environment

The environment you study in has a big impact on your learning. Studying in a coffee shop, while probably more enjoyable, is not likely to be as fruitful as studying in a quiet room. It's important to keep distractions to a minimum. You're only planning to study for a short block of time, so make the most of it. Don't pause to check your phone or get up to find a snack. It's also important to **avoid multitasking**. Research has consistently shown that multitasking will make your studying dramatically less effective. Your study area should also be comfortable and well-lit so you don't have the distraction of straining your eyes or sitting on an uncomfortable chair.

The time of day you study is also important. You want to be rested and alert. Don't wait until just before bedtime. Study when you'll be most likely to comprehend and remember. Even better, if you know what time of day your test will be, set that time aside for study. That way your brain will be used to working on that subject at that specific time and you'll have a better chance of recalling information.

Finally, it can be helpful to team up with others who are studying for the same test. Your actual studying should be done in as isolated an environment as possible, but the work of organizing the information and setting up the study plan can be divided up. In between study sessions, you can discuss with your teammates the concepts that you're all studying and quiz each other on the details. Just be sure that your teammates are as serious about the test as you are. If you find that your study time is being replaced with social time, you might need to find a new team.

Secret Key #2 – Make Your Studying Count

You're devoting a lot of time and effort to preparing for this test, so you want to be absolutely certain it will pay off. This means doing more than just reading the content and hoping you can remember it on test day. It's important to make every minute of study count. There are two main areas you can focus on to make your studying count.

Retention

It doesn't matter how much time you study if you can't remember the material. You need to make sure you are retaining the concepts. To check your retention of the information you're learning, try recalling it at later times with minimal prompting. Try carrying around flashcards and glance at one or two from time to time or ask a friend who's also studying for the test to quiz you.

To enhance your retention, look for ways to put the information into practice so that you can apply it rather than simply recalling it. If you're using the information in practical ways, it will be much easier to remember. Similarly, it helps to solidify a concept in your mind if you're not only reading it to yourself but also explaining it to someone else. Ask a friend to let you teach them about a concept you're a little shaky on (or speak aloud to an imaginary audience if necessary). As you try to summarize, define, give examples, and answer your friend's questions, you'll understand the concepts better and they will stay with you longer. Finally, step back for a big picture view and ask yourself how each piece of information fits with the whole subject. When you link the different concepts together and see them working together as a whole, it's easier to remember the individual components.

Finally, practice showing your work on any multi-step problems, even if you're just studying. Writing out each step you take to solve a problem will help solidify the process in your mind, and you'll be more likely to remember it during the test.

Modality

Modality simply refers to the means or method by which you study. Choosing a study modality that fits your own individual learning style is crucial. No two people learn best in exactly the same way, so it's important to know your strengths and use them to your advantage.

For example, if you learn best by visualization, focus on visualizing a concept in your mind and draw an image or a diagram. Try color-coding your notes, illustrating them, or creating symbols that will trigger your mind to recall a learned concept. If you learn best by hearing or discussing information, find a study partner who learns the same way or read aloud to yourself. Think about how to put the information in your own words. Imagine that you are giving a lecture on the topic and record yourself so you can listen to it later.

For any learning style, flashcards can be helpful. Organize the information so you can take advantage of spare moments to review. Underline key words or phrases. Use different colors for different categories. Mnemonic devices (such as creating a short list in which every item starts with the same letter) can also help with retention. Find what works best for you and use it to store the information in your mind most effectively and easily.

Secret Key #3 – Practice the Right Way

Your success on test day depends not only on how many hours you put into preparing, but also on whether you prepared the right way. It's good to check along the way to see if your studying is paying off. One of the most effective ways to do this is by taking practice tests to evaluate your progress. Practice tests are useful because they show exactly where you need to improve. Every time you take a practice test, pay special attention to these three groups of questions:

- The questions you got wrong
- The questions you had to guess on, even if you guessed right
- The questions you found difficult or slow to work through

This will show you exactly what your weak areas are, and where you need to devote more study time. Ask yourself why each of these questions gave you trouble. Was it because you didn't understand the material? Was it because you didn't remember the vocabulary? Do you need more repetitions on this type of question to build speed and confidence? Dig into those questions and figure out how you can strengthen your weak areas as you go back to review the material.

Additionally, many practice tests have a section explaining the answer choices. It can be tempting to read the explanation and think that you now have a good understanding of the concept. However, an explanation likely only covers part of the question's broader context. Even if the explanation makes perfect sense, **go back and investigate** every concept related to the question until you're positive you have a thorough understanding.

As you go along, keep in mind that the practice test is just that: practice. Memorizing these questions and answers will not be very helpful on the actual test because it is unlikely to have any of the same exact questions. If you only know the right answers to the sample questions, you won't be prepared for the real thing. **Study the concepts** until you understand them fully, and then you'll be able to answer any question that shows up on the test.

It's important to wait on the practice tests until you're ready. If you take a test on your first day of study, you may be overwhelmed by the amount of material covered and how much you need to learn. Work up to it gradually.

On test day, you'll need to be prepared for answering questions, managing your time, and using the test-taking strategies you've learned. It's a lot to balance, like a mental marathon that will have a big impact on your future. Like training for a marathon, you'll need to start slowly and work your way up. When test day arrives, you'll be ready.

Start with the strategies you've read in the first two Secret Keys—plan your course and study in the way that works best for you. If you have time, consider using multiple study resources to get different approaches to the same concepts. It can be helpful to see difficult concepts from more than one angle. Then find a good source for practice tests. Many times, the test website will suggest potential study resources or provide sample tests.

Practice Test Strategy

If you're able to find at least three practice tests, we recommend this strategy:

Untimed and Open-Book Practice

Take the first test with no time constraints and with your notes and study guide handy. Take your time and focus on applying the strategies you've learned.

Timed and Open-Book Practice

Take the second practice test open-book as well, but set a timer and practice pacing yourself to finish in time.

Timed and Closed-Book Practice

Take any other practice tests as if it were test day. Set a timer and put away your study materials. Sit at a table or desk in a quiet room, imagine yourself at the testing center, and answer questions as quickly and accurately as possible.

Keep repeating timed and closed-book tests on a regular basis until you run out of practice tests or it's time for the actual test. Your mind will be ready for the schedule and stress of test day, and you'll be able to focus on recalling the material you've learned.

Secret Key #4 – Pace Yourself

Once you're fully prepared for the material on the test, your biggest challenge on test day will be managing your time. Just knowing that the clock is ticking can make you panic even if you have plenty of time left. Work on pacing yourself so you can build confidence against the time constraints of the exam. Pacing is a difficult skill to master, especially in a high-pressure environment, so **practice is vital**.

Set time expectations for your pace based on how much time is available. For example, if a section has 60 questions and the time limit is 30 minutes, you know you have to average 30 seconds or less per question in order to answer them all. Although 30 seconds is the hard limit, set 25 seconds per question as your goal, so you reserve extra time to spend on harder questions. When you budget extra time for the harder questions, you no longer have any reason to stress when those questions take longer to answer.

Don't let this time expectation distract you from working through the test at a calm, steady pace, but keep it in mind so you don't spend too much time on any one question. Recognize that taking extra time on one question you don't understand may keep you from answering two that you do understand later in the test. If your time limit for a question is up and you're still not sure of the answer, mark it and move on, and come back to it later if the time and the test format allow. If the testing format doesn't allow you to return to earlier questions, just make an educated guess; then put it out of your mind and move on.

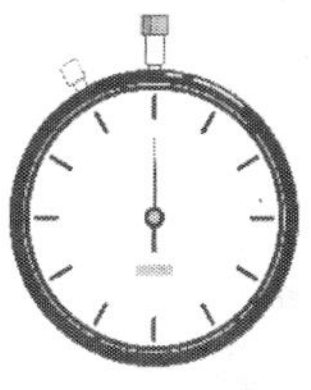

On the easier questions, be careful not to rush. It may seem wise to hurry through them so you have more time for the challenging ones, but it's not worth missing one if you know the concept and just didn't take the time to read the question fully. Work efficiently but make sure you understand the question and have looked at all of the answer choices, since more than one may seem right at first.

Even if you're paying attention to the time, you may find yourself a little behind at some point. You should speed up to get back on track, but do so wisely. Don't panic; just take a few seconds less on each question until you're caught up. Don't guess without thinking, but do look through the answer choices and eliminate any you know are wrong. If you can get down to two choices, it is often worthwhile to guess from those. Once you've chosen an answer, move on and don't dwell on any that you skipped or had to hurry through. If a question was taking too long, chances are it was one of the harder ones, so you weren't as likely to get it right anyway.

On the other hand, if you find yourself getting ahead of schedule, it may be beneficial to slow down a little. The more quickly you work, the more likely you are to make a careless mistake that will affect your score. You've budgeted time for each question, so don't be afraid to spend that time. Practice an efficient but careful pace to get the most out of the time you have.

Secret Key #5 – Have a Plan for Guessing

When you're taking the test, you may find yourself stuck on a question. Some of the answer choices seem better than others, but you don't see the one answer choice that is obviously correct. What do you do?

The scenario described above is very common, yet most test takers have not effectively prepared for it. Developing and practicing a plan for guessing may be one of the single most effective uses of your time as you get ready for the exam.

In developing your plan for guessing, there are three questions to address:

- When should you start the guessing process?
- How should you narrow down the choices?
- Which answer should you choose?

When to Start the Guessing Process

Unless your plan for guessing is to select C every time (which, despite its merits, is not what we recommend), you need to leave yourself enough time to apply your answer elimination strategies. Since you have a limited amount of time for each question, that means that if you're going to give yourself the best shot at guessing correctly, you have to decide quickly whether or not you will guess.

Of course, the best-case scenario is that you don't have to guess at all, so first, see if you can answer the question based on your knowledge of the subject and basic reasoning skills. Focus on the key words in the question and try to jog your memory of related topics. Give yourself a chance to bring the knowledge to mind, but once you realize that you don't have (or you can't access) the knowledge you need to answer the question, it's time to start the guessing process.

It's almost always better to start the guessing process too early than too late. It only takes a few seconds to remember something and answer the question from knowledge. Carefully eliminating wrong answer choices takes longer. Plus, going through the process of eliminating answer choices can actually help jog your memory.

Summary: Start the guessing process as soon as you decide that you can't answer the question based on your knowledge.

How to Narrow Down the Choices

The next chapter in this book (**Test-Taking Strategies**) includes a wide range of strategies for how to approach questions and how to look for answer choices to eliminate. You will definitely want to read those carefully, practice them, and figure out which ones work best for you. Here though, we're going to address a mindset rather than a particular strategy.

Your odds of guessing an answer correctly depend on how many options you are choosing from.

Number of options left	5	4	3	2	1
Odds of guessing correctly	20%	25%	33%	50%	100%

You can see from this chart just how valuable it is to be able to eliminate incorrect answers and make an educated guess, but there are two things that many test takers do that cause them to miss out on the benefits of guessing:

- Accidentally eliminating the correct answer
- Selecting an answer based on an impression

We'll look at the first one here, and the second one in the next section.

To avoid accidentally eliminating the correct answer, we recommend a thought exercise called **the $5 challenge**. In this challenge, you only eliminate an answer choice from contention if you are willing to bet $5 on it being wrong. Why $5? Five dollars is a small but not insignificant amount of money. It's an amount you could afford to lose but wouldn't want to throw away. And while losing $5 once might not hurt too much, doing it twenty times will set you back $100. In the same way, each small decision you make—eliminating a choice here, guessing on a question there—won't by itself impact your score very much, but when you put them all together, they can make a big difference. By holding each answer choice elimination decision to a higher standard, you can reduce the risk of accidentally eliminating the correct answer.

The $5 challenge can also be applied in a positive sense: If you are willing to bet $5 that an answer choice *is* correct, go ahead and mark it as correct.

Summary: Only eliminate an answer choice if you are willing to bet $5 that it is wrong.

Which Answer to Choose

You're taking the test. You've run into a hard question and decided you'll have to guess. You've eliminated all the answer choices you're willing to bet $5 on. Now you have to pick an answer. Why do we even need to talk about this? Why can't you just pick whichever one you feel like when the time comes?

The answer to these questions is that if you don't come into the test with a plan, you'll rely on your impression to select an answer choice, and if you do that, you risk falling into a trap. The test writers know that everyone who takes their test will be guessing on some of the questions, so they intentionally write wrong answer choices to seem plausible. You still have to pick an answer though, and if the wrong answer choices are designed to look right, how can you ever be sure that you're not falling for their trap? The best solution we've found to this dilemma is to take the decision out of your hands entirely. Here is the process we recommend:

Once you've eliminated any choices that you are confident (willing to bet $5) are wrong, select the first remaining choice as your answer.

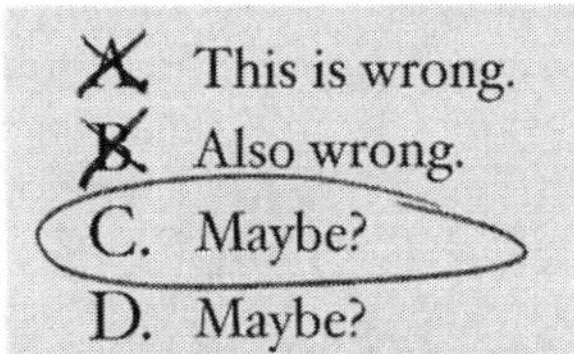

Whether you choose to select the first remaining choice, the second, or the last, the important thing is that you use some preselected standard. Using this approach guarantees that you will not be enticed into selecting an answer choice that looks right, because you are not basing your decision on how the answer choices look.

This is not meant to make you question your knowledge. Instead, it is to help you recognize the difference between your knowledge and your impressions. There's a huge difference between thinking an answer is right because of what you know, and thinking an answer is right because it looks or sounds like it should be right.

Summary: To ensure that your selection is appropriately random, make a predetermined selection from among all answer choices you have not eliminated.

Test-Taking Strategies

This section contains a list of test-taking strategies that you may find helpful as you work through the test. By taking what you know and applying logical thought, you can maximize your chances of answering any question correctly!

It is very important to realize that every question is different and every person is different: no single strategy will work on every question, and no single strategy will work for every person. That's why we've included all of them here, so you can try them out and determine which ones work best for different types of questions and which ones work best for you.

Question Strategies

READ CAREFULLY

Read the question and the answer choices carefully. Don't miss the question because you misread the terms. You have plenty of time to read each question thoroughly and make sure you understand what is being asked. Yet a happy medium must be attained, so don't waste too much time. You must read carefully and efficiently.

CONTEXTUAL CLUES

Look for contextual clues. If the question includes a word you are not familiar with, look at the immediate context for some indication of what the word might mean. Contextual clues can often give you all the information you need to decipher the meaning of an unfamiliar word. Even if you can't determine the meaning, you may be able to narrow down the possibilities enough to make a solid guess at the answer to the question.

PREFIXES

If you're having trouble with a word in the question or answer choices, try dissecting it. Take advantage of every clue that the word might include. Prefixes can be a huge help. Usually, they allow you to determine a basic meaning. *Pre-* means before, *post-* means after, *pro-* is positive, *de-* is negative. From prefixes, you can get an idea of the general meaning of the word and try to put it into context.

HEDGE WORDS

Watch out for critical hedge words, such as *likely, may, can, sometimes, often, almost, mostly, usually, generally, rarely,* and *sometimes.* Question writers insert these hedge phrases to cover every possibility. Often an answer choice will be wrong simply because it leaves no room for exception. Be on guard for answer choices that have definitive words such as *exactly* and *always.*

SWITCHBACK WORDS

Stay alert for *switchbacks.* These are the words and phrases frequently used to alert you to shifts in thought. The most common switchback words are *but, although,* and *however.* Others include *nevertheless, on the other hand, even though, while, in spite of, despite,* and *regardless of.* Switchback words are important to catch because they can change the direction of the question or an answer choice.

✓ Face Value

When in doubt, use common sense. Accept the situation in the problem at face value. Don't read too much into it. These problems will not require you to make wild assumptions. If you have to go beyond creativity and warp time or space in order to have an answer choice fit the question, then you should move on and consider the other answer choices. These are normal problems rooted in reality. The applicable relationship or explanation may not be readily apparent, but it is there for you to figure out. Use your common sense to interpret anything that isn't clear.

Answer Choice Strategies

✓ Answer Selection

The most thorough way to pick an answer choice is to identify and eliminate wrong answers until only one is left, then confirm it is the correct answer. Sometimes an answer choice may immediately seem right, but be careful. The test writers will usually put more than one reasonable answer choice on each question, so take a second to read all of them and make sure that the other choices are not equally obvious. As long as you have time left, it is better to read every answer choice than to pick the first one that looks right without checking the others.

✓ Answer Choice Families

An answer choice family consists of two (in rare cases, three) answer choices that are very similar in construction and cannot all be true at the same time. If you see two answer choices that are direct opposites or parallels, one of them is usually the correct answer. For instance, if one answer choice says that quantity *x* increases and another either says that quantity *x* decreases (opposite) or says that quantity *y* increases (parallel), then those answer choices would fall into the same family. An answer choice that doesn't match the construction of the answer choice family is more likely to be incorrect. Most questions will not have answer choice families, but when they do appear, you should be prepared to recognize them.

✓ Eliminate Answers

Eliminate answer choices as soon as you realize they are wrong, but make sure you consider all possibilities. If you are eliminating answer choices and realize that the last one you are left with is also wrong, don't panic. Start over and consider each choice again. There may be something you missed the first time that you will realize on the second pass.

✓ Avoid Fact Traps

Don't be distracted by an answer choice that is factually true but doesn't answer the question. You are looking for the choice that answers the question. Stay focused on what the question is asking for so you don't accidentally pick an answer that is true but incorrect. Always go back to the question and make sure the answer choice you've selected actually answers the question and is not merely a true statement.

✓ Extreme Statements

In general, you should avoid answers that put forth extreme actions as standard practice or proclaim controversial ideas as established fact. An answer choice that states the "process should be used in certain situations, if…" is much more likely to be correct than one that states the "process should be discontinued completely." The first is a calm rational statement and doesn't even make a definitive, uncompromising stance, using a hedge word *if* to provide wiggle room, whereas the second choice is far more extreme.

☑ BENCHMARK

As you read through the answer choices and you come across one that seems to answer the question well, mentally select that answer choice. This is not your final answer, but it's the one that will help you evaluate the other answer choices. The one that you selected is your benchmark or standard for judging each of the other answer choices. Every other answer choice must be compared to your benchmark. That choice is correct until proven otherwise by another answer choice beating it. If you find a better answer, then that one becomes your new benchmark. Once you've decided that no other choice answers the question as well as your benchmark, you have your final answer.

☑ PREDICT THE ANSWER

Before you even start looking at the answer choices, it is often best to try to predict the answer. When you come up with the answer on your own, it is easier to avoid distractions and traps because you will know exactly what to look for. The right answer choice is unlikely to be word-for-word what you came up with, but it should be a close match. Even if you are confident that you have the right answer, you should still take the time to read each option before moving on.

General Strategies

☑ TOUGH QUESTIONS

If you are stumped on a problem or it appears too hard or too difficult, don't waste time. Move on! Remember though, if you can quickly check for obviously incorrect answer choices, your chances of guessing correctly are greatly improved. Before you completely give up, at least try to knock out a couple of possible answers. Eliminate what you can and then guess at the remaining answer choices before moving on.

☑ CHECK YOUR WORK

Since you will probably not know every term listed and the answer to every question, it is important that you get credit for the ones that you do know. Don't miss any questions through careless mistakes. If at all possible, try to take a second to look back over your answer selection and make sure you've selected the correct answer choice and haven't made a costly careless mistake (such as marking an answer choice that you didn't mean to mark). This quick double check should more than pay for itself in caught mistakes for the time it costs.

☑ PACE YOURSELF

It's easy to be overwhelmed when you're looking at a page full of questions; your mind is confused and full of random thoughts, and the clock is ticking down faster than you would like. Calm down and maintain the pace that you have set for yourself. Especially as you get down to the last few minutes of the test, don't let the small numbers on the clock make you panic. As long as you are on track by monitoring your pace, you are guaranteed to have time for each question.

☑ DON'T RUSH

It is very easy to make errors when you are in a hurry. Maintaining a fast pace in answering questions is pointless if it makes you miss questions that you would have gotten right otherwise. Test writers like to include distracting information and wrong answers that seem right. Taking a little extra time to avoid careless mistakes can make all the difference in your test score. Find a pace that allows you to be confident in the answers that you select.

✓ Keep Moving

Panicking will not help you pass the test, so do your best to stay calm and keep moving. Taking deep breaths and going through the answer elimination steps you practiced can help to break through a stress barrier and keep your pace.

Final Notes

The combination of a solid foundation of content knowledge and the confidence that comes from practicing your plan for applying that knowledge is the key to maximizing your performance on test day. As your foundation of content knowledge is built up and strengthened, you'll find that the strategies included in this chapter become more and more effective in helping you quickly sift through the distractions and traps of the test to isolate the correct answer.

Now that you're preparing to move forward into the test content chapters of this book, be sure to keep your goal in mind. As you read, think about how you will be able to apply this information on the test. If you've already seen sample questions for the test and you have an idea of the question format and style, try to come up with questions of your own that you can answer based on what you're reading. This will give you valuable practice applying your knowledge in the same ways you can expect to on test day.

Good luck and good studying!

Where To Begin (Read First!)

Depending on where you are in your project management journey, **you may not need to read everything** we've included in this guide. Refer to the outline below to determine which sections of the guide ought to be given your time and attention.

MOMETRIX'S PMP GUIDE FOR PMBOK 6

The PMP exam still requires knowledge of the processes and practices used prior to PMBOK 7. This section of the guide provides a refresher on that content in case you're new to PMI.

AGILE

The PMP exam now requires knowledge of Agile processes and practices as well. For those new to Agile, this section will provide a useful reference for the questions requiring knowledge of Agile.

PRINCIPLES

PMI identifies 12 key principles that underlie all project management activities. This section gives an overview of these guiding principles.

PERFORMANCE DOMAINS

PMI identifies 8 performance domains that describe the activities undertaken within project management. This section outlines those activities.

TAILORING

Not all projects are the same, and not every approach, method, or process will be equally effective on every project. This section discusses the process of tailoring the management of each project to its particular needs.

MODELS, METHODS, AND ARTIFACTS

This section reviews the basic models (ways to conceptualize real-world phenomena), methods (means of accomplishing goals), and artifacts (documentation created for a project) that will be used or produced during a project.

PMP EXAM TIPS

The PMP exam has some peculiarities that test takers would do well to understand going in. Review this section for some practical advice on how to approach the questions you will encounter.

PMP PRACTICE TESTS

Following the content sections, you'll find two full-length practice tests with questions that model the rigor, complexity, and coverage of those that you will encounter on the PMP exam. Use these to gauge your readiness for the exam. Although one test is printed in the book for your convenience, we recommend taking them both via the online interactive interface to better model your actual test day experience.

Mometrix's PMP Guide for PMBOK 6

Note: This is not the entirety of our previous study guide edition, but it includes all of the most essential elements for the current version of the exam.

Foundational Elements

Project

A project is officially defined by the Project Management Institute as "a temporary endeavor undertaken to create a unique product, service, or result." A project typically consists of many phases that essentially serve to plan, procure, execute, and communicate the project. Projects—and their subcomponents, called deliverables—are the events that are performed to achieve broader organizational objectives. The project is temporary in the sense that a defined start date and end date are expected and essential to planning. Examples of projects include quality improvement initiatives, building construction, developing a new consumer product, launching a space satellite, conducting field research in economics, and retooling a factory.

Unique services or the ability to perform such services may be considered a deliverable. Unique products as a deliverable can be a new consumer good, a part or component to another good, or an improvement upon an existing product or service. Unique results as a deliverable may include finished research, gained knowledge or skill, and marketplace performance. The final form of deliverable is a combination of the three.

Projects, especially those that are tied to organizational or strategic objectives, are evidence of organizational change. Projects serve to transform all or part of organizations from a lower former state to an improved, stronger, and more competitive future state. Projects can vary in how much change they create and how widely across an organization or marketplace they can influence. Nonetheless, the incremental progress of project deliverables and completion of projects serves to transform and ultimately create business value or stronger achievement of an organization's mission. For example, a for-profit company can undertake an operational improvement project to reduce costs by several hundred million dollars. Business value may materialize as stronger stock performance, greater market share, higher profits, higher revenues, or brand reputation. A nonprofit organization may perform a project to launch a new fundraising initiative in a new continent or country where their mission can grow. Nonprofit value creation can include stronger financial security, wider influence, higher membership, lower costs, and public benefits.

Importance of Project Management

Project Management

Project management is defined as the discipline of achieving project objectives through the skillful use of communication, knowledge, tools, and resources. Project management is used in order to efficiently and effectively achieve planned project objectives. It facilitates organizational improvement and achievement of the desired future state of the organization. As a set of tools and behaviors, project management also allows individuals, teams, and organizations to satisfy stakeholders, meet broader strategic or business goals, better use limited resources, and execute projects on time and on budget. When executed effectively, project management is a transformative discipline for organizations seeking growth, improvement, and excellence.

Project, Portfolio, Program, and Operations Management

Projects, Portfolios, and Programs

Organizations may use a hierarchy of project management systems to achieve larger organizational change and meet objectives. At the base of the hierarchy is the project itself. A program is defined as a collective series of interrelated projects and related supporting program administrative activities that all support a related objective or strategic goal. Programs are often used to coordinate the resources and benefits of multiple projects, though not necessarily on a wide or expansive scale. Portfolios are used by larger organizations and multinational corporations to coordinate programs and subprojects on a larger scope. Project, program, and portfolio managers all utilize project management principles, yet must be cognizant of the resource constraints created with multiple layers of management working towards strategic accomplishment. Practices such as portfolio review, project executive oversight, and strategic alignment can all play important roles in coordinating these hierarchical project scales.

Program Management and Interdependency Management

Program management is a broader classification of the project management discipline where multiple projects within an affiliated scope or strategic focus can be grouped into a larger collective called a program. Program management has a longer life cycle, broader scope, and higher-level planning than underlying projects. The high-level planning by program managers must account for the interdependency of the components, subprojects, and shared resources within the organization between other programs and projects, not simply within one project itself. Program managers must monitor interdependencies such as continued scope alignment, risks, resource conflicts and constraints, change requests, budget overlaps, and benefits realization.

Portfolio Management

Portfolio management is defined as the oversight and management of an array of programs, projects, and supporting activities, but it is more closely tied to execution of overall organizational strategy and objectives. Though the projects and programs within portfolios are often interdependent and interrelated, this is not necessarily always the case. The function of portfolio management includes steering programs and projects to maximize organizational return on investment, steer program and project economics, optimize project and program timing to meet organizational strategy, centralize common tasks and resources where needed, provide strategic decision-making, and influence investment decisions by the organization as they relate to strategy.

Operations Management

Operations management is the planning and execution of day-to-day and year-to-year business operations activities to meet customer demands for goods and services. Operations management is concerned with the activities that are required to transform raw materials and inputs into sellable outputs meeting customer quality expectations. Though this is not directly an aspect of project management, both disciplines can occur simultaneously in an organization and have to compete for shared financial, personnel, and scheduling resources. Projects may be undertaken that positively or negatively affect operations. Likewise, operational needs may influence when projects can be scheduled and completed.

Organizational Project Management

The interaction of projects, programs, and portfolios within an organization seeking to achieve strategic business objectives often requires that an organization use organizational project management (OPM) to better coordinate all such efforts efficiently. The correct allocation of resources, and selection of projects that align with and best achieve strategic objectives, are the primary goals of OPM.

Key Project Components

Project Life Cycle and Development Life Cycle

Project life cycle is defined by the Project Management Institute as the ordered set of phases that a project flows through from its start through its completion. The project life cycle has a common framework pattern that generally remains consistent regardless of the specific goals or outcomes being sought: start, preparation, execution, and closing. Project life cycles are classified as either predictive or adaptive, depending upon when planning and adjustments are made to the cycle. Adaptive projects have a predetermined scope in the start phase but continue with increased agility in the face of changes. Predictive project models are more traditional and take a waterfall approach. Early scope, cost, and resource decisions are made, and strong control is placed on the flow of the project. Development life cycles also include iterative models (where the project scope is set, but cost and resource decisions are made as the project evolves over time) and incremental models (where functionality is added over a set schedule to achieve the deliverable).

Project Phase

A project phase is defined as a group of common and logically similar activities that are performed simultaneously or sequentially in a project in order to complete a deliverable or milestone that signifies the transition into a new or next phase. Phases can be labeled with numbers or letters, or they can be labeled by duration, by the types of resources being developed, or using the key deliverable(s) that conclude the phase. Furthermore, projects may be broken down into common colloquial terms based on the typical deliverables that similar projects require. For example, a project to launch a new consumer product would likely include phases such as research and development, consumer testing, and packaging design. The phase concept in projects allows compartmentalization of the tasks and milestones, division of labor, and paced execution needed to achieve the final goals.

Phase Gate

The phase gate is a figurative point at the end of each phase where project management and/or organization decision-makers determine if the phase outcome has been successful and how the project should continue. Previous performance indicators are reviewed based on what was performed in the phase to that point. Decision-makers determine based on the data if they should move on to the next phase, adjust their approach to the project and move to the next phase, repeat the phase, continue working on elements of the current phase, or end the project entirely. Decision-makers are likely to use the project management plan, the project charter, strategic objectives, and other business-related data to make their determination to either go through the gate to the next phase or not. Phase gate steps are very common in product or service development projects where feasibility and design must be proven before launch.

Project Management Processes and Process Categories

The execution of project management processes serves the project manager in keeping the project life cycle on track. The concept of project management (PM) process is applicable across many industries that use project management techniques. The underlying concept of their use is that inputs entering a process become transformed using tools and techniques to create an output or outcome. That output or outcome of one process becomes either the input for a downstream process, a phase-completing deliverable, or a final project deliverable. Generally, PM processes can be categorized by their frequency of use: one-time predefined, recurring, or continuous. One-time predefined processes can include writing the charter or other unique actions to be taken. Recurring processes can include phase gates, resource procurements, or data analysis. Continuous processes are those that are fundamental to effective project management and can include examples such as monitoring, communication, and control activities.

Project Management Process Groups

Project management process groups are created when assessing and logically grouping related processes and activities into collective groups that support achievement of specific objectives in the project. While project phases follow a more time-based flow, process groups are not necessarily chronological and may draw from tasks in various points in the project. Process can be classified into five major groups: monitoring, planning, executing, initiating, and closing.

Process Group	Description
Initiating	Grouped activities that define the charter, team, working rules, new phases, and project authorization.
Planning	Activities that create the project scope, objectives, and project work-breakdown and schedule.
Executing	Activities that perform the planned work in the project.
Monitoring	Processes that oversee the use of time, resources, quality, and change management.
Closing	Processes used to complete phases or the project itself.

Project Management Knowledge Area

Project management knowledge areas (PMKAs) are essential disciplines within the Project Management Professional body of knowledge. Each knowledge area is characterized by the relatively unique skill that the project manager must have to be successful in it. Similar to process groups, knowledge areas are defined by their typical tasks, inputs, and outputs, and the tools used to transform. Each knowledge area requires different skill sets to achieve mastery, such as communication, time management, financial management, and stakeholder analysis.

Knowledge Area	Description
Quality management	Involves processes related to product or service quality parameters, voice of the customer, and project management process quality.
Cost management	Area based on financial and budget constraints involving cost management, financing, planning, estimating, and cost control.
Schedule management	Processes related to accurately scheduling the project and keeping it on schedule thereafter.
Scope management	Processes involved in ensuring that only the defined work in the project scope gets completed.
Integration management	Involves integrating and coordinating the activities within the project process groups.
Stakeholder management	Involves analyzing internal and external stakeholders and how the project progress and outcomes impact these important persons or organizations.
Procurement management	Processes involved in buying or obtaining the goods, services, and outcomes needed from contributors outside of the project team.
Risk management	Involves risk management studies and mitigation.
Communications management	Includes timely and accurate collection, distribution, and control of information.
Resource management	Involves the identification and attainment of the right resources for project completion.

Importance of Project Management Data and Information

An expected result of project management planning and execution is the generation of various forms of data that are analyzed, communicated, and ultimately transformed into useful information throughout the project life cycle and further used for project decision-making. The resulting data and information can be both stored in a repository and communicated in progress reports to various stakeholders as necessary to the project team. The terminology commonly associated to the project management process is work performance. The term is used to refer specifically to data, information, and reports that arise from the project management process. Work performance data —such as activity completion dates, quality measurements, and completion progress—is raw data collected during the execution of the project and its knowledge areas. Work performance information is the result of data transformed through analysis to make project insights and decisions. Work performance reporting refers to relevant communications and summaries of critical data and information gained through the project management process.

Tailoring

Tailoring is defined as the appropriate application of the necessary inputs, tools, techniques, and phases to manage a given project effectively. The tailoring concept is used for project management because there is no one methodology applicable to all projects. Methodology for project management can vary based on expert insights, professional groups, third-party vendors, and government agencies. Project managers are responsible for collaborating with stakeholders, the project team, organizational leadership, and persons overseeing resource allocation to tailor the project approach accordingly. Many factors must be considered, including timeframe, quality requirements, resource constraints, financial needs, internal and external stakeholders, and risk. These constraints can compete with each other and will invariably drive tailoring decisions by the project manager. This concept is discussed in a separate chapter of this guide.

Project Management Business Documents

Business Cases

The project business case document is used in the life cycle of the project to establish the economic feasibility and validity of the planned project. The business case justifies the start and continuation of the project. Business case files demonstrate, especially to stakeholders and public shareholders, that the undertaking of a certain project will be of benefit to the organization and will be a value-added use of limited capital and human resources. The importance of such an approach is reflected in the preference for projects that align with organizational objectives and are a wise use of resources towards stated goals.

Business Benefits Management Plans

The business benefits management plan is a precursor document that describes how and when the benefits of the project itself will be realized by the organization. The benefits management plan explains the specific mechanics of how the benefit is realized; business case files often serve as the input to create the benefits plan. The benefits plan serves to specifically show the financial and measurable gains that will be achieved. It begins with baseline data analysis of the current state. The proposed future state is described in the early phases of the project. As the project nears completion, actual measurements of the improved state can be compiled and demonstrate the true benefit.

Project Charters

The project charter is an official documentation of the project's authorization—generally issued by the project sponsor or champion to a project manager—and signals the approval for the project to begin initial phases and resource procurement. **The charter is a critical milestone in a project and reflects the organization's acknowledgement that the project meets strategic objectives and has a satisfactory business case and benefit to be pursued. The charter names and authorizes the project manager to begin work on the project.** The charter also initiates the use of the project management plan—a detailed account of how project resources will be utilized during the project life cycle. Key elements of the charter include project objectives, purpose, and deliverables needed for success. Secondary but important elements include explanation of risks, financial and time constraints, project assumptions, identification of the manager and project team, and information about key stakeholders. Under Project Management Professional criteria, a project is not authorized to start without an approved charter.

Key Success Measures in Project Management

Key success measures are established at the start of the project by the project manager and key stakeholders. The measures of success are determined, as well as how success is to be measured and what aspects of the project will impact the desired success. Key success measures are likely to include traditional measurements, such as time, budget, quality, and scope. However, it is in the interest of the organization and project stakeholders that success is also measured by how well the project meets organizational objectives and achieves the planned benefit. Key success measures can be included as an element of the project charter. Common measurements include customer satisfaction, schedule attainment, return on investment, cost savings realized, payback period, meeting strategic objectives, or meeting business case objectives.

Project Operating Environment

Enterprise Environmental Factors

Internal to the Organization

Enterprise environmental factors (EEFs) are circumstances that occur outside of the control of the project management team that may influence the actions taken by the team. Internal EEFs are those factors that occur within the organization performing the project. These factors are indicative of how the organization is designed and operated.

Factor	Description
Organizational design, culture, and governance	The mission and vision established for the organization, the cultural behaviors, and the levels of authority that exist.
Physical location of the operations	Where the operations and teams are located geographically.
Infrastructure	Facilities, telecommunications, information technology, operating capacity, and related equipment.
IT software	Software programs used and available, such as project management software, enterprise resource planning, and design software.
Resources	Vendors and related approval processes, subcontractors, and contractual agreements.
Employees	Human resources, skill sets, training, and competencies.

External to the Organization

All organizations operate within an external ecosystem of influences from various markets, governments, geopolitical events, social forces, cultures, and natural phenomena. Project managers and organizational leadership must be attentive to the external factors when designing business strategies and project charters, as well as project risks and deliverables.

Factor	Description
Government regulations	Local, state, national, and international laws that determine permitted and restricted actions by an organization.
Legal business restrictions	Laws related to employees, business conduct, and purchasing.
Fiscal influences	Access to capital markets, interest rates, inflation, trade factors.
Marketplace barriers	Intellectual property, competitive forces, market share.
Social and cultural factors	Ethics and social norms, identity politics, public perception.
Environmental impacts	Geographic locations, weather, seasons, climate changes, working conditions.
Project management commercial databases	Compiled data regarding risks, benchmarking, and cost estimates.
Scientific research	Evidence-based studies, expert knowledge, and benchmarking.

Organizational Process Assets

Overview

Organizational process assets (OPAs) are both historical practices and the knowledge that any stakeholders or supportive elements involved in the project are able to bring to its execution to influence the project management process. Many supportive persons, organizations, vendors, and stakeholders are involved with project phases and execution. These individuals or organizations have various levels of **policies, procedures, expertise, and processes** that can add value to any current project they are involved in. Project managers benefit from identifying and using these OPAs to their advantage to achieve project deliverables. Although organizations often may house a dedicated project management office that oversees project policies, procedures, and plans, organizational knowledge bases represent assets—in the form of lessons learned, adjustments, quality issues, and financial performances—that are gained during the course of the execution of the project's phases. Successful organizations using project management are apt at managing expertise assets, as well as learning from the inconsistencies as they occur.

Policies and Procedures

Project Policies and Procedures Related to Initiating, Planning, and Closing Projects

Within the context of OPAs, an organization has at its disposal well-defined polices and historical practices for project process groups, including the initiating, planning, and closing activities. OPAs in the initiating and planning groups include foundational approaches to organizational behavior and project quality. Policies focused on health, safety, environmental and quality standards, human resource standards, and security are common in these asset groups. Furthermore, organizational policies on tailoring, project life cycles, metrics, and management methods serve as administrative norms. Other common assets for initiating and planning include project management templates commonly used in the process. The closing assets often include evaluation methods, policies on follow-up auditing, agreement closure, and steps necessary to transfer ownership of an asset or service to another stakeholder.

PROJECT POLICIES AND PROCEDURES RELATED TO EXECUTION, MONITORING, AND CONTROLLING PROJECTS

OPAs utilized in an organization's project management system would be commonly used and available to project managers as standards and guidance for actionable project process groups, such as execution and monitoring. These critical phases often contain unexpected risks and delays to the project; having well-defined procedures to manage through these difficult parts of the project inevitably improves project outcomes. Common policies and procedures in the execution process group can include change management processes, financial controls and accounting practices for projects, quality milestones and policies to be monitored throughout the project, communication policies, workflow prioritization, verification procedures, and validation methods.

ORGANIZATIONAL KNOWLEDGE REPOSITORIES

Organizations performing multiple project management streams simultaneously and over the course of many periods benefit from the shared knowledge gained from each project. Databases and knowledge mines give project planning and management stakeholders the advantage of organizational learning, faster lead times in the early project phases, more rapid execution, and lower unforeseen risks in future projects. Tools such as quality management systems, shared document servers, resource planning platforms, and unified communication methods all reduce the barriers to repeat success. Project management-specific repositories often include shared project management software platforms, shared project document templates, financial databases, vendor management databases (such as enterprise resource planning specifically used for projects), and formal project final reports from past projects. Furthermore, these repositories are ideal places to store past metric performance data, past data on schedule attainment and risk analysis, and past decision-making on project tailoring and business cases.

ORGANIZATIONAL SYSTEMS OVERVIEW

THEORY OF BUSINESS ORGANIZATION SYSTEMS

Organizations—whether for-profit or nonprofit—operate under the constraints and influence of organizational behavior and dynamics. Organizations consist of people, and those people have various levels of influence, power, leadership, and capabilities that can have degrees of benefit or detriment to any project. Foremost, top leadership of an organization must be accountable to develop a well-functioning organizational design and culture that both establish the means to effective project management. The project manager and related stakeholders must be able to recognize the power, influence, relationships, and competencies that they and their other stakeholders have towards the successful completion of a project. It is likewise important for project managers to understand the organizational governance and norms as they relate to individual projects, and in terms of how these can impact project metrics.

SYSTEMS THINKING AND SYSTEMS DYNAMICS

Systems thinking is defined as the ability to analyze how an organization or project's goals, elements, and interconnectivity are joined and become impacted as progress or change is made over the course of functioning. Project managers that use systems thinking are aware that decisions made in one part of the project may affect different parts of the project in the present or the future. The project management plan and its sub-elements are highly interrelated; project managers must be aware of and review how changes to certain project elements will alter project trajectory. Systems dynamics are defined as the behavior of complex systems in nonlinear patterns charted and tracked to better understand systems behaviors, decision-making, and change in a project, process, or organization. Projects are highly interrelated and can be highly complex. A project manager with the ability to monitor complex behaviors is able to make better decisions and adjustments to the project towards expected outcomes.

ORGANIZATIONAL GOVERNANCE FRAMEWORKS

Organizational governance is defined as the interactive and structural configuration—such as hierarchical or matrix formats—of personnel within an organization that is used by management to influence the behaviors, culture, and objective outcomes of the organization itself. The oversight of organizational governance thus requires framework considerations such as roles, responsibilities, and human resources to objectively monitor effectiveness and change the governance structure as needed. How an organization is governed is often a result of the culture within its ranks. Norms such as rules, policies, standard operating procedures, business systems, quality systems, and modes of communication can all influence how governance is executed and in turn how effective project management can be. Aligning these elements—especially as projects become more complex in size and scope—reinforces effective use of project resources. Governance frameworks can become inhibitory when organizations are performing project portfolios and programs with many active projects running at the same time. Governance frameworks must be factored into the tailoring process in early planning phases of projects.

Project Scale	Common Governance Elements
Project	Common governance domains: alignment, risk, performance, communications.
Program	Each domain with common functions: oversight, control, integration, decision-making.
Portfolio	Each function has a governance supporting process.

MANAGEMENT ELEMENTS

Modern management has multitudes of practices and methods to be effective in management of a system, group, or process. The organizational governance and structure will influence what general management principles are both used and effective in various parts of the organizational structure. Key principles can be grouped by common themes: standards, efficiency, top-down management, and matrix management. These principles are not all-inclusive; many more principles are used and likely highly effective based on the organization's governance and the culture of the business.

Group	Common Principles
Efficiency	Division of labor and specialization
	Skills development
	Economic use of resources
Matrix	Unity of goal
	Balanced goals and objectives
	Innovation and contribution by stakeholders
	Discipline of action and rules
	Compensation and fair labor
Standards	Effective communication modes
	Quality of execution and performance
	Safety and security
	Morale and culture management
Top-down	Authorization
	Unity of command

Organizational Structure Types

Tradeoff Between Organizational Structure Types and Structure Optimization

The elements to an effective organizational structure often depend on the desired outcomes of the project or strategy sought by the organization and its stakeholders. Many organizational structures are available to use, each with different elements that can be adjusted to create permutations and flexible structure styles based on desired outcomes. The project management process benefits from well-designed and well-planned organizational structures; often multiple organizational structures may be used within a project or portfolio. The most influential characteristics of a project include:

- Work group arrangement
- Degree of project manager authority
- Project manager's role
- Degree of resource availability
- Budget ownership
- Scope of project administrative staff

Degrees and combinations of these factors can create a continuum of organizational structures ranging from simple organic projects with little complexity to matrix and hybrid styles with various sub-structures and work arrangements.

Complexity Scale (low)	**Simple/Organic**	Flexible, with little project manager (PM) authority. Limited resources and part-time focus. Usually a small business.
	Functional	Work group focused on job at hand, little PM authority, and few resources outside of work group.
	Multidisciplined	Multiple org functions working part-time, little PM authority. Few resources overseen by functional manager.
	Matrix	PM involved; varies with strong, weak, or mixed forms of matrix teams. Increase in resources as project grows more complex.
	Virtual	Distributed network of colleagues and stakeholders. Limited face-to-face work. PM can be full or part time, and resources depend on complexity.
	Hybrid	Mixed attributes from all styles.
Complexity Scale (high)	**PMO**	High resource needs, full-time dedicated PMs leading teams and budgets. High levels of authority for PMs.

Factors to Consider When Implementing or Changing an Organizational Structure

The task of designing and continuously adjusting an organizational structure to fit strategic and project needs requires awareness and consideration of several factors common within organizations. These factors can be grouped into categories such as strategic, hierarchical, flexible, and functional.

Strategic factors center on those that link to the overall organizational strategy and objectives: (1) how well the structure aligns with those broader objectives and (2) how accountability and responsibility are upheld against those aligned objectives.

Hierarchical factors provide a structural operating norm among the organization's members. The culture of the organization must be considered against hierarchical factors. Factors include (3) clear authority and decision escalation, (4) authority to delegate, (5) clear communications, and (6) span of control.

Flexible factors include (7) adaptability and simplicity of design.

Lastly, functional factors focus on time and logistics: (8) performance efficiency, cost, and physical locations of the structure.

Project Management Office

The project management office (PMO) is an organizational division used in some organizations to provide coordination of project-related activities via facilitation, resources, and governance support to projects within the organization. Depending upon the scale and scope of organizational projects, the PMO will have various levels of indirect or direct involvement with projects themselves. PMOs are not likely to directly lead projects; their role is largely advising other project managers. A controlling style of PMO involves more hands-on guidance and methodology building for co-project managers. These services aid in standardizing forms, procedures, and governance practices. Directive PMOs involve project managers from the office taking direct control of one or more projects, so the project team reports directly to the PMO.

Role of The Project Manager

Definition of a Project Manager

Project Manager's Function

The project manager (PM) functions within an organization to lead the team selected to achieve the objectives of a defined project. This management role differs from traditional jobs, such as functional manager or operations manager, in that the PM does not directly supervise a business function, business unit, or operating efficiency within the organization. Rather, the PM must lead the team to accomplish the project objectives using spheres of influence within the organization, clear mandates from senior management, and the stakeholder relationships available. The PM is responsible for meeting the project objectives for the outcomes of the project, for team communication and motivation, and ultimately for stakeholder satisfaction. Effective PMs are skilled at management, technical aptitude, planning, leadership, and finance.

Project Manager's Influence

The PM must lead a team, project stakeholders, and other supportive colleagues through a transformative process to achieve a positive outcome for the organization with net positive financial and/or competitive advantage for the organization. Very often the PM does not have role power over the people who work with or impact the project. Just as much as planning and execution skills, the level of expertise and relationship strength the PM holds can influence how results are obtained. A PM must convince, influence, support, and lead the project team and stakeholders through to the success of the project.

Sphere of Influence

Project

Project Manager's Role and Function Within the Project

The PM is analogous to a sports team head coach or a symphony conductor. The PM serves to navigate the team through the project schedule while keeping stability through resource limits and challenging obstacles. The PM also serves to direct and empower the team members to perform their respective roles. Relationship and communication skills across the project team and stakeholder network can distinguish the top PMs from their peers. Essential elements to the role include formal communication plans, multiple communication mediums, and clarity and consistency in communications. Relationship skills essential to the role include formal and informal network development. Formal networks are those that are within the PM's reporting structure. Informal networks include subject matter experts, executive champions, and other stakeholders that can provide support and solutions to the project team. Relationship management is an important way that PMs can navigate the team through the organizational complexities.

Organization

Project Manager's Role and Function Within the Broader Organization

Within the broader organization, PMs interact most commonly with senior executives, functional managers, specialized colleagues, and other PMs. Senior executive interaction occurs in the form of project chartering, stakeholder buy-in, and business case review. PMs may often also report to a senior executive for special strategic projects. PMs are likely to share resources with, report to, or support functional managers—such as operations managers—in order to achieve project objectives. Resource constraints and communication are critical functions for PMs and functional leaders. The PM's role in the organization includes strengthening organizational competency in project management, improving the state of efficiency and performance of the organization as a result of successful projects, and developing relationships within the organization that will help achieve the project team's deliverables. The PM must also promote their profession and champion the project management discipline and system from within. This role can be achieved by building strong relationships with other internal PMs, by demonstrating the value-added outcomes of projects, and by supporting improvements in efficacy of the organization's project management function.

Influence on and by the Industry, Profession, and Across Other Disciplines

External influences such as technology advances, efficiency tools, economic shifts, market forces, regulatory changes, project discipline improvements, and resource availability changes may require PMs to adjust their planning and execution in projects. As many of these influences precipitate change in the project management body of knowledge or force new technologies onto industry, it is wise for PMs to perform continuing education and professional development within their profession or in related skills. Continuing certifications in project management, operations management, and related industries where projects may be initiated are also recommended. PMs are also able to influence professionals in other industries, persuading them of the value of using project management skills to enhance their own achievement. Skills that are highly developed in PMs—such as project quality, budgeting, resource management, and schedule adherence—are beneficial educational options for non-PMs.

Project Manager Competencies

Skills in the PMI Talent Triangle

The Project Management Institute recognizes that competent PMs exhibit three essential skill sets: leadership, technical project management, and strategic management.

The leadership skill set is evidenced by a PM's ability to engage, motivate, and aid a project team and its stakeholders to the successful achievement of organizational goals. For example, a PM helps the project team negotiate severely constrained resources to help keep a critical project on schedule.

The technical project management skill set is characterized as knowledge and behaviors represented in project, program, or portfolio management itself. For example, a PM achieves above-target schedule, budget, and quality adherence for multiple simultaneous projects.

Strategic management skill sets are defined as the awareness of internal organizational and external industry knowledge and can positively impact business and project results. For example, a PM is deeply aware of pending industry technology advancements and can adopt their use in projects to maintain a competitive advantage.

While each skill by itself can be impactful, the role of the PM is incomplete and insufficient unless all three skills are finely developed in PMs and the project management organization.

Technical Project Management Skills

Technical project management skills are those that are executed by the PM and team to achieve the planned project outcomes within the project performance indicators and body of knowledge. Technical expertise is necessary for effective project management; knowing when to obtain outside assistance or subject matter support is equally important to successful PMs. Technical expertise must also be balanced with effective execution and use of the tools available to PMs. The most effective PMs can balance the competing needs of schedule adherence, financial reporting, issue resolution, focus on critical success factors of any given project, tailoring of approaches, and thorough planning.

Strategic and Business Management Skills

Strategic thinking combines awareness of the broader internal organization, external market forces, and organizational goals to make effective and innovative decisions to improve or sustain a competitive advantage. As projects tend to include elements from many different organizational disciplines (such as financial, quality, procurement, operations, engineering, and customer awareness), PMs must also be adept at multiple business management skills in order to be maximally effective. This domain knowledge allows the PM to provide maximum benefit and value to the organization, collaborate with domain experts to meet project deliverables, and promote the benefits of projects and project management systems to the organization's strategic objectives. The PM should be aware of and able to explain key aspects of the organization (e.g., organizational strategy, vision and mission statement, key performance indicators, products and/or services, competition and market forces, as well as how operations function).

Importance of Leadership and People Skills in Project Management

Leadership is essential to project management and is demonstrated by the ability to motivate, guide, and instruct a team or network of contributors. These abilities are achieved when PMs exhibit certain underlying talents, including conciliation, problem-solving, critical decision-making, communication skills, and relationship-building with stakeholders and team members. These "people skills" are a vital talent in project management that can elevate a leader's ability to achieve project outcomes consistently. All projects need people to direct, execute, and influence outcomes. Successful PMs understand the motivations, strengths, and weaknesses that their team and stakeholders exhibit and are able to adjust their own plans, communication, and influence accordingly to stay focused on the objectives. Leadership styles and attributes are discussed within the Team performance domain section of this guide.

Performing Integration

Process Level

Integration in project management is defined as the coordination of the elemental parts of the project management process into a smoothly functioning system. Integration results in deliverables, including the project charter, the project plan, and the project scope. The PM has two primary responsibilities in performing project integration. First, the PM must work with the project sponsor to ensure project deliverables and objectives are aligned with organizational strategy and other portfolios and programs. Second, PMs must filter out the nonessential distractions and clear a path for the team to concentrate on the objectives, scope, deliverables, plan, and charter of the project facing them. The most direct form of project integration is on the underlying processes involved in project management. These processes can occur as mutually exclusive events or as overlapping, repeated, and consequential events where integration and interaction must be managed by the project leader.

Cognitive and Context Integration

Cognitive-level project integration is defined as the ability of a person to combine subject matter knowledge and expertise with qualitative skills, such as leadership, vision, and organizational acumen to form an integrated skill set in managing a project. The PM must be able to balance and perform the necessary combination of knowledge-based expertise and interpersonal skills to achieve the objectives of the project or organization. Furthermore, the integration of various skill sets, both knowledge and interpersonal, requires the ability to morph from one set of behaviors to slightly different behaviors as a PM, depending upon the progression and challenges facing the project.

PMs must think beyond cognitive-level integration—such as direct project and subject matter knowledge and interpersonal skills—and must be aware of broader contextual influences upon the project, such as the project's relevance to overall business or organizational objectives, business case relevance for the project, or marketplace impacts of the project outcomes. Additional context awareness is needed towards the organization's broader strategy and objectives. Behavioral alignment with and integration of cognitive and contextual roles gives the PM advantages in project performance and the organization's progress towards its overarching goals.

Project Integration Management

Develop Project Charter

Overview

The project charter is a summary document that serves as valid authorization to perform the project and to use organizational resources against the project. It is a concise collection of all key details related to the deliverables, plan, scope, and resources needed to be successful. The charter links the organization's strategic objectives to the project plan and its execution via business case files, internal and external factors, and the benefits management plan. From the charter, many supporting materials and information can be created with accuracy and validation. Materials that flow forth after the charter include the project management plan, project schedule, cost management, quality plan, resource allocation, risk management, procurement, and the appropriate project documentation. **The project charter provides official authorization for the project manager to begin work on the project.**

Inputs

Utility of Business Documents in Creating Charters

The two most significant business documents used as inputs into the charter process are the business case and the benefits management plan. The business case documents the justification to perform the project under the analysis that the investment outlays in monetary, time, and personnel resources will benefit the organization. The business case also includes a cost-benefit analysis and has several data sources, including market research, external competitive environment studies, the state of technology in the marketplace, customer feedback, market demand, or organizational strategy. The benefits management plan is a collection of analyses such as a pro forma statement that demonstrates how the benefits are likely to be obtained as the project is completed.

Use of Agreements in Developing Project Plans

Agreements are types of business documents more commonly used when a project management team is working for an external firm as a contracted service provider. Agreements serve to document terms and bind behaviors between the project team and the organization receiving the benefit of the project management services. Agreements can come in many forms, the most familiar of which (for an external provider) would be a contract or service agreement, memorandums of understanding, letters of intent, verbal agreements, or emailed statements.

Enterprise Environmental Factors and Organizational Process Assets

The project charter includes cost-benefit analysis, risk assessment, and functional validation references that require awareness of several external and internal factors. External validation ensures that the project benefits and focus are relevant to the marketplace and the organization's strategy. Internal validation ensures that the project is consistent with internal objectives and organizational culture factors. Organizational process assets support the project charter as inputs that set standards in policies, procedures, monitoring methods, reporting, governance framework, work templates, and organizational learning databases. These standards and history provide a pathway to future charter development without having to start from scratch.

Tools and Techniques

Benefit of Using Expert Judgement When Developing Project Charters

When developing the project charter, especially in new and complex projects that the organization has little to no experience performing, an external expert is beneficial to the management team. Expert judgement is the judgement of an individual or group developed through expertise, skill, training, and education to provide deliberate direction to an inexperienced project team to build confidence and increase the likelihood of good decision-making. The specialization of knowledge and skill is beneficial when complexity enters a project or is a necessary force to be overcome. Expert judgement beneficial to project managers is commonly seen in organizational optimization, risk analysis, budget and schedule management, and industry technical knowledge. External consultants are commonly used, but other sources can include government agencies, nonprofits, and academia.

Project Charter Data-Gathering Techniques

Project charter development requires input from various stakeholders, subject matter experts, team members, and even customers in order to align with the problem or weakness needed to be overcome. Brainstorming is a tool that involves ideation and analysis. Diverse stakeholders, experts, and team members perform facilitated, open, and collaborative idea generation to solve the problem(s) facing the project team. The ideas are analyzed, and top concepts are incorporated into the project charter. Focus groups use open communication approaches and draw upon stakeholders, subject matter experts, and product (or service) end users to provide the project team with unbiased perspective on project risks, quality criteria, and success factors. Interviews are more intimate and candid ways to get high-level information about project risks, constraints, and approval criteria from stakeholders. Project managers and their teams assess the relative need for each of these techniques based on the project and situational needs.

Key Traits of Project Managers When Facilitating Project Charters

Project managers must effectively manage the human element in the charter development process and lead the team through techniques that bring positive outcomes to charter development meetings and discussions. Conflict and differing personal goals and values are common in many charter development phases. The project manager can use conflict management to bring stakeholders and team members together on differences in objectives, scope, success criteria, and milestones. The project manager must be skilled at meeting management in order to stay on track with the process and to gather information from the meeting and stakeholders.

Outputs

Purpose and Elements of Project Charters

The project charter serves as a validation and authorization from the project sponsor that the project will receive resources and will be executed. The charter also provides the project manager with responsibility and authority to lead the project initiative as detailed in the charter. The charter communicates key information to internal and external stakeholders regarding the project scope and execution plan. Several elements are commonly added to the charter to maximize its effectiveness.

Charter Element	Description
Responsible parties	Lists the project manager, sponsor, and other persons responsible for carrying out or overseeing the project
Key stakeholders	Persons or organizations that impact or benefit from the project
Project description	Description is high-level and describes the project, scope, and any problems needing solved
Objectives	Listed objectives of the project, along with measurable success criteria
Purpose statement	Describes the project purpose in terms of example data and problem statements
Approval requirements	Lists how success is defined, how it is decided, and who has authority to sign off on the project
Resources allocated	Financial, human, and goods resources are defined

Problem Statement

The problem statement must clearly describe, in objective terms, the problem or challenge that the team must overcome through use of the project process. Measurable data is highly useful in validating that the problem statement actually reflects the true problem, that the objectives of the project align with resolving the problem, and that the statement does not draw premature conclusions. In lean Six Sigma projects, the statement is often written in terms of the customer's needs and benefit. The objectives, success measures, and milestones must be a skeletal support structure to achievement of problem resolution.

Develop Project Management Plan

Overview

The project management plan is a comprehensive document that provides a thorough summary of the project work and the way in which the project components will be executed. The purpose of the development of the project management plan is to perform the consolidation of the separate subcomponents into one comprehensive work. Key inputs into this process include the project charter and outputs from preliminary processes, such as business case development, enterprise environmental factors, and organizational process assets. Project management teams must be skilled at using several tools to analyze, compile, and communicate an effective project management plan. Along with professional judgement, project managers must also use team facilitation, leadership skills, and data collection methods to achieve the plan. An important feature incorporated into the plan is baselining. Baselining refers to defined reference points documented for cost, time, and scope so that performance can be measured against these reference points. Through the course of the project, these baselines can be adjusted, but only through a formalized change management process.

Inputs

Impact on Development of Project Management Plans

Enterprise Environmental Factors

Many sub-plans developed within the context of the project management plan are interdependent upon enterprise resources and systems. Two key internal enterprise factors are the organizational design and the infrastructure used to support it. The organizational design includes how hierarchies are structured, the internal culture, management behaviors, and how the organization is governed through policies and practices. The infrastructure factors include telecommunications, technology available for performing project work, and the physical assets of the organization.

Organizational Process Assets

These factors represent the norms and approved procedures used by the organization for projects or in support of project management. Core organizational policies and procedures, the project management process norms, and project tailoring procedures are examples. Other assets of the organizational processes include policies and norms regarding change management, monitoring of sub-plans, reporting and information sharing, and how the organization learns from project progress and outcomes.

Tools and Techniques

Impact of Well-Planned Meetings on Project Management Plans

Development of the project management plan involves planned meetings—varying in duration and frequency—in order to communicate project execution strategy, objectives, and methods of monitoring and control. The development of the project management plan precedes the first team meeting and marks the transition to the implementation phase of the project. The size of the project can also determine when the kickoff meeting is held and within which project phase that meeting is held. Larger projects where the planning team is separate from the execution team will have a kickoff meeting in the implementation phase of the project. Smaller projects, where the planning team is also performing the execution, will have the kickoff meeting in the planning phase because the team memberships are the same. Generally, kickoff meetings are intended to give team members information about their roles, responsibilities, objectives, and measurement tools for the project. The kickoff is also an opportunity to gain commitment from all team members regarding the project deliverables, objectives, and key performance indicators.

OUTPUTS

CENTRAL COMPONENTS OF PROJECT MANAGEMENT PLANS

Subsidiary plans function within the project management plan to control key performance indicators, resources, communications, and scheduling of the plan. Common types of subsidiary plans include the schedule management plan, a cost management plan, and a communications management plan. The schedule management plan includes the criteria and monitoring steps needed for schedule management. The cost management plan describes how the team will plan and monitor project costs. The communications management plan oversees the veracity, control, and spread of the project communications. Baselines are validated and approved versions of key components of the project plan upon which team members and stakeholders may draw reference as the project progresses. Baselines are used for essential and frequently reviewed components, such as the scope, schedule, and cost plans. These approved standards are used when comparing actual performance as the project moves forward. Additional elements to the project management plan include those that focus on changes, management review, and information configuration plans. Project documents support many of the subsidiary plans within the project plan and serve as evidence and analytical tools for performance assessment and continuous improvement.

DIRECT AND MANAGE PROJECT WORK

OVERVIEW

Following the completion of the project management plan, the project team must begin managing project work. Directing and managing project work is the process group of following the project management plan, its subsidiary plans, and approved changes, and leading the execution of the project tasks and systems towards completion of the schedule, objectives, and deliverables. This part of the project is ongoing and is hands-on execution of tasks. Inputs of this project element include the project management plan itself, enterprise environmental factors, and organizational process assets. Accomplishment and execution are key behaviors of the project team. The project manager leads the completion of project tasks, planned activities, and achievement of deliverables in the schedule. It is equally important that the project team manage change effectively during the project work phases. Also, the project manager must ensure that work performance data is sufficiently collected, analyzed, and communicated for the subsequent control process group and for future improvements to the organization's project management processes.

INPUTS

NECESSARY PROJECT INPUT DOCUMENTS

During the phase of directing and managing project work, several document sources can be used as inputs to achieve successful outcomes. These documents, commonly employed at other project steps and supplementary to the project management plan, include schedules, registers, and reports. Project schedules describe the work breakdown and timing around all tasks and milestones. The milestone list coincides with the schedule by listing dates planned for each milestone in the schedule. The requirements traceability record serves to link the project requirements for quality and performance to the project milestones. Project communications provide obvious critical importance in the documentation process. Furthermore, the risk register and risk reporting tools serve as preventative inputs against unplanned threats to the project and quantitative assessments on overall project risks, respectively. Lastly, the project documentation change log supports documentation of updates and adjustments made during the project work.

IMPORTANCE OF THE CHANGE LOG AND APPROVED CHANGE REQUEST PROCESSES

Project managers, often with the support of a change control board of advisors or project stakeholders, must carefully control changes to mutually agreed project plans, schedules, and deliverables. Changes to project documentation are widely communicated and can drive the decisions of many stakeholders and contributors. This control process is called the change management and approval system, or the perform integrated change control (PICC) process. When project managers approve change requests, they must schedule the change's resources and implementation and integrate it into the ongoing project. In a less formal sense, change logs document change actions taken to project documents and plans during execution.

Tools and Techniques

PMIS and Project Work Meetings

The project management information system (PMIS) is a component of the project work phase that is often overseen by the organization's information technology (IT) division. PMIS is commonly computer software that collects, analyzes, and communicates project data into useful information for the management of project work. PMIS systems include all software applications needed to execute the project, such as word processing, email, digital communication, data storage, and specialty applications. The PMIS is often integrated with enterprise resource planning software tools for procurement, costing, and human resource planning. Advanced information systems can also be very positive when larger project scopes exist with more detailed deliverable performance indicators to report.

Project work meetings are very common for the communication and execution of project work. The project manager, project team, and relevant stakeholders are fixtures in attendance of project work meetings. Various meeting types are performed at different points in the project life cycle.

Technical meetings	Scrum daily standup meetings	Iteration meetings
Steering committee	Kickoff meetings	Technical meetings
Progress update meetings	Lessons learned meetings	Problem-solving meetings

Outputs

Deliverables

A deliverable is an outcome (of a process, phase, or project) whose quality is valid and supported. This outcome is often in the form of a built capability, tangible object, process result, or product. The deliverable can be an outcome listed as the final step of the project or as several intermediary stages within the project. Deliverables may need to have change control processes applied when completed as an intermediary step and where subject to adjustments or forthcoming phases of the project that may alter the qualities of the deliverable. A deliverable may be internal or external. An internal deliverable can be a product, service, or result that is intended to satisfy the requirements or fulfill an objective of an internal stakeholder. An external deliverable serves to meet similar needs for an external stakeholder. The external customer verifies that the deliverable meets the quality and performance expectations.

Use of Work Performance Data as an Output of the Project Work Phase

Work performance data is the measured and elemental result of the project activities performed in the course of executing the project phases. Work performance information is generated from the analysis of such raw performance data. Systems are used to capture raw work performance data, store it appropriately, analyze it, and transform the analysis into meaningful work performance information that can be used to report, communicate, and draw conclusions about the current project performance. Work data sources include KPIs, actual begin and end dates for tasks in the project, change requests, quality measurements, cost figures, schedule attainment, and communication records. These data sources are considered the outcomes of directing and managing the project work as scheduled.

Issue Log and Change Requests

During the course of performing project work against schedule, financial, quality, and resources constraints, the project team will often encounter issues that occur and will need to be resolved in order to meet performance objectives, deliverables, or milestones as expected. These issues can be in the form of conflicts, resource constraints, performance lags, and unforeseen errors. The issue log serves as a data source for such problems and as a location to document the corrective and preventive actions agreed upon by the project team. Data also found in the issues log include dates when issues were identified and resolved, persons finding the issues, risk or prioritization scores, and elements that define who resolves the issue and by when.

Project managers and executives expect to be aware of issues and, more importantly, of the efforts being performed to resolve the issues. **Once an issue is identified, a single team member should be designated the "owner" of the issue to monitor, document, and report on the issue's final resolution.** Future project planning can benefit from the knowledge gained from issue log accuracy. Change requests are related documents that create a formal paper trail and process around changing elements of the project plan while performing project work. These requests can alter deliverables, schedules, scope, cost, budget, resources, or quality parameters. The requests must be submitted, reviewed, and approved by the PICC process and team within the organization.

Project Document Updates Commonly Occurring During Project Work

Changes can occur at various points within a project plan. Changes to a project plan must be formally documented and submitted through the organization's change control process—often referred to as the PICC process. Several documents in the project work processes are commonly adjusted as the work is executed. The project has several supporting guidance tools used to steer decision-making during the work phases. Risk models created in early project planning phases may need to be updated or added as tasks are completed. Stakeholders are documented and defined prior to beginning project work. Tools such as RACI matrices (responsible, accountable, consulted, informed) may need updating as stakeholder relevance changes. Prior to beginning project work, assumption logs are used to inform the team of constraints. As those assumptions are tested, updates are likely needed. Requirements registered as critical to the outcome of the project may require changes and additional items based on customer needs. Furthermore, the activity list documenting the tasks needed for completion can be changed through the process due to unforeseen impactful issues. Lastly, the lessons learned register, a common source for documenting improvement opportunities, requires updating as such information is discovered.

Manage Project Knowledge

Overview

Knowledge management during the course of the project serves to better achieve the project objectives using existing knowledge from past projects and new knowledge from the current project. Both sources serve to expand and improve the organizational learning and knowledge repositories for improving the likelihood of stronger future project performance. Past history, and knowledge captured and assessed, benefits future project performance. Nearly all phases of the project management process serve as sources for knowledge capture. Inputs include the project management plan, various project documents, external environmental factors, and organizational assets. Tools used to transform inputs into outputs include knowledge and information management techniques, as well as interpersonal and team performance skills. Outcomes are those that fall within the lessons learned register, changes approved to the project management plan, and improvements made to the organizational process asset process.

Input

In all aspects of the project knowledge management process, it is important that organizations build trust among their leaders and contributors so that the benefit of the knowledge process is maximized. As an input to the project knowledge process, the project management plan details the project's execution, monitoring, and closeout, as well as the relevant details of supporting plans to the project. These essential details give insight into how the project was performed and can aid future planning efforts. Project documents such as the stakeholder register, team assignments, and the lessons learned register provide knowledge on how such influential persons were managed, how individual contributors made up the project team, and what lessons were gained from each executed project. Environmental factors within the enterprise such as positive-learning culture, working relationship strength, and blame-free employee relationships all help to reinforce the knowledge-centered organization. Lastly, the cultural routines and behaviors of the organization can support the value placed on knowledge capture and internal learning. Norms such as formal procedures for information sharing, confidentiality policies, and opportunities for informal discussions and innovations all reinforce the human element of project knowledge capture.

Tools and Techniques

Knowledge Management

Knowledge management is defined as using specific internal processes to create and apply knowledge to the benefit of the project management process. The definition can be further broadened to include the sharing of diverse knowledge and backgrounds for the benefit of projects and team members. Several tools and techniques are employed in the knowledge management process. These include social interactions, community networking, meetings, seminars, conferences, collaborative research, workshops, interactive training, and learning review meetings. The use and balance of these tools depends upon the cultural norms and acceptance of knowledge management techniques.

Information Management

Information management refers to the processes that transform data and results into useful information and the processes that allow stakeholders and project teams to access such information. Information, as a source of knowledge to be shared, can be documented and shared within a project team or within an organization through several tools: the lessons learned register, project performance libraries, knowledge capture processes, information compilation, and software systems such as project management information systems (PMIS). Because people have many differences in preferred learning styles, the transfer of information and knowledge may require differing delivery approaches for different recipients. For example, project managers may benefit from face-to-face discussions of past lessons learned from those previous project managers themselves. Thus, capturing information alone does not sufficiently ensure that that information is being absorbed by those seeking the information. Furthermore, available resources, subject matter experts, and consultants with highly tuned and relevant skills can often provide answers and information sooner than if someone simply went searching for it.

Expert Judgement and Interpersonal Skills

The knowledge management process can benefit from external support by subject matter experts. Such support is preferable when coming from experts with skills specifically in project knowledge management, information management, related software and tools for managing these systems, and organizational learning. Project managers and their teams can utilize and strengthen their organization's knowledge management system by adopting interpersonal skills, such as facilitation (especially in meetings), active listening, and leadership. Facilitation refers to the skill set of leading a team through the processes of decision-making. Active listening improves communications by infusing validation and verification behaviors to ensure understanding is certain between parties. Leadership refers to the ability to champion the organization's vision and strategy while inspiring the team and stakeholders towards peak performance. Two additional interpersonal skills desired of the project team are political awareness and networking. The former serves to discover and capture information and knowledge that may be asymmetrical based on power positions within an organization. The latter refers to the ability to gain information through formal and informal connections between colleagues, acquaintances, and professionals to gain implied or unambiguous knowledge.

Outputs

Lessons Learned Register, Plan Updates, and Organizational Process Assets Updates

The lessons learned register is a transitioning tool where project leaders and team members document valuable content such as issues, problems, risks, or opportunities that were experienced. These lessons—and the way in which each problem was resolved—are documented as outputs of processes in the project so the register can then be used as an input in other or subsequent project phases. The life cycle of the lessons learned register is fluid throughout the project. When the project is complete, the register is added to the lessons learned repository within the organization as an organizational process asset for future project planning. Changes to the project management plan resulting from a formal change request and review through a change control system such as the PICC process are known as plan updates due to knowledge capture. Template or standard content within project management plan development procedures may be updated with new knowledge as well. Organizational process assets are also components that are commonly updated as knowledge is mined or gained.

Monitor and Control Project Work

Overview

The monitor and control project work process serves to document, assess, and communicate project progress towards the achievement of the project's validated objectives. Such status reports of the project work provide stakeholders with informative progress updates and allow them to be aware when intervention or support is needed. Financial, schedule, and resource performance can also be assessed and shared. Monitoring serves to collect project data as inputs to continuous improvement opportunities. Control refers to the acts of planning, implementing, and verifying corrective and preventive actions that are taken following a deficiency or when a weakness is found. Nine components are considered essential to the monitor and control process.

Component	Description
Risks	Verifying the condition and impact of project risks
Key performance indicator	Actual performance versus project management plan
Corrective and preventive action (CAPA)	Identifying and assigning corrective and preventive actions as needed
Cost and schedule	Maintaining cost and schedule forecasts and performance
Business alignment	Monitoring alignment of project against business needs
Product specification	Maintaining product or service attributes and information as developed
Data collection	Recording data on performance and forecasting
Change execution	Implementing changes from control processes
Reporting	Project progress reporting and communications

Inputs

Project Documents Used as Inputs to the Monitor and Control Project Work Process

Many project documents may be applicable as inputs to the monitor and control project work processes, but 10 project documents typically stand out as most commonly used. These documents can be grouped into forecasts, reports, and registers (or logs).

Forecasts	**Schedule forecasts**—Forecasting for schedule attainment is based on the projected plan, allowed tolerances to the plan, and actual schedule attainment performance. **Cost forecasts**—The actual financial performance against planned budget is calculated, and changes are implemented as necessary. **Milestone list**—Milestone lists, often also listed in the Gantt chart or project schedule, are indicated on a schedule and used to compare planned versus actual attainment.
Reports	**Quality reports**—Serve as a compilation of quality issues, corrective and preventive actions taken, and performance against quality parameters as set in the project planning phases. **Risk reports**—Summarizes individual as well as overall project risks into one report. **Basis of estimates report**—For estimates within the project plan, this set of information explains the basis of those estimates and guidance in the event of variances to the estimates.
Registers and Logs	**Risk register**—Documents the encountered threats and opportunities throughout the project. **Issue log**—The issue log tracks problems encountered during execution and who is responsible for resolving within agreed timeframes. **Assumption log**—Defines the assumptions and constraints analyzed as being impactful to the project. **Lessons learned register**—A knowledge-capturing tool used in the future improvement of project planning, variance prevention, and continuous improvement.

Work Performance Information

Work execution data generated and collected within the monitoring and control phase of the project is transferred into work performance information in order to be utilized in reporting metrics and project performance. Work execution data is collected and compared against the project management plan and the project documents in order to gauge project performance. The work performance information is stored securely for retrieval by stakeholders needing the information for reporting or variance planning. Metrics around work performance are determined within the project management plan at the early phases of the project. The information is embedded into reports and communicated among stakeholders to demonstrate how the project is being executed to plan. Metrics are targeted performance goals. Work performance data is the result of raw measurement. Work performance information applies analysis to the raw work performance data to glean understanding and make decisions. Work performance reports are formalized findings interpreted for the stakeholders.

Utility of Agreements in Controlling Project Work

Agreements, such as those made between a project manager acting as the buyer of services and a service provider acting as the seller of services, are methods used to control project performance when outsourced to a third party or independent entity to support the efforts of the project. It is wise for the project manager and team to design clauses, criteria, and performance metrics within any agreements or contracts made with third-party providers. Such agreements most often align with the objectives and metrics of the project itself. Oversight of contractor work may also be reviewed in part by a procurement division of the organization within which the project is being performed. Procured contractors supporting a project should be aligned and following similar if not identical performance standards. In some cases, it is advised to have contractors held to tighter standards than the project itself.

Tools and Techniques

Types of Data Analysis in Monitoring Project Work

Alternatives analysis provides a project team with a selection of alternative actions to be taken as corrective actions when faced with variations or deviations from the plan.

The cost-benefit analysis is a commonly used financial tool that allows the project team to financially weigh corrective action approaches based on expense and benefit or efficacy towards the problem itself.

Earned value analysis tools combine the schedule, cost, and scope data into an analysis that provides a budgeted cost of work performed. Both the scope statement and the work breakdown structure (WBS) are key elements to the earned value analysis.

The root cause analysis—for example, using a 5 Whys tool—provides clarity about the true reason for a nonconformance or variance as a clear path to what the corrective and preventive actions should be.

The trend analysis tools are widely applicable and focus on collecting data and searching within that data using mathematical models for trends that provide explanations for the data behavior.

Lastly, variance analysis focuses on the reasons for differences between expected results and actual results, as well as how those differences can be overcome.

Outputs

Work Performance Reports and Change Requests

Work performance reports are the result of work data as the project is executed. These reports include information that is created from the recording and analysis of project work data. Work performance reporting is intended to communicate progress and drive future decisions within the project. These reports include schedule attainment, costs incurred and variance, earned value reporting, and burnup/burndown information. These performance reports are often presented in a variety of formats, including scorecards, written reports in prose, financial charts, and schedule graphs. Key stakeholders that rely on this information receive the reports in a timely manner in order to track progress and make project or resource decisions. Change requests are used when analyzing actual project outcomes against the project plan. Where adjustments need to be made to cost, schedule, scope, quality, and procurement, the performance reporting supports those adjustment decisions. The PICC process drives the review and action upon any change requests. A change derived as an output of the project work processes can take the form of a corrective action, a preventive action, or a defect repair.

Project Documents That May Be Revised Due to Outputs of the Control Project Work Phase

As a project transitions out of the control project work processes, outputs are generated, including work performance reporting, change requests, project management plan updates, and document updates. Document updates that are commonly encountered at this transitionary point include those to forecasts or registers used within the project. As the work is executed, issues are tallied on the issues log, and individual items are delegated to a responsible person to resolve by an agreed timeframe. Additionally, the risk register is updated as the project team discovers new risks to the success of the project plan. The output can also be translated into lessons learned; such information is documented into a register and used for continuous improvement for future phases or projects by the organization. Output data is very useful in assessing and changing cost and schedule forecasts. The respective cost management and schedule management processes dictate how these adjustments are made.

Perform Integrated Change Control

Overview

The perform integrated change control (PICC) process is a centralized system for the review of all project change requests, decision-making upon those requests, directing the changes to project management plans and related documents, and conveying the changes and decisions through communications with stakeholders. The controlled process by which the changes occur allows for a structured and disciplined approach to adjusting key information and tools used in project execution. An important factor considered by the centralized process is the relative risk or impact to project risks presented by the proposed change(s). The change control process is owned by the project manager, can be performed at any point within the project after baselines (initial costs, scope, and schedule) are set, and must be well documented. When baselines are impacted by the change request, the PICC process must be followed. The PICC process may sometimes be orchestrated by a change control board that performs the review, evaluation, decision-making, and communication of change dispositions. In highly customer-centric organizations, customer representatives may sit on the change control board.

Inputs

Project Management Plan, Project Documents, and Change Requests

Several foundational project materials serve to ensure the PICC process is executed consistently and with validation. These inputs are in the form of either plans or baselines. Primarily, the change process relies on the project management plan as a basis for evaluating the proposed change. The PICC process and change control board, if used, employ a formal written change management plan that gives guidance and steps necessary to the organization for the change evaluation process. The related configuration management plan serves as a documented guide for the version control upon the elements of the project that keep the final product or service in a functioning state. The three baselines acting as inputs to the PICC process are scope, cost, and schedule. A baseline is an agreed and set standard against which project performance is measured. Project documents used as inputs to the PICC process include risk reports; basis of estimates reports that explain how cost, scope, and schedule estimates were determined; and the requirements traceability matrix. Change requests that get processed through the PICC may impact the project baselines and may include corrective or preventive actions or updates to formal documents and plans. Baselines are only updated after completing the PICC process via the change control board.

Tools and Techniques

Use of Change Control Tools

Configuration control is defined as the control of the features and attributes of the product or service deliverable being created by the project. Change control is defined as the control and documentation of the changes in the project, plan, baselines, and supporting documentation needed to execute the project. Change control tools, both manual and automated versions, are used to capture and govern such changes. Tools utilized will depend upon the unique needs of a project and the phases(s) where the changes are necessary. Configuration tools differ from change management tools in their scope and degree of impact towards the deliverables.

Configuration management tools include:

- **Identification of the configuration item**—A task serving to define and validate the configuration change to be made. The tool also includes verification of labeling, performance, and accountability.
- **Record and report**—Includes procedures and tools for documenting and communicating configuration changes.
- **Verification and audit**—These tools provide proof and assurance that the functional requirements are implemented in line with the configuration change documentation.

Change control tools include:

- **Analysis for need of change**—The identification of changes needed in documents or processes.
- **Change request form**—Used to document the proposal.
- **Change decision-making**—The process where supporting evidence is used to guide project leadership or the change control board (CCB).
- **Tracking changes**—Includes tools used to register documents, approval for changes, and rationale for making such changes.

Function of Data Analysis, Decision-Making, and Meetings

Commonly used tools for data analysis in the PICC process include cost-benefit analysis and alternatives analysis. Cost-benefit uses financial assumptions to determine if the benefit of the change outweighs the expense. Risk avoidance may be an alternative means to assess benefit and should be considered by project management. Alternatives analysis weighs all competing alternatives against the proposed change to determine the optimal outcome. Decision-making tools used in the PICC process include voting, multicriteria decision-making, and autocratic decision-making. Voting provides a variety of ways to accept or reject changes by majority or plurality. Multicriteria decision-making involves a matrix approach to analyze the change against several criteria. Autocratic decision-making involves one person making the choice to accept or reject the changes. Lastly, CCB meetings are beneficial to the PICC process as a means to review the change, assess impact to the project, and discuss alternatives. The CCB may also serve to perform configuration management reviews.

Outputs

Utility of Outputs

After the change request has been processed through the change management plan by the project manager or an appointee, the changes are implemented where necessary. The process includes steps for executing these changes. A project plan change log houses the details of all approved changes during the project life cycle. Significant project updates may be made to the project management plan or to a variety of project documents. Changes to baselines are not retroactively effective against past data. Once approved changes are implemented, appropriate project team members or stakeholders should be notified, and any retraining should be scheduled.

Close Project or Phase

Overview

Closeout and Closure

Closeout is the process where the project manager and/or team completes all remaining tasks or activities for the phase or project itself. The closure completes remaining tasks and prompts finalized reports to be archived for future learning, and the team disbands in order to pursue new or other projects in progress. Inputs include the project charter, the management plan, various documents such as the lessons learned log and milestone list, and accepted deliverables documentation. Tools include data analysis and meetings. Outputs include the lessons learned register; a final project deliverable such as a product, service, or transition; and a final report. Many actions and activities are to be reviewed during the closeout process. These can be categorized as documentation, resource allocation, waste disposition, deliverable, contractual, and summarization activities. Most importantly, the final deliverable(s) must be issued to the customer. Also, procurement and contract closure may be needed as the project or phase is completed.

Inputs

Project Documents Serving

Closeout documents may require completion, final sign-off, reporting, communication, or storage for later retrieval. The documents can be grouped into logs/registers, standards, and reports:

- Logs and registers
  - Risk register—Summarizes the risks that have been identified through the previous phases or activity.
  - Milestone list—Provides verification of the specific dates when project or phase milestones have been met.
  - Lessons learned register—All lessons learned from the phase or project are finalized before being added to the organization's central database.
  - Issue log—Closeout serves to ensure no outstanding issues are left open.
  - Change log—Any changes that were requested and executed during the project or phase are referenced here.
  - Assumption log—A pre-work summary of the project assumptions gets saved for future reference.
- Standards
  - Requirements documentation—Provides verification that the execution was within the scope of the project or phase.
  - QC measurements—Provides evidence that quality parameters were met for the phase or project deliverable(s).
  - Basis of estimates—Summarizes the performance of actual cost, duration, and resource use compared to estimated usages.
- Reports
  - Project communications—A summary of all project or phase-related communications from the project team.
  - Quality reports—Generally include quality metric summaries, suggested improvements, and all resolved quality issues.
  - Risk report—Serves to summarize risk status and verify if any risks need to be resolved before closeout.

Agreements and Procurement Documentation

Agreements are managed within the procurement management plan of the project. During closeout, contractual terms and conditions generally state what is required for agreement closure. Complexity of a project scope and its deliverables may make the agreement closeout more elaborate, especially as criteria for closure are numerous. When closing out the contractual agreements, the project team, through the procurement management plan, compiles and archives all related documentation. Examples of archived information include performance evidence on cost, scope, quality, and schedule, as well as supporting specifications, manuals, and inspection records. The summary information for each contract closeout is beneficial to the lessons learned database for future projects or future contracts with contractors.

Tools and Techniques

Expert Judgement, Data Analysis, and Meetings

Expert judgement is beneficial in the closeout process as a means to ensure contractual agreements are fulfilled, legal language is understood, any final regulatory reviews are achieved through the right government agencies, and project results and processes receive any required closeout auditing per stakeholder requirements. Expert analysis at closeout can often identify and resolve risks that the team does not want to linger beyond closeout.

Data analysis is used as a closeout tool to analyze documents and information to benefit the lessons learned repository. Furthermore, analysis techniques can be helpful; for example, variance can give reliable information on performance metric improvement, trending can improve future planning models, and regression can gather more confidence on the variables that drive project success.

Meetings are used primarily to communicate status on the closeout process and deliverable completion; for final reporting on metrics and performance to stakeholders; and to ensure relevant knowledge and documentation is captured in the correct repositories.

Outputs

Final Changes Made to Project Documents and Common Organizational Process Asset Updates

Closure moves the project or phase documents into their final version and into archiving for knowledge capture. The project team(s) update and finalize project documents and the lessons learned register. The final lessons learned register is a highly important output of closure and often includes significant topics such as business case accuracy and handling risks and issues. Organizational process assets are also likely to be updated. Documents used in the closure or transfer process—such as agreements, specifications, and prior phase information—are reviewed by the project manager as a prerequisite to closure. Furthermore, organizational and operational support documents and project template documents may also be reviewed and updated as outputs of the closure process. The deliverables must be formally accepted by the sponsor, and the final documentation must be updated, before the team can be released. The project manager then gives the accounting department the final approval to finalize payment and billing for all contracts and agreements based on their relative terms.

Issue of the Final Deliverable and Typical Elements of Final Project Reports

The final deliverable is issued to the recipient party, who is one of the stakeholders defined early in the project. The method of transfer depends on the form the deliverable takes. For example, the completion of a warehouse as a deliverable has an occupancy transfer process that officially transfers responsibility when milestones are met and closeouts are verified. On the other hand, deliverable transfer may be an established process, service, or product that gets delivered verbally, physically, or electronically.

Accompanying the final deliverable is a final report. This report may be provided to the stakeholder or customer receiving the deliverable, or it may remain within the project organization as reference and evidence of completion and lessons learned. Key elements of the final report include:

- Executive summary
- Scope summary and confirmation that scope was met
- Quality performance against objectives
- Performance against cost, schedule, and resource metrics
- Explanation of how the project and deliverable met business needs
- Risk summary and how risks were managed

Project Scope Management

Plan Scope Management

Overview

Project scope management is the process of ensuring that the project includes the required activities, and only those activities, in order to produce the deliverables within performance metrics to complete the project. Scope management is important in that it ensures clarity regarding what is in and out of the project's focus. Project scope management consists of six key elements.

Element	Description
Plan scope management	Creating a scope management plan showing how all elements will oversee the scope itself
Collect requirements	Capturing customer and stakeholder requirements to translate into scope language
Define scope	Clearly expressing the project and deliverables into a scope in objective terms
Create work breakdown structure	Parsing out each smaller activity that is needed to achieve deliverables and project work
Validate scope	Obtaining evidence that the described deliverables are sufficient
Control scope	Monitoring performance compared to the project or product scope, keeping performance aligned to the scope, and adjusting scope baseline where necessary

Scope Management Approaches in Predictive and Adaptive Project Life Cycles

The use of predictive or adaptive scope management approaches depends on the degree of uncertainty and change inherent to the subject matter. Predictive scope management is relatively low uncertainty, and the scope is well defined as a prerequisite to project start. Adaptive scope management is described as the repetitive adjustment of the scope given acquired knowledge of change, stakeholder input, and deliverable performance data. The feedback loop is used as an Agile development of the deliverable and progressive reduction of requirement work backlogs. The process adjusts the deliverable and project scope several times, each time ironing out development issues important to stakeholders. Predictive scope management has well-defined work breakdown, baselines, and change control processes. Agile scope management adjusts based on feedback from the iterative results of working through requirements backlogs. The status of the backlog is an indicator of forthcoming work.

Tailoring Considerations

Given that each project will have distinct characteristics, the project manager and project team must be cognizant of how the six key scope management elements may need to be tailored to fit the project. Though tailoring will be discussed more thoroughly in this guide, five key tailoring considerations are:

Tailoring Approach	Description
Governance	Consideration of how the organizational design, hierarchy, and audit practices upon the scope process should proceed.
Knowledge management	Consideration of how the organization captures and uses knowledge and stakeholder requirements in scope management.
Stability requirements	Does the organization gather and address unstable scope requirements? Does this impact the decision to be predictive or Agile in scope management?
Development approaches	Does the organization need to use a predictive, an Agile, or a hybrid approach to scope management, given the stakeholder needs?
Validation and sustainability	What are the validation systems and control methods used by the project organization?

Inputs, Tools, Outputs

Plan Scope Management and Inputs

Plan scope management is a process where the project manager and team develop a plan to create the project scope using a variety of customer inputs, analysis tools, and formalized communications tools. The team must ensure that a valid, clear, and controlled scope is created to guide the project, its team, and stakeholders as the project moves forward. The plan scope management knowledge area consists of a procedure or plan that will describe how the scope is to be created, how it is to be controlled, and what sources are used to give it validation. Key inputs to the scope management plan include the project charter and the project management plan. The scope must encompass the purpose, assumptions, constraints, quality parameters, and life-cycle features that are within these two input documents. Also, there may be several organizational process assets and enterprise environmental factors that are used as inputs, such as marketplace behavior, organizational norms, and past project scope lessons learned.

Transformational Tools and Resulting Outputs

Common tools such as expert judgement, meetings facilitated by the project manager, and data analysis are used to transform the scope management plan inputs into the resulting output: a clearly defined scope management plan. The **scope management plan** is an important part of the overall project management plan in that it will provide the project team with the procedures and constraints required to create the project scope. More elementally, the plan describes how the scope will be validated, monitored, controlled, created, and defined. Furthermore, the plan will describe acceptance of deliverables, defining and maintaining the scope baseline, and how the work breakdown structure will be drafted. The **requirements management plan**, also called a business analysis plan, explains as part of the project management plan how the stakeholder and customer requirements will be defined, analyzed, and controlled. The requirements management plan will also include explanations of how the requirements will be prioritized, what metrics will be monitored for performance, and how configuration activities will be performed.

Collect Requirements

Overview

Within the project scope management process, the collecting requirements sub-element refers to the process by which the project team gathers, documents, analyzes, and manages key stakeholder and customer requirements needed to meet the project objectives. An effective project scope must include feedback from stakeholders and have their concerns be met by the project as well. Project success can be heightened with active involvement from stakeholders and customers. Requirements themselves are attributes or conditions that must be found in the final product, service, or project result in order to satisfy a contractual agreement made with the customer or stakeholder. The stakeholder and customer requirements must be thoroughly captured, translated into the project scope and baseline, and controlled. The requirements are very important in the scope process because they are the foundation of the WBS and the performance measurement tools to be developed later.

Inputs

Usefulness of Inputs into the Collect Requirements Sub-Element

The project charter provides the project team with authority from the project sponsor to do the work and allocate resources to the project. The charter is the product of information from the business case, risks, high-level requirements and deliverables, and measurable objectives. The charter provides very key information to ensure the project scope is well defined and consistent with the chartered intent of the project. The project management plan includes several components that support the development of the project scope during the collection of requirements. The plan includes a stakeholder engagement plan that details communication modes, engagement strategies, and stakeholder participation activities. The project management plan also includes the requirements management plan and the newly created scope management plan finished prior to beginning to collect requirements for the scope itself. Key project documents used include the assumptions log, the lessons learned register, and the stakeholder register. Last but not least, any contracts or agreements with stakeholders, customers, or sponsors must be factored into this element of scope management.

Tools and Techniques

Techniques for Data Gathering When Collecting Stakeholder Requirements

Effective data-gathering tools used for stakeholder requirement compilations include benchmarking, focus groups, surveys, interviews, and brainstorming. Benchmarking is defined as the comparison of intended or proposed deliverables or processes to standard models or comparative existing versions from other organizations in order to obtain best practices, innovations, and performance goals. Focus groups serve to gather key demographics and potential users, stakeholders, subject matter experts, or impacted persons in an interactive group setting for data on their perspectives and advice on the proposed product, service, or process being proposed in the project. Surveys are electronic or paper-based means to collect data from a large, dispersed population and provide quick statistical analysis to drive the project scope process. Interviews are one-on-one collections of stakeholder and expert data regarding the impact of the proposed project deliverable(s) and perspectives on features and deliverables themselves. Lastly, brainstorming involves grouping stakeholders to compile a multitude of relevant innovative ideas regarding product, scope, or project requirements.

Data Analysis, Decision-Making, and Data Representation

Data analysis in project scope management is largely focused on document reviews designed to find key data and draw that data into the scope-defining process. A wide variety of documents may be reviewed to extract the relevant requirements. Documents commonly contained in this review include proposals, regulations, policies, procedures, process flows, business cases and processes, business plans, contracts, and agreements.

The collection of requirements for scope management can also involve decision-making tools designed to narrow down choices. Similar tools such as majority voting, unanimous voting, multicriteria decision-making, and autocratic decision-making are used just as in the perform integrated change control (PICC) process.

Data may also be visualized and analyzed in representation formats to help effectively gather and communicate requirements. Mind mapping is a tool used to capture related brainstormed ideas and organize them into groupings. Affinity diagrams are similar mapping tools where related brainstormed topics are grouped based on common characteristics. Both tools make analysis easier than with a large, unsorted data set.

Interpersonal and Team Skills Used to Collect Requirements for Project Scope Management

The nominal group technique translates brainstorming event ideas into a more manageable list of choices for action based on preference from the participants in the group. Teams consisting of stakeholders, subject matter experts, and project team members will provide validation to the nominal group rankings. Observations used in project scope management refer to the physical observation by a project team member or manager upon the process or activity of a stakeholder in order to obtain a greater understanding of requirements that are not easily or readily communicated from the stakeholder. Observations are similar to job shadowing, but may also include participation in the activity itself, where the participating observer would get a greater understanding of requirements. Facilitation refers to workshops where project team members serve to facilitate discussions and meetings with key stakeholders to define requirements and build trusting understandings between the two parties. This facilitation approach is especially helpful when stakeholders disagree with the priority of requirements for the project.

Quality Function Deployment

Quality function deployment (QFD) is a tool used to systematically translate stakeholder-defined requirements into technical specifications, controls, and engineering requirements. The tool uses four combined matrices to create a summary of relationships between customer requirements and resulting process parameters to create goods or services that meet those requirements. QFD also translates the customer voice into salesforce language and further into engineering and operations understanding. Cross-functional experts from the organization are important support to the project manager seeking to create a QFD successfully. To further strengthen the analysis of customer voice, the QFD matrix often includes competitive data, co-relationships of requirements, and weighted scores for communicating significance to requirements.

Context Diagram and Prototypes

The context diagram is used to model the scope in a project. The diagram provides a visual representation of how customers use the deliverable and how the business systems create and deliver the product or service. Furthermore, the diagram maps the inputs to the business transformation systems, the actors that provide the inputs, the outputs generated from the business process, and the actors receiving the process outputs.

Prototypes are effective in validating stakeholder requirements by providing a testable model to obtain performance feedback. Prototypes are generally iterative versions made and adjusted in multiple cycles to confirm these requirements and validate performance to expectations.

Prototypes can come in several forms, including simulations, computer models, engineered physical versions, and mock versions of the desired final product. The end of the prototype phasing results in a production-ready product with all requirements captured and performance validated.

Outputs

Types of Requirements Documentation

Solutions requirements are outputs of the collection element that most completely detail the parameters, functions, and features of the service or product that will best meet the stakeholder requirements collected. Solutions requirements are divided into functional and nonfunctional groups based on characteristics. Functional solutions requirements are tangible features and behaviors that the product or service will exhibit, such as parts, actions, and processes. Nonfunctional solutions requirements are intangible features that are not visibly present but can be determined through statistical analysis or deeper evaluation of the product or service. Stakeholder requirements are also documented as an output. Related quality requirements detail the tests, parameters, and audits necessary to ensure the project and results meet quality expectations. Project requirements detail the milestones, resource constraints, and processes needed to achieve a successful project outcome. Business requirements list the higher-level business relevance of the project. Lastly, the transition and readiness requirements describe how the project team, its stakeholders, and participants will develop the resources and systems in order to effectively begin the forthcoming project.

Requirements Traceability Matrix

The requirements traceability matrix is a tool used in scope development to bond the deliverables to the originating customer and stakeholder requirements from which they are derived. A full traceability of deliverables to requirements ensures that the project activity delivers economic value, uses resources appropriately, and meets project objectives. As performance is tracked in the project life cycle, measurement of performance against the requirements using the matrix reinforces validation. Elements of the requirements traceability matrix include high-level validated requirements, project scope and objectives, business objectives, and work breakdown deliverables. Quality attributes are documented within the traceability matrix in sufficient detail that each requirement can be effectively understood, measured, monitored, controlled, and compared for performance reporting needs. The requirements traceability matrix may also include final deliverable or phase acceptance criteria.

Define Scope

Overview

The core part of the project scope management process involves the activity of using relevant inputs to formally develop the scope of the project and product/service considered to be the primary deliverable. The scope also delineates what is inside and what is outside the purview of the project. The process of defining the scope could potentially use any part or all of the collected requirements outputs. Iterative projects may have the scope change as the project evolves, while predictive projects have the scope well defined in the project scope management phase, with no changes thereafter. The resulting output of the define scope step is a clear, detailed depiction of the project and its deliverables, including resulting products or services.

Outputs

Project Scope Statement

The project scope statement serves to describe the project scope as well as the product/service scope. It also contains highly important details, including the constraints, the deliverables, and any assumptions relevant to the project. The scope statement is written for stakeholders as the primary audience. The scope statement provides a baseline perimeter from which the project team and the PICC or change control board can base their decisions when confronted with change requests. After the scope statement is completed, the project team has more guidance and a path forward for creating more detailed plans and executing the project work.

The four main features of the scope statement are acceptance criteria, deliverables, scope description, and exclusions.

- The acceptance criteria explain key features, parameters, or requirements that must be met before the deliverable(s) can be considered accepted.
- The deliverables are any type of product, service, or phase transition that meet the compiled requirements. The description of deliverables is included in the scope statement with sufficient detail to ensure it is clearly communicated.
- The scope description defines the expected project deliverables using the referenced and compiled requirements as well as the project charter.
- Exclusions to the scope description are also defined in the exclusion section to ensure added clarity about what is in scope in the project.

Project Charter vs. Project Scope Statement

The project charter represents the authorization for the project manager and team to begin procuring resources and performing activities for the assigned project. The charter also signals that the project meets organizational strategic objectives, and the business case exemplifies an endeavor that makes financial sense to pursue. The charter also lists project objectives, purpose, deliverables, and the resources needed to complete the project.

In contrast, the project scope statement reflects the input of customer and stakeholder requirements in order to ensure the project is focused on what matters most to the client and not focused on irrelevant details. In some projects, the scope statement is a critical element to the project charter. For example, it is common in lean Six Sigma projects to have a scope statement within the project charter. Furthermore, the charter describes purpose, high-level requirements and deliverables, and summary details for the project (such as schedule and objectives). The scope statement details the deliverables, acceptance criteria, and any scope exclusions.

Create WBS

Overview

Work breakdown structures (WBSs) divide a project into smaller, manageable activities to help the team make sense of the steps necessary to complete the project. The WBS can provide the team with the actions necessary to enact the vision and deliverables in the project within schedule and budget. The structure is an element of the project scope management process. The WBS deconstructs the entire scope of the project. The defined goals or objectives are important parts of the WBS, with all tasks and subtasks being derived from the goals. WBS plans are depicted as a hierarchy of the project by creating layers, including work packages, tasks, and subtasks. Details such as precursory and subsequent tasks, costs, and performance expectations are all included in each level of the WBS.

Tools and Techniques

Decomposition

Decomposition is defined as the division of the project scope and deliverables into smaller and more manageable subcomponents. Specificity is indicated in the decomposition as more detailed breakdowns reflect the degree of control desired by the project team. The smallest elements resulting from the decomposition process are work packages. Work packages themselves are not simple activities or tasks; the packages consist of several highly related tasks to be completed. Decomposition includes five key steps: deliverables analysis, WBS organization, upper-level WBS decomposition into subsidiary workings, tagging WBS steps with identification codes, and verification of effective and accurate decomposition.

Outputs

Scope Baseline

The purpose of the scope baseline as a WBS output and a key part of the project management plan is a validated scope statement combined with the WBS and its associated WBS dictionary. The baseline is a controlled comparison that requires a formal change process in order to be revised.

The five key components of the scope baseline are the WBS itself, the WBS dictionary, the project scope statement, the work package, and the planning package.

- The WBS is a detailed breakdown of the total work forthcoming in the project.
- The WBS dictionary provides further detailed information about deliverable, schedule, and activity for each WBS constituent. Other information provided in the dictionary includes work descriptions, milestones, resource requirements, and responsibilities.
- The project scope statement lists the scope itself, listings of the deliverables, constraints, and key assumptions for the project.
- The work package represents identified, elemental-level tasks within the WBS. Each package has a unique identifier and includes related cost, schedule, and resource data linked to that identifier. Multiple work packages form a control account.
- The planning package is an intermediary part of the WBS without schedule details but with relevant work content included.

Validate Scope

Overview

The validate scope process involves the project manager and team obtaining objective validation for the project scope and deliverables. Such validation of each deliverable supports the allocation of resources towards the final outcomes of the project—such as a product, service, or transition—and makes commitment towards a high-quality project outcome more likely. Customers are a primary source of validation in this element; deliverables from the project control quality process are reviewed for acceptance by project customers. Inputs to the validate scope element include the scope baseline, requirements documentation, and work execution data.

Inputs

The validate scope element to the project scope management phase includes the project management plan itself, several key project documents, deliverables, and work execution data. The subcomponents of the project management plan used as inputs include the scope baseline, the requirements management plan, and the scope management plan. Several common but important documents used as inputs include the stakeholder requirements documentation and the related requirements traceability matrix; the lessons learned register; and any quality reports generated in the project to date, such as quality assurance issues or corrective actions. Deliverables used in the scope validation process must be those that have supporting proof reflecting their alignment with customer expectations in the control quality phase. Lastly, work execution data represents an input that demonstrates the validation performance amassed in the project. These records may include measurements showing compliance to requirements, nonconformances issued, and the results of previous validation activities.

Tools and Techniques and Outputs

Inspection and Decision-Making

Decision-making is a common aspect of leadership in project management. Decision-making is important in the scope validation process because of the amount and impact of the information collected to derive an effective scope statement and project scope management planning. One element of the decision-making technique is voting. Voting is utilized when the stakeholders develop the validation material. Inspection is a common approach to validate and verify systems. In the project scope management process, inspections are used to verify deliverables and customer relevance of the scope. The inspections, also commonly known in project management as reviews or walkthroughs, verify whether work and deliverables meet the acceptance criteria and are in line with expectations. Inspections often include several facets, such as observations, record reviews, data analysis, measuring processes or workflows, and even destructive testing of finished outputs.

Control Scope

Overview

The control scope element serves to sustain the project's central scope and monitor progress in relation to that scope. The scope baseline is a key component of this element. The baseline is the validated model against which progress is monitored. Deviation from the scope baseline would prompt reporting and communication to relay those deviations to key stakeholders and project leadership. The control scope process also ensures that the perform integrated change control (PICC) unit is utilized for any recommended baseline or scope changes and corrective actions. Limited resources committed to the project are at risk of being overused or deviating from plan in a situation called scope creep. The control scope element also serves to ensure that the defined scope is met, and that scope creep is minimized or prevented entirely. When change is a necessity for valid reasons, the control scope process ensures that those changes are well managed and communicated. The control scope process flow begins with inputs of the project management plan, project documents such as the requirements traceability matrix, and work performance data. Through the element, outputs include work performance information, activity for the PICC unit, potentially revised project management plans, and updated project documents.

Inputs

Project Management Plan Components and Project Documents That Serve as Inputs

The process to control the scope must include critical validation documents, including the project management plan and its subcomponents. Subcomponents include primarily the scope management plan and the scope baseline. To control the scope against creep and uncontrolled changes, project managers and stakeholders must closely monitor performance against the scope baseline. The scope management plan serves as a standard operating procedure defining how the organization will execute the control functions upon the project scope and product scope. The baseline is the calibration model against which performance is monitored. Additional project plan components include the configuration management process, the performance measurement baseline, and the customer/stakeholder requirements management plan. These plans serve as guides of validation when monitoring scope.

Project documents used as inputs include the requirements traceability matrix, all related requirements documentation, and the lessons learned register. These components and documents are also supplemented by work performance data and various associated organizational process assets.

Project Schedule Management

Plan Schedule Management

Overview

Process	Description
Plan schedule management	The encompassing policies and procedures that describe how the project schedule is to be created, managed, performed, and verified by the project team.
Define activities	The project team determines the specific activities and tasks needed to accomplish the defined deliverables of the project. This component includes the use of decomposition and rolling wave planning techniques.
Sequence activities	The process by which the project team constructs sequential and relational order to the defined activities and tasks. The schedule begins taking a rough format during this step.
Estimate activity durations	Using validation material, history, and expert opinion (among other resources) to affix time durations or work periods to each task in the body of defined activities needed for deliverable completion.
Develop schedule	This part of the schedule management process involves the analysis of the define, sequence, and duration estimate work and develops a project schedule to be followed for execution and control.
Control schedule	Procedures that serve to monitor and verify the adherence to the project schedule and use formal processes to adapt or prevent change from impacting performance against baseline.

Emerging Trends in Project Schedule Management

Alternative scheduling is a change-friendly option that uses adaptive life cycles and is similar to rolling wave planning and Agile product development schemes. Information is collected and translated into product features within sequential timeframes. During the course of each of these timeframes, value is added to the deliverable and the project in an incremental manner. On-demand scheduling relies on downstream demand or pull for intermediary inputs or signal to progress through the sequenced activity of the project schedule. The organization's throughput capacity and its ability to forecast demand are often weaknesses for on-demand schedule performance. On-demand scheduling is similarly used in lean manufacturing principles, such as Kanban and Goldratt's theory of constraints.

Inputs

The plan schedule management process is similar to the scope development process in that it involves the development of policies and standard operating procedures regarding planning, implementing, and controlling the project schedule. Just as with the scope management plan, the schedule management planning process documents procedures, policies, and metrics that will be used to ensure that schedule development, monitoring, and sustainability are achieved. Key inputs used when developing the schedule management plan include the project charter, the project management plan, the scope management plan, and enterprise environmental factors.

Tools and Techniques

Expert Judgement, Meetings, and Data Analysis

Expert judgement focused on effective project schedule development provides the project leadership with experience and insight into optimizing the schedule early. Experts may be selected from within the organization, or they may be exterior consultants or stakeholders. Expertise most valuable to supporting plan schedule management can include adaptive life cycle or predictive methods, scheduling software implementation and interpretation, scheduling basics such as creation and control, and advanced considerations within specific industries.

Meetings are important approaches to collect stakeholders that impact or influence the schedule and develop the project schedule and its supporting activities.

Data analysis is a common tool used when there are alternatives that need to be weighed by the project team before selecting a life-cycle model. Data analysis tools are also supportive when calculations must be made regarding rolling wave planning, lead and lag times, and related resource planning.

Outputs

Schedule Management Plan

The schedule management plan is a key component of the project management plan and serves to communicate how the schedule will be created, monitored, and controlled by the project team, and by relevant stakeholders and experts as needed. The level of complexity of the schedule management plan is determined by the scope of the project. The schedule management plan, as an output, will provide the team with several standards and instructions needed for the schedule life cycle.

Results of the Plan	Description
Control thresholds	Acceptable schedule variation levels to be monitored.
Level of accuracy	Ranges acceptable in the estimation of activity durations.
Organizational procedure linkage	Linkage to the work breakdown structure (WBS).
Project schedule model development	The chosen scheduling development tools are defined.
Project schedule model maintenance	The procedures for updating schedule execution status.
Release and iteration length	Commonly occurs when using time-boxing in adaptive life cycle scheduling.
Reporting formats	Specific controls on schedule performance reporting.
Rules of performance measurement	Performance measurement rules such as earned value management are set.
Units of measure	Elemental units of measure are defined for consistency.

Define Activities

Overview

The define activities element is a process where work activities are defined as necessary to accomplish the project deliverables. The work breakdown structure results in work packages—small breakdowns of the project but not at the most elemental task level. The define activities process hashes out the specific tasks and activities needed to fulfill these packages. Inputs into the define activities process include the project management plan, the schedule management plan, the scope baseline, enterprise environmental factors, and various organizational process assets.

Tools and Techniques

Decomposition

Decomposition is defined as the creation of manageable pieces and activities from the scope and deliverables. The analogy used is that of organic matter decomposing into elemental nutrients that are the building blocks of the organic material itself. Fittingly, decomposition is a collaborative tool used in the creation of elemental activities needed to complete work packages. Distinct from the work breakdown process, decomposition takes deliverables a step further by breaking them into manageable tasks. The WBS packages are each decomposed into the activities or tasks needed to complete each deliverable. The WBS dictionary is also essential to creating the activity breakdown.

Rolling Wave Planning

Rolling wave planning is a technique for focusing on planning the finite details on near-term activities with increased importance while looking at more distant planning activities from a broader perspective. The rolling wave plan is repeated routinely as near-term activities are planned and executed and future activities come due. Longer-term work is kept in work packages, and near-term planning is broken down into activities and details through decomposition. The technique is highly useful in Agile and waterfall project life cycles.

Outputs

Change Requests, Milestone List, Activity Attributes, and Activities List

Change requests that arise in the context of the define activities process often occur as work packages are broken down into activities and new information is obtained that exposes a weakness in the initial baselines. As with other change requests, such endeavors are routed through the PICC group in the organization.

The milestone list functions within the activity schedule as markers—with no technical duration—that collections of activities have been completed and/or deliverables have been achieved during the project schedule execution. Milestones are often indicated as contractually mandatory or strongly recommended based on organizational lessons learned.

Activity attributes are collections of more detailed information for each activity decomposed from work packages. These attributes provide key stakeholders and activity executors. The attributes also include details such as lead and lag times, assumptions, constraints, activity relationships, and resource requirements. The additional information provides support for leadership analysis of the schedule and greater clarity and context to each task.

The activities list delineates, by ordered activity ID, the tasks in the schedule. A work description is also included in the list to give additional context. Iterative life cycle approaches to project schedule planning expand the activities list and activity attributes in sequential batches as the project progresses.

Sequence Activities

Overview

Sequencing activities is the act of linking project activities based upon their relationships with each other. Relationship mapping and sequencing can be based on individual linkage or grouping using related features. The intent of sequencing activities is to give added efficiency in the execution of the schedule and lead/lag time as necessary for certain activities. Inputs to the sequencing process include activity attributes, activity lists, the milestone list, and assumptions. Transformation of the inputs results in the creation of project schedule network diagrams and updates to the input documents as necessary. Sequencing involves the use of predecessor and successor linkage, lead and lag time estimations, and duration calculations to make a visual map of the various work activity streams in parallel or sequence through every milestone and deliverable in the schedule.

Inputs

Function of Key Inputs

Input	Use in Sequencing
Activity attributes	Added detail within the activity attributes often provides unambiguous durations, sequences, predecessor relationships, and duration uncertainty (in the form of lead and lag times). These details provide straightforward sequencing input.
Activity lists	The activity list provides a summary of all activities that must be sequenced in the sequencing phase.
Milestone list	The milestone list describes the collective activities that must be completed before each milestone is considered to be achieved. Similarly, the milestone list may also have defined dates or elapsed days that dictate how activities are to be scheduled.
Assumptions	The assumptions and constraints documentation influences the sequencing activities because the lists contain information on uncertainty in lag and lead times, risks, and relationships among activities. These variables impose the need to plan for uncertainties in the sequence.
Schedule management plan	The plan gives validated guidance and requirements for how the schedule management and sequencing must be performed.
Scope baseline	The scope baseline gives boundaries regarding assumptions, constraints, work breakdown structure (WBS), and deliverables necessary to sequencing.

Tools and Techniques

Precedence Diagramming Method

The precedence diagramming method (PDM) is a tool used to visually depict the activities in the compiled sequence schedule using nodes and logical relationships. Activities will have one of four distinct relationships—or dependencies—between themselves and other activities. These dependencies can be predecessor-type or successor-type. Predecessor dependencies imply an activity that comes prior to a dependent activity. Successor dependencies imply a dependent activity that comes following a prior activity. The PDM also categorizes four types of relationships based on the possible dependency permutations. The available relationships are based on sequential, parallel, complementary, and overlapping uses.

Relationship Types

Start to finish (SF)	An overlapping relationship where the successor activity does not finish until the predecessor activity starts.
Start to start (SS)	A complementary relationship where the successor activity does not start until the predecessor activity also starts.
Finish to start (FS)	The most common relationship, where sequentially the successor activity does not start until the preceding activity finishes.
Finish to finish (FF)	The successor activity is not considered finished until the predecessor activity finishes.

Dependency Determination

Dependency relationships are determined in the sequencing process by first categorizing relationships as internal or external and as mandatory or optional. The classification of each dependency influences the prioritization each activity receives in the sequencing process. These two dimensions of dependency focus on the degree of control the project team has over the implied dependencies. For example, internal dependencies are generally more controllable than external dependencies. Likewise, discretionary dependencies are more flexible and can be variable based on the needs of other activities and resource constraints. However, mandatory dependencies are generally nonnegotiable and must be completed before downstream activities begin.

Internal dependencies are based on internal limitations and precedence. External dependencies are outside the direct control of the project team, as with a government agency. Mandatory dependencies can include contractual obligations or legal requirements, or may be influenced by mathematical or physical limitations. Discretionary dependencies are those where flexibility is available, and sequencing can take advantage of that trait. These soft logic dependencies expose the project to schedule attainment variance if not tightly controlled.

Lag and Lead Times

Lead occurs in activity scheduling in finish-to-start dependencies and provides the opportunity to hasten the successor activity given the predecessor. In contrast, lag occurs commonly—but not exclusively—in start-to-start dependencies. In lag situations, a downstream successor activity is delayed pending the completion of a predecessor. Lead is denoted in project schedule network diagrams or in planning software with the type of relationship, the numerical lead duration, and a negative sign. Similarly, lag is denoted with the relationship type, the numerical duration, and a positive sign. The process of sequencing activities must factor in the dependencies that need lead and lag times. The calculations and mapping of sequencing activities and schedule network diagrams is commonly performed with project management information systems. Such software is able to perform mapping; document leads, lags, and dependencies; and help arrange logical relationships for the project team.

Outputs

Project Schedule Network Diagram

The project schedule network diagram is a visual depiction of the sequenced activities and their dependencies. The diagram is created as an output of the sequence activities step of the project schedule management process. The diagram shows logical relationships, indicates lead or lag durations as appropriate, and displays any divergence or convergence routes of the activity flow. Network diagram divergence occurs when a predecessor activity has multiple successors. Convergence occurs when a successor activity has multiple predecessors. Regardless of whether the diagram is created manually or through project management information systems (PMIS), the diagrams provide a roadmap of the sequenced schedule. Diagrams may often include descriptions of the process used to create the map—a summary narrative—and unique clusters of activities may have supporting detail added for clarity.

Estimate Activity Durations

Overview

The process of estimating activity durations involves using valid project data and information inputs to attach an estimated number of work cycles to each activity in the schedule. This process adds a layer of mathematical and temporal utility to the schedule and sequence. A very significant amount of input information—such as the project management plan and project documents—is needed to perform the estimations. Several of these inputs involve data on resource sourcing and availability. Generally, the stakeholders or team members with the most relevant experience regarding certain activities also perform the duration estimations for those activities. The estimations derive the amount of work necessary to complete activities, all while factoring in constraints and external requirements on the usage of time. Many factors contribute to the estimations of each activity, including resource availability and effectiveness. Duration estimates exclude lead and lag times; these are added when mapping network diagrams.

Factors to Consider When Estimating Durations

Diminishing returns occur in duration estimation when resources are increasingly added towards the effort of producing work output for an activity and the additional effort does not yield any improvement in obtaining the outputs sooner or with better quality. Technology serves as an estimation factor because of the gains in speed, efficiency, and accuracy with advances in technology. For example, automated sorting operations may complete an activity at a fraction of the estimated duration versus when hand-sorting methods are used. Resource quantity refers to the caveat that a linear increase in resources applied to an activity does not necessarily result in a corresponding decrease in duration. Resources at some point become a burden upon the duration as more support and work must go into each activity. Lastly, organizational motivation serves estimation work by preventing procrastination as well as expansion of work performed to fit the pre-existing duration.

Inputs

Function of Key Inputs

Input	Description
Activity attributes and list	The activities list is a compendium of all activities to be sequenced and executed. Attributes are attached as supplementary cut sheets that provide added detail, such as logical relationships and lead/lag durations.
Assumption log	Useful assumptions and constraints known to the project team and valuable to factor into duration estimates.
Milestone list	Ordered listing of key milestones marking progress through the project schedule.
Lessons learned register	Past knowledge gained from experience in the organization and compiled for repeating successes and avoiding mistakes in the future.
Schedule management plan	Provides guidance on accuracy and other requirements for duration assessments.
Scope baseline	Project scope information as well as WBS dictionary.
Resource breakdown and calendars	A detailed account and breakdown of the resources needed for each activity and their temporal availability to work at each activity. For example, human resources and equipment resources must be adequately scheduled to maximize schedule attainment.
Resource requirements	Requirements linked to the resources needed for each activity. These requirements serve as specifications that need to be met by resources in order to meet duration and quality expectations.
Risk register	A compendium of identified risks that may impact the project.

Tools and Techniques

Analogous Estimating

Analogous estimating is a version of benchmarking whereby past objective duration and cost data is used to estimate similar parameters in a present or future project. Parameters such as budget size, project scope, and schedule duration of the project, when comparable to the present project undergoing activity duration estimations, can be used to support these estimates, especially when reliable present information is not available. The technique is a relatively modest investment of time and cost, but it can be riddled with inaccuracies.

Parametric Estimating

Parametric estimating uses computer software calculations, as well as past project cost and temporal data, to derive duration estimates based on statistical models. Other variables are factored into the calculations based on the past project parameters. The process can also provide statistical estimates of cost. The assumptions included in the calculations become increasingly accurate as the historical data is more reliable. Though the underlying assumptions of total necessary hours for an activity need calculating, the durations for each activity can be easily calculated by multiplying the work quantity and the labor capability. These calculations support resource allocation, costing, scheduling dependencies, and relationship determination.

Three-Point Estimating and Bottom-up Estimating

Three-point estimating of durations is an average calculation of the most likely, best case (optimistic), and worst case (pessimistic) activity durations calculated. This average provides a useful duration value when indicators and uncertainties provide differing estimates with similar probabilities; it is especially useful when historical precedent for duration is lacking. This resulting average is based on the (non-statistical) range of possibilities. The most likely duration (tM) has the highest probability given the resource productivity, availability, and dependencies. The optimistic duration (tO) is the analyzed best outcome given the inputs and assumptions. The pessimistic duration represents the worst-case outcome (tP). By calculating the mean of these three durations, the triangular distribution (tE) is calculated.

Bottom-up estimating is similarly useful when the project duration is difficult to estimate. The most elemental branches of the WBS are decomposed into work; the work is estimated individually to the farthest extent possible; and the aggregated durations (including dependencies) are summed to represent the activities, packages, and project itself.

Reserve Analysis

Reserve analysis is useful in deriving the level of contingency or management capacity needed for a project. When uncertainty exceeds an acceptable threshold, the project management allocates reserves to the schedule, generally in the form of additional percentage of the estimated duration or in the form of additional work hours. Given the uncertainty as the project work is performed and actual durations and resource requirements are experienced, the reserve quantities may be reduced or eliminated. The project schedule often denotes core durations from reserve proportions and distinguishes both in performance reporting. Furthermore, management reserves are built-in contingency resources that are available to project management in the event that unforeseen variation in project risks, assumptions, and external factors diverge the project from its scope or schedule unexpectedly. These management reserve resources allow the project manager and stakeholders to make on-the-fly resource allocations to get the project back on track. These reserves are outside of the schedule baseline but may require a baseline change process if it is determined that the management reserves need to be used.

Outputs

Features of Duration Estimates as Outputs of the Activity Duration Process

Duration estimates that result from the estimate activity duration process are characterized as a duration of time estimated to complete the activity, phase, or project. The estimates may also have a calculated range of variation that the team may experience when executing the activity or larger portion of the project. Such indicated variation can be displayed as additional work periods (e.g., days or hours) or as probabilities of exceeding or meeting the expected duration. The basis of the duration estimates includes several factors that were used to create the estimated durations. Such supporting data can be in the form of project risks, assumptions made, constraints known to the project team, the approach used to develop or calculate the estimates, how much statistical confidence exists for each estimate, descriptions of variance around the estimate, and the calculations of three-point or bottom-up calculations. The basis information can be highly valuable as historical information when planning future projects or iterations within a project life cycle.

DEVELOP SCHEDULE

OVERVIEW

The develop schedule element reflects precisely what its name describes. The collective analysis of activity sequencing outputs, duration outputs, resource requirements, assumptions, and constraints yields a schedule of the activities and work to be executed by the project team and stakeholders. The schedule includes start dates, divergent and convergent work streams, and milestones in a format that is easy to understand. Such an important element to the schedule management phase requires careful and often repeated analysis to reach optimization. Key inputs include the project management plan, several project document sources, agreements, and organizational factors. Key steps include schedule compilation (often by software), schedule review by the project staff to identify conflicts or resource constraints, review of dependencies for correctness, and approval/baselining of the schedule itself.

INPUTS

ESSENTIAL PROJECT DOCUMENTS

Essential project documents needed to effectively develop the project schedule:

Document	Explanation
Duration estimate	Details the specific quantity of work periods the estimation work has determined for completing activities.
Basis of estimates	The supporting details used to derive the duration estimates.
Resource calendars	Calendars that show the ebb and flow of resource availability during the project.
Activity list	The ordered list of all activities to be included in the schedule.
Activity attributes	Specific details that supplement each activity and support determining the schedule.
Milestone list	Markers within the schedule on specific dates that represent required achievements and demonstrating performance.
Project schedule network designs	A visual representation of the predecessor and successor dependencies between activities.
Resource requirements	Specific data on what resources are needed for each activity and in what quantity.
Project team assignments	Defines the human or personnel resources required for each activity; in other words, who is performing each activity.
Project management plan	An essential reference source that includes the schedule management plan, scope baseline, lessons learned, risk register, assumption log, and risk register.

TOOLS AND TECHNIQUES

SCHEDULE NETWORK ANALYSIS

Schedule network analysis is a broad term that represents the process of using schedule development input materials to create the schedule model. The process is rarely straightforward and often requires review and reanalysis throughout the project in order to reach an ideal network relationship between activities and phases. Furthermore, the network analysis includes supplementary practices of slip prevention and risk attack as iterations and reviews are performed. Part of scheduling is baking in management reserve resources in the event the project goes off track for unplanned reasons. Reserve execution can correct slip, especially at activity convergence or divergence points in the schedule. Such activation of reserve resources is also positive where critical path methodology indicates the potential for slip and delay. The critical path method is one of several commonly used network analysis tools.

Critical Path Method

The critical path is the primary constraint throughout the project and is also the length of the longest single chain of activities linked together, showing the shortest collective duration of start to finish. The critical path generally has no available slack time. Within this path, all other noncritical path activities can be scheduled with varying degrees of slack time. Slack time refers to the flexibility of delaying one or more project activities without causing delay to the overall project. The method uses relationships, sequence, duration, early start, late start, early finish, and late finish estimations to visually depict the critical path. Late and early finish and start dates provide the model with estimations of timeframes where activities could be completed.

Resource Optimization, Leveling, and Smoothing

Resource optimization refers to the modulation of activity start and finish dates to better align with the supply availability of resources such as labor, equipment, and funding. The optimization ensures that resource constraints due to overloaded demand are avoided where possible. Optimization can vary based on which variable is modified: the activity durations or the schedule sequence.

Resource leveling is a type of optimization where start and finish dates are aligned to the availability of resources. Resource constraints that may prompt leveling include multiple activities requiring the same resources or severe time or quantitative limitations on the availability of those resources.

Resource smoothing is the second alternative in optimization options and has the added benefit of not impacting the critical path. Smoothing changes the sequence variable; the activities are adjusted in the schedule so that resource constraints do not exceed a predetermined threshold.

Benefits of Simulations, Probability Distributions, and What-If Analysis

The use of simulations in schedule development is based on virtual experimentation with scenarios, where risk and error can be evaluated safely without wasting valuable project resources. Simulations can help explain the effects of changes and alternatives when uncertainty is abundant during schedule development. For example, Monte Carlo analysis analyzes risk and uncertainty to provide different schedule outcomes and probabilities that each model will meet timeframe expectations.

Probability distributions that arise from such simulations allow project teams to reduce the uncertainty in their model schedule as they are able to optimize the activity sequencing and durations. As adjustments are made, probability distributions reach higher certainty that models will meet the schedule and end date expectations.

What-if scenarios are evaluations where different combinations of factors are created to predict the effect upon objectives. What-if analysis provides tested outcomes and quantitative project impact as different variables are adjusted for one or multiple activities within the project. This analysis also supports the project team's preparation for reserve resources and contingency planning.

Schedule Compression Techniques

Schedule compression is a technique where the project team can analyze the project activities and durations against objectives and contractual dates to squeeze the schedule duration to a shorter timeframe. Crashing is a form of schedule compression where resources are added while controlling cost increases so that the critical path activities are prioritized and given a greater chance to be performed faster. Some additional resource allocation to the critical path activities may yield diminishing returns. Added labor or parts may not shorten completion; a threshold may also exist for resource allocation where more effort is needed to manage the additional resources. Fast-tracking refers to the maximized use of parallel work execution where the baseline schedule may indicate sequential work. The parallel activity in fast-tracking is only beneficial as a compression option if it can hasten the critical path. Cost overruns and risk introduction must also be managed in both compression techniques and have a net benefit if able to hasten the project timeframe.

Agile Release Planning

Agile release planning is a deliverable schedule management process that works in reverse from a fixed deliverable date. Batches of completed work are planned sequentially prior to the expected deliverable (or release) date. Each batch, termed a sprint, is an iteration of customer-centered features that are developed by the project team to satisfy stakeholder and customer requirements. Generally, these requirements are gathered through quantitative and qualitative customer data collection methods. Work is broken down within each iteration among the team members. The team works with higher levels of flexibility and agility when given a fixed schedule and batch-separated sprints. The process is ideal for dispersed and non-collocated work teams, as with software developers. The schedule can be adjusted based on customer needs and virtual work efficiencies.

Outputs

Schedule Baseline, Project Schedule, and Graphical Representations of the Schedule

The schedule baseline represents the confirmed schedule model to be followed as work execution begins. As with other baselines in the project management process, changes to the schedule baseline must be controlled and routed through a formal process such as the perform integrated change control (PICC) group. Performance against this baseline is monitored and reported so that stakeholders and team members understand if schedule attainment metrics are being met.

The project schedule itself visually depicts the activities, their dependencies, time durations, milestones, and supporting detail as needed to convey the sequential process to complete the project work.

Schedules are commonly constructed with a combination of listed sequential activities and a visual guide to their durations, relationships, and sequence. Network diagrams may be used to show durations as well as interconnectivity between activities. Simpler models, such as bar charts and milestone markers, explain durations and sequence sufficiently in low to moderately complex projects.

Project Calendars, Schedule Data, and Document Updates

Project calendars provide workers with more realistic timeframes, defining work days where scheduled activities and work are performed, as opposed to times when work is not expected to be scheduled. For capturing faster schedule completion, workforces and their associated activities are likely to be scheduled in parallel, around the clock in shifts, and/or with added overtime or human capital. Project calendars provide a more focused and granular version of work to the persons performing the work.

Schedule data is generated for the schedule model and should be able to capture all features and information in the schedule. The data can also be in the form of supporting material, such as reserve information; simulated alternative schedules as contingencies; resources needed per timeframe of the schedule; financial reporting; and resource histograms.

The most significant document updates resulting from the schedule development include assumption logs, resource requirements, duration estimates (especially if crashing or fast-tracking), and the cost baseline.

CONTROL SCHEDULE

OVERVIEW

Schedule control implies that the baseline schedule—which was thoroughly created, validated, and optimized—will be followed as work is executed. Tools must be implemented that can reasonably ensure control to baseline is achieved. Where changes must occur to the baseline, a formalized schedule change process is employed. For example, the PICC process serves to control proposed changes to the schedule, the reserves (if any), and the progress on the active schedule execution. Agile project life cycles are similarly concerned with maintaining control over the schedule and performance against its baseline. Agile—an iterative planning process—promotes controlling the schedule, including backward-looking reviews for future improvement, numerical estimations of project completeness, and managing any work backlogs.

TOOLS AND TECHNIQUES

COMMON DATA ANALYSIS TECHNIQUES USED IN SCHEDULE CONTROL

Iteration burndown is a technique for visual communication of work commitment and completion during iterative schedule planning. Displayed in a linear chart or bar chart, the visual shows the progress of smaller amounts of remaining work as the iteration days continue and work is completed. The burndown chart can also show differences between actual and predicted work remaining in the iteration. Earned value analysis (EVA) is a set of calculations to objectively show schedule performance variance compared to baseline. The analysis includes calculating schedule variance and a schedule performance index for the purposes of performance appraisal and reporting. Similarly, variance analysis can be performed on the actual and planned start and finish dates for all tasks to identify a quantitative variance compared to baseline. Weighted calculations may be imposed for variances within the critical path, as opposed to variances outside the critical path having less impact on the project duration overall. Trend analysis provides a longer-term visual on how performance changes over time.

Project Cost Management

PLAN COST MANAGEMENT

OVERVIEW

Project cost management refers to the set of processes where project costs are estimated, the budget planned and implemented, and the costs controlled through formal procedures. The cost management is coordinated through a cost management plan. The plan details how costs must be estimated, monitored, and controlled. The plan also describes the budgeting process and cost management steps. The budget process results in an approved cost baseline against which the project leadership can perform variance analysis with actual expenses. Lastly, costs are expected to be well controlled compared to the cost baseline.

Financial analysis and modeling are likely different between projects based on the industry where the project is being executed. How costs are allocated may also be different depending on accounting standards within the organization. These accounting practices may be very different in private versus publicly traded companies. Independent financial performance prediction may occur by third-party analysis or by analysts within the same organization. Project managers are expected to consider tailoring approaches regarding cost management so that the uniqueness of any given project would not be hindered.

INPUTS

The plan cost management process involves the project team determining and documenting how project costs will be estimated, budgeted, distributed, monitored, and controlled. Several essential documents support this process, including the project charter, the schedule management plan, and the risk management plan. The resulting cost management plan guides the team through cost estimation, budgeting, and cost control. Other inputs to the cost management plan process include external environmental factors, like regional or global market conditions, productivity, monetary exchange, and overhead costs. Several organizational assets, such as financial skill, costing and estimating expertise and tools, and past project history, provide a positive influence on the cost plan development.

OUTPUTS

COST MANAGEMENT PLAN AS AN OUTPUT TO THE PLAN COST MANAGEMENT PROCESS

The cost management plan guides the team in performing cost estimation, budgeting, cost management, cost monitoring, and cost control procedures. The plan resides within the overall project management plan and clearly describes all important financial factors to the project execution. The plan often conveys key details to stakeholders.

Type of Feature	Description
Additional cost details	Further footnote-type financial information may be included for reference, such as exchange rates.
Control thresholds	When cost control weakens to where variance would exceed a threshold, it provides a warning to key stakeholders and the project manager.
Accuracy	Cost estimate level of accuracy acceptable to the organization. Expressed as a percentage about a mean.
Organizational procedures	Reflected in the work breakdown structure; costs are represented as a control account.
Precision	Rounding is defined according to the accounting practices of the organization.
Reporting	The financial reporting requirements and frequency are defined for the project.
Rules of performance monitoring	Describes how performance measurements (such as earned value management) will be calculated.
Unit of measure	Defining the unit of measure for time, weight, distance, and currency for consistency across all stakeholders.

Estimate Costs

Overview

Cost estimation is the series of work performed by the project team to assess the expected costs associated with the activities to be performed in the project schedule. The estimation derives quantitative figures of the predicted expenses for labor, resources, and services to complete the project. Assumptions and constraints are factored into the estimations. Alternative cost models are also generated with differing scenario options for buying, leasing, or making parts and services needed in the activities. The cost estimation process is iterative during the life of the project. More information is gained as the project work is completed and as purchasing decisions become due during that project progress. Several rounds of review of the cost estimation are expected. It is also helpful to stakeholders to understand the degree of confidence around each cost estimate.

Input

As the preliminary task performed prior to using inputs to create the project cost estimates, the cost management plan outlines the procedures and specifications to be used for performing the estimations. Similarly, the quality management plan is incorporated as an input into the cost estimation process. The quality plan includes customer and stakeholder requirements and measures of project success. The scope is also highly important to the cost estimation. Thus, the scope baseline serves as another key input to the cost estimation process. Within the scope baseline, key elements such as the WBS, the WBS dictionary, and the scope statement itself give more specific reference information for cost estimation. Other inputs include common project documents such as the project schedule, resources requirements, and the risk register. External factors such as market conditions, exchange rates, and trade fluctuation are inputs that may vary in usefulness from project to project.

Tools and Techniques

Use of Common Estimating Tools

Analogous estimation is defined as the use of past project cost estimation data to derive similar (or analogous) estimates for the current project, under the assumption that similar expenses, project execution, and constraints exist in the present project. Scope, cost, schedule, and resources may all be derived from analogous projects.

Parametric estimation uses more statistical analysis with past data and parameters when analyzed against similar parameters in the current project. The uncertainty of the estimation may be reduced if the analytical model is validated and uses sound technique.

Bottom-up estimations focus the estimation analysis on the most granular work in each activity within the project. This uses the line of thought that estimations of the lowest elements of the work will aggregate into a highly accurate estimation of total project costs. The roll-up of costs may, however, overlook macro-level risks, cost assumptions, and market forces.

Three-point estimations use a range of probable cost analyses to derive a triangular distribution representing a pseudo-confidence interval of the likely costs. Three-point estimations can also employ a beta distribution calculation that adds weight to the most likely activity cost scenario. In both calculation approaches, confidence in the optimal estimation is gained.

Cost of Quality

The cost of quality is the expense incurred by an organization to meet customer and stakeholder quality expectations, or to rectify product or service quality and customer satisfaction when quality has deviated from the acceptable limits. Quality costs can come in four different types, based on the degree of failure: conformance costs (preventive and appraisal) and nonconformance costs (internal failure and external failure).

Preventive costs have little failure evident and are designed to use resources to avoid the multiples of quality costs in failure when preventive controls are not in place. Appraisal costs are those that perform quality evaluations and control upon processes, products, or services in order to ensure that customers are going to receive expected satisfaction and that the process worked as designed. Shifting appraisal costs towards preventive costs is an ideal to quality professionals.

Internal and external failure costs occur when finished products or services do not meet specifications and must be reworked, scrapped, or recalled from the client. External failures incur the most significant expenses in retrieval of nonconforming output and in legal fees and remuneration. Cost estimates balanced heavily on prevention likely require little expense on failure.

Outputs

Format and Features of Resulting Cost Estimates

Cost estimates that result from the process are quantitative in nature and show a monetary value after historical, risk, external, and customer analysis of what the cost should be. This is expressed for the project as a whole, and for each activity or phase within the project schedule. Contingencies are also tallied within the cost estimate given risk and constraint input. Specific direct cost details summarized within the cost estimate can include equipment, supplies, labor, materials, facilities, and financing interest. Furthermore, the cost estimate output includes a basis of estimates summary that describes the decision-making baked into each estimation. This basis also summarizes constraints, assumptions, risks, and ranges considered in the analysis. Once the cost estimation is complete, there may be more document revision in the project plan, including the lessons learned log, risk register, and assumptions log.

Determine Budget

Overview

After the activity costs have been estimated using one or a combination of estimation approaches, the project team (or the organization's financial experts) compile the estimated costs into an approved baseline budget. Setting the baseline gives the project team and stakeholders a benchmark against which performance can be measured. Because the charter formally authorizes the use of resources towards the project, the budget creates the boundaries of authorized funding. The budget often includes contingency reserve funding in the event of unplanned issues or threats to the project schedule. The budget determination process is the aggregation of the cost estimation work. Several inputs are required for the budget process. Foremost, the cost estimations are needed. Additionally, the cost management and resource management plans, project schedule, and scope baseline are pulled from the project management plan.

Tools and Techniques

Historical Information Review, Data Analysis, and Funding Limit Reconciliation

When analyzing the cost estimates and supporting input documents, the project team must use history and data analysis as primary means for arriving at a budget. A straightforward approach is the aggregation of activity costs following the pattern of the WBS. Phases and levels of the project have their aggregated costs tallied, as well as the project as a whole.

Historical information is reviewed to ensure analytical estimates, such as parametric or analogous methods, are as consistent with past patterns as possible. Accuracy of historical data, validity of the mathematical models, and scalability of the analysis are features that support effective historical review.

Funding limit reconciliation is a budgeting element that monitors and identifies funding variances between budgeted limits and planned commitments of expenditure. Figurative red flags indicate expenses are exceeding planned costs, which would prompt adjustments in the scheduled allocation of funds as well as date constraints for future project work.

Outputs

Cost Baseline

The cost baseline is a detailed budget that includes cost allocations approved at various intervals throughout the schedule. The cost baseline, as observed with other project baselines, serves as the comparison point for actual performance when monitoring adherence to budget. The cost baseline covers all budget elements for the project, including contingency reserves but excluding management reserves. The baseline is commonly portrayed as a time-based graphic of the cost estimates incurred as the scheduled activities occur over time. When the project team factors in the management reserve funds, the complete project budget takes shape. The baseline is also used as a planning model for financial resource allocation as the project work progresses in time. This projection ability allows for smoothing or planning of expenditures by the organization. The baseline, when presented as a graph, would show stepwise increments of funding allocations as the cost curve increases over time. For comparison, actual expenditures are plotted with the cost baseline and funding outlays to provide a performance visual.

Control Costs

Overview

The control costs element involves ensuring that budgeted costs planned in the project schedule are monitored against the known cost baseline for performance assurance and expected use of resources. The control costs phase relies heavily on tracking value added per project expenditure (earned value analysis), implying that the metric of expenditures compared to completed project work is important. Several important factors and deliverables are achieved through the cost control element. These factors can be grouped into monitoring, managing, and preventing activities. The PICC group must have oversight on cost baseline or budget change requests.

Deliverables Found in Effective Cost Control Outcomes

Control Costs Activity	Description
Monitoring	Cost variances as they occur, work performance based on actual funds expended, monitoring funding use by various segmentations of the project schedule (WBS, phases, activity, etc.).
Managing	Timely evaluation, execution, and communication of change requests and approvals in real time, regaining control of cost overruns.
Preventing	Leading baseline revisions through the change process, employing systems and controls to prevent unauthorized use of funds or change to baselines.

Tools and Techniques

Earned Value Analysis

Earned value analysis (EVA) is used in cost control to monitor actual expenditure and schedule progress compared to the budget and schedule. This metric provides an assessment of the value—in financial and schedule terms—of the investment spent to date in the project. EVA has three primary monitoring dimensions: planned value, earned value, and actual cost.

- Planned value (PV) is defined as a roadmap of the project work expected to be completed at any given point in the scheduled budget allocation. Budget at completion (BAC) is a term used for the project's total planned value.
- Earned value (EV) is the proportion of work completed compared to the budget authorization distributed to date. EV is commonly used to express the percentage completion or work in progress in a project.
- Actual cost (AC) is the booked expenditures truly incurred and accounted for the work activity performed. AC can be monitored and reported at intervals in the schedule. AC is the true cost incurred given the budgeted funds.

Variance Analysis

Variance analysis is the process of mathematically expressing actual performance against an expected baseline performance. Variance analysis in the context of cost control and earned value analysis can mathematically express variances in costs and schedule. Variance analysis is a precursor to root cause, corrective, and preventive actions for resolving and preventing variances found.

- Schedule variance (SV)—The difference between EV and PV. The calculation factors in work performed against budget (EV) and negates the authorized budget for the planned work to derive a schedule metric.
- Cost variance (CV)—The difference between EV and AC, expressing the degree to which the project is over/under budget with current performance.
- Schedule performance index (SPI) is the ratio of EV to PV. Cost performance index (CPI) is the ratio of EV to AC. SPI represents schedule efficiency, while CPI, arguably a more important metric, represents cost efficiency for the work finished to date.

Schedule variance (SV)	Cost variance (CV)	Schedule performance index (SPI)	Cost performance index (CPI)
$SV = EV - PV$	$CV = EV - AC$	$SPI = \frac{EV}{PV}$	$CPI = \frac{EV}{AC}$

FORECASTING

As the project team standardizes and effectively monitors project costs and value, the team may seek to predict an estimate at completion (EAC) that represents the expenditures estimated to be incurred at the time of schedule completion. Such forecasts are made using work performance information collected and analyzed from the project activity made prior to initiating the forecasting. Bottom-up summation, where actual costs are summed with an estimate to complete (ETC), is an effective approach for estimate at completion forecasting. Risk is an important factor when developing forecast scenarios. Multiple options are available for deriving an EAC forecast for the estimate to complete metric.

EAC Model	Description	EAC Calculation
For ETC work performed at budgeted rate	Uses actual cost data to represent work performed and forecast ETC at budgeted rates.	$EAC = AC + (BAC - EV)$
For ETC work performed at present CPI	Bases forecast on present performance, assuming continuation of that performance and at same CPI. Expressed as a rate.	$EAC = \frac{BAC}{CPI}$
For ETC work using SPI and CPI	Expressed as a rate of efficiency by factoring in schedule and cost indices, and allows for more management judgement in the calculation.	$EAC = AC + \frac{BAC - EV}{CPI \times SPI}$

TCPI

A to-complete performance index (TCPI) metric provides cost control efforts with an endgame perspective on the cost control performance necessary to meet a defined management goal. TCPI is a ratio of the remaining cost to the remaining budget. Using the BAC value, the earned value and the actual costs are factored to derive the ratio. Work remaining is the difference between budget at completion and earned value. Cost remaining is the difference between BAC and AC. By setting control limits around the TCPI index, the team can assess the budgetary behavior needed to keep the expenses within range of the budget at completion. The TCPI can indicate performance above baseline (estimate at cost) or below baseline (budget at cost).

Project Quality Management

PLAN QUALITY MANAGEMENT

OVERVIEW

FUNCTION

Project quality management serves the project management process by collecting and enforcing project and customer quality requirements upon the project work. The quality management system involves methods for monitoring, controlling, and managing quality requirements significant to stakeholders and customers. Related activities in the quality management system include continuous improvement programs. Similar to other project management plan elements, quality management begins with setting a quality management plan, followed by monitoring and controlling quality performance. Quality systems tend to have wide-reaching impact and influence on the organization or project processes. Interrelation between key quality processes—such as the quality management plan itself, scope validation, management activities, and quality assurance—are unavoidable. Behaviors such as product or service testing, quality reporting, auditing, and quality metric tracking are all supportive of effective oversight of project quality.

Quality

Quality is defined as the degree to which a product or service meets expected performance characteristics. Quality is primarily based on stakeholder and customer requirements or preferences. Quality can be expressed both qualitatively and quantitatively. The latter uses descriptive statistics, attribute measurement, and various graphical methods. Statistically, quality can be defined as the prevention of variation from the expected performance. Forward-thinking quality assessments must also account for the changing needs and desires of stakeholders and customers so that quality expectations are continuously being monitored and controlled for customer satisfaction.

Quality is kept at high levels when balanced towards preventive activities. The costs and efforts associated with prevention are more effective and valuable than failure recovery and expenses. Preventive actions include auditing, design for experiments, and obtaining the critical-to-quality specifications and voice of the customer for quality parameter development. Attribute sampling is an appraisal activity that performs in-process evaluations of quality performance as outputs and in-progress work are performed. Tolerances are the measurable boundaries that separate acceptable quality from unacceptable. Organizations often set internal tolerances tighter than customer-approved tolerances in order to deliver higher customer satisfaction over time.

Inputs

Plan quality management is the set of processes that result in having well-defined customer-based quality parameters established for the project and its deliverables. The process is further defined as having documented procedures executed to monitor and control quality via assurance practices. These two elements ensure that customer requirements are captured, and activities and outcomes of the project are verified to meet those expectations. The plan details how quality parameters are defined and controlled throughout the project. Common inputs are required for plan development, including the project charter, requirements management plan, risk management plan, and stakeholder engagement plan. Furthermore, inputs such as requirements documentation, customer specifications, regulatory references, and the requirements traceability matrix serve as essential data sources for setting quality standards.

Tools and Techniques

Baseline Data Collection Techniques

Interviews serve as qualitative data collection, primarily to gather quality specification, customer preferences, and stakeholder concerns. Interviews capture and aggregate such data to be translated into critical-to-quality specifications, ideally to the point where they can be monitored and controlled quantitatively through statistical and mathematical means. Various formats of interview data can be collected, including formal and informal feedback, as well as implicit and explicit details. Relevant stakeholders are subjected to the interviews in unbiased and positive settings so that the most high-quality information can be collected.

Benchmarking refers to the practice of evaluating other projects, organizations, or industries for best practices or optimal approaches to managing output quality and performance. The organization performing the benchmarking studies seeks to obtain and emulate such best practices in their own project operations.

Brainstorming involves the collective participation of stakeholders, project staff, and leadership in thinking of and compiling ideas and approaches for the quality plan development. The unbiased collection of innovation serves to build incremental creativity to prevent and solve problems.

SIMILARITIES AND DIFFERENCES BETWEEN COST OF QUALITY ACCOUNTING MODELS AND COST-BENEFIT ANALYSIS

Cost of quality is a management and accounting tool that tracks organizational or project costs based on impact to the quality of the product or service being created. The logic behind cost of quality is that of a dichotomy between costs of conformance and costs of nonconformance. The objective is to balance more costs onto the conformance activities to prevent costs in the nonconformance bucket. Often, the more resources spent on conformance activities, the less overall total quality costs are incurred, at least up to a point of diminishing returns. Conformance costs include preventive expenses, such as audits. Conformance costs also include appraisal expenses, such as product testing, raw material analysis, and record reviews. Nonconformance costs include internal and external failures. Internal failures are costs related to waste, defects, and inefficiency. External failure costs are those related to recalls, market withdrawals, insurance claims, and reputational damage.

Cost-benefit analysis refers to the analytical comparison and decision-making between two or more alternatives. The cost or resources to be used must not outweigh the benefits likely to be obtained if the decision is accepted. Cost effectiveness is the objective when using the cost-benefit tool. It is important that project managers be wary of focusing solely on cost for decision-making. Such shortsightedness can miss the opportunity to strengthen preventive quality costs.

QUALITY DATA REPRESENTATION APPROACHES

Mind mapping is defined as an information organization tool to group thoughts, ideas, and topics into groups based on shared characteristics. The technique can help capture all relevant details related to product or process quality so that key controls may be developed.

A matrix diagram gives insight into the relationships between different datasets facing an improvement project or quality initiative. It is an essential management tool that comes in many forms based on how many types of sources are to be analyzed. By comparing relevant datasets among each other using any of the several diagram methods, a team can gain useful information and knowledge for improvement or strategic planning. The six common types of matrix diagrams used in quality and continuous improvement systems are X, Y, C, L, T, and roof-shaped diagrams.

Stakeholder	Unaware	Resistant	Neutral	Supportive	Leading
USDA		C			D
FDA			C	D	
US Dept of Commerce	C		D		
US Customs			C D		
Customer				D	C
City Health Dept		C		D	

Flowcharts are visual diagrams that map a process and show the interrelations or sequential workflow of a process. Flowcharts are useful when a quality or improvement team needs to fully understand all aspects of complex processes to control all steps and ensure the overall process functions appropriately to deliver compliant output. Examples of flowcharts include failure mode mapping, SIPOC diagrams (suppliers, inputs, process, outputs, customers), and swim lane diagrams.

OUTPUTS

QUALITY MANAGEMENT PLAN AND QUALITY PARAMETERS AND METRICS

Once complete, the quality management plan must outline how the project team and stakeholders will manage, monitor, and control project quality requirements and ensure deliverables meet customer quality expectations. The quality plan also outlines how policies, procedures, and performance measurement systems for project quality will be implemented for the project. Stakeholders and the project team members must be very familiar with the quality plan and how it will be executed. The plan also includes quality standards or specifications, quality objectives and measurement approaches, roles and responsibilities, planned quality control and assurance activities, the frequencies of quality activities, and relevant standard operating procedures regarding quality impacts to the project.

Common quality parameters and metrics include:

- First pass quality percent
- Defects per million opportunities (DPMO)
- Six Sigma
- Audit scores
- Defects per million units
- Net weight control
- Statistical process control conformance
- Cost of quality performance

Manage Quality

Overview

Quality Assurance

Quality assurance is the practice of ensuring that quality systems are being used as designed and are operating with a high probability of producing outputs that meet or exceed customer expectations. The manage quality element of the project management process involves performing quality assurance activities in the project execution process so that customer and stakeholder expectations are verified as met. Data collected from the quality management element is communicated to stakeholders of the project. Manage quality also includes product or service design elements of the project and process improvements. Four essential facets to the manage quality process within projects are:

- Verifying that quality standards are being followed, and that they meet project quality objectives.
- Performing product or service design processes to ensure deliverables meet customer expectations.
- Performing preventive and process control functions to ensure outputs are highly reliable with little unwanted variation.
- Using quality tools to drive improvement in efficiency and customer satisfaction.

Although larger organizations are likely to have dedicated quality assurance personnel working as key stakeholders or project team contributors, the responsibility for quality performance lies with all employees in the organization, especially those with direct impact on project results. Quality assurance leaders may also be project managers, which is common with lean Six Sigma project initiatives.

Tools and Techniques

Data Analysis Techniques and the Procurement of Strong Data to Be Monitored

The old saying of "garbage in, garbage out" applies when considering the analysis of quality assurance data. First, data collection must be reliable, accurate, and representative of the systems being monitored for conformance. Traditional approaches such as checklists, run charts, and inspections are good examples. Second, the analysis methods must be appropriate in order to obtain relevant and useful information that helps the project team and stakeholders understand quality performance against requirements and objectives. Though there are many quality assurance tools useful for data analysis, four common tools for project quality management are root cause analysis, document analysis, alternatives analysis, and process analysis.

- **Root cause analysis**—The deliberate and structured analysis of the underlying reasons that led to a result or nonconformance. Finding the true root cause allows quality teams to deliver the most effective solution to the problem. Common tools include 5 Whys analyses and fishbone diagrams.
- **Document analysis**—A form or record review that finds quality issues and feeds into corrective action processes.
- **Alternatives analysis**—The analysis of different options based on criteria, weights, or customer requirements.
- **Process analysis**—The assessment of processes and any opportunities to implement improvements for increased efficiency, increased customer satisfaction, and lower waste.

Data Presentation Tools

Scatter diagrams plot coordinate datasets where observations have two related parameters. For example, a plot of the number of defectives output over time has a quantity value and a time value associated with each measurement. Scatter plotting shows the relationship between two variables, and best-fit or trend lines can be added to further define those relationships and create predictive models.

Matrix diagrams translate variable and factor relationships between multiple criteria to derive meaningful information that is otherwise hidden.

Histograms are bar-chart plots of data by frequency in order to show a distribution pattern across a range of likely output values. Visualization gives insight into process behaviors and cause/effect.

Flowcharts are mapped steps that show the direction of a process to help others better understand the flow of materials and information.

Affinity diagrams can be used in project management to group common types of nonconformance causes, allowing greater focus on the most important causes.

Cause-and-effect diagrams visualize the relationship between an effect and the underlying cause or causes. This allows quality teams to attack multiple contributing causes and change outcomes in the future.

Auditing

Auditing is the planned review of an organization's performance compared to a set of agreed criteria or parameters. The audit is performed by one or more auditors and looks to gain objective and firsthand evidence to assess how strongly a process, organization, product, or service meets expectations. The expectations or standards used as the criteria for the audit are typically compiled or enforced by stakeholders, leadership, customers, or regulatory agencies with a vested interest in ensuring conformance. Auditing benefits the quality assurance process as a preventive cost of conformance. Proactively seeking out performance weaknesses or conformance risks encourages the project team and organization to adopt and enforce the behaviors that ensure quality standards are met or exceeded.

Outputs

Outputs unique to the quality management process include quality reporting and quality testing documentation. Quality reporting includes aggregated performance measurements against customer quality requirements and quality objectives for the project. The reporting that is derived from the quality assurance and quality management procedures provides key status information to the project leadership and stakeholders. Reporting also includes current quality risks, probabilities of nonconformance, defect rates, waste and rework, and any open corrective actions or continuous improvement opportunities. The reports themselves can contain a variety of data and information formats, including observed quantitative and qualitative graphs and summarized statistics. Quality testing and evaluation documentation includes performance and durability testing on finished outputs of the project to confirm consistency with specifications. Stakeholders to the project may request certificates of analysis or other verifications that outputs of the project were tested and proven to conform to requirements.

Project Resource Management

Plan Resource Management

Overview

Project managers and project teams must have resources available in the necessary quantities and at the right points in the project schedule. Project resource management ensures that resource needs are determined, procured, and made available to the project team when and where needed. Resource management involves creating a resource management plan, estimating activity resources, acquiring the right resources, and controlling the resources. This management process must also develop strong team performance to strengthen project performance. After all, personnel and employees that support the project are resources too. Risks are mitigated when project managers can effectively manage and control both physical and human resources. Emerging trends in resource management include constraint management, the development of emotional intelligence in personnel, and non-classically distributed (or virtual) teamwork.

Inputs

Self-Organizing Teams, Tailoring Considerations, and Inputs

Self-organizing teams (SOTs) are used in Agile iterations of projects in decentralized organizational structures. No single person serves as the sole project manager. A person may be loosely designated to give support and guidance to the other team members. Decentralized SOTs share common characteristics among members: strong commitment to the vision, trustworthiness, self-reliance, and high levels of team performance. These people must be able to adapt well to changes.

Tailoring the resource management process must consider human resource acquisition, specific industry requirements, organizational management and design approaches, and the range of the project team's skill and expertise.

Key inputs to the development of a resource management plan include the quality management plan, scope baseline, project schedule, requirements register, and risk catalog. Human resources are a critical element to the resource management plan. Thus, organizational process assets, including expertise in organizational design and leadership, are important inputs.

TOOLS AND TECHNIQUES

IMPORTANCE OF SUBJECT MATTER EXPERT SUPPORT AND ORGANIZATIONAL THEORY

Subject matter experts (SMEs) skilled in project resource management give a project manager important guidance. Expert consultants or organizations can provide guidance in three main areas: resource selection, procurement, and performance. SMEs can have specialized training or skills in determining the resources needed for activities and the levels of support needed. Furthermore, SMEs improve procurement practices by having skill in negotiating buying terms, managing supply chain details, navigating resource risks, and coordinating resource lead times with the project schedule. Lastly, SMEs can drive project performance by developing talent, resource management performance metrics, and communications.

Organizational theory collects data regarding how human capital interacts and behaves in groups, teams, and the organization as a whole. Organizational development uses this people data to design better work structures, operating policies, and leadership approaches to get the highest performance possible from personnel.

DATA REPRESENTATION TOOLS FOR RESOURCE MANAGEMENT

The RACI matrix is a communication chart used by the project manager so team members, stakeholders, and other personnel resources understand responsibilities, accountabilities, consulted experts, and information flow.

The chart lists several tasks relevant to the project, or may list all activities in the project schedule. On an opposing axis, the chart lists relevant names—team members, stakeholders, or experts supporting the team. For each combination of name and task, the letters R, A, C, and I are documented to indicate who is **responsible** for completing tasks, who is **accountable** to ensure tasks get done, and how **communication** and **information** are to flow among the team and stakeholders.

The responsibility assignment matrix (RAM) shows the resources assigned to each activity or work package in the project. This allows the project team to clearly visualize resource requirements, team member responsibilities, and resource usage over the life cycle of the project.

Hierarchical charts express how physical and/or personnel resources are divided among all activities of a project. The work breakdown structure, organizational breakdown structure, and resource breakdown structure illustrate how deliverables, the organization's personnel resources, and the physical and team resources are all broken down through a hierarchy into elemental packages or groupings for the project.

OUTPUTS

OUTPUT FEATURES

The finalized resource management plan describes to the project leadership how resources are organized, decided, allocated, managed, and issued to each activity or work package within the schedule. The two pieces to the plan are instructions for people management and for materials management. Each piece requires different management approaches and different procedures. Resource management plans generally include details on roles and responsibilities, how the resources will be obtained and managed, and how resources will be inventoried and verified for performance capabilities. Also, the plan typically includes personnel organizational charts, corrective action procedures, training requirements, team development guidance, and approved methods for rewarding or recognizing successful team members. Other documents and plans can be updated as a result of the resource management plan creation. These updates can occur to the charter, risk register, and assumption log.

Estimate Activity Resources

Overview

After the resource management plan is completed, the project team must estimate the resources needed for each activity within the project schedule. The team makes estimates for human and material resources. The estimations focus on several key dimensions: quantities, duration of time, cost, type of equipment, and any service provider support. Inputs for the activity resource estimation process include the resource management plan, the activity list and attributes, cost estimates, project schedule, and resource calendars. Procurement of resources requires financial investment. The methods and tools used in estimating activity resources are similar to the methods for estimating costs. Subject matter experts are also selected to support the estimation process.

Outputs

Activity Resource Estimation Process

The resource estimation is a documentation package that explains the resource requirements of the project activities. Details in the package include quantities, types, and sources. The resource requirements are aggregated and tallied in a way that is similar to the costs in the cost estimate output. To ensure clear communication of decision-making, the package also includes a summary basis of estimates. The basis outlines several factors, including risk and confidence level information, estimate ranges, detailed methods used to create the resource estimates, assumptions and constraints considered, and the references or resources used to create the estimation itself. The estimation provides a road map for the project team regarding procurement and inventory for project activities. Project document updates, updated from the resource estimation process, include the lessons learned register, the assumption log, and (most significantly) the activity attributes.

Resource Breakdown Structure

The resource breakdown structure (RBS) is a tool like the work breakdown structure. The RBS outlines the resources as categories—materials, equipment, services, and labor—needed for the project and separated by category and type. Each breakdown level may also include quality or grade information to identify the quality level of each resource needed. The breakdown makes the resource procurement quantities clear. The breakdown also makes the labor qualifications and material quality clear so that procurement and work assignments can begin.

Acquire Resources

Overview

The acquire resources process involves hiring or assigning labor and procuring materials and services needed to complete project activities. Project teams and stakeholders must have clear descriptions of the acquisition requirements and the needs for each activity over the course of the project schedule. Inventory, labor, and expertise within an organization may be sufficient to keep procurement internal. Most organizations working in complex projects must make external resource acquisitions. The process of acquisition must be well managed to ensure project success. The project leadership must have several key skills, including negotiation, substitution, and alternatives planning.

- Specialists assigned to purchase materials for the project must be skilled in negotiation. This enables the project team to be more likely to out-compete other sources requesting the same resources.

- When resources are limited, especially resources critical to the project, the project team must have alternative resource options available so that delays or project failures are not likely.
- The failure of the project team to acquire materials, labor, services, or equipment for completing the project tasks may lead to scope changes, major delays, or project cancellation. Project leadership must be aware of procurement risks and ways to mitigate the impact to customers.

Tools and Techniques

Decision-Making and Negotiating

Resource acquisition for project management often has many factors and risks to consider before selecting a material source or making a personnel hire. Instinct and expertise are positive examples of decision-making ability. Analytical approaches to decision-making can benefit project resource acquisition decision-making through rational calculations. Multicriteria decision analysis is a tool that combines several important factors and scores several resource options against one another to derive the best sourcing to pursue. The criteria are weighted based on internal stakeholder criteria and project team assessment of importance. Commonly cited criteria for materials or services include capability to meet performance expectations, cost, and availability. Commonly cited criteria for labor include emotional intelligence, knowledge, expertise, attitude, and skill set. Negotiations are an important element to acquiring resources. The ability of a project manager to cut through the various acceptance criteria should be documented and communicated or enforced in a distinct way. Negotiating is a beneficial skill when scarce resources are required by the operation and limitations are abundant (or at least negatively impacting the operation).

Virtual Teams

Virtual teams consist of team members operating from a variety of physical locations, time zones, and work schedules within the same project. The virtual nature of the team means that its members are led and evaluated remotely across discontinuous communication methods such as internet, email, conference call, video conferencing, and shared computer-based work platforms. Several other staff resources may be included virtually, including home-based employees, remote consultants, off-shift activity execution, and follow-the-sun project teams in multiple continents. The coordination and monitoring of project performance are increasingly important when the team shifts towards virtual. Deliverables, milestones, progress reporting, and verification gain importance to ensure commitment is high with the remote staff. Resource needs may also be lower because some virtual contributors do not need infrastructure such as offices; other virtual or freelance contributors may be contracted as well.

Outputs

Resource Assignments, Calendars, and Project Management Plan Changes

Resource assignments are categorized as physical or team assignments. The physical assignment of tangible procured materials, parts, and equipment occurs as detailed in the activity resource estimation process. These resources are acquired in the indicated quantities, locations, and timing per the previous estimates. Team assignments include the personnel who will be completing the work. Personnel are hired or assigned to the team with roles and responsibilities defined. The assignments are documented accordingly in project plans.

Resource calendars are a compilation of team member work shift details. The resource calendar indicates all open and available work time for each resource: personnel, equipment, or facilities. Utilization can be monitored and reported as a metric when collecting calendar data. Geographic location, skill level, and resource cross-utilization are also factored into the resource calendar data.

Lastly, and in a way similar to previous project phase outputs, the project management plan elements are subjected to updates throughout the resource acquisition process. Updates may be needed in the resource management plan, the cost baseline, the project schedule, the resource breakdown structure, and the resource requirements.

Develop Team

Overview

Team Development Process and Characteristic Behaviors of High-Performing Teams

Once acquired, the team members performing project work must be assimilated into the system and culture of the project team. Development must involve expansion of abilities, team building, training to work standards, and leadership support of a positive work culture. Project leadership must also be aware of methods to sustain high morale, develop interpersonal skills, and utilize team members by maximizing their strengths. Project and organizational leadership should develop several key behaviors in team members to make high performance more likely:

- Boost and champion collaboration in problem-solving and decision-making.
- Provide team-building opportunities.
- Promote honest and open communication lines to make conflicts less likely.
- Resolve conflicts quickly and effectively.
- Focus on crafting high levels of trust between team members.

Objectives and Stages of Team Development

Foremost, the first objective of the development of a well-functioning project team is to effectively complete project work within plan parameters. Team development should also enhance trust, skills, productivity (both individual and team), cross-training, and decision-making skills among team members. Teams hasten the development process when beginning with a prepared set of team norms or organizational cultural standards. Although these norms may adjust or change as the team develops, the baseline of cultural behaviors sets a strong foundation.

Tuckman's Stages of Group Development break the common path for team development into five characteristic steps. Team dynamics shift as the project team interacts with each other and faces challenges together. The development phases may not all occur, and some may not be in the same order as the model process describes.

- Forming—As the team begins working together, each person learns of their roles, responsibilities, and basic processes.
- Storming—As the team begins evaluating and working through activities, collaboration is minimal and team functioning is minimal. Conflict is highly likely.
- Norming—As more work is performed, behaviors that work well for the team are taking shape. Collaborative work strengthens.
- Performing—The team functions smoothly together and demonstrates interdependence when problem-solving.
- Adjourning—When the project work is completed, the team most often disbands without any further deliverables.

Tools and Techniques

Utility of Communication Tools, Colocation, and Virtual Work

Communication between team members and with project management helps shorten the time required to reach high performance. Various situations of team work locations require multiple communication options. Collocated project teams, virtual teams, and blended styles will require savvy use of tools available. Common tools include email, conferencing, video/audio, shared scheduling, and information-sharing tools within localized intranet or cloud-based services. Virtual teams require distributed online platforms to share information and communicate. Virtual teamwork may enhance development if outside experts participate from a distance when physical presence may not be feasible. Colocation is an effective approach where all team members work from the same location and can strengthen team bonding and performance quickly.

Interpersonal Skills

Negotiation is a skill used to derive compromise outcomes on decisions within the project team. Conflict management is very important to maintaining a high-performing team without strife that may reduce performance and engagement. Conflict is inevitable, but unhealthy conflicts are detrimental to performance. Influence is a skill that builds trust and aligns team members and stakeholders with reliable evidence, persuasion, and relationships. Motivation is enabled in team members through healthy empowerment of team members to contribute to the mission of the project. Motivation is also enabled through respect, fair treatment, accountability, and a clear and positive mission for the project team. Rewards, including financial rewards, can also be motivators of performance. Lastly, skilled team building, where the right people are given the skills to perform the right jobs optimally, will lead to higher performance. Common themes in effective team building include fostering a collaborative environment, effective communications, and interpersonal skill development.

Outputs

Team Performance Assessments

The project team development phase produces team performance assessments as evidence of monitoring and opportunities for improvement. Team performance data collected periodically will help both project and organizational leadership to assess where efforts at team facilitation and development are working effectively and where such efforts need change or support. This evaluation of performance often includes assignment performance data, turnover rate, net competencies held by the cumulative project team, and strengthened team solidarity. By collecting team development and performance data, project leadership can analyze strengths and weaknesses in skills, training, coaching, and realignment necessary to improve project performance and team development.

Manage Team

Overview

The project team management process involves monitoring, evaluating, adjusting, and coaching team members and defusing conflicts to collectively ensure the team executes project work at high performance levels. The team management process focuses on optimization of human resources, behaviors, and skills for project success. Project leadership must have key project plans, information logs, and performance data. These sources are analyzed with various tools or techniques to achieve team optimization. Ongoing or periodic team member assessments are also used as means to ensure the team is functionally ideal.

Tools and Techniques

Conflict Resolution

A low to moderate level of conflict among a project team is common and supports a healthy level of team performance and decision-making. When conflicts become detrimental to performance, it is important for project leadership to defuse conflicts quickly. Disruptive conflicts occur due to variation in resource expectations, schedule fluctuation, cost constrictions, and insufficient team development. The project manager or organizational leadership can help prevent disruptive conflicts by creating a culture of collaboration, trust, and communication. The project manager must assess the most effective approach to conflict resolution on a case-by-case basis while considering conflict intensity, team relationships, and impact to team motivation. Five key techniques—differentiated by degrees of active or passive engagement as well as win/lose combination—are commonly used in management to resolve conflicts.

Approach	Active/Passive	Description
Collaborative	Highly active (win-win)	The conflict is assessed from multiple viewpoints in a shared approach to solve the root cause problem(s).
Forced resolution	Active (win-lose)	The authoritative party (the project manager) forces the decision upon the team or individuals without feedback.
Compromise	Neutral (neutral)	Both sides of the conflict make concessions to a satisfactory outcome. The root cause of the conflict may not get resolved, and the situation may be win-win or lose-lose.
Accommodation	Passive (lose-win)	One party's desires are accommodated to avoid conflict, so the underlying root causes remain for a future day.
Avoid	Very passive (lose-lose)	The conflict resolution is avoided and may increase in severity if ignored further.

Leadership, Emotional Intelligence, and Influence

Leadership, emotional intelligence, and influential abilities are traits that can be developed in project managers.

Leadership is defined as the ability to motivate and inspire other people towards a common mission. Strong leaders are passionate about the project and about driving their team towards success.

Emotional intelligence is defined as a leader's ability to gauge and respond effectively to their own emotions and the emotions of those in their sphere of influence. Emotional intelligence also includes the ability to be empathetic, acknowledge others' concerns, and reduce team tensions.

Influence is developed skillfully over time by project leaders. Their influence can have three dimensions: role-based, relationship-based, or expertise-based. Influence based on role power, or one's authority over others, is effective only in the short term. Relationship and expertise influence are more sustainable options for influence.

Control Resources

Overview

Resource control is focused on resource utilization against the project schedule and resource management plan. The expected timing and usage of physical resources are monitored and controlled. Corrective actions are implemented where deviations from the baseline plan create a negative performance impact. This level of control helps ensure that the necessary resources are made available, costs incurred, and schedules maintained in the sequence expected. Key parameters monitored in the resource control phase include resource costs, quantity variances, accuracy in release and timing, navigating resource availability constraints, and change management.

Tools and Techniques

Problem-Solving

Problem-solving is a technique used by project managers to face challenges with a defined process so that the obstacle is overcome or eliminated, and the project work can continue within the expectations established. Project managers and teams are faced with internal or external problems, each presenting different methods to approach solutions. Many problem-solving techniques are available. Generally, problem-solving techniques follow a similar set of steps. Identifying and defining the problem begets the ability to collect the right types of data before beginning analysis. Analysis searches for possible solutions to the problem's root causes. Implementing solutions resolves the immediate issue, but resolution is not sustained without methods to verify and control the improvement in the future.

Project Communications Management

Plan Communications Management

Overview

Project communications management involves the implementation and support of project communication systems used to share project information to stakeholders within and outside the organization. The management system components include strategic communications planning and the execution of that plan. Essential aspects of communication in effective project management include body language, choice of media, level of formality, and whether the communication is written or verbal. Various approaches may differ in effectiveness when considering multiple potential dimensions to communication. In addition to internal, external, formal, and informal dimensions, communication activities may be along organizational design paths—for example, up or down the chain of command, or laterally among colleagues. Communication dimensions can also be public and formal, such as securities filings or press releases. Communications could also be unofficial, such as stakeholder meetings and working groups.

Trends

Social computing is best defined as the beneficial use of public communication networks, such as public internet, social media, and mobile systems, to challenge or improve project collaboration and performance. Stakeholder engagement can diverge into two subcategories: stakeholder participation in project meetings and stakeholder participation in project reviews. The former subcategory gives a greater voice to stakeholders that will be impacted by the project work or its outcomes. Participation in periodic project meetings opens an opportunity for the project team to receive feedback, ideas, or low- to mid-level conflict for better decision-making and focus on stakeholder needs. The latter category ensures stakeholders are informed of project work, status, and performance through reviews. Stakeholders that are considered essential to project success are primary recipients of review communications. Multifaceted communication strategies exist, in which project management delivers project communications in a variety of forms, platforms, and styles to ensure all participants and stakeholders receive information and messages in the model they prefer.

5 C's of Written Communications

The 5 C's of written communications are as follows:

- Control of idea-flow—Using mixed approaches (written, verbal, charts, graphs) to convey ideas and information smoothly.
- Clear purpose—The content and purpose of the information must be relevant to the audience.
- Concise phrasing—Communications delivered without unnecessary wording will keep audience misunderstandings minimized.
- Coherent flow—The art of denoting sections, topics, and a logical flow of information to the audience. Also, providing summary and introductory elements.
- Correct grammar—Accuracy of language and grammar used will prevent misunderstandings.

Supplementary ways to enhance the 5 C's of written communications are as follows:

- Active listening—Capturing and summarizing the speaker's words to ensure understanding.
- Skill enhancement—Using several concepts to enhance team performance: coaching, persuasion, motivation, negotiating, and conflict resolution.
- Stakeholder expectation management—Ensure stakeholders are satisfied that the project will meet their expectations.
- Cultural intelligence—Developing empathy and cultural understanding among team members.

Inputs

Plan Communications Management and Key Inputs to the Preliminary Process

The communication management plan is a set of standards and policies set by the project management team to ensure that the communication needs of stakeholders are met. The approach to meeting these expectations involves balancing the available communication assets within the organization as well as the project needs. The project team collects the communication preferences and needs from stakeholders early in the project life cycle and implements communication systems to ensure those preferences are met in a timely manner. Information management is an important element to the plan.

Key inputs to the development of a communication management plan include the resource management plan and the stakeholder engagement plan. These inputs are part of the overall project management plan and detail communication needs for personnel resources and project stakeholders. Related documents to these plans, including the stakeholder register and the requirements documentation, are also used.

Tools and Techniques

Technologies and Analysis

Important technologies used for developing the project communication plan are implemented based on underlying characteristics of the project. The project manager must adapt the communications technologies to the project using several potential approaches. Foremost, security of the communication is considered based on the sensitivity of the project objectives. Confidentiality may be increased if the project is within a military or highly competitive environment. The physical environment where the project will take place—virtual, blended, or collocated—and the geographic distribution of the project team will require consideration of cultural, time zone, and technology considerations. The methods of communication must also be easy to use for the project team and stakeholders.

Many sources are investigated to obtain input for development of the plan. These inputs can include:

- Stakeholder requirements
- Regulatory requirements
- Communication path network diagrams
- Organizational charts
- RACI matrix and related responsibility documents
- Internal and external information requirements
- Project staffing levels to gauge level of involvement with communications

Baseline Interactive and Cross-Cultural Communication Model for Project Management

The interactive communication model presents the standard flow of effective communication within a project between a sender and receiver. The baseline process involves the recipient acknowledging the information, reviewing it, and issuing their feedback to the sender. The sender must take responsibility to ensure the communication is clear and delivered correctly to the recipient. The recipient must take responsibility for receiving the complete communication, interpreting the material, and providing an acknowledgement or response to the sender. As layers of complexity are added to this model, communication effectiveness can decline if care is not taken. Cultural differences in language, ethnicity, socially acceptable behaviors, work methods, and social roles will impact how well senders encode their message and how recipients interpret and affirm their feedback. Furthermore, each individual within the communication will have personal influential factors impacting encoding and decoding the communication. The project manager must be aware of these factors and adjust communications accordingly.

Communication Methods for Sharing Project Information with Stakeholders

The three main types of communication methods for project stakeholder communication are push, pull, and interactive.

Push communications involve the project manager and/or team distributing communication materials downwards to the stakeholders on a schedule and format that is dictated by the project leadership. These results are discontinuous and are only provided periodically by select persons. Information asymmetry may exist between sender and recipient. Push techniques include reports, emails, newsletters, blogs, and meetings.

Pull communications result when recipients can access and retrieve relevant project communications and reporting when they so desire. Real-time information is obtained by the recipient as desired. Pull systems are better suited for larger stakeholder groups. Pull technologies include intranets, training portals online, and knowledge databases.

Interactive methods involve multiple persons or parties sending and receiving information among each other simultaneously. This common approach is found in meetings, conference calls, and seminars.

Outputs

Project Communications Plan

The project communications plan is the result of the analysis of stakeholder communication requirements, cultural and organizational communications characteristics, organizational technology dedicated to communications, and project standards for communications. The plan describes to internal and external stakeholders how project communications will be designed, executed, and controlled. Plan elements can be grouped into several categories: linguistics, stakeholder, resources/responsibilities, and methods. The plan may also include controlled documents and templates for effective communications during the project, likely developed from previous work in the lessons learned register.

Plan Element Category	Description
Linguistics	Glossary of familiar terms used
	Information in the appropriate language, content, and format
Stakeholder	Stakeholder communication rules and preferences
	Regulatory constraints
Resources/ responsibilities	Designated responsible person for communicating
	Defined distribution frequencies of communications
	Authorization controls for confidential information
	Defined resource allocation for communications
	Information flowcharts and control requirements
Methods	Information flowcharts that map out the distribution
	Procedures on how to escalate communications issues for more senior support
	Receipt acknowledgement process
	Approved technologies and media for communications

Manage Communications

Overview

Communication Management Process and Concepts for Effective Project Communication

The process of managing the project communications will follow the project's communication management plan. Managing communications involves the effective and accurate oversight of project information among the project team and with relevant stakeholders. Communications management addresses all steps in project information flow, including information creation, storage, distribution, control, monitoring, and review. The management process also addresses the functionality of communication methods, systems adjustments, and change requests. The communication management process also explains how the project team will address seven key aspects of communication.

Aspect	Description
Active listening	Strengthening comprehension by sending clear communications, actively acknowledging receipt, and achieving understanding between both parties.
Choice of media	Selection of the right communication medium (one or more) to deliver with effectiveness to all stakeholders.
Facilitation	Management of decision impasse and conflict to keep team member engagement strong.
Meetings	Performing effective meeting behaviors such as using agendas, timeliness, taking minutes, action lists, and participation.

Aspect	Description
Presentations	Conveying information through effective visuals, concise content, and clear delivery.
Sender/receiver models	Lowering barriers to effective feedback and interactive communications to strengthen understanding.
Writing style	Maintaining active voice and using effective writing skills.

Tools and Techniques

Communications Skills for Effectively Managing Project Communications

Competence is a communication skill characterized by strong leadership qualities, delivery with clear purpose, and effective information sharing. Experience in managing project communications develops project manager communication competence.

Feedback is a communication tool commonly used in the speaker/listener model. Interaction by the recipient when digesting the sender's information results in providing a feedback loop to clarify and verify understanding between the two parties. Furthermore, leadership behaviors such as coaching and performance evaluation are considered effective project communication behaviors related to feedback.

Nonverbal communication skills can supplement the written and spoken delivery of information. Body language, preparation, facial expression, and tone of voice serve to enhance communication delivery.

Presentations are most effective when delivered with relevant information of importance to the concerns and schedules of the audience. Effective presentations in the project process are often focused on performance reports, key challenges, and creating project scope and deliverable understanding.

PMIS

The project management information system (PMIS) is a component of the project work phase that is often overseen by the organization's information technology (IT) division. PMIS is commonly computer software that collects, analyzes, and communicates project data into useful information for the management of project work. PMIS systems can often be integrated with enterprise resource planning software tools for procurement, costing, and human resource planning. PMIS provides a reliable and easy information retrieval source for communicating project status and information to stakeholders. Assuming the data in PMIS is accurate, several PMIS tools are available to support these communications:

- **Electronic communications**—Tools and integrations are common so that information can be pushed or pulled with stakeholders through email, web portals, and conferencing.
- **Social media platforms**—Information and feedback systems may integrate with social media and mobile platforms for ease of stakeholder interaction.
- **Digital management tools**—Computer-based technologies that support project communications, including collaboration software, project management software, and office platforms.

Monitor Communications

Overview

Project leadership performs monitoring activities on the communications systems and processes to ensure effective, timely, and accurate delivery of project information to stakeholders and team members. Project leadership is responsible for ensuring that the information and communication expectations are met or exceeded for all stakeholders. The monitoring process for communications uses predefined information flow diagrams, stakeholder information requirements, and relevant sub-plans in the project to ensure the expectations and plan requirements are met. Activities including the collection and analysis of customer data, satisfaction surveys, complaint summaries, and collected corrective actions ensure that communications monitoring remains valid. As communications are issued or received, monitoring practices may need to be changed through formal project change systems.

Project Risk Management

Plan Risk Management

Overview

Key Elements and Non-Event Risks to Consider

Project risk management is an element of the project management plan that focuses on identifying, analyzing, and subverting project risks. The element also includes risk monitoring and response planning. By identifying, addressing, and monitoring project risks, the project manager is better able to prevent risks from negatively impacting project performance. The risk management plan includes components such as risk identification, quantitative and qualitative analysis, responses, and risk monitoring. The two types of project risks of concern are individual risk and overall project risk. Individual risks may impact certain objectives in the project, while the overall risks are those, from multiple potential sources, identified to impact the project as a whole.

Non-event risks are defined as those in a project that are not tied directly to future uncertain events. Rather, the non-event risks, including variability and ambiguity, are quantitative, statistical, or probability-based variations that add risk to the achievement of the objectives. Ambiguity risk arises where assumptions and available knowledge are weak and may impose a positive or negative risk.

Project Resilience and Integrated Risk Management

Resilience is defined in project management as the preparation in project planning to absorb and overcome unknown project risks as they impact the work. Resilience is created when project managers perform several strategic approaches. Three key resources must have allocated flexibility for unknown risk management; these three are schedule time, material and human resources, and budget. Continuing the flexibility theme, the project processes and personnel must remain flexible to unknown risks and be confident in using procedures to overcome the risks when faced. Clear project objectives, mission, and scope allow the team to get back on track when they face unknown risks. Preventive assessment of risks before they require resources and action is a way the project manager can avoid unknowns becoming detrimental to the project. Lastly, high levels of communication between project leadership and key stakeholders is essential, especially if these unknown risks require adjustments to the project scope, deliverables, or plan.

Integrated risk management is defined as the process of organizational risk management when the organization has many subdivisions or teams working on separate and possibly related projects, programs, or portfolios. Some risks are best managed at the lowest level, while collective or higher-scale risks can be managed using broader resources.

Inputs

Risk Management Plan and Inputs

The risk management plan is developed as the first step in the plan risk management element. The plan describes how the project team will perform risk analysis and management processes for the project. The plan and its execution highlight risks and make known the strategies necessary to minimize their impact to achieving project objectives and deliverables. The risk management plan is developed early in the project life cycle and is often revised or reviewed during various project phases. Inputs to the risk management plan development include essential material like the charter, project management plan, scope, and stakeholder requirements. Other key inputs from the parent organization overseeing the project can include a broader risk management policy, organizational risk management tools such as a risk breakdown structure, and the use of contracted experts skilled in risk analysis.

Outputs

Features and Impact of the Risk Management Plan

The risk management plan itself is a document that outlines the risk strategy, risk management methodology, and team roles and responsibilities regarding risk management. Furthermore, the plan describes how risk management will be financed and scheduled, and the levels of severity for certain risk classifications. The risk strategy gives stakeholders a thorough understanding of how the project team and the organization will assess and manage through risks. The methodology section details the specific tools the team will use to identify and manage the risks. Roles and responsibilities provide stakeholders confidence that tasks in the management plan are assigned to specific functions or team members. Resource allocation is described in the financing and timing sections. Both describe how money is allocated and how human resources are scheduled for risk management functions. Project budgets are expected to include risk management funds based on the analysis. Finally, risk categories are detailed in the plan; the categories are organized in a risk breakdown structure that groups like risks or bases the dichotomy on organizational knowledge.

Impact Matrix and Scoring Scheme

The impact matrix is a prioritization tool that gives project managers a quantitative method for ranking risks relative to each other. The matrix is preceded by a set of definitions for known risk probabilities and impact. This set defines risk severity based on several factors, such as time, cost, quality impact, and probability of occurrence. The impact matrix plots probability of occurrence against degree of impact on either a positive or negative scale. Positive impacts are considered opportunities, while negative impacts are considered threats to project performance. The matrix is filled in with unitless scores in which higher values represent high-impact/high-probability risks, while lower scores represent lower-impact/lower-probability combinations. The rankings give management a tool to visualize the likelihood of positive or negative risk impacts to the project.

Identify Risks

Overview

The risk identification process includes detection of likely risks, including their sources and features. The collection of profile information on the known risks supports project decision-making and risk mitigation strategies as the risk plan is further executed. Knowing the risk enemy well can allow a project team to attack it correctly. It is wise for the risk profiles to have similar formats and information captured. Stakeholders and team members reviewing these risks benefit when viewing familiar information and categories. Identification may also lead to assigning risk observers and documenting initial responses the team will take if the risks occur. The risk identification process occurs throughout the project life cycle. As the project progresses, new risks may be identified, especially when deviations from the project plan occur.

Inputs

Input	Description
Baselines	Documents including schedule, cost, and scope baselines. Each document is assessed for uncertainty in estimates or assumptions made. External factors may also impact the risk profile of each baseline.
Cost management plan	Uncertainty elements are included within the cost management plan.
Logs and registers	Commonly used documents include the assumption log, issue log, lessons learned register, and stakeholder register.
Quality management plan	The quality plan often lists areas of uncertainty regarding quality performance and stakeholder perceptions. Risks to shifts in quality perceptions are also commonly addressed.
Requirements management plan	Describes the project objectives highly subjected to risk impact.
Resource management plan	Details the risks associated with material and personnel resources.
Risk management plan	Provides the framework for analyzing and managing the known and unknown risks.
Schedule management plan	Details the risks associated with the project schedule and its assumptions.
Estimates	Documented quantitative estimates for cost and duration contain underlying variance. Risk occurs if estimates lose accuracy over time.
Requirements documentation	Stakeholder and resource requirements documentation used as a frame of reference for which requirements are exposed to varying degrees of risk.

Tools and Techniques

Brainstorming, Checklists, and Interviewing

Brainstorming is a tool used for collecting all comprehensible risks to individual project elements and collectively to the project overall. The team assembled includes project team members, stakeholders, and often subject matter experts; an unbiased flow of ideas culminates in a comprehensive list of risks to be analyzed. Checklists are a basic quality tool that is used to remind a person or group of important points to be inspected or assessed routinely. The items within the checklist have been added with insight and justification based on lessons learned, regulations, or project policies. The checklist can gather objective data on risk exposure in project operations. Lastly, interviewing is a project risk data gathering technique when the interviewees have experience in risk management scenarios like what is found in the project. In all data gathering, the project team must prevent bias, untruthfulness, and inaccuracy in the results collected.

Document Analysis, SWOT Analysis, Constraint Analysis, and Root Cause Analysis

Document analysis is a simple review of the relevant project documents for signs of project risks. These documents can include plans, schematics, policies, schedules, budgets, contracts, and stakeholder reports.

SWOT analysis is the assessment of strengths, weaknesses, opportunities, and threats from collective sources internal and external to the project or organization. These compilations can be further analyzed in permutations to develop approaches to prevent the identified risks.

Constraint analysis involves validation of the assumptions and constraints that were baked into the project. Validation can expose the true likelihood of impact for each of the assumptions and constraints. Validation is best performed early in the project, soon after the constraints and assumptions are identified.

Root cause analysis is a technique used to derive the right corrective and preventive action for project issues or nonconformances requiring resolution. When a project is a continuous improvement initiative, the root cause analysis follows the crafting of the problem statement.

Prompt Lists

Prompt lists are a compilation of known risk categories that serve as a useful reference and reminder to the project team. When the team encounters risk or must use risk identification, the prompt list will provide supportive ideas for assessing the type of risks observed. Risk prompt lists can be generated in multiple ways. The most common approaches include the risk breakdown structure (RBS) and broader mnemonic acronym devices. The lowest identified risks on the RBS can be tallied into a prompt list. These are especially useful for identifying individual risks in a project. More strategic prompt lists may focus more on overall sources of risk. Examples of strategic project management prompt lists include VUCA (volatility, uncertainty, complexity, and ambiguity) and PESTLE (political, economic, social, technological, legal, and environmental).

Outputs

Risk Register and Risk Reports

The risk register is a central file where known individual risks are documented. The risk register is the primary output of the identify risks subprocess of project risk management. The results of other subprocesses—such as qualitative risk analysis, planning risk responses, implementing risk responses, and risk monitoring—are also documented in the risk register. The risk register lists all identified risks categorized with a unique identification number. It is essential that the identified risks are described as completely as possible. The register may also include contributor names designated as the responsible owner for each risk. Additionally, the register may offer response concepts for each risk so that action can be performed when risks are monitored in the project execution. Risk registers may also vary between different projects or organizations; relevant information is included based on organizational needs. Sufficient information to tie the risk to WBS activities, timing, and severity are common considerations.

The identified risks are compiled into a risk report that summarizes overall project risk as well as individual risks that may occur. The report eventually includes risk-related information and performance from several points in the project. The report typically lists sources of overall project risk, summarization of individual risks, and relevant analysis of risk across the project life cycle.

Perform Qualitative Risk Analysis

Overview

After the risks have been identified, the qualitative risk analysis process serves to analyze each known risk in terms of severity and likelihood of occurrence. The analysis results in a risk profile ranking where the project team or organization can prioritize certain risks over others. While the severity and likelihood rankings can generally be subjective, internal or external studies may be available that can provide a more objective assessment of the risk profile. Some risks may be regulatory or customer-driven in nature, and these risks are more easily defined for priority. The internal team that performs the qualitative risk assessment must be calibrated so that bias and variation in risk perception is absent or minimized from the analysis work. Once all risks are provided a prioritization score, each is assigned an owner, and efforts may be made to eliminate or reduce the risk severity to a more acceptable score. The risk quantitative analysis and response is continuous throughout the project, especially as new risks are encountered.

TOOLS AND TECHNIQUES

RISK DATA QUALITY ASSESSMENT AND RISK PROBABILITY AND IMPACT ASSESSMENT

Risk data quality assessments examine the accuracy and precision of data generated for the individual quantitative assessments. This check of risk data reliability ensures that decision-making is not weak. The quality assessment is performed by surveying stakeholders regarding several risk data perspectives, including data relevance and objectivity. The project team takes the weighted average of the returned rankings and derives quality scores for each measured perspective.

The risk probability and impact assessment are related tools used to gauge the likelihood and effect severity of the identified risks. These concepts are very similar to failure mode and effects analysis (FMEA) in lean Six Sigma projects. The effect focuses on how the risk would impact cost, schedule, resource, quality, and performance objectives. The impact analysis is gauged on a scale where negative impact represents threats while positive impact represents opportunities. By plotting the impact against likelihood, a graphical impact matrix of the risks improves interpretation. The project team must gather meaningful and well-supported probability and impact data using qualitative techniques.

ASSESSING ADDITIONAL RISKS TO THE PROJECT

Additional risks that must be assessed by the project team beyond likelihood and impact are categorized into those affecting control, social interconnectivity, and time.

Category	Risk parameter	Description
Control	Controllability	High controllability occurs when the project team (or owner of the risk itself) is best able to govern the outcome of a given risk.
	Detectability	Highly detectable risks are those that the project team can most easily identify as they are occurring or are forthcoming.
	Manageability	Highly manageable risks are those that the project team or risk owners are best able to manage the effects of.
Social interconnectivity	Connectivity	Connectivity refers to how extensively the risk is related and connected to other individual risks. High connectivity implies many other risks are connected.
	Perception	Termed propinquity, the level is high when multiple stakeholders perceive the risk to be very significant.
	Strategic impact	High strategic impact refers to those risks that will have a very significant effect, either positive or negative.
Time	Dormancy	High-dormancy risks are those where there is a long period of time between the occurrence of the risk and the point when the risk was detected.
	Proximity	High proximity occurs when a risk's occurrence is a short duration of time prior to impacting a project objective.
	Urgency	High urgency is reflected in a short period of time between when the risk occurs and when an effective resolution is implemented.

HIERARCHICAL BUBBLE CHART FOR VISUALIZING PROJECT RISKS

Bubble charts are used to visually express more than two risk parameters within the same chart. A traditional *x*- and *y*-axis plots two of the three variables, while the size of the bubbles represents the third risk parameter to be visualized. Any applicable combination of three risk parameters relevant to the project can be plotted and visualized using a bubble chart. Further expanding on the chart model, each quadrant can be qualitatively categorized to communicate a label or grouping of certain risk combinations. The added information to the chart provides improved decision-making when assessing multi-risk impact to the project. Large bubbles in the high proximity/high detectability fields are unacceptable. Small bubbles in the low/low area are ideal. The bubble size reflects the intensity of the third parameter, such as impact to the project.

PERFORM QUANTITATIVE RISK ANALYSIS

OVERVIEW

QUANTITATIVE RISK ANALYSIS AND INPUTS

The quantitative risk analysis takes mathematical approaches to analyze the effects of all identified individual project risks, as well as their impact on the project objectives. Numerically quantifying the risk levels benefits data-driven organizations and stakeholders. The project team performing the risk analysis must rely on strong data collection techniques; thorough data analysis for the risk quantification; and the support of well-crafted assumption and baseline documentation, including that of the scope, schedule plan, and cost plan. Quantitative risk assessment is highly reliable and must have necessary costs allocated within the project for its execution. Larger or more complex projects often require this form of analysis, especially where the project is of high strategic importance to the organization. The qualitative risk analysis phase outputs of high significance are used as inputs into the quantitative analysis phase. Thereafter, the mathematical analysis results in planning risk responses. Inputs to the quantitative risk analysis include the project management plan and its sub-elements, baselines such as cost and schedule, and nearly the full gamut of project documents.

TOOLS AND TECHNIQUES

EXPRESSION OF UNCERTAINTY AND S-CURVE OF QUANTITATIVE COST ANALYSIS

Uncertainty can be expressed in the quantitative risk analysis by transforming data for schedule, cost, or resource uncertainty into one of several probability distributions. This transformation communicates the likelihood of different outcomes across a distribution of all potential outcomes. Common distributions used in this phase include uniform, beta, normal, and lognormal. Individual project risks are either directly covered with an assessed probability distribution or with a probability branch model to visualize likely impacts that would occur as potential risks happen. The S-curve is an output of a Monte Carlo simulation of risk. The simulation factors in the effects of multiple individual risks in the project and provides greater certainty on the effects those risks may have upon the project achievement of objectives. The S-curve is a cumulative probability distribution of the simulated outcome for a given project objective, such as schedule adherence, cost, or other performance metric. Being further up the S-curve indicates a higher probability—approaching 1.0—of a certain outcome along a continuum.

TORNADO DIAGRAM AND DECISION TREE ANALYSIS

The tornado diagram is a visual output of a sensitivity analysis used in the quantitative risk analysis phase. Sensitivity analyses take the risk analysis of individual risks one step further than simply defining them. It is positive to analyze how much impact individual risks may have on the project outcomes. The tornado diagram plots the relative correlation coefficient for each analyzed element in the quantitative model. Correlation is between each risk or uncertainty and the outcome of concern. Stronger-correlated risks are plotted on top, descending downward to lesser-correlated risks. Correlation can be either a positive or negative direction on the plot. The resulting graph resembles a tornado and expresses risk correlation intensity and direction for each outcome.

Outputs

Project Document Updates

After a quantitative risk analysis, the project manager should update the risk report with an assessment of the overall project risks and validated likelihood for those identified project risks. The assessment of overall risks contains two key measures: success probabilities and inherent remaining variation among potential risks still pending in the project at the time of the assessment. The probabilistic success information is based on the individual project risks and compiled sources of uncertainty. The second most common element updated in the risk report is the detailed likelihood analysis for the project. This update contains the analysis information, including S-curves, tornado diagrams, and criticality for the project risks. Additional updates include individual project risks listed and described by priority, identified trends captured from the quantitative analysis, and the risk analysis team's recommended responses to each risk.

Plan Risk Responses

Overview

The risk response planning phase involves the project team defining specific actions that will be taken, presently or in the future, to diminish the impacts of the proposed risks. The subjugation of the risks through action generally begins with tasks that carry the highest risk probability. Prioritization can be done through a combination of quantitative likelihood and severity and detectability measurements. The process also must have allocated budget resources to execute these potential response plans as needed. Responses must be valid for the risk presented. Constraints may still force the organization to have several contingency strategies for each response, should full planned resource allocation be a challenge. Multiple strategies, including backup procedures, are important. Key inputs include the resource, risk, and cost management plans; the resource calendar; the risk register; and the risk report.

Tools and Techniques

Strategies for Neutralizing Project Risk Threats

Strategy	Description
Accept	Acceptance strategies allow the risk to occur with full understanding that there may be positive or negative impact to the objectives. This strategy is generally used for low-priority risks, and the related resource constraints that occur can easily be absorbed by the project plans. Active acceptance includes budgeting a reserve of resources in time, money, or resources. Passive acceptance keeps an ongoing view of the risk level and impact rather than setting aside reserves.
Avoid	Avoidance occurs when the project team works to neutralize the risk threat. Elimination can be achieved by significant adjustment to the schedule, scope, objectives, or strategy within the project.
Escalate	Escalation occurs when project experts assess that the project manager is not suited to manage the risk and the resolution must be performed at the organizational level. Program- and portfolio-level leadership may also take on the responsibility of risk neutralization.

Strategy	Description
Mitigate	Actions are performed to lessen the impact and/or likelihood of risks. The mitigation strategy is preventive when started as early as possible when valid risks are identified. Mitigation may also require organizational investment to add redundancies or scale-up simulations.
Transfer	The transfer of risk responsibilities and mitigation towards competent providers can occur, so that the project leadership can focus on the project work. Insurance and warranties are examples of risk transfer.

STRATEGIES FOR CAPITALIZING ON PROJECT RISK OPPORTUNITIES

Strategy	Description
Accept	Acceptance is a passive activity regarding the acknowledgement of an opportunity without acting. Low impact of the opportunity, cost-benefit considerations, and resource constraints may prevent these opportunities from being pursued.
Enhance	Known opportunities are deliberately strengthened early after they are recognized to effectively increase the probability the opportunity will reoccur or have further positive outcomes. Enhancement increases the benefit that is derived from the opportunity towards the project. Enhancing the causes will increase the benefit derived.
Escalate	Escalation refers to the hand-off of the opportunity to another leader of the organization, program management, or portfolio levels. This is generally due to the opportunity being outside the scope of the project or outside the capabilities of the project manager and team.
Exploit	A beneficial strategy for high-benefit opportunities, where the project team or organization acts to manipulate the opportunity to increase the likelihood of stronger positive outcomes. For example, exploiting process bottlenecks by adding more processing capacity.
Share	Opportunities may be transferred to another team or to a third party for further pursuit, especially if the opportunities are out of the project scope. Companies may also form spin-off organizations or new corporations built around the shared opportunity. Negative risk-sharing may also involve paying risk premiums to the firm overtaking responsibility.

OUTPUTS

PROJECT DOCUMENT UPDATES AND REVISION OF THE RISK REGISTER BASED ON OUTCOMES

Updated project documents contain several project management plan sub-plans, including those for quality, cost, schedule, resources, and procurement. Key baseline documents such as the cost, schedule, and scope baselines are updated as a result of the risk response determination. Project document updates outside of the project management plan itself are highlighted by changes made to the risk register. The risk responses must be captured in the risk register, and the process includes many informational elements. Foremost, the agreed response and specific related actions are detailed for each relevant risk. To support decision-making, the conditions or causes that would lead the team to activate each risk response are detailed for clarity. Also included are relevant budget or schedule actions that must be added when the responses are activated. Contingency and backup plans are also described where necessary, should the planned risk response not work as expected. Lastly, each response details secondary risks that may remain after the initial response is performed.

Implement Risk Responses

Overview

The implement risk responses element serves as a process to establish the agreed risk responses and the underlying support systems needed for effective execution. Detailed plans laid out in the risk response planning process support effective execution in the implementation phase. Implementation serves to minimize known risk impacts to the project and minimize individual known threats. Key inputs to the process include the project management plan, the risk register, and risk reports. Techniques for implementation include effective interpersonal skills and sound judgement. For more complex projects or organizations, a project management information system (PMIS) would also drive implementation. The output of the process, other than implemented responses, includes project document updates, notably to the risk register and the risk report.

Monitor Risks

Overview

Monitor Risks Element and Inputs

The monitor risks process includes oversight by the project manager and team on the progress of risk response implementation. The process also evaluates conditions for adding new risks to the project and to monitor the effectiveness of the risk process. Monitoring also serves to ensure project team members and key stakeholders are kept updated on the status of risk exposure as the project continues. The objective information gathered regarding project performance aids the risk monitoring function to ensure that risk responses are adequate and effective, that assumptions remain valid, and that contingencies are available. Key inputs include the project management plan, the risk register, the risk report, and work performance data.

Tools and Techniques

Reserve Analysis and Technical Performance Analysis

Reserve analysis provides information to stakeholders on the relative ratio of resource reserves allocated for risk mitigation compared to the amount of remaining risk at any given point within the project execution process. The resulting figures provide stakeholders and project members with an assessment of the capability of the reserves to meet the ideally expected demand.

Technical performance analysis benchmarks the expected technical performance progress with the actual technical performance achievement. This ratio of planned versus actual performance must ensure that data collected is reliable without bias. The measurements and actionable limits for each performance parameter commonly include defects, transfer times, and capacity.

Audits

Auditing is the planned review of an organization's performance compared to a set of agreed criteria or parameters. The audit is performed by one or more auditors and looks to gain objective and first-hand evidence to assess how strongly a process, organization, product, or service meets expectations. The expectations or standards used as the criteria for the audit are typically compiled or enforced by stakeholders, leadership, customers, or regulatory agencies with a vested interest in ensuring conformance. Risk-focused audits serve to ensure that the risk management processes are effective. The organization creates detailed risk audit criteria and executes the audit (or has a third party perform the audits) on a defined frequency. The project manager bears responsibility for scheduling and preparing for risk audits during the project.

Project Procurement Management

Plan Procurement Management

Overview

Project Procurement Management Process

Procurement management focuses on obtaining resources, services, or results effectively and within constraints from outside of the project team. These assurances are obtained using formal contracts, purchase agreements, and service agreements with clearly defined criteria and terms. Procurement stakeholders and responsible persons are part of either the project team or the organization at large. The process includes having a defined procurement plan, executing that plan, and performing control methods to ensure providers meet their responsibilities. The contractual process and language influences many of the outcomes in the procurement process.

Various parameters are commonly included in procurement contracts, such as cost, timing, quality, and customer service metrics. There are also many laws that impact the contractual deliverables for procurement. The financial, legal, and executive level of the project's parent organization may have full responsibility for entering into procurement agreements; such situations may require careful planning and influence by the project manager. Alternatively, smaller organizations without dedicated procurement teams likely have the project manager lead procurement efforts for projects. Risk mitigation is critical when contracting services or supply, and contracts and service agreement language, audits, and performance evaluations can help mitigate likely risks. Procurement strategies may also require supply chain systems working concurrently to ensure cost and schedule parameters are met.

Features of Purchasing Contracts and Relationships Between Buyers and Sellers

Purchasing contracts describe the transactional, legal, and deliverable requirements that the buyer will impose on the seller should the two parties enter into the agreement mutually. Project management responsibilities include ensuring that the contracts include all relevant terms, conditions, specifications, and requirements necessary to receive goods or services that help achieve the requirements of the project. The project manager may also need to adhere to organizational procurement requirements or defer procurement responsibilities to the organization's support colleagues. The agreement can take one of many forms, including service-level agreements, purchase orders, contracts, or memorandums of agreement. Buyers seek to include all necessary details, requirements, and restrictions so that the seller output will meet their expectations; otherwise, claims and penalties may be imposed. The seller seeks to obtain the business to service the buyer in favorable terms within their known capabilities and for an equitable fee.

Procurement Management Plan

The procurement management plan ensures that the project team has a formal procedure for selecting suppliers, defining how procurement decisions are made, and outlining the procurement requirements and process. The plan also describes the project resources to be obtained from within the organization or obtained externally. Lastly, the plan outlines the roles and responsibilities within the project team and organization for procurement related to the project. When preparing the project procurement plan, key steps are grouped into preparation, evaluation, and selection:

- **Preparation**—The project team, with or without support from the parent organization, documents the specifications in the form of a statement of work (SOW) or a terms of reference (TOR) file. The team prepares a cost estimate and budget for the total project procurement using supporting project documentation.

- **Evaluation**—After advertising the opportunity, the team narrows down a short list of qualified suppliers and opens the bidding process. Suppliers submit bids. The project team analyzes the bids compared to criteria and project expectations.
- **Selection**—The final analysis of cost and quality among the narrowed bids identifies the winning provider or supplier. The procurement negotiations and contract signing finishes the process.

Tools and Techniques

Cost-Reimbursable Contracts, Fixed-Price Contracts, and Time and Material Contracts

Cost-reimbursable contracts are defined as terms where the buyer makes payments to the seller for approved incurred costs as they occur. The model benefits buyers when project work variation is relatively high. No up-front payments are made prior to the phased completion of work elements. Three self-evident variants of the cost-reimbursable model are cost plus award, cost plus incentive, and cost plus fixed fee.

Fixed-price contracts define the overall total price to be paid for the procurement agreement without embedded payments or incentives based on variation or flux in work. The fixed-price contract is useful when the deliverable purchased is highly familiar and procurement variation is limited.

Time and material contracts are a blend of fixed-cost and cost-reimbursable versions. Time and material contracts are common when there is no clear statement of work available from prospective sellers.

Source Selection Analysis

All projects and organizations have competing spheres of influence that impact which criteria are prioritized when making procurement decisions. It is advantageous for buyers and sellers to ensure that all parties are aware of the buyer's selection method and criteria. Sellers must prepare proposals and may invest significant resources to submit a strong bid, especially if the contract is very large or the proposal is very complex. Several common selection methods are used, though they differ on which project element is the highest-priority parameter.

Selection Method	Description
Quality-based	A technically superior product or service with high quality may cost more but will inherently be more reliable and meet expectations better. Financial perspectives are considered after firms exceed technical baselines.
Low cost	When supplies or services are of minimal variation among providers, cost is often the key differentiator.
Qualifications	A streamlined approach where the cost-benefit ratio of the project team performing a formal procurement analysis is weak. The team selects based on commonly known reputational factors.
Sole source	The buyer does not seek out bids among providers; rather, the buyer negotiates with one provider only.
Combo (quality and cost)	The two criteria are blended; quality becomes more important when the seller's performance is not well known.
Fixed budget	The sellers are made aware of a fixed value of the procurement offer, and a top bid is chosen from several choices that have adjusted cost and quality parameters to fit the budget.

Output

Procurement Management Plan and Guidance Features

The completed procurement management plan outlines the procurement processes that the project team will perform. The plan describes the bidding procedures and controls to be used, as well as the resource allocations available for each procurement need. The plan also describes how the procurement process ties into the overall project management plan elements. For example, it describes linkage to the schedule plan, cost plan, and the stakeholder requirements information. The degree of formality of the procurement plan is determined by the scope and complexity of the project itself.

Guidance Detail	Description
Coordination	Advising the project team how procurement requirements link to other elements of the project management plan (e.g., schedule, cost management, quality, and performance management).
Timetable	Temporal map of when procurement activities must occur relative to the project plans.
Metrics	Procurement metrics for ensuring performance is achieved.
Stakeholder involvement	Defining the roles and responsibilities needed from key stakeholders in the procurement process.
Assumptions	Constraints and assumptions that drive procurement decisions.
Legal awareness	Details of any legal boundaries impacting the procurement.
Independent estimates	Advice on when external independent guidance is needed.
Risk mitigation	Details on insurance and risk mitigation options to prevent major negative impact to the project.
Prequalification	Preapproval of trusted suppliers and providers.

Procurement Strategy

The procurement strategy is outlined within the procurement management plan, specifically when the team decides to purchase from sources external to their organization. The procurement strategy provides functional instructions for the logistics, legality, contract development, and flow of obtaining the goods or services contracted. The logistics and delivery of the goods or services is chosen based on whether the team is procuring professional or commercial services. Professional services include options such as direct purchase, subcontracting, joint ventures, and buyer-directed. Each option carries a different level of control and risk-taking. Commercial construction service options typically include design-build, design-bid-build, design-build-operate, and turnkey delivery methods.

Contract payment approaches are typically managed by the project team's financial colleagues, not by the project team itself. Verification may be requested by the financial team to ensure expenses are accurate. Several variations of procurement payment methods are used in projects, including cost plus incentive fees, labor/time and materials, and fixed price. Different methods may be desired depending on whether the nature of the project work is familiar or variable.

Procurement flow is monitored by the project manager through phased implementation, key performance indicators for sellers, stage-gate progress criteria, and phase knowledge transfer. Described below are four primary types of business bid documents: RFP, RFI, RFQ, and SOW.

Bid Document Type	Description
Request for proposal (RFP)	The project team is seeking proposed solutions to a problem needing external expertise. The formal request seeks specific content and parameter responses from prospective sellers before a decision is made.
Request for information (RFI)	A preliminary step in procurement. Requesting further information on goods or services helps the project team request a quotation or proposal.
Request for quotation (RFQ)	A quotation is a commonly used document where the seller outlines how they intend to meet the buyer's expectations and at what costs. Buyers should be expected to communicate their needs and constraints prior to receiving a quotation. Accuracy in the quotation communication prevents project errors.
Statement of work (SOW)	A compilation of relevant parts of the project scope that a prospective seller would have to achieve to successfully meet expectations. Sellers use the SOW to determine if they can meet those requirements. Clarity is important when the project team creates the SOW. SOW information can also include quality parameters, cost requirements, specifications, work location, and supply levels.

Conduct Procurements

Overview

Conduct Procurements Process

The conduct procurements process is the activity of comparing formal agreements from sellers, making a choice, and completing a legal contract with the chosen seller(s). Prerequisites to the decision-making process include the compiled RFQ, RFP, and/or RFI documents that the project team may have requested from each potential vendor. The decision itself can reference much of the project management plan, including sub-plans for risk, resources, requirements, communications, procurement, configuration, and cost. The combination of these references used in the conducting of procurement can vary between projects. When making yes-or-no decisions regarding conducting procurement with each potential vendor, teams are wise to keep good documented evidence of the decisions made. Supporting documentation for the conduct procurement element includes the independent cost estimates, statements of work from the potential vendors, bid documents (RFI, RFQ, RFP), and the source selection criteria. Furthermore, there are enterprise environmental factors and organizational process assets that are factored into the decisions, such as prior contractual agreements still ongoing, regulatory restrictions, internal policies that influence procurement choice, and internal accounting practices.

Tools and Techniques

Data Analysis, Advertising, Bidding Conferences, and Team Skills

Data analysis techniques used in procurement execution mainly focus on ensuring the proposal details match the bid expectations, the statement of work, and related criteria incumbent upon the chosen vendor.

Advertising of procurement searches may be a prerequisite for certain projects, such as government contracts. Advertising is also likely to expand the pool of interested or available sellers of a resource or service.

Bidding conferences may involve large gatherings of vendors or contractors to collectively and competitively show and discuss their capabilities to prospective buyers or project organizations with relevant needs. More commonly, one buyer may arrange a bidder conference where all potential sellers present their proposals on a level playing field and benefit the single buyer with fair decision-making.

Team skills such as negotiation tactics are important for both the buyer and seller in the conduct procurement process. Reaching an equitable decision where both the buyer and seller feel successful is the ideal outcome. Fine details often must be negotiated, such as payment terms, legal wording, corrective action obligations, performance capabilities, and service schedule. Ideally, the project organization should have financial authority to perform the negotiations, with clearance to sign the contract when finalized and consult the project manager as necessary.

Output

Completed Procurement Agreements

Completed procurement agreements share common features. Foremost is the approved statement of work that both parties agree will be provided contractually. Related details regarding schedule, cost, and milestones are included to support the achievement of the statement of work. Accounting details regarding payments and terms are included. Any relevant performance reporting requirements placed upon the seller are detailed in the agreement. Key quality and performance requirements are also detailed in the agreement as needed. The agreements are also likely to include common legal clauses, warranties, hold-harmless details, and termination language. Lastly, the agreements may include details of incentives or penalties, should either party exceed or not meet expectations.

Document Updates and Project Management Plan Updates Resulting from Procurement Decisions

Procurement agreements with sellers can disrupt previously planned elements of the project management plan based on the seller's capabilities or the available options buyers have in a marketplace for procured supply. The project manager may need to adjust quality and requirements plans based on seller capabilities. The project manager may also need to revise the risk management plan if the procurement agreement introduces new uncertainty. Changes are likely to the cost, schedule, and scope baseline (including the WBS) when initiating a procurement agreement. When outsourcing the supply or service, sellers introduce variation to the schedule and cost expectations because of the uncertainty that can impact their own ability to meet demands of buyers, often multiple buyers simultaneously. As the project becomes more dependent upon outside work and factors, the inherent supply chain risks become more likely. Documents that are often updated after procurement decisions include the requirements documentation and traceability matrix. Both documents expand to include supplier technical requirements, multiple levels of compliance standards that the suppliers are expected to meet, and the seller's capabilities that impact the requirements traceability. Any added risks from contracting a supplier would be added to the risk register, while any stipulations that must be met with the seller (performed by the project team) must be updated in the stakeholder register.

Control Procurements

Overview

Control Procurements Process and Administrative Control Tasks

Procurement control involves seller-buyer relationship management by the project team, contract performance monitoring, and related corrective actions when performance is not meeting expectations. Monitoring is performed by the project team continuously during the project while the seller or provider is expected to perform work. It is wise for the project manager to monitor the project team and organization's performance to the expectations listed in procurement agreements. These control processes must be replicated across multiple suppliers and vendors.

Administrative tasks that must be performed in the control procurements process include data collection from procurement activities (including financial), schedule adjustments for procurement activities, procurement-related reporting to the project team and any impact procurement has upon the project objectives, payment of procured vendors by the organization, and quality assurance analysis upon project elements that are impacted by procurement behaviors and performance.

Input

Agreements, Procurement Documentation, Change Requests, and Work Performance Data

Agreements are contractual documents that place legally binding conditions upon the seller and buyer regarding the goods and/or services to be procured. Specific conditions within the agreements must be reviewed and implemented by both parties. The project manager and team must monitor procurement performance as part of the project management plan.

Procurement documentation includes all contracts and supporting information related to their evaluation, execution, and performance monitoring. Key procurement documents include the performance evaluations, communications, contractual payment processes, and statement of work.

Change requests must be approved by the project manager and, in some cases, the vendor. Subsequent revisions may be performed on related procurement documents, such as the vendor's statement of work, deliverable specifications, and payment terms. The project team must be cautious to avoid changes and disruption to a vendor's supply that may impact the supply of other procurement deals simultaneously.

Lastly, work performance data is compiled for vendors with active procurement agreements. Relevant data includes work that is in progress or recently completed, financial transaction data, performance metrics, and schedule accuracy.

Tools and Techniques

Claims Administration, Earned Value Analysis, Performance Reviews, Trend Analysis, and Auditing

Claims administration is the technique used to resolve conflicts and poor performance issues between buyer and seller, though primarily directed towards the seller side of the relationship. A claim indicates that either party has evidence or subjective opinion that argues that the other party has not maintained the expected level of quality, performance, or service necessary. The claimant seeks remuneration and/or corrective action from the other party. Claims may also include contested changes or disagreement regarding whether a change occurred. Both the buyer and seller have a desire to effectively negotiate an equitable resolution to any claim situation; the procurement agreement should indicate claims procedures and recourse.

Earned value analysis is used in procurement performance monitoring to track expected schedule and cost performance against actual performance, with the variances being the key performance indicator.

Performance reviews are documented and shared evaluations of a vendor or contractor's performance against the predefined measures from the agreement. Periodic performance communication to vendors supports continuous improvement and collaborative dialog to prevent future major problems with deliverables.

Trend analysis may be included in performance reviews as a proactive tool.

Lastly, auditing serves as an independent assessment of vendor performance and can be the basis for continued procurement agreements.

Output

Closed Procurements, Work Performance Information, and Organizational Process Asset Updates

Closed procurement agreements are a key outcome of the procurement control process; the closed agreements indicate that both parties met their overall responsibilities and that the deliverables were achieved. Formal written notice from the buyer to the seller serves as confirmation of the closure of the agreement after fulfillment. The closure implies that no outstanding and unfulfilled deliverables or payments remain. The project team has also approved all deliverables and performance.

Work performance information is collected following the procurement control process. Such data can be used to gauge future procurement searches among the same or similar vendors and benchmark procurement in future projects. The statement of work is used to compare actual vendor technical performance, budget adherence, and deliverable performance.

Furthermore, organizational processes may be improved or revised to account for experiences and information gained after contracts are closed. Payment processes, performance evaluations, seller pre-qualification records, lessons learned, and procurement history databases are all valuable information sources benefiting from contract closure.

Project Stakeholder Management

Identify Stakeholders

Overview

Project Stakeholder Management Process

Stakeholder management begins with identifying and compiling all relevant stakeholders that have an impact on or could be impacted by the project in positive or negative ways. From there, the expectations of each stakeholder are defined and prioritized based on their impact to the project. The project team then creates targeted stakeholder management plans so that such persons, groups, or organizations are engaged, are supportive of the project's objectives, and are involved in good communication. The process begins with creating a stakeholder management plan and continues with monitoring and managing the engagement of each stakeholder. Stakeholder management is a primary objective of the project manager, and the effective management of expectations and requirements can drive success of the project. Periodic reviews of identification, prioritization, engagement, and satisfaction of stakeholders is the responsibility of the project manager, at least during project phase transitions, the influx or release of stakeholders, and during any significant changes to the project objectives or plans. Project team members have an important supportive role in stakeholder management; consultation with key stakeholders for their feedback and critique of project performance gives the manager room for improvement.

Tools and Techniques

Inputs and Analysis of Inputs to Create the Stakeholder Register

Input	Description	Analysis
Business case	An early project document that outlines the organizational and stakeholder benefits to doing the project.	The business case includes information regarding how initially identified stakeholders will be impacted by the project.
Benefits management plan	The plan that is derived after the business case and explains how the benefits to the organization and stakeholders will be achieved.	Select groups of stakeholders or individuals are described regarding the benefits they will see from the project.
Communications management plan	The project sub-plan that describes how the project team will execute communications with stakeholders and the organization.	Information and reporting needs in the form of communication are listed in this plan. Responsibilities to communicate with stakeholders are vital to stakeholder management.
Stakeholder engagement plan	The output of the first iteration of the stakeholder identification process. This document can be a reference for ongoing reviews of the stakeholder register and engagement.	Stakeholder engagement details are compiled in this plan and should correlate with the stakeholder register.
Change and issues logs	Documented sources for project changes and issues that arise during planning and execution.	Changes and issues that have an impact on all or select stakeholders. Change and issues may also identify new stakeholders to the project.
Requirements documentation	Summary of the key requirements expected of the project and its deliverables.	Requirements may directly or indirectly identify stakeholders to the project.

Stakeholder Analysis and Stakeholder Mapping and Representation

Stakeholder analysis is the process of compiling several key details about each stakeholder to the project and each individual's stake in the project. The compilation allows the project team to prioritize and strategize stakeholder management practices. The analysis begins with certain vital information, including each stakeholder's relative attitudes and expectations of the project, their role as a stakeholder to the project, and how much each is concerned with project communications. The stake component of the analysis includes several sub-parts:

- Contribution—The individual may have provided resources, such as finances, labor, materials, or advice towards the project and may expect some form of share of the project's benefits in return.
- Interest—Decisions made by the project team will have an impact on some stakeholders more than others.
- Knowledge—Knowledge can be powerful when a project team must navigate the workings of an organization and the nuances of human behaviors.

- Ownership—The stake may be a legal title or ownership of some part or asset of the project.
- Rights—Certain stakeholders have either moral or legal rights to common or competing interests to the project.

Stakeholder mapping involves creating characterization analyses of the stakeholders to find and strategize around stakeholder relationships and connections. Common versions include the power/interest grid, stakeholder cube, salience model, and directions of influence model.

Outputs

Stakeholder Register and Updates to Project Documents and Plans

The stakeholder register lists all key details and requirements from each project stakeholder. The register begins with vital information for each individual or organization, including names, organization name, roles, and contact information. The stakeholders are classified by several binary terms that provide simple categorization to the stakeholders. These categories may include levels of power, influence, and impact; interest, whether internal or external; and direction of influence classifications. Assessment information is the third and most significant set of classification data in the register. Assessment information includes project life cycle relevance, stakeholder expectations, and key requirements held by each identified stakeholder. As the register is created and stakeholder requirements become well understood, changes may be necessary to project documents and plans. For example, the requirements plan, communications management plan, risk management plan, and stakeholder engagement plan may need to be revised to align with stakeholder data. Along those lines, other related documents such as the issues log and risk register may need to be revised given stakeholder data realization.

Plan Stakeholder Engagement

Overview

Stakeholder Engagement Planning Process and Inputs

Stakeholder engagement planning is the activity of the project team and/or organization to draw stakeholders into the project, increasing their involvement, and being attentive to their expectations and impact to the project. The stakeholder identification is performed early in the project life cycle, while the engagement plan is reassessed routinely throughout the project as new information is gained from stakeholder interactions. Events or milestones in the project should prompt the project manager to reassess the engagement process. Situations including the addition of new stakeholders to the register, parent organizational structure change, project phase transitions, and changes in project deliverables or objectives would all prompt a reassessment of the register. Key inputs to the engagement plan development include the resource, risk, and communication management plans; the assumption and issues logs; the risk register; and the stakeholder register. Related agreements for procurement or with stakeholders would also be factored into the plan development.

Tools and Techniques

Mind Mapping and Assessment Matrices

Mind mapping is defined as the organization of ideas and information according to their relationships with other thoughts, information, and ideas. The organization leads to greater understanding of the information and obtaining of key relationships and innovations from studying the connections made. Mind-mapping stakeholder engagement information and register details stimulates creativity on how the team can effectively engage and manage stakeholders. Assessment matrices plot the current engagement conditions for each stakeholder against the desired state of engagement as defined by the project plan. The matrices include scales that define engagement levels in several buckets based on the degree of engagement observed. Buckets include unaware, resistant, neutral, supportive, and leading. Resistant stakeholders are aware of the benefits of the project but do not want to accept the outcomes, as they may disrupt perceived aspects of their function. On the positive end of the spectrum, leading stakeholders are fully engaged and are helping to drive the outcomes of the project. The matrix plots "C" for the current state for each stakeholder and "D" for the desired state.

Stakeholder	Unaware	Resistant	Neutral	Supportive	Leading
USDA		C			D
FDA			C	D	
US Dept of Commerce	C		D		
US Customs			C D		
Customer				D	C
City Health Dept		C		D	

Manage Stakeholder Engagement

Overview

The engagement management process follows the development of the engagement plan. The physical work of meeting, communicating, and performing improvements related to engagement highlights this process. Furthermore, communications must meet stakeholder expectations and provide the information each individual or organizational stakeholder desires. Active engagement and management of stakeholders provides the project manager with leverage, flexibility, and support with impactful stakeholders. Key inputs include the project management plan and many of its sub-plans and project documents. These inputs are transformed into engagement activities with techniques such as communication skills development, internal or external expert judgement, and the development of interpersonal skills. Interpersonal skills such as active listening, conflict resolution, emotional intelligence, negotiation, and political awareness all serve to improve and maintain engagement. The primary outputs of the process include measurably engaged stakeholders, verified by assessment matrices, and potential updates to the project plans or documents via change requests.

Stakeholder Engagement Monitoring Process

Monitoring stakeholder engagement follows the development of a stakeholder engagement management plan. Monitoring involves continuously assessing the stakeholder relationships, reviewing granular data regarding performance on factors most important to stakeholders, and revising engagement strategies based on performance results. Monitoring the relevant data and information allows the project team to be more effective at engaging the stakeholders, most notably those highly prioritized. Inputs include project management sub-plans such as the resource, communications, and stakeholder engagement plans. Also, the stakeholder register serves as a primary document input. Work performance data is included with these monitored materials. Analysis techniques such as alternatives, stakeholder, root cause, multicriteria decision-making, and data visualization all allow the project manager to derive effective monitoring and engagement strategies. Interpersonal skills such as active listening and networking also support effective monitoring. Work performance reporting and related updates to project plans and documents result from the monitoring process, all of which may be used as supporting information to reinforce customer satisfaction and involvement with the project.

Agile

Agile is a term used to describe adaptive project development where the scope is fluid and subject to frequent change. Created for the software industry, Agile values **stakeholder satisfaction at its core**. However, since software is now an integral part of all modern business workflows, and due to the number of competitive advantages that adaptive development presents, Agile has within the last few years migrated into other areas of business, finance, and industry. The PMP Exam will have several questions related to Agile methodologies, frameworks, concepts, and strategies; most will test Extreme (XP), Scrum, and Kanban methodologies, but you should be familiar with Lean development concepts as well. In addition, there will be several question scenarios that emphasize a hybrid approach to project management.

Though you should have already received comprehensive coverage of Agile during your required 35-hour PMP training, we have included this **brief overview of the most common Agile terms and concepts** you should be familiar with for the exam.

Agile Manifesto—Developed in 2001.

The 4 key **Agile values** that software developers should follow are:

- Individuals and interactions over processes and tools.
- Working software over comprehensive documentation.
- Customer collaboration over contract negotiation.
- Responding to change over following a plan.

The 12 **Agile Principles** are:

- The highest priority is to satisfy the customer via **early and continuous delivery of valuable software.**
- **Welcome change**—even late in development. Harness change for the customer's competitive advantage.
- Deliver working software frequently.
- Business people and developers must work together daily.
- Build projects around **motivated individuals**; give them the environment, tools, and support they need, and trust them to get the job done.
- **Face-to-face conversation** is the most effective method of conveying information.
- Working software (or a working deliverable) is the primary measure of progress.
- Agile processes **promote sustainable development**; strive to maintain a constant pace indefinitely.
- Continuous attention to technical excellence and good design enhances agility.
- **Simplicity**—the art of maximizing the amount of work *not* done—is essential.
- The best architectures, requirements, and designs emerge from **self-organizing teams.**
- At regular intervals, the team should reflect on how to become more effective, then adjust its behavior accordingly.

Agile Mindset

Projects are done, solved, and created by and for **people**. Compared to traditional predictive projects, Agile projects build in increments, conduct planning throughout versus up front, and deliver products over time so the customer sees value sooner versus waiting until the end of the project. Agile is also responsive to stakeholders' frequent needs or requests for change. Risk identification and response is more fluid as well.

With predictive projects, the scope is fixed while the time (schedule) and cost (budget) must be adapted to achieve the scope. With Agile projects, however, the time and cost are fixed over a predicted period while **the scope changes instead.** The development team and the Agile project manager are kept on a financial "retainer" until the product owner and development team agree there is no longer any value to be produced from the project.

The Merits of Agile

The Agile Declaration of Interdependence (DOI) touts an increased return on investment based on a developmental focus on a **continuous flow of value.** Improved reliability stems from engaging customers in frequent interactions and shared ownership. Agile also boosts team performance through group accountability for results and shared responsibility for team effectiveness. Note that these ideas are not dissimilar to the best practices of predictive project approaches.

Common Agile Terms

The terms may change based on the framework, but the purpose remains the same.

Agile project manager or Scrum master—Leads the team and guides the organization through the process.

Product owner—The designated representative of the organization (like a predictive project sponsor).

Scrum artifacts—The tangible items produced during the Agile process: the product increments, the product backlog, and the sprint backlog.

Product backlog—The list of required design features and functionalities of one or more project deliverables prioritized by the **product owner** according to the market value to the organization.

Sprint backlog—The segment of work chosen out of the product backlog **by the team** as the focus for a sprint.

Sprints—Periods of work (ideally, 4 weeks each) focused only on the sprint backlog. (These are also referred to as iterations on the exam. Sprints are from Scrum, while "iterations" are XP work periods.)

Sprint planning meeting—The product owner, Scrum master (a.k.a. the Agile project manager), and development team meet after the product owner has prioritized the backlog. The team looks at the updated product backlog and utilizes work point estimation to determine which components will be developed within the next 4-week sprint. **The output of this meeting is the sprint backlog.**

Daily scrum (Scrum) **or daily standup** (XP)—A brief daily meeting, preferably held in the same place every time, no more than 15 minutes long. It is a spot check of the current progress of the entire team and an opportunity to address any impediments to productivity for the next 24 hours.

Team members should be ready to announce what they accomplished yesterday, what they will accomplish today, and what assistance they will need in order to finish on schedule.

Sprint spike—These are special meetings or pull-asides to work on a particular problem that is outside of the sprint backlog but necessary to keep the project progressing. Architectural spikes are used to gather information, refine approaches, or clarify user stories before continuing product development. Risk-based spikes are used to reduce or eliminate a possible risk.

Release—This occurs when several sprints' worth of work or a project component increment are completed and ready for implementation testing and possible roll-out.

Sprint review—At the end of the sprint, the project team—consisting of the Agile project manager (Scrum master), product owner, and developers—meet to share the current completed work and evaluate it for additional improvement. Other stakeholders may be invited to attend and give feedback as well. Afterward, the product owner will then begin reprioritizing the product backlog prior to the next sprint planning meeting. **Allow no more than one hour per number of weeks in the sprint.**

Sprint retrospective—This meeting is held after the sprint review and is solely for the development team and the Agile project manager or Scrum master to document lessons learned. They discuss what went well, what needs improvement, and how the team should implement those improvements during the next sprint cycle. Retrospectives have a 2-hour time limit and are highly structured.

- **Set stage**—6 mins. Call to order, encourage participation, outline agenda, get group focused.
- **Gather data** for improvement—40 mins. Break into groups and assess what happened during the sprint.
- **Generate insights**—25 mins. Share via brainstorming, fishbone analysis, "Ask why 5 times," dot voting.
- **Decide** on improvement—20 mins. Short subjects (start doing, stop doing, do more of, do less of), SMART goals.
- **Close retrospective**—20 mins. Reflect on the retrospective itself, summary chart of improvement suggestions.

Definition of done—The definition of done (DoD) is agreed upon by the development team and the product owner at the beginning for the project as a whole. A DoD may also be applied to specified phase components (e.g., Module 1 testing or Module 4 documentation). Projects can also be declared "done" when the development team or product owner agree there is no more value to be obtained from working on the project.

Rolling wave planning (a.k.a. progressive elaboration)—Unlike predictive projects, which conduct most of the planning up front, Agile projects conduct planning, estimation, design, and development of test scenarios throughout the project as updated information and detail requests emerge.

Timeboxing—Many sprint or iteration planning sessions have prescribed, fixed durations. Work or planning that is not completed during the timeframe gets moved to a later timebox. Daily standups are 15 minutes, retrospectives are 2 hours, and sprints are 1 to 4 weeks (but most commonly 4 weeks for Scrum and 2 weeks for XP). Default to 4 weeks for exam questions.

Pre-mortem—This is a risk analysis meeting to consider sources of project failure before work begins. The process includes listing possible failures, listing reasons they would cause failure (the impact), and reviewing the project plan to see how to remove the risk or reduce the impact.

Technical debt—The messy backlog of extra work caused by not organizing and cleaning up the work as you go. Keeping code standardized, fixed, and cleaned up as you go is referred to as **refactoring**.

Value stream map—This looks similar to a network diagram but is used to diagram a process workflow in a linear array of boxes. Steps are then combined and rearranged for the **purpose of fixing a process to reduce waste.**

Scrum versus Extreme (XP) Framework Terms—Different Names for Similar Purposes

Definition (Predictive Equivalent)	Scrum	XP
A "timebox" of a fixed length of time (milestone phase)	Sprint	Iteration
The business representative (project sponsor)	Product owner	Customer
Lessons learned meeting	Retrospective	Reflection
Release to production	Release	Small release
The Agile project manager (project manager)	Scrum master	Coach
Agile planning meetings	Sprint or release planning	Planning game
Cross-functional developers (project team)	Development team	Team
15-minute daily meeting	Daily scrum	Daily standup

For the PMP exam, a **sprint is synonymous with an iteration.** A question scenario might refer to either the "project manager" for predictive projects or the "Agile project manager" for nonspecific Agile framework projects. Sometimes, however, the type of manager will be deliberately omitted as part of the test to see if you can determine the project approach. Pay attention to "pro**ject** sponsor," a predictive project organization representative, versus a "pro**duct** sponsor," a predictive project representative for a single deliverable; predictive projects can have both working on the same project. For example, a new hospital construction project could have a pro**ject** sponsor to represent the medical organization for the project in its entirety, plus a pro**duct** sponsor for the main hospital building, a different product sponsor for the technology components, and a third product sponsor for the parking structure and campus exterior. These product sponsors could also be referred to as "customers" for a predictive project. Meanwhile, the "product **owner**" or a "customer" could refer to the organization's representative for an Agile project based on whether it's a Scrum versus an XP framework. On the exam, "customers" can refer to product sponsors as well as organization representatives for a predictive project, or a "customer" could be an XP Agile product owner, depending on the context cues in the question scenario. The terms "product" versus "project" are visually confusing when viewing them on a screen while under the timeboxed pressure of the PMP exam constraints. Therefore, for each question scenario, discern **who is the actor** directing the activity or **whose perspective** needs to be considered to derive the answer. Is it the project manager, a team member, a stakeholder, the project sponsor, the product owner, a generic client, a predictive customer, or the XP customer?

Agile Frameworks

Frameworks include the rules, roles, goals, structure, boundaries, and ideologies of a process for development. There are 12 or more recognized Agile frameworks. SAFe applies Agile principles to the whole-organization management processes in multiple industries outside of software development. Feature-Driven Development plans and creates a prototype or wireframe first, then breaks the work into iterative development components. For the exam, however, you should be most familiar with Scrum, XP, and Lean development.

Scrum Framework

The following are Scrum-specific terms and concepts you will probably encounter on the PMP exam. Scrum is based on **empiricism**—observing events and artifacts, or data and past experiences, to make informed decisions. The Scrum approach is built upon **Three Empirical Pillars—transparency, inspection, and adaptation**.

- **Transparency**—Visible to all who are responsible for the outcome.
- **Inspection**—An open-door policy for stakeholders to conduct timely checks on progress toward product goals, to provide feedback for problematic deviation from the plan, and to reduce the Gulf of Evaluation.
- **Adaptation**—Adjust processes to minimize issues or make improvements after periodic inspection.

Scrum values give direction to the team. (Be prepared for at least one exam question on these.)

- **Commitment**—to the team and goal
- **Focus**—on one task at a time
- **Openness**—about work and challenges
- **Respect**—each other and each other's work
- **Courage**—to do the right thing and take risks

Accountability in Scrum

Product owner—Owns the product vision, defines features, and sets release date. The product owner is responsible for marketing and compliance as well as maximizing product value for the organization by prioritizing ("grooming") the product backlog.

Scrum master—Acts as a "servant leader" by guiding team interactions and removing obstacles to team productivity. This Agile project manager assists and trains the product owner and organization stakeholders on the Scrum and Agile process. Note: Current versions of Agile have dropped "servant" and now refer just to the "leader"; be prepared for both on the exam.

Developers—Provide steady delivery of high-quality work for incremental development; they self-manage team productivity, and they determine the sprint backlog, sprint production schedule, and tool selection.

Extreme (XP) Framework

Extreme (XP) Development originated with Scrum. (The "P" stands for "programming," reflecting XP's software development origins.) Combined with Kanban, where work in progress is limited, XP is one of the most popular frameworks for software development today.

XP Core Values

The team should function as a single unit. Everyone is accountable for everything versus having one sole responsibility.

- **Simplicity**—Reduce complexity and extra features to find the simplest thing that will work.
- **Feedback**—Collect feedback early in order to **fail fast** for faster recovery and improvement.
- **Communication**—Daily stand-up meetings are necessary and ensure that everyone knows who is doing what and the status of the work.
- **Courage**—Allow work to be entirely visible to others.
- **Respect**—Everyone is accountable for success or failure, so work together as a team to do it correctly.

XP Roles

- **Coach** (a.k.a. the Agile project manager)—Leads the team, acts as mentor, guides the development process, and keeps the team on track. The coach also trains stakeholders on the merits of an Agile approach.
- **Customer**—Represents the organization, provides the project priorities, drives the marketing and business aspects of the project, and is ultimately responsible for compliance.
- **Programmers**—The development team members who build the software.
- **Testers**—Help the customer plan and write acceptance criteria tests for the user stories.

XP-Specific Concepts and Practices

- **Release planning**—A release is a phase of development where a major component or milestone of development will be created. Release planning allows the customer to itemize functionality and features required while the programmers estimate the time required to build the component. This is the "big picture" meeting for the phase.
- **Iteration planning** (like Scrum sprint planning meetings)—This meeting is held at the start of every iteration (often 2 weeks for XP) so the customer and programmers can break the release features into granular tasks and work estimates. This is the "fine-tuning" meeting for the phase.
- **3 types of iterations**—Iteration 0 is the first iteration of the project that establishes the team and sets the tone for development efforts yet **doesn't build anything**. The development iteration is when the product development gets done. Iteration H (the "hardening" sprint or release) is done after the product is developed to create the documentation and clean up code for formal presentation.

Since XP is a framework specific to the software development industry, you will need to know some development buzzwords for the exam.

- Focus on **collective code ownership** and consistent coding standards and procedures.
- Use test-driven development (TDD), continuous integration, and paired programming so code can be tested and fixed as soon as it is created.
- The best architecture comes from **self-directed teams.**
- **Refactor** to remove redundancy and eliminate unused functionality throughout the entirety of the development—not just at the end.
- **Use simple code design** and ensure code is testable, "clean," and understandable.
- Utilize frequent small releases for customer testing.

Agile Personas and User Stories

User personas—These are fictional representations of an end user that serve as a perspective for product development. By creating a character with career goals, skills, needs, hobbies, personal ideologies, and values, a development team can target features for development that will provide value for the user. Traditional and digital marketing services also utilize this technique in order to target their product development and advertisement to specific groups of customers.

User stories—Developers write these based on real-world users' needs. They include a user type ("who"), a product functionality goal or need ("what"), and a justification of value for the need ("why"). (Example: "As a hospital admittance clerk, I need a way to scan a driver's license or official ID and capture all pertinent data for our records. This would save valuable time during the rush of emergency room processing.") These user stories provide depth and context for feature analysis and test development for the final product. Note: An exam question scenario that mentions a nondescript "backlog" is referring to a user story; each user story is a separate product functionality component. The "product" backlog is the overall list of product functionalities that gets reprioritized by the product owner. The "sprint" backlog is the section of the product backlog that the development team has determined will be completed during the four-week sprint work period.

INVEST and the 3 C's

For the exam, know the INVEST acronym and the 3 C's. (Remember, this applies most often to software development.) The most effective user stories are:

- Independent—Each user story is unique so it can be prioritized as a product functionality or element.
- Negotiable—Based on the cost or duplication of functions, user stories can be negotiated.
- Valuable—Clearly state their value justification. (How will it contribute to the organization?)
- Estimable—The user story should include a way to measure or quantify value and development time.
- Small—Should require between half a day to no more than a week's worth of software development.
- Testable—A user story function should be testable once completed.

The 3 C's of Agile are the **card** (sticky note of the user story), **conversation** (discussion of the user's functionality request from its inception through the end of its development), and **confirmation** (the final testing by the customer or product owner that affirms the product fulfills the requirements of the user story). Newer variations of Agile interpret the C's differently and may include collaboration and communication. Stick with the more traditional "card, conversation, and confirmation" for the PMP exam.

Epic Breakdown of Agile Development

XP projects are broken into a hierarchy of requirements and work packages. These are theoretical "containers" or bundles for work that have similar aspects in common. There is no right or wrong way to define these containers; how they are classified depends on the culture of the development team as part of the adaptability of the Agile mentality. Each unit in the hierarchy has a specific value-driven goal that contributes to the parent task above it in the hierarchy. Here is a general-purpose explanation, for the exam, ranked from highest to lowest amount of work:

Themes—Some teams utilize the concept of "themes" as containers that apply to the initiatives of the entire organization. A theme is similar to an organization's portfolio of programs and projects, focused on delivering targeted value to the entire company.

Epics—Consider these big "user stories" to represent the value of the deliverable(s) to the overall organization. Epics would be similar to a program consisting of smaller projects. For example, a construction program for a new golf resort could consist of two epics (big, but distinct projects)—the hotel accommodations and the golf grounds.

Features—These can be separate areas of value and functionality grouped by related work. The new golf resort project may have a technology integration "feature" to capture all of the work necessary to establish the technology infrastructure and operational software. It could include the design and installation work for the interior aesthetics as a separate feature. A third feature might be the golf course development. All of these are key components or deliverables for the bigger, "epic" golf resort, yet the work activities and development teams for each respective feature are different from the other features in the project. (You wouldn't use the interior design team to plan and build the golf course.)

Stories—These are the technical development "short stories" or quick-finish sub-projects that are associated with their feature "parent" in the hierarchy. The golf course feature will have a course design story, a maintenance shed development story, a refreshment stand story, etc. The size of the story depends on the initial scope of the project and the estimation techniques utilized by the project team when creating a structured breakdown of the work. For software development, many teams try to keep a story length to no more than a week's worth of work. However, **Agile uses "relative" estimating based on the size, complexity, and number of deliverables in the overall project.** The bigger the overall project, the more levels of hierarchy will be needed; the tier components, such as features and stories, will be larger in either length or number as well.

Tasks—These are subtasks of the stories and are the smallest unit of development in the hierarchy. A task for the golf course design story might be to confirm and hire the designer. The refreshment stand story might require tasks such as "hire architect" and "plan list of fare."

Lean Development

Lean development was first implemented by the Toyota auto manufacturing company. The principles and processes have been adapted and refined for a variety of industries, including software development. Regardless of the version of Lean, **defining *customer value* and subsequent delivery is the primary goal or principle**. Team-specific principles include:

- Empower the team by respecting their superior knowledge.
- Amplify learning among the team and stakeholders through frequent, early, and open communication, feedback, sharing, and implementation.
- Deliver value fast and iterate through designs. (Create a minimum viable product, or MVP, for release and improve upon it later.)
- Defer decisions until as late as possible to limit team focus to the current work. This reduces wasted focus.
- Build quality into the product and continually assure quality.
- Optimize the whole by seeing the system as more than the sum of its parts (a.k.a. "systems thinking").
- Maximize value by **eliminating the 7 "wastes" of Lean:** partially done work, waiting, extra features, extra processes, task switching, motion via extra travel or steps, and defects or rework.

Kanban

Kanban, Japanese for "sign board," developed from the Lean process used at Toyota. Kanban uses a physical whiteboard and sticky note "cards" as an information radiator for visualizing the backlog. It is big so everyone can see it, and it is "low-tech and high-touch" so everyone can use it. A Kanban board consists of an item or task column, an "in progress" column, a "testing" or "bug" column, and a "done" column. It uses a "pull" system, where anyone with free time can take work from others by selecting a sticky note user story "card" of work, completing that portion of the work, then placing the card back on the board in the appropriate column to the right. The Kanban system is effective because it **limits the work in progress**. Once the team establishes rules and procedures for the use of the board, new work cannot be added to the board until enough work gets classified as "done." Group collaboration is an integral component of the process since everyone must communicate and work together to manage the flow of work "cards" through the process.

A Scrum board also utilizes a whiteboard, sticky notes, and columns. However, the rules and procedure for use are defined by the team. Instead of limiting the number of cards in the "item" or "task" column, the entire project backlog might be posted. "Swim lanes" are special columns outside of the normal productivity flow to allow more time to find a solution for a problem.

Most project management tools—like Jira, Monday, Asana, Smartsheet, and Microsoft Project—have digital forms of either Scrum or Kanban boards that can be tailored for productivity by the team. This allows distributed teams, those with remote workers who cannot be collocated, to plan and produce smoothly.

Agile Planning

Use these backlog prioritization techniques during planning meetings to get the stakeholders engaged and involved in prioritizing features.

"Monopoly money," dot sticker voting, or 100-point methods—Stakeholders are given a certain amount of voting currency to distribute among product feature and functionality suggestions or to prioritize components.

MoSCoW technique—Ask stakeholders what features the product **M**ust have, **S**hould have, **C**ould have if time permits, and **W**ould like but not now.

Kano analysis—Present stakeholders with a list of features and chart their perceived value based on whether the feature is preferred or expected. This helps developers understand product feature needs based on "satisfiers" and "dissatisfiers." Consider the features that may be considered for the base model development of a new sports sedan.

- **Delighters**—Features that are "extra" or "bonus" and beyond customer expectations (e.g., seat warmers, a moon roof, super acceleration).
- **Satisfiers**—Necessary features to make the buyer happy with the product (e.g., stereo, sporty body style).
- **Dissatisfiers**—Must-have features that don't add value when present but will make buyers unhappy when absent (e.g., power steering, cup holders, USB ports).
- **Indifferent**—Features that have neither a positive nor negative influence on customer happiness (e.g., self-driving feature).
- **Reverse**—Features that may have a negative impact on customers (e.g., limited color palette, no hybrid or electric option).

Techniques to Maximize Group Participation and Discussion

You want everyone to feel comfortable and empowered to provide genuine and equal input and feedback while minimizing conflict.

- Round robin—Pass a token around, and only one can speak at a time. This ensures no one monopolizes the conversation.
- Group brainstorming—Everyone writes their ideas on a sticky note to avoid a cacophony of shouting.
- Simple voting—Ask the group for a thumbs up, a thumbs down, or a thumb sideways for "ambivalent."
- Fist of five—Ask the group to rate their level of agreement by showing fingers (1 is lowest, 5 is highest).

Promote "green zone" communication that is group focused, is positive, takes responsibility, uses persuasion, seeks excellence versus victory, and listens well. For the exam, green zone examples help the group.

Discourage "red zone" communication that blames others for everything, sees conflict as a battle to win, feels threatened and responds defensively, uses blame and shame, or won't forgive. For the exam, red zone examples hinder the group.

Avoid these ineffective group participation strategies or dilemmas.

- **Simple scheme**—Ask the group about the first priority for the product, the second priority for the product, etc. However, there is rarely group consensus on priorities.
- **HIPPO**—The highest-paid person's opinion (or the most influential person's opinion).
- **Bandwagon**—Tendency to favor an idea because others are in favor of it.
- **Groupthink**—Not offering alternatives to the consensus to avoid conflict or making waves.

Collaboration games you may see on the exam:

Agile project tweet—Sum up the product feature or function by creating an advertising slogan in a set amount of characters.

Remember the future—Ask stakeholders to imagine they are looking back on a product after it has already been released. As they "remember" the product, ask what they think users will say about the product. This helps define the project success criteria.

Speedboat (or sailboat) game—Draw a line pointed toward the project goal. Tell the group a project "boat" is moving on the water line toward the goal. Give them sticky notes to identify and label what makes the boat move toward the goal (wind) and what holds the boat back (anchor). This helps identify opportunities and threats.

Prune the product tree—Draw a tree trunk with branches. Ask the group to write product features on sticky notes and place them on the tree. Group them by category. Features dependent on others should be placed higher up the tree. This helps stakeholders understand the importance of identifying priorities during a development process.

ESTIMATION OF STORY (WORK) POINTS

Agile product development occurs during timeboxed sprints of **2 to 4 weeks**. The project team breaks product components into granular tasks for "relative" estimating based on the overall size of the project as well as the complexity and number of deliverables. The tasks will vary in length, so they are estimated as "points" of work that can be completed in a fixed unit of time. Affinity estimating determines points of work and cycle times based on similar or "like" categories or collections. T-shirt sizing breaks points of work into metaphorical shirt sizes to describe the approximate size of a task. (XP uses metaphor concepts frequently as common descriptors for Agile processes that clients and team members can understand. The T-shirt sizing for estimation generates quick understanding. A client will understand the difference between a task that's a "medium" versus a "2X." Many of the collaboration games listed above utilized metaphors as well.) Wideband Delphi is used when a group of experts is queried anonymously; it's fast and accurate because it's done by experts with no need to collaborate.

Fibonacci estimating uses the Fibonacci sequence to generate a size approximation as well. The Fibonacci sequence starts with 0, adds the next digit to get a sum, adds the next digit to the previous total to get a new sum, and continues to infinity. ($0 + 1 = 1, 1 + 1 = 2, 2 + 1 = 3, 3 + 2 = 5, 5 + 3 = 8$, etc.) You don't need to know the formula on the test, but you do need to know it's used for estimating work points.

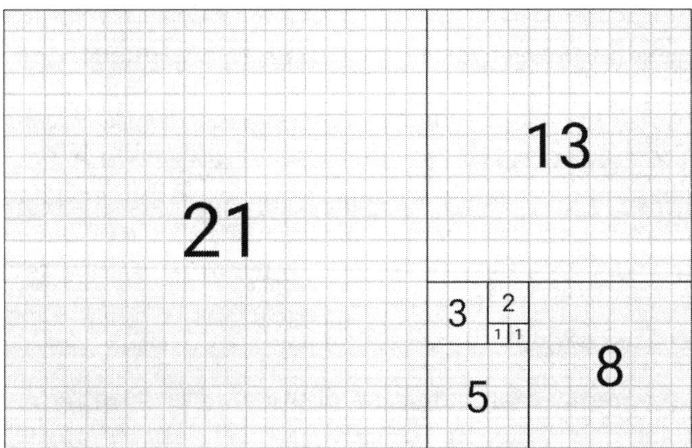

Once the initial estimation activities are completed, the stakeholders help create a **"story map"** as a preliminary product roadmap. The **product roadmap** is a refined story backlog that will be used to tentatively schedule project milestones. The product owner will continue to prioritize the backlog prior to each sprint or iteration along the roadmap until each milestone is achieved.

LEAD TIME AND CYCLE TIME

Lead time is the entire duration of the process (e.g., a 4-week sprint). Cycle time, a subset of lead time, is the amount of time it takes to complete a part of the process, or the amount of time it takes to get the work done.

$$\text{Cycle Time} = \frac{\text{WIP}}{\text{Throughput}}$$

WIP is the amount of work in progress, and throughput is the amount of work (in work points) that can be done in a time period. If a team needs to build "Module X," estimated at 100 points of work (the WIP), and the team is capable of completing 5 points of work per day (the throughput), what would be the cycle time for Module X? Calculate: $\frac{100}{5} = 20$ days.

Little's law concludes that cycle times are proportional to the queue lengths; **you can predict completion times based on the queue size or backlog**. If the team knows how much work needs to be done and knows how much work they can do in a day, the team can determine with fair accuracy the number of days until completion. (This is just algebra.)

Parkinson's law states that the cycle time will always fill the lead time; **workers will take all of the time they have to complete a job.** (This is just human nature.) Therefore, teams should utilize Agile estimation strategies to accurately reflect the appropriate story points' worth of work. The lead time should be kept short or tight to limit the work in progress—to focus on doing one thing completely and well—while avoiding the Parkinson's effect.

SUMMARY

Compared to predictive projects, Agile delivers value quicker, decreases costs, and reduces risk. Value delivery occurs more frequently and increases over time. Risk is generally lower since it is identified and analyzed more frequently. Product work is transparent throughout development, and a useful product or feature is delivered often. Also, the cost of change is reduced due to integrated and reactive planning.

Agile teams should be composed of **cross-functional "generalist specialists"** who can share and exchange responsibilities easily. Teams should be small, with a maximum of 11 members including the project owner (Scrum master) and the product owner. Teams should also remain adaptive and promote self-learning and skills development for the sake of individual motivation and improved overall team performance. Finally, teams should be self-managing and empowered to determine their own cadence, as well as the developmental process and tools.

This has been a brief review of concepts you are likely to encounter at least once on the PMP exam. We encourage you to utilize other online resources for Agile concepts as well. Keep these Agile buzzwords in mind when selecting "best" answers for any project approach on the exam: just-in-time delivery, feedback loops, continuous improvement, stakeholder satisfaction, delivering value early and often, low-tech and high-touch tools and information radiators like whiteboards where everyone can participate, and collocation and face-to-face communication.

Principles

Stewardship

According to PMI, the following are the key points in understanding Stewardship:

- Stewardship encompasses responsibilities within and external to the organization.
- Stewardship includes integrity, care, trustworthiness, and compliance.
- A holistic view of stewardship considers financial, social, technical, and sustainable environmental awareness.

A steward has a responsibility to a project, both to those funding it and to those who will benefit from it. This responsibility will often require the project manager to play the mediator in some cases and the unyielding opponent in others. A good parallel is a fiduciary who has a fiscal responsibility to perform tasks designated as being in the best interest of the client. In the context of project management, a **caring** steward makes use of sound judgment and common sense to act in the best interest of the project and on behalf of the sponsoring organization. This requires a deft hand and shrewd consideration of logistical, technical, and environmental concerns to perform the triage necessary to maintain balance among the project constraints; the project manager must monitor scope, budget, and schedule while ensuring quality, reducing risk, and optimizing resources. Therefore, the project manager "steward" must first ensure the project is justified via the business use case developed as part of the project charter. Then, the project manager must ensure the project is well-planned and tailored within the context of the organizational process assets and the enterprise environmental factors. The steward must also endeavor to optimize stakeholder engagement and open communication with the organization's stakeholders throughout the project. Not only does this frequent interaction with stakeholders provide invaluable opportunities for feedback to improve project processes and deliverables, but it also demonstrates to the organization that the project is in the good hands of a capable steward who truly cares about the project's success.

The project manager is often faced with dilemmas related to **integrity**. Integrity refers to a project manager's trustworthiness based on honesty, earnest effort, and capability. Can the organization depend on you to get the job done well and in a manner that reflects positively on the organization? Opportunities to demonstrate integrity arise every time you advise on the status or make a decision on a project. The project manager must respect the law, or maintain **compliance**, above all other considerations. Then, he or she must act in the "best interest" of the organization. This supersedes the actual goal of a project—to produce the deliverables by achieving the requirements defined by the scope. How should you as the project manager proceed when the project constraints, stakeholder agendas, regulatory changes, and environmental factors conflict with one another? Do you concede to demands from high-profile customer stakeholders or the project sponsor representing the organization that is paying the bills? Do you compromise by reducing the project scope, substituting inferior materials, or crashing the project without approval in order to keep it on schedule? If the project is two months behind, should you reflect that in the status report? Guidance for "good steward" answers to these dilemmas can be found in the project planning documentation.

The PMI structured approach to project management integrates the detailed planning of each of the Knowledge Areas and distributes the implementation of the planning across the process phases. This procedural approach establishes the bright-line standard for the project goal, implementation, and measurement in a manner designed to eliminate these ambiguities or "gray areas" of interpretation. When addressing project conflicts and risks, a change in one project aspect will have a ripple effect on the rest of the project. Therefore, the project manager must first consult project planning documentation in order to evaluate the impact of project-altering decisions. A PMI project manager should recognize that the integrated change control process represents a dependable procedure for weighing and instigating project changes for any project approach. Though Agile projects often entail less documentation and more fluidity in approaches to product development, there will still be overarching planning and corresponding documents associated with the holistic project management that should be reviewed regularly to ensure the project is progressing appropriately.

Regardless of the project's status, maintain regular and frequent communication in accordance with the methods prescribed for your stakeholders detailed in the communication management plan. Project managers will often have to make compromises, so it is best to determine based on the Knowledge Area Plan's documentation which project aspects you can be flexible on, versus those components you cannot. Thus, the PMI process generates the appropriate plans. The integrated change control process manages adaptations to the plans. As part of competent stewardship, the project manager is responsible for knowing when to make a change, when not to alter the plan, and the appropriate strategies for optimizing flexibility while keeping a project on course. The project team and stakeholders should always be able to **trust** that the project manager steward will neither overpromise nor underdeliver and will accurately portray whatever authority they have to make meaningful change. This should include proactively recognizing potential conflicts of interest and actively avoiding unethical or illegal behaviors that could jeopardize the deliverable or contribute to a suboptimal outcome.

With respect to compliance, the project manager should understand that industry standards and local laws can vary, so it is prudent to review them—not only to verify the legality of your project, but also to understand your role as the responsible party in charge of the project. An illegal contract is never binding, but the laws will determine the level of accountability demanded by those in charge of the project. And, according to PMI, the predictive project sponsor (or Agile product owner) is ultimately responsible for compliance with the law. However, as part of proper project stewardship, the project manager should monitor regulatory compliance as well. Have you or the organization's compliance body had an attorney review the contract, or binding documentation? Are there clearly articulated statements of work? Is there any ambiguous language? Raise concerns before undertaking any project work to avoid legal issues. If your project requires periodic legal review, diligently record this in your risk register and inform your project sponsor. If these concerns cannot be properly mitigated, then the project should not be undertaken.

Team

According to PMI, the following are the key points in understanding Team:

- Projects are delivered by project teams.
- Project teams work within organizational and professional cultures and guidelines, often establishing their own "local" culture.
- A collaborative project team environment facilitates the following:
    - Alignment with other organizational cultures and guidelines
    - Individual and team learning and development
    - Optimal contributions to deliver desired outcomes

During the Lessons Learned (a post-project analysis phase), some of the most reviewed items are losses and inefficiencies caused by project members failing to work well together. Successful project managers will need to hone the soft skills of collaboration and emotional intelligence, knowing that *soft* does not in any way imply *nonessential*. If anything, these interpersonal skills are some of the most important skills for the profession of project management and will be pivotal in establishing team agreements.

The complexity and variety of projects you will be called to work on will require a vast array of skills and expertise. In fact, this is true individually for most-large scale projects. As the list of required skills increases, so will the number of people involved. This means more personalities and work habits to deal with. The more diverse the resource pool, the more challenging it is to forge these individuals into a single productive team. Add into the mix the potential for widely differing time zones or compact work schedules, and it is clear how facilitating collaboration can become one of the more time-consuming parts of the job for the project manager. PMI promotes the ideal of colocation, or in-person, face-to-face communication for team and stakeholder collaboration. However, contemporary work dynamics may continue to rely on remote work from different locations and time zones around the world. To promote collaboration, consider the different work norms and behaviors of your team members. Are they used to face-to-face meetings, virtual meetings, conference calls, or emails? Do they require special work equipment or spaces? Do they speak the same language with operational fluency? Are there potential cultural conflicts that may impact team cohesiveness? How will you inspire the team to self-manage interactions with colleagues when differences in sociopolitical viewpoints create conflicts among team members? It will be your job to ask these questions, and the more comfortable you are during the initial interview stage, the greater your understanding will be of how to properly compile your work schedule.

But collaboration is more than just the impact on you as the PM. You must also consider how disparate team members must work together and what challenges may be present. Some skilled professionals have very rigid ideas of how others should interact with them, and how they should interact with others, so consider their suitability when preparing work assignments. However, there really is no substitute for the PM having touchpoints with the team to ensure collegiality. This means you should meet with your team members initially and regularly for every significant phase of work. You must also ensure that all team members participate in the development and approval of the team charter to govern team operations; the team members should determine collectively what their obligations to each other and the project vision will be. This pulse-checking is integral, not just for keeping your project on track, but for gauging the collaboration of your team. It is paramount that everyone has clarity on the tasks they have selected or been delegated, as this prevents unnecessary confusion about who has **authority**, **accountability**, and **responsibility**.

Team members feeling uninformed, or overly compartmentalized, is a common refrain in post-analysis meetings. This feeling of alienization is likely to increase when team members are asked to utilize tools or processes that are new or unfamiliar. Be sure to ease their concerns by using one-on-one meetings, or joint meetings with their functional manager (if practical), to ensure proper opportunities for participation and discussion. Also vital to team management is your obligation to hold team members accountable for their productivity. If a team member is not performing at an optimal level, discuss the concern with the team member to discover the root of the problem. Is he or she having problems at home? Having a conflict with another team member? Does he or she need more training? Demonstrate empathy, discuss alternative solutions, and find training solutions when needed. Meet with team members privately to discuss your concerns with regard to project performance and conflict management concerns. Once you have addressed a concern, always follow up to ensure your solution has solved the problem.

Stakeholders

According to PMI, the following are the key points in understanding Stakeholders:

- Stakeholders influence projects, performance, and outcomes.
- Project teams serve other stakeholders by engaging with them.
- Stakeholder engagement proactively advances value delivery.

In practice, a stakeholder is any individual or organization who will be affected by the implementation of the project (e.g., taxpayers, local residents, rival organizations, political activists, or lower-level employees whose workflows might change). Consider who will gain or lose money, property, status, job responsibilities, and influence as a result of the project. During the initiating phase of the project, the stakeholder register will be established to list, define, and categorize the key organization players, the project sponsor (and related customer representatives), local and regional legislative representatives who may weigh in on the project, pre-selected contractors, vendors, and team members, and any known groups who may have interest in or may object to the project. As the project progresses, the stakeholder register will need to be updated as new stakeholders are discovered and existing stakeholders change roles. Although the definition of "stakeholder" can seem arbitrary or non-specific, if a person has a financial, social, or political interest in the project outcome or bears some responsibility for consulting, producing, or validating any portion of the project processes or deliverables, then they should be considered a stakeholder.

Because stakeholders may be responsible for approving phase gates, change orders, and possibly even the project deliverable itself, the project manager should develop a stakeholder engagement plan to properly identify how to engage with each stakeholder group. Predictive projects should include opportunities for stakeholder groups to provide feedback throughout the project; the goal, modality and preliminary planning details for these events would be detailed in the stakeholder engagement plan. This plan is different from the communication management plan, which is a matrix a project manager will refer to, identifying what to communicate to each stakeholder group, as well as the frequency and format of delivery. Though supplemental prototype review and testing opportunities for lower-tier stakeholder groups can be scheduled at key milestones, Agile projects include frequent product owner and stakeholder feedback opportunities during sprint reviews.

The simplest path to successful engagement is to utilize surveys and conduct in-person meetings with stakeholders. Encourage the stakeholder to self-identify their respective roles, awareness of and interest in the project, and individual communication preferences. Additionally, note the different time zones of the individuals or organizations. Many individuals will make a concerted effort to join regular status calls or other online meetings regardless of their local time, as they are vested in the project and wish to see a good outcome. If they are members of an organization, a simple consultation of the organization chart may be all that is needed. Emails or more formal communication can be exchanged to introduce your project and invite stakeholders to participate in project engagement events. There are some individuals or organizations who will refuse to participate in the project due to disinterest or objection, but they should still be kept on your stakeholder register; lack of awareness of a policy or procedural change, or even vindictive behavior, can pose a risk to the project. As the project moves forward, continue to send formal communication when possible, and record these attempts. Keep in mind, however, you will never achieve a 100% read or response rate to an email or survey. Establishing a centralized repository of project information—and reports from which interested (and obligated) stakeholders may "pull," as well as utilizing "push" notifications of key reports to the appropriate stakeholder groups at scheduled intervals—will help minimize late-project deliverable dissatisfaction from groups of stakeholders declaring, "We didn't know about it!" Make certain there is "no excuse" for any stakeholder to remain uninformed. Then allow the organization's functional management to do their part to ensure stakeholders comply with expectations of awareness.

Finally, make sure the communication method used accommodates the schedule of your stakeholders to the extent it is possible. Many executive stakeholders prefer quick meetings (ten minutes or less) rather than emails, since their inbox fills up quickly with email to a point where timely correspondence becomes difficult. Other stakeholders may be double- or even triple-booked with meetings during their day and prefer email or other indirect communication. Additionally, the information regarding stakeholders may be confidential, so considerations should be extended regarding its accessibility to other members of the project management team. This sensitivity makes it necessary to discuss when the plan should be accessed and who has permission to make updates. The stakeholder engagement plan will be preserved as an artifact of the project and can be inspected by the project management office (PMO) or other select stakeholders.

Value

According to PMI, the following are the key points in understanding Value:

- Value is the ultimate indicator of project success.
- Value can be realized throughout the project, at the end of the project, or after the project is complete.
- Value, and the benefits that contribute to value, can be defined in quantitative and/or qualitative terms.
- A focus on outcomes allows project teams to support the intended benefits that lead to value creation.
- Project teams evaluate progress and adapt to maximize the expected value.

Value is a metric that is usually external to a project manager; it is determined by its benefit to the end user, not to the project manager. Due to its inherently subjective nature and its role as a key determinant of measuring success, it is necessary for the project's value proposition to be explicitly defined in the business use case of the project charter *before* undertaking project work. It cannot be left as some vague moving target, since this will cause the project to fail for lack of clear goals, or almost assuredly be plagued by conflict due to competing priorities. Project managers should ensure that the same standard is always applied when measuring value, whether it is quantitative or qualitative.

Project managers will use their various skills and tools to design their projects to deliver value. By creating work packages with quality as an output and with consistent measurement, project teams should be able to achieve the quality goals of their deliverable. If your value metrics are largely qualitative, be sure to involve the project sponsors or other senior stakeholders on a regular basis to ensure the project teams are on the right track. Leverage this feedback positively when communicating course corrections to your project teams, allowing them to adapt and update their work accordingly.

One of the fundamental ways a project manager can contribute value is by being highly prepared. The quest to drive value in your project is intentional, and must therefore be the result of thorough, if not exhaustive, analysis of how to get the deliverable past the milestones defined by the contract. Questions to ask are: Does the cost of providing the value exceed the budget? Are there technical or other product considerations to consider that exceed the scope in the charter? Are there hard deadlines that have been imposed? If these or any other blockers (things that cause the work to stop) exist, it is important for the project manager to review this with the sponsor or senior stakeholders.

As stated at the beginning, value is a metric that is derived from the contract or charter as specified by the sponsor. Therefore, before the project can conclude, the sponsor or client must validate that the desired value was achieved. However, before they inspect it, the project management team should also do their own validation to ensure all of the team's target values were achieved. The temptation to produce more than what was enumerated in the charter or contract is real and must be avoided, as excessive ornamentation or "gold plating" of the deliverable could expose the project to validation failure and increased risk. Created work packages should achieve what was contractually or verbally specified; if additional value can be created, mention it to the client or sponsor and let it be determined by their decision. If this change is approved, the change control process must be followed to fully document this update to the deliverable.

Systems Thinking

According to PMI, the following are the key points in understanding Systems Thinking:

- A project is a system of interdependent and interacting domains of activity.
- Systems thinking entails taking a holistic view of how project parts interact with each other and with external systems.
- Systems are constantly changing, requiring consistent attention to the internal and external conditions.
- Being responsive to system interactions allows project teams to leverage positive outcomes.

A system is any set of functioning components that can act both independently and as part of a larger whole in any dynamic environment. This is a more abstract, conceptual view, but it's also a highly effective notional construct as you start the project, because it compels you to ask some vital questions, such as "What does my project need to function?" and "How many subsystems or supersystems are involved?" This ideological framework is useful when complications and complexities arise because it can offer clarity as to which pieces of a project are truly necessary and how best to focus efforts into them. For example, think of making a movie as a project. If a change is made to the script, then the resultant changes must be considered for all other aspects of filming: casting changes, location changes, scenery changes. Any of these changes would be enough to consider the impact on budget, schedule, and availability. The producer would be wise to carefully weigh the changes to make the best decision, and in this way, they are acting as a project manager using systems thinking in a dynamic environment.

Because most systems reside in dynamic environments, it is important to consider all external conditions and how they intersect with your project. The project manager, the project sponsor or product owner, key organization stakeholders, and other stakeholders of influence should meet as a planning team; multiple and relevant perspectives are key to this process. Start by considering the gamut of changes that can occur and ensure they are clearly articulated and charted. While a 360-degree view is not always achievable, the possibility of future changes and potential risks should be explored early in the project planning of a system. The project manager should enlist the project sponsor, key organizational decision-makers, and any other subject matter experts (SMEs) to form the brainstorming "think tank." If your budget allows, it may be wise to hire experts in the field if you do not have SMEs on your project team. Leveraging their expertise is usually worth the cost, as they can provide invaluable insight about not only the nature of the change potential but scheduling concerns as well.

It is also important to note how systems thinking applies to your individual team members. Philosophical differences in the way some team members view their roles may be internalized to a degree where they can unintentionally challenge team cohesion. While most project members take great pride in being flexible, be aware of how they view their roles, as their assumptions, preferences, and work methods may be too singular for a team environment. Keep the team focused on the project vision and the fact that it will be accomplished by a team of many—not just one. Once you do have philosophical alignment, ensure the skills of your team members represent the widest set possible to allow a greater chance of sniffing out potential issues, system constraints, or variables. Leveraging skills like empathy, flexibility, and big-picture thinking can help the project manager minimize risk by identifying, managing, and traversing issues as they occur. Use the integrated change control process when a change element cannot be ignored.

Leadership

According to PMI, the following are the key points in understanding Leadership:

- Effective leadership promotes project success and contributes to positive project outcomes.
- Any project team member can demonstrate leadership behaviors.
- Leadership is different than authority.
- Effective leaders adapt their style to the situation.
- Effective leaders recognize differences in motivation among project team members.
- Leaders demonstrate desired behavior in areas of honesty, integrity, and ethical conduct.

While leadership is the quality most associated with project managers and is easily understood with conventional definitions, it does have a more specific context in the project management narrative. In broadly conventional terms, leadership is simply the capacity to guide or direct. For the project management realm, however, leadership is instead the ability to create a common vision that, when adopted, influences others to realize it. It is an internal quality that compels external adherence to a strategy and is entirely distinct from management. While management is the discipline to produce repeatable results, leadership is the ability to inspire and motivate. Not all good managers are effective leaders, and not all good leaders are effective managers. The most successful project managers are often both good leaders and good managers.

Good leaders establish direction by first knowing the outcome they would like to achieve, then promoting it to the project team as early as possible. The initial team meeting is the best place to start. Once vision is established, consider the best ways to align your project team to collaborate in the same direction. This is a difficult task, as some project members need more buy-in or commitment than others. Once team alignment has been reached, the project manager should endeavor to inspire and motivate the team while always promoting the project vision. If inspiration and motivation are sufficiently internalized, the team will be more willing to handle and overcome obstacles using their own enthusiasm and creativity. Good leaders unleash the potential in their teams, ensuring all members have a voice or platform, and creating safe spaces where team members can cooperatively work together. Conversely, good managers ensure proper adherence to the standards needed for project success.

Inherent in leadership is authority, which is defined as the right to enforce rules or commands to control outcomes. The organization's structure determines the project manager's authority and ultimate control of the project resources and decision-making permissions. Often, organizations will contract with a project manager who will coordinate instead of leading a project since he or she must appeal to the functional manager for approval to make decisions and deploy resources. If this happens, approach the sponsor and seek to formalize a strong matrix or project-oriented matrix scenario that will allow you to lead and manage your project with confidence and without hindrance from the organization's functional managers. Also constantly assess the leadership of your project—the leadership of not only the leaders on your team, but also yourself. Ineffective leadership is corrosive and can be devastating to morale. If you feel uncertainty or deficiency in your capabilities, seek out trusted peers and mentors who can help you refine your skills. Project managers should always be seeking ways to improve their abilities, whether it is stretching themselves by learning new skillsets or allowing (sometimes painful) feedback when solicited—especially from within the project team. Effective leaders surround themselves with people who are willing to offer frank and candid feedback, so be sure to listen when they share their thoughts and try to accept the truth of any critiques.

Tailoring

According to PMI, the following are the key points in understanding Tailoring:

- Each project is unique.
- Project success is based on adapting to the unique context of the project to determine the most appropriate methods of producing the desired outcomes.
- Tailoring the approach is iterative, and therefore is a continuous process throughout the project.

The procedural approach to tailoring represents a key shift in project management in the 7th edition of the PMBOK Guide. This guide contains an expanded section that discusses the steps of tailoring the project approach, tailoring for the organization, tailoring for the project, and ongoing tailoring required throughout the project.

Tailoring is the process of intentionally adapting a unique aspect of a project to ultimately produce a better outcome, within the complexities of a dynamic environment. This may include altering the approach, the schedule, the systems or subsystems, or the underlying processes to make them as efficient as possible for meeting the deliverable. When done well, tailoring boosts efficiency and eliminates waste, saving money in your budget that can be used elsewhere. For example, if you are developing a marketing program for a new industry, you may start with a standard marketing program but will soon solicit input from experts to create a newly tailored standard for your demographic. This approach allows you to save some time and expense and balance the needs to fulfill the deliverable, while also accommodating the dynamic environment your workplan demanded.

All projects are dynamic, and no two projects are alike. All projects will require some level of tailoring. Three of the four official PMI tailoring process steps occur during the initiating and planning stages of the project and well before the actual project work activity begins. The fourth tailoring step involves adapting to the myriad of obstacles and opportunities that emerge throughout the project's duration. Regardless of the tailoring step, consulting with your project team and SMEs throughout all process phases of the project is vital to discovering, analyzing, and evaluating potential risks, opportunities, new stakeholders, pending legislation, changes in relevant industries, and other considerations that may impact the success or ultimate value of the project.

If your organization has a project management office (PMO) that provides methodology oversight, or some other parent organization policy directive, it is still your responsibility to consider all relevant factors and decide where the project needs tailoring to be successful. Finally, ensure all tailoring decisions are properly documented and communicated to the sponsor and relevant stakeholders.

Quality

According to PMI, the following are the key points in understanding Quality:

- Project quality entails satisfying stakeholders' expectations and fulfilling project and product requirements.
- Quality focuses on meeting acceptance criteria for deliverables.
- Project quality entails ensuring project processes are appropriate and as effective as possible.

Delivering quality can be one of the more challenging aspects of managing projects. Quality is the degree to which the deliverable fulfills the project requirements and satisfies the customer's needs. Quality in Agile software projects is generally measured by whether or not the software deliverable works according to the operational features required. Agile quality management processes are monitored and adjusted continuously during development via paired programming, daily stand-up meetings, and sprint reviews.

"Quality" in traditional or predictive project management is assessed at two levels. First, the quality management plan is developed during the planning phase to document the processes that will be used for producing the deliverables and managing aspects of the project. Designated stakeholders, whether part of the development or quality control team, will conduct periodic process audits as the deliverables are produced to verify that the production processes are being followed according to the quality management plan, as well as to document areas of the project and production processes that can be improved.

The "quality" of the project deliverables is also evaluated. Quality requirements, or the declared condition or capability that must be present in the deliverable to satisfy the terms of the contract, should be recorded in the requirements documentation as part of the Plan Scope Management process. These quality requirements will be utilized during the final Validate Scope process prior to sponsor approval of the final project deliverables. Thoroughly integrating quality into project work compels the project manager to consider every aspect, whether novel or established, to achieve the project goals. Consider carefully "benchmarking" parallel applications that have been successfully implemented in other industries, as unproven process steps carry risk that must be properly understood. For example, when devising a new software application where you have no previous experience, a common practice is to follow test scripts that have been proven to work in similar applications. While the software might serve a completely different industry or function, there is still enough commonality between the applications to allow one testing method to be co-opted by the other.

Project teams need to understand how to properly measure the performance characteristics of the deliverable, and this requires metrics. A metric is a measure of performance that can be computed in a repeatable process to track the success of a project requirement. Determining how you will track performance is essential to the project team's ability to ensure the quality stipulated in the requirements for the project, allowing the project manager to plan the project work.

Because this process requires signoff by either the customer or stakeholders, it must be transparent and verifiable. It is the role of the project manager to properly track and log the project work. If the quality standards are not being met, analysis of the issue by the quality control team should begin immediately to understand why and remedy the issue. If the analysis of the project team determines that the issue is the result of a risk factor, it must be logged, analyzed, and reported to the customer or senior stakeholders for resolution if the project is to continue. It is the role of the project manager to ensure that quality standards help, not hinder, the deliverable, and if newly discovered activities or steps are used successfully, they should be recorded in the lessons learned register for future project work.

Complexity

According to PMI, the following are the key points in understanding Complexity:

- Complexity is the result of human behavior, system interactions, uncertainty, and ambiguity.
- Complexity can emerge at any point during the project.
- Complexity can be introduced by events or conditions that affect value, scope, communications, stakeholders, risk, and technological innovation.
- Project teams can stay vigilant in identifying elements of complexity and use a variety of methods to reduce the amount or impact of complexity.

PMI defines complexity as the "characteristic of a project or its environment that is difficult to manage due to human behavior, system behavior, and ambiguity." It is a continually moving and evolving interaction between the different systems your project resides in, or in simpler terms, complexity is the property of something that makes it difficult to understand or work around. Because complexity cannot be completely mitigated, it must instead be managed using as much preparation and understanding as possible. Prudent project managers should carefully undertake the project using the best available information, risk management processes, and phased project work to ensure project success.

Complexity in a system is the result of interactions between various sources, and PMI has identified four targeted areas:

- **Human behavior**—People generally act in a self-interested way, with agendas that may run into conflict with goals or deliverables. Human behavior is an incredibly rich display of personal demeanors and attitudes that may not always align with project work. While the project manager can ensure certain behaviors of project members align with organizational values and policy, the authority to ensure compliance is limited by factors such as cultural norms, language barriers, or in some cases, detrimental conduct. Project managers should work with whatever authorities provide oversight. In cases where the behavior of individuals outside of the project team is a factor, the project manager may have to rely on outside assistance from the community at large, regional policymakers, or even law enforcement.
- **System behavior**—While more common in some industries than others (IT for example), consideration must be given to whether interdependencies exist within a system that might compete with each other, even inadvertently. It is possible that a system is dynamic because elements within the system compete for the same resources or cannot be properly integrated. Sustained challenges remain for the project team if they cannot harness these components, possibly injecting risk into the project.
- **Uncertainty and ambiguity**—Uncertainty is a state where a lack of understanding or awareness produces inhibition when making decisions in a complex environment. While seemingly related, this is different than ambiguity, which is a state where a lack of clarity exists in a situation, resulting in a condition where more information is required to act. Simply stated, uncertainty means not having enough data to make an informed decision, whereas ambiguity is having enough information to make a decision—but without confidence it is the best one. Understanding uncertainty and ambiguities is crucial to effectively address complexity in your project and is a relevant narrative for healthy discussions with the project team.

- **Technological innovation**—A helpful method for understanding the concept of technological innovation is to think of your first time using a new technology—whether it was in social media, a new graphical user interface in your email, or in your vehicle. Using it for the first few times presented challenges and possibly even slowed your progress until you got used to it. This is the hurdle presented by technological innovation. You may be present at the onset of an innovative but complex technology that must be used. Account for the challenge this represents to your project team when assessing the impact of adoption.

Risk

According to PMI, the following are the key points in understanding Risk:

- Individual and overall risks can impact projects.
- Risks can be positive (opportunities) or negative (threats).
- Risks are addressed continually throughout the project.
- An organization's risk attitude, appetite, and threshold influence how risk is addressed.
- Risk responses should be:
    - Appropriate for the significance of the risk
    - Cost effective
    - Realistic within the project context
    - Agreed to by relevant stakeholders
    - Owned by a responsible person

The proper handling of risk is one of the chief duties of any project manager, and some even consider this the only true role. A risk is an uncertain event or condition that falls into one of two categories—positive or negative. While it is perhaps not intuitive, risk can be a positive if viewed as an opportunity. For example, suppose a risk that threatens the timely completion of the project is identified. In response, your project team creates a mitigation that can also be used for future projects, creating cost savings for the portfolio and/or the organization. So, risks become positive if the actions can produce upside or value to the deliverable. By contrast, when an action taken to offset risk fails to reduce the potential threat to the deliverable, this is deemed a negative risk. Risks are further subdivided into external or internal buckets, where each risk can be assessed on probability of occurrence and severity of impact.

The range of acceptable risk is determined by your stakeholders and should be discussed at the onset of any project, or when a risk is newly detected. When initial discussions take place, the project manager should carefully note the risk appetite—the tolerance or degree of uncertainty a stakeholder is willing to accept to achieve the deliverable. The risk threshold is the quantifiable variation of the risk appetite expressed as a measurement that is acceptable to the stakeholders. If a work order comes in for $10,000 and your budget limit is $12,000, then your risk threshold is $2,000. The willingness of the stakeholders to assume the extra cost above budget is their risk appetite. As the complexity of the risk analysis increases, it may require the use of more sophisticated tracking tools or methods. In some projects, especially where safety is a concern, it may be worth the expense to seek an SME for best practices and extra analysis. The identification, understanding and evaluation, and mitigation of risks are principal tasks that must be undertaken not just initially, but continually, throughout a project.

Effective risk management requires enacting strategies to keep the risk profile within an acceptable range. Employ regular risk reviews throughout the project to monitor emergent risks, categorize them, and ensure all project team members understand the protocols for risk reporting. Because a risk has the potential to become a crisis, diligent risk identification by the project team is vital, though even the most vigilant measures may not be enough to identify all incoming risks. Not all risks can be mitigated, and risk must therefore be tolerated by the stakeholders to some degree if the project is to reach completion. In this event, properly catalogue and report the risks to the stakeholders, so they can decide if they want to continue the project. If you are to go forward, be sure to record the results and—if necessary—obtain formal signoff and maintain this as an artifact of the project. Once the project manager understands the risk profiles of their stakeholders, risk responses can then be considered to address each risk as a potential threat or opportunity.

Adaptability and Resiliency

According to PMI, the following are the key points in understanding Adaptability and Resiliency:

- Adaptability is the ability to respond to changing conditions.
- Resiliency is the ability to absorb impacts and to recover quickly from a setback or failure.
- A focus on outcomes rather than outputs facilitates adaptability.

Dwight D. Eisenhower once stated: "In preparing for battle I have always found that plans are useless, but planning is indispensable." Unlike President Eisenhower, PMP reveres the "plan" as the documentation of the planning process for the PMP exam. However, no matter how impeccable a plan a project manager and the planning team may develop, obstacles and opportunities are an integral component of project implementation. Adaptability is the level of ease and anticipation with which you are willing to adjust to a circumstance. Resiliency is the measure of how much difficulty you are willing to absorb to undertake that change. These traits are both complementary and necessary for all successful project managers to hone and possess. For example, an athlete in a team sport may be asked to change positions to fulfill the needs of the team. The degree of willingness to accept this change is adaptability. The level of difficulty in successfully performing the new position is a measure of resiliency.

There are several tools in the project manager's toolkit that can be used to leverage adaptability, such as establishing an up-to-date skills matrix of all project team members, as well as ensuring that project team diversity is rich enough to facilitate collaboration and engender innovative solutions. You could utilize the Agile practice of holding short daily stand-up meetings of 15 minutes or less to encourage team members to offer their opinions and to speak up about any inefficiencies or struggles they have recognized. The objective of this is to regroup, rethink, and replan to maintain a steady project development flow while utilizing short feedback loops whenever possible to quickly adjust to changes as they come. (Many industries are now looking at Agile methodologies to optimize team productivity. Making this type of daily change to the "traditional" team's workflow will require time for training and for gradual acceptance as part of the new workflow.)

Because adaptability and resiliency are empowerment attributes driven by a project management culture, the teams can be stimulated to produce novel and even unorthodox solutions. With the encouragement of the project manager to foster this kind of environment, project teams may often come up with solutions that exceed the original proposed solution. However, innovation needs time for exploration, development, and refinement. If the project is predictive or traditional, the brainstorming and planning for these innovations should be conducted before beginning project work activities, and appropriate time should be scheduled to allow for prototype development and testing. Any changes to the project scope on a traditional or predictive project, once work on the final deliverables begins, must be thoroughly analyzed as part of the integrated change control process. Ensure you have received official approval from the project's change control board on a change order, and that the cost of the change is acceptable to the sponsor before proceeding with the change.

Change

According to PMI, the following are the key points in understanding Change:

- A structured approach to change helps individuals, groups, and the organization transition from the current state to a future desired state.
- Change can originate from internal influences or external sources.
- Enabling change can be challenging, as not all stakeholders embrace change.
- Attempting too much change in a short time can lead to change fatigue and/or resistance.
- Stakeholder engagement and motivational approaches assist in change adoption.

Resistance to change is normal. Think of a time when you decided to create a new habit—regular exercise, earlier bedtime, or any other personal initiative. The difficulty it takes to form a new habit, whether to neutralize bad ones or create new positive ones, is due to the very human tendency we all possess to remain the same. PMI defines change management as a "comprehensive, cyclic, and structured approach for transitioning individuals, groups, and organizations from a current state to a future state in which they realize desired benefits."

Your effectiveness as a project manager may often be viewed by your stakeholders as your ability to adapt to, accept, deflect, and harness change for strategic project advantage, whether those changes are of internal or external origin. For example, if you are overseeing a project where an organization is upskilling the workforce, you might encounter hostility from some of the workers who resist this initiative, preferring known skills and habits over new ones. In anticipation of this, you might host town hall–style meetings or smaller group discussions where you provide transparent information about the project's target outcomes and benefits before inviting workers to express their concerns. Ask these workers what additional features or inclusions they would like to see to improve their workflow as a result of the inevitable process change. Ask them to participate in future planning or testing sessions, then utilize their feedback. As a result of worker feedback, you and the project sponsor might decide to add more increments or phases, or additional time between phases, to facilitate a more gradual adjustment and eventual acceptance. Achieving the deliverable doesn't have to mean begrudging compromise. It could instead mean focusing on incorporating change as part of your strategy.

Because an opportunity or stimulus for change can appear at any time, the versatility of the project manager is often "on display" to the project team and to your stakeholders. Their resistance to change must be managed, and an effective tool to combat this is to remind the team of the project vision and goals. Sometimes, however, there is too much change within a given timeframe, and PMI refers to this as "change saturation." Consider reordering the timing of project tasks that are easier or have more familiarity to give everyone time to acclimatize to the changes, especially if they will result in new paradigms.

Finally, recognize that the propensity to resist change exists as a matter of natural order, so don't be surprised to encounter resistance from internal or external sources. The project manager will need to regularly employ strategic initiatives to quickly recognize and address change. It is perfectly fine to seek out the advice and counsel of other project managers if you are unsure if your initiatives are effective. In fact, the best course of action is to refer to SMEs and deploy strategies that worked for them, tailored to the specifications of your project.

Performance Domains

Stakeholder

According to PMI, effective execution of the Stakeholder performance domain results in the following desired outcomes:

- A productive working relationship with stakeholders throughout the project.
- Stakeholder agreement with project objectives.
- Stakeholders who are project beneficiaries are supportive and satisfied, while stakeholders who may oppose the project or its deliverables do not negatively impact project outcomes.

PMI defines a stakeholder as "an individual, group, or organization that may affect, be affected by, or perceive itself to be affected by a decision, activity, or outcome of a project, program, or portfolio." Stakeholders are not only the project team members and the organization's key decision-makers; stakeholders can also range from individuals to millions of people outside of the organization. Also, the stakeholders on your project may vary depending upon the phase of your project and even the actions being taken by the project team.

As a **project manager, you are ultimately accountable for stakeholder satisfaction.** You will need to identify and analyze known stakeholders early during the project and continue to add stakeholders to your stakeholder register as the project progresses. Through proactive engagement and communication with stakeholders throughout the project life cycle, you can gain a better understanding of their requirements during planning. You can then utilize feedback to manage expectations, resolve issues, and make informed decisions as the project progresses.

Stakeholder Engagement

While effective execution of the Stakeholder performance domain relies heavily on communication, interpersonal skills, emotional intelligence, and other intangibles, the tangible artifact of this performance domain is the stakeholder engagement plan. The stakeholder engagement plan identifies the strategies and actions required to promote productive involvement of stakeholders in project or program decision-making and execution. It should be tailored to suit the needs of your project. This should include a stakeholder register with contact and/or contextual information about stakeholders, such as their communication preferences or what time zone they reside in. The stakeholder register should also include an assessment of each stakeholder's relative level of power, influence, and interest in the project outcomes to help you design more effective interaction with the stakeholders. It is important to note that **any documentation related to your stakeholder analysis should be kept confidential** due to the personal nature of the assessments. Through identification, understanding and analyzing, prioritizing, engaging, and monitoring project stakeholders, project managers can not only develop but successfully *execute* a stakeholder engagement plan.

Identifying Stakeholders

Remember that the term "stakeholder" refers to more than the project sponsor, project manager, and project team. The term includes anyone who will be affected by the implementation of the project. Will their taxes increase? Will their workflow and tools change? Will the project result in an eyesore that irritates members of the community? Will one department become obsolete and risk a layoff due to the project deliverables? Will the industry be turned on its head as a result of your project deliverables? Not all stakeholders are known at the start of a project; job roles may change, new vendors may emerge, or a new group of activists might focus their attention on your project mid-development. Therefore, the process of stakeholder identification and engagement is continuous throughout the project.

But remember, this process is about more than just filling out a form or planning for planning's sake. Ultimately, project managers need to build trust with key stakeholders by developing an understanding of their perspectives and interests. Seek to understand stakeholder motivations and expectations and, when necessary, manage those expectations to ensure they are aligned with project objectives. Through proactive engagement with project stakeholders, project managers can understand the needs and expectations of a stakeholder, while also having the ability to anticipate what will be of greatest importance, interest, or concern to that stakeholder as issues arise throughout the project.

As the project manager, you don't get to choose who the stakeholders are, but you do need to make decisions and prioritize the necessary level of stakeholder engagement to contribute to project success. Through your efforts to better understand and analyze key stakeholders on your project, you can begin to make decisions on how to balance and prioritize their multiple viewpoints, while also determining how, when, how often, and under what circumstances stakeholders want to be—and should be—engaged. Not all stakeholders will have an equal say or the same level of influence or permissions on decisions. Though the project manager may coordinate with the organization to accommodate stakeholder requests, the project manager is not officially required to honor all requests or demands. A project manager needs clear delineation via the project charter and stakeholder register as to which stakeholder is a "boss." Apart from the project sponsor or product owner, which stakeholders have been sanctioned by the organization to influence scope change? And which stakeholder groups increase project risk?

Stakeholder Analysis and Mapping

The stakeholder analysis process entails gathering information to determine whose interests should be considered throughout the project. This information may be quantitative or qualitative and is gathered in a variety of ways. One-on-one or group meetings, surveys, questionnaires, a project manager's use of subject matter experts, or personal experience with a project stakeholder are just a few ways that information can be gathered. According to PMI, the project manager should consult the individual stakeholder as the "best" source of information regarding his or her role, influence, and interest in the project.

The analysis begins with certain vital information about each stakeholder, including their relative attitudes and expectations of the project, their role as a stakeholder to the project, and how much they are concerned with project communications. The analysis that determines how much a stakeholder actually has at stake includes several sub-parts:

- **Contribution**—The individual may have provided resources, such as finances, labor, materials, or advice toward the project, and may expect some form of share of the project's benefits in return.
- **Interest**—Decisions made by the project team will have an impact on some stakeholders more than others.
- **Knowledge**—Knowledge can be powerful when a project team must navigate the workings of an organization and the nuances of human behaviors.

- **Ownership**—The stake may be a legal title or ownership of some part or asset of the project.
- **Rights**—Certain stakeholders have either moral or legal rights to common or competing interests to the project.

Stakeholder mapping involves creating characterization analyses of the stakeholders to find and strategize around stakeholder relationships and connections. Common versions in predictive projects include the power/interest grid, stakeholder cube, salience model, and directions of influence model. Agile projects may utilize user stories to develop project goals for deliverables.

Mind-mapping stakeholder engagement information and register details stimulates creativity on how the team can effectively engage and manage stakeholders. Assessment matrices utilize scales to define and plot the current engagement conditions for each stakeholder against the desired state of engagement as defined by the project plan. Resistant stakeholders are aware of the benefits of the project but do not want to accept the outcomes, as they may disrupt perceived aspects of their function. On the positive end of the spectrum, leading stakeholders are fully engaged and are helping to drive the outcomes of the project. The matrix plots "C" for the current state for each stakeholder and "D" for the desired state.

Stakeholder	Unaware	Resistant	Neutral	Supportive	Leading
USDA		C			D
FDA			C	D	
US Dept of Commerce	C		D		
US Customs			C D		
Customer				D	C
City Health Dept		C		D	

A power and interest grid depicting a stakeholder's estimated influence in the organization versus their level of interest in the project may be a useful tool in determining the appropriate level of detail and amount of communication to provide that stakeholder. As a rule of thumb, project managers can assess communication needs according to each stakeholder's level of influence and importance to the project. For example, a stakeholder with low interest or importance to the project may not need the same frequency or level of detail in project communications as someone with a higher level of interest and/or influence.

		Interest		
Power/Influence		*Low*	*Medium*	*High*
	Low	Monitor	Keep Informed	Keep Informed
	Medium	Monitor	Keep Informed	Keep Satisfied
	High	Monitor	Keep Satisfied	Manage Closely

Stakeholder Communication and Reporting

Perhaps the most effective way to gauge a stakeholder's interests and expectations is through frequent, two-way communication with that stakeholder.

When selecting a communication method, always consider the nature of the information to be communicated and its intended audience. "Push" communications (e.g., memos, emails, status reports) can be used for one-way communications, and should be used deliberately, since they inhibit the ability to immediately gauge reaction and assess understanding of the receivers. "Pull" communications allow stakeholders to access information at their leisure and may be used for less timely information. The nature of the information being communicated, and the stakeholders intended to receive that information, may also influence whether the communication is verbal or written, formal or informal.

The most effective project managers coach, guide, and mentor project stakeholders throughout the project, sharing information whenever possible or appropriate. Providing project transparency through project reporting is an excellent way to establish and maintain trust with stakeholders. Utilize regular reporting via push emails or newsletters to keep all stakeholders informed of the project in its broadest sense. Then utilize more focused reports for targeted stakeholder groups, as indicated in the stakeholder register, to provide more detail on a need-to-know basis.

Remember that not all stakeholders will be as familiar with the project environment as the project manager or other members of the project team may be. They may lack interest in the project and may decline to read reports. However, the fact that the information is available helps affirm your trustworthiness. Stakeholders may rely on your judgment and expertise on unfamiliar topics, such as how to interpret certain project metrics, how the project would respond if certain risks were to come to fruition, and what plans you have in place, or even recommended communication channels for regular status updates. If you've taken the time to understand and continually assess stakeholder needs, preferences, and desires for the project, you'll be able to employ proper communication strategies to get stakeholders the information they need in a timely manner. In addition, you'll continue building trust and be able to utilize your network to implement solutions to remove impediments, obstacles, and blockers for the team when necessary.

Reporting and open communication about the project status will engender greater positivity at the conclusion of the project as well. Since project managers are responsible for enabling change to achieve a vision, they must also prepare the organization and relevant stakeholders for any changes the project will bring by ensuring awareness, understanding, and support through the transition. Consider that low-level organization employees, community members, or displaced industry workers may still be impacted by the project result long after the project is finished. If they are not properly prepared and informed throughout the project, they may not be eager to support the result once it is delivered. Delayed information may lead to increased resistance and slower adoption, resulting in an even greater delay to the realization of benefits from the project. To maximize the project value in the end, take the time throughout the project to build productive stakeholder relationships. Continue the iterative process of identifying and analyzing new stakeholders throughout. Monitor engagement strategies to determine if current engagement strategies are effective, then make adjustments to the stakeholder engagement strategies to optimize your results.

SUMMARY

Stakeholder management is a primary objective of the project manager; effective management of expectations and requirements drives the project's success. Stakeholder management begins with identifying and compiling all relevant stakeholders that have an impact on or could be impacted by the project in positive or negative ways. During the Initializing phase of the project, the stakeholder register is created to document pertinent details of each known stakeholder and stakeholder group. From there, the expectations of each stakeholder or stakeholder group are defined and prioritized based on their influence, impact, and interest in the project. The project team then creates a targeted stakeholder management plan so that such persons, groups, or organizations are engaged, well informed, and supportive of the project's objectives. The project manager manages the engagement of each stakeholder group by conducting periodic reviews of identification, prioritization, engagement, and satisfaction of stakeholders. The project manager must monitor engagement efforts to ensure the stakeholder management plan is being followed. Project team members have an important supportive role in stakeholder management; consultation with key stakeholders for their feedback and critique of project performance gives the project manager room for improvement.

The Stakeholder performance domain is all about engaging stakeholders proactively, to the degree needed to contribute to project success and customer satisfaction. Failing to properly engage with stakeholders can lead to misunderstandings, false expectations, and wasted time and resources. By working with stakeholders to maintain alignment, you create shared understanding between stakeholders and the project team, you engender trust in your capabilities and decisions, you are better informed to help manage project uncertainty (risk), and you help ensure the ultimate success of the project.

Team

The Team performance domain provides the blueprint for the team's performance and accountability for the project work. This domain directly aligns with the Develop and Manage Team processes under the Resources Management knowledge area. It includes execution of the assigned work, leadership and management of the team, development of knowledge and skills, team collaboration, ownership, and performance in the delivery of projects and value.

According to PMI, high-performing teams have these characteristics:

- Aligned with clear goals and project vision
- Have well-understood roles and responsibilities
- Are motivated to provide quality work

The following components of the Team performance domain aid in ensuring that project investments deliver the targeted business value:

- Leadership
- Skills development
- Team culture
- Feeding team performance
- Team performance and accountability

Regardless of skills, experience, and organizational maturity, when people form a team, they cannot operate successfully in a vacuum. All teams require leadership, support, and a plan to guide them in performing tasks, navigating the scoped work, and owning their responsibilities.

Leadership Styles

Because no single person on the team holds all the required knowledge and skills for a project, each team member plays a co-dependent role in the team's leadership. Managers direct work activity, while leaders inspire work excellence. Project managers must do both; leadership techniques will vary depending on the organization, the project conditions, and the inherent skills and personality of the project manager. For example, projects using a waterfall (flow in a sequence) methodology are often under the leadership of a program or project manager responsible for overseeing all aspects of the project life cycle. This model requires the program or project leader to direct regularly scheduled meetings, a fully scoped project plan, and a schedule to drive the team. In an ideal Agile environment, a team operates as a self-contained unit responsible for its own self-management. The Agile project manager, often referred to as Scrum Master, acts as a "servant leader" to the project team by promoting the project vision or goal, guiding productivity through conflicts while removing obstacles to productivity. Whether on predictive or Agile projects, leaders need to adopt a management approach that enables the project team to deliver the project successfully while helping the team develop their skills and mature as a team.

Styles of leadership used by project managers are likely to be adjusted based on several different groups of characteristics exhibited by the project and/or team itself. The ethics, needs, values, and attitudes of the leader, as well as each team member, will be variable, subject to many underlying factors and influences. The characteristics of the organization itself, such as the vision and structure, will force leadership adjustments on the project manager. Environmental characteristics occurring external to the organization, including economics, marketplace changes, and geopolitics, are generally outside of the project manager's control. However, the project manager will need to adjust leadership approaches in response to these influences as well.

Given these leadership characteristic groups, there are six leadership styles that are commonly used, solely or in combination, to stay successful in project management.

Leadership Style	Description
Charismatic	Extroverted, energetic, and inspiring style with high confidence that motivates others
Hands-off	Loose oversight, allowing team to make choices and actions themselves
Interactional	Blended approach combining charismatic, transactional, and transformational styles
Servant leadership	Service to others is primary role; team growth and learning, relationship and collaborative focus
Transactional	Goal and objective oriented; results matter and drive rewards
Transformational	Supporting team through vision and example behaviors; innovation and creativity are priorities

Understanding the leadership approach to use for a project or team is critical and can either significantly aid success or cause undue harm if the undertaking is misaligned or ill-applied. Project leaders need to be well-versed in the leadership options and techniques available, and must understand their own inherent strengths and weaknesses. For example, a project that has tight timelines or requires specific skills may benefit from autocratic leadership, which delivers clear expectations and real-time feedback to support the team's alignment to deliverables and goals. Also, teams that are newly formed or not co-located may require more support to communicate and interact effectively. In these environments, governance and policy for the tools, times, and methods to facilitate the team's ability to work together are invaluable to their success.

Ideal Leadership Qualities—Emotional Intelligence and Focus

These are considered the ideal leadership qualities related to emotional intelligence and focus:

- **Having a vision**—Leaders fully understand and live by the mission, objectives, and values of the project or organization. They help others reach the same ideals with passion.
- **Empathy toward others**—Strong leaders have strong emotional intelligence and are able to grasp the sensitivities, needs, and concerns of others while still leading their teams and stakeholders to achieve the desired goal.
- **Integrity and respect**—Leaders behave ethically, responsibly, and with integrity and respect for others.
- **Systems and critical thinking**—Strong leaders are collaborative and cognizant of situations where systems thinking, critical thinking, and difficult decision-making must occur to achieve outcomes. Leaders also know that many factors influence decision-making, and decisions can impact many other elements.
- **Focus on what matters most**—Strong leaders are decisive when necessary, fair when recognizing those who perform, and clear when setting expectations for others. Leaders keep their focus on priorities, revising priorities routinely, being flexible when necessary, and knowing ways to avoid distractions.

Communication and Conflict Management

The following are ideal leadership qualities related to communication and conflict management:

- **Communication**—Strong leaders are skilled at actively listening to colleagues, team members, and stakeholders. Active listening involves giving attention, comprehending, and relaying back to the presenter a verification that they are understood. Strong leaders routinely give and accept constructive feedback about performance and communication so that they and others can grow and improve. Communication is also something that leaders spend significant time doing.
- **Conflict and relationship management**—Leaders manage expectations and are cognizant of when organizational behavior can lead to interpersonal conflict. Identifying, resolving, and preventing conflict is vital for a leader, especially one who leads complex and multi-disciplinary teams. Leaders build trust and actively work to prevent and resolve disagreements. Leaders are honest when dealing with conflict and relationships; they hone their skills at negotiating, persuasion, and diffusion. Lastly, a strong leader actively grows their professional relationships for mutual benefit and the benefit of the organization.

Versions of Power Within an Organization

There are four types of organizational power. Any or all of these may be available to the project manager seeking to influence stakeholders or overcome internal politics to achieve objectives. Role-based powers rely on the organization's hierarchy and chains of command as leverage over others. Relationship-based powers rely on language, behaviors, and connections with colleagues and stakeholders to achieve results. Expertise-based powers rely on knowledge and reputation. Information-based powers use the premise that the control of information can yield power over others. The project manager role must be aware of these forms of power, how they can implement these forms themselves or with their team, and how other stakeholders may use these toward the project team to gain influence and achieve results.

Power Group	Typical Styles	Example Uses
Role-based power	Positional	A formal title and role in the organization
	Punitive	Negative consequences issued by hierarchy
	Pressure	Limiting choices or freedom to get desired action
	Avoiding	Decline to participate as means to influence results
Relationship-based power	Personal	Charismatic attraction
	Connection	Building alliances and networks
	Cooperative	Finding common ground
	Guilt	Enforcing a sense of obligation
Expertise-based power	Referent	Admiration or respect based on reputation
	Situational	Experience in unique situations
	Expert	Formal education, training, or skills
	Persuasive	Using argumentation and mental prowess
Information-based power	Informing	Control over the collection or sharing of useful information
	Incentivization	Using monetary incentives and objectives to drive behaviors

Team Growth and Skills Development

Project leaders who want to build a high-performance team understand that both individual and team accountability are essential. To be accountable, teams need to know what they are doing and when it needs to be done. To support accountability, the project plan and schedule should be developed collaboratively to ensure that project team members are aware of the planned tasks and timelines. This is a form of shared ownership that is central to the concept of every team and their ability to cooperate and commit. Additionally, prioritization of work enables the team to focus on the right activities at the right time and avoids distractions and misunderstandings that may cause them to deviate from the plan. In this way, project leaders enable the team to operate effectively by keeping them on task.

Skills development is key to the Team performance domain; it also impacts the Project Work performance domain positively by increasing team capabilities. A capable leader helps align team member skills and interests to the right tasks and activities while enabling them to acquire skills and knowledge to reinvest in the team, the organization, or individual pursuits. Thus, the project manager should engage with individual team members to learn about their motivations, interests, strengths, and weaknesses, then facilitate opportunities for ongoing growth and satisfaction; this benefits the entire team. **A project manager should then build time into the production schedule for training and development.** By prioritizing time for training, team members will increase excellence in their project performance and ultimately add value to the project deliverables.

Growth and development of skills, knowledge, and performance cannot happen without clear goals. Goal setting and measurement sets the right tone and expectations for the team's delivery of the project as well as their performance. One method is the use of SMART (specific, measurable, achievable, realistic, time-bound) goals to establish performance standards that help to grow and advance team skills.

Collaborative goal setting builds interest and commitment to the project objectives, and it influences team performance positively. Using this type of framework provides goals that are meaningful, well-defined, and achievable, which empowers the team to succeed. For example, instead of setting a goal to reduce costs for computer installation, set a specific and measurable goal to reduce those costs by $5,000. This can be broken down further to a measurement of the variables affecting costs, to establish viability within the scope of the project. Additionally, ensuring that the goal can be supported within the confines of the project resources (human and material) and establishing a target date to finish provides a method to align the team, provide clarity, and track performance.

Training and learning opportunities are key to team motivation toward growth and development, and they must be identified and employed to provide benefits. Even if teams perform the same kind of projects repeatedly, project leaders can evaluate quality and performance to expose inefficiencies and convert those into performance targets. The more practiced a team becomes, the greater chance that performance improves when aligned to goals for improvement or quality. The teams' knowledge and capabilities can be elevated through a regular practice of refining tasks, processes, or procedures, providing measurable value to the project and business. Agile projects already allow time for this via the sprint retrospective meetings. Predictive projects, however, will need to allocate specific time for this activity.

TEAM CULTURE

Organizational policies and processes that govern the team also shape the habits and practices of the team. The development of a team's culture—through its traditions, mantras, and charter-enforced policies—can be a prime motivational force in the team's level of productivity. However, the project manager must also modulate and refine team-cultural practices to prevent conflicts with the overall project scope and vision. For example, if there is an unanticipated issue that arises to threaten the project, the organizational governance indicated by planning documents and the project sponsor or product owner provides a foundation for the team response. However, the team culture frames that response in quality, depth, and timing. The project manager should make sure that when in conflict, the project vision and project sponsor's requests take precedence over team cultural practice.

Team culture also has a role in productivity and organizational capacities, facilitating how the team works together and the level of quality and sophistication they display. Teams who have been together a long time may have high productivity because of the shared experiences and self-knowledge. In contrast, new teams may demonstrate lower productivity because of their lack of shared experiences and self-awareness. Projects change, and new members may be added at any time. Therefore, project managers should strive to develop an inclusive team culture to optimize project and team performance while minimizing distractions and potential conflicts.

FEEDING TEAM PERFORMANCE

The most successful teams have essential elements in common; they communicate, collaborate, challenge each other, and share responsibility and success. The team, when managed in a manner that creates an environment in which they can thrive, is enabled to perform reliably and consistently. When team members use their knowledge and experience individually, and integrate it with their team members while using prescribed tools and methods, it establishes a culture that facilitates team capabilities regardless of the project's complexity.

Feedback, when used to improve team performance, can also serve as a platform to establish a team culture that encourages measurable performance growth. Based on targets set for a project and individuals, team members need to understand how they have performed against the predetermined measure for success. Absent this, neither the project nor the team can confidently ensure that the outcomes match the goals. Feedback should be ongoing through structured reviews, coaching, mentoring, and real-time observation. It should be meaningful, constructive, and motivational in order to inspire a team member to improve. Though project managers should hold team members accountable for their performance and seek understanding and solutions when the performance is subpar, criticism that may be perceived as negative or punitive by the team member should be conducted privately and on a limited basis. Find out why your team members aren't performing well, then see if you can find a solution to help, like more time, more training, or an altered schedule to deal with family or personal issues. Follow up and keep documenting to help the team members get and stay on track.

Team Performance and Accountability

Projects provide the focal point for every team to unite around the project vision. The project's purpose and goals establish the team's existence and fuel its activities. The ability of the team to complete tasks, design solutions, solve problems, manage conflict, make decisions, and find agreement requires a combination of technical skills and knowledge, self-awareness, and strategic and systems thinking. To accomplish this balance, teams must be able to interact and build relationships to accomplish the work together. Therefore, interpersonal skills are vital to optimizing team productivity.

Teams are inspired and motivated not only by the project goal and future benefits, but also by each other as they learn, fail, and succeed individually and together in their efforts. Projects are demanding and dynamic by nature, so risk, uncertainty, and conflict are regular occurrences that teams must navigate. Using the tensions that arise from these conditions to build deeper knowledge and fortitude affords teams an opportunity to understand and exceed their limits and collectively take on and resolve difficulties. Overcoming hardships can serve to bond the team and build their common awareness and aptitude. **Project managers must therefore utilize emotional intelligence, as well as strong leadership skills, to combine the tools, methods, and behaviors needed to achieve the project goals and promote the team's development.**

The Team performance domain exchanges inputs and outputs with the other seven project performance domains. It is an essential member of the larger system of project management to facilitate the business value packaged in each project. The project manager and team should understand that no matter how thoroughly the project has been planned in the beginning, every project maintains a degree of uncertainty; change will be required to repair defects, respond to risk, and capitalize on new opportunities. Predictive projects endeavor to minimize the need for change through early project planning, then make changes only when absolutely necessary—to repair defects, avoid a threat, or seize an opportunity. Agile projects are expected to welcome change as part of continuous improvement. Regardless of the project approach, the project manager should promote "change" among team members as a positive and necessary aspect of the project's success.

Leading Team Performance

Leaders are responsible and accountable for project outcomes and team performance. They use their skills and authority to bring organization and harmony to the team. Leaders also facilitate and promote communication and transparency as critical elements of project and business success. Team morale can be negatively impacted without good tools, the training to use them effectively, and the absence of leadership support to solve problems and remove barriers. Therefore, **leaders must enable teams to have the appropriate autonomy by ensuring they have the information, tools, and support needed to accomplish the work.**

The project leader should **continually promote the project vision** to refresh the team and stakeholder alignment to the project objectives. The project vision can also act as a launchpad to help align team interests and goals with individual skills development.

Leaders may build team performance by applying success metrics to establish the standard of performance and measuring the degree of fulfilment against the assigned tasks or activities. This helps to identify strengths, weaknesses, and opportunities to improve or leverage for future work. Rolling this information into feedback to continually aid performance and skills development adds value to the project, the performer, and the business.

SUMMARY

Human needs include the factors that support both performance and job satisfaction, so project leaders will encourage success through attention to the variables that impact team performance and engagement, such as trust, conflict management, respect, and collaborative equity. Teams who have the freedom to engage openly and acknowledge limits without fear of reprisal are better positioned to mature and evolve their performance.

Equally important is acknowledging and celebrating accomplishments and growth. Teams need to know that they matter and are valued. Good leaders incorporate acknowledgement of robust performance and achievements to both boost and thank the team and provide feedback about what is working well. Without this information, the team's motivation and commitment may dwindle, resulting in underperformance and poor project delivery. When the project team understands and commits to the larger picture and project outcomes, they can also envision the value they are responsible for delivering for the project, as well as the direct benefit to themselves. This factor can be used to encourage and inspire optimal team performance.

Team performance is impacted and inspired by numerous variables but must be thoughtfully considered and integrated into the management of project work. Ultimately, the project manager should focus on developing and maintaining the qualities of a high-performing team—a team that is aligned with clear goals and a project vision, has a thorough understanding of roles and responsibilities, and is well-motivated to deliver quality work.

Development Approach and Life Cycle

The Development Approach and Life Cycle performance domain involves the establishment of the appropriate development approach, delivery cadence, and project life cycle phases that best suit the project and its deliverables. According to PMI, effective execution of this performance domain results in the following desired outcomes:

- Development approaches that are consistent with project deliverables.
- A project life cycle consisting of phases that connect the delivery of business and stakeholder value from the beginning to the end of the project.
- A project life cycle consisting of phases that facilitate the delivery cadence and development approach required to produce the project deliverables.

PMI defines a deliverable as something unique and verifiable produced to complete a process, phase, or project. This could be in the form of a tangible product, a process or process improvement, a targeted result, the execution of an event, or even the improved capability to perform a service. Deliverables are the lasting outputs produced by the project team. The types of deliverables to be produced on the project determine the way in which those deliverables can be developed through a development approach—a method used to create the deliverable(s) during the project life cycle. Together these factors influence the delivery cadence on a project, or the timing and frequency of project deliverables. And each of these factors plays a role in determining the project life cycle and its phases.

It's important to understand the relationship between these key terms:

- The type of project deliverables determines how they can be developed.

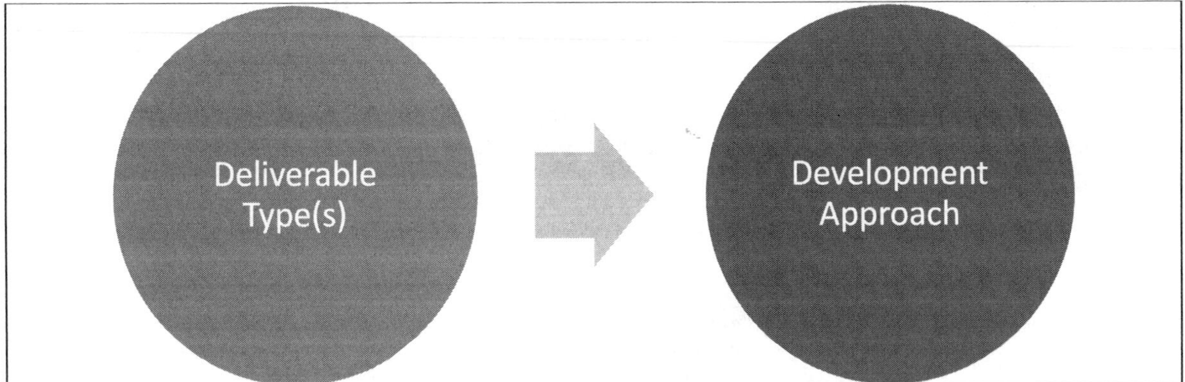

- The deliverables and selected development approach influence the delivery cadence.

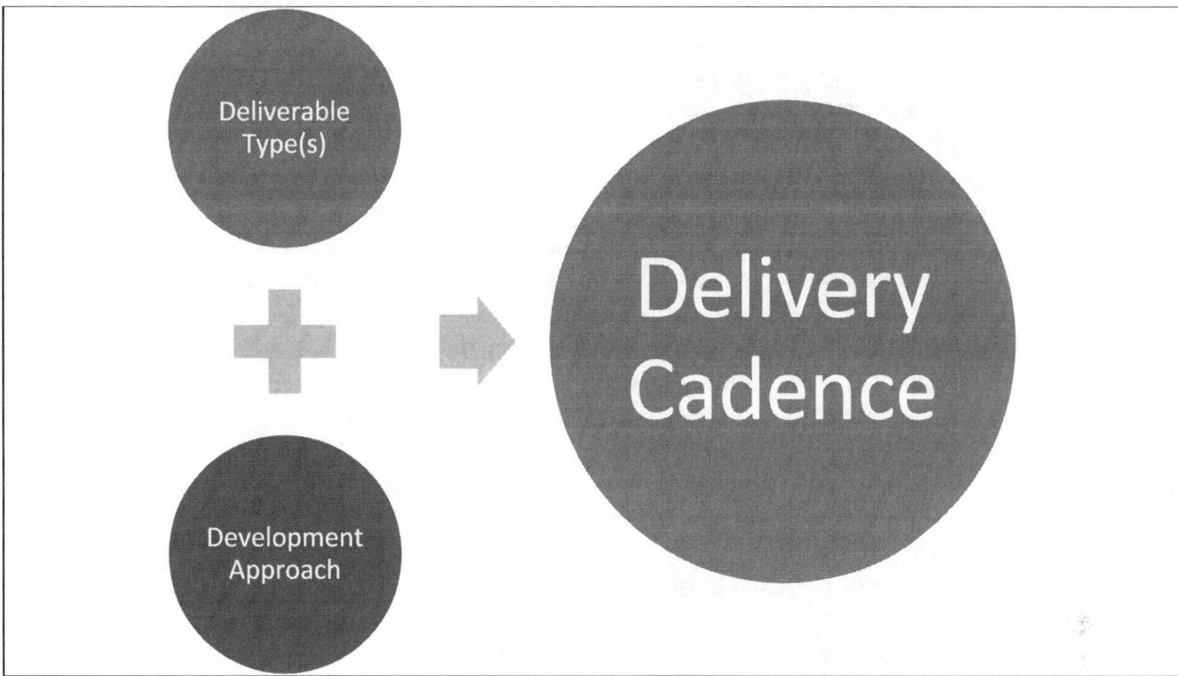

- And all these factors play a role in formulating the project life cycle and its phases.

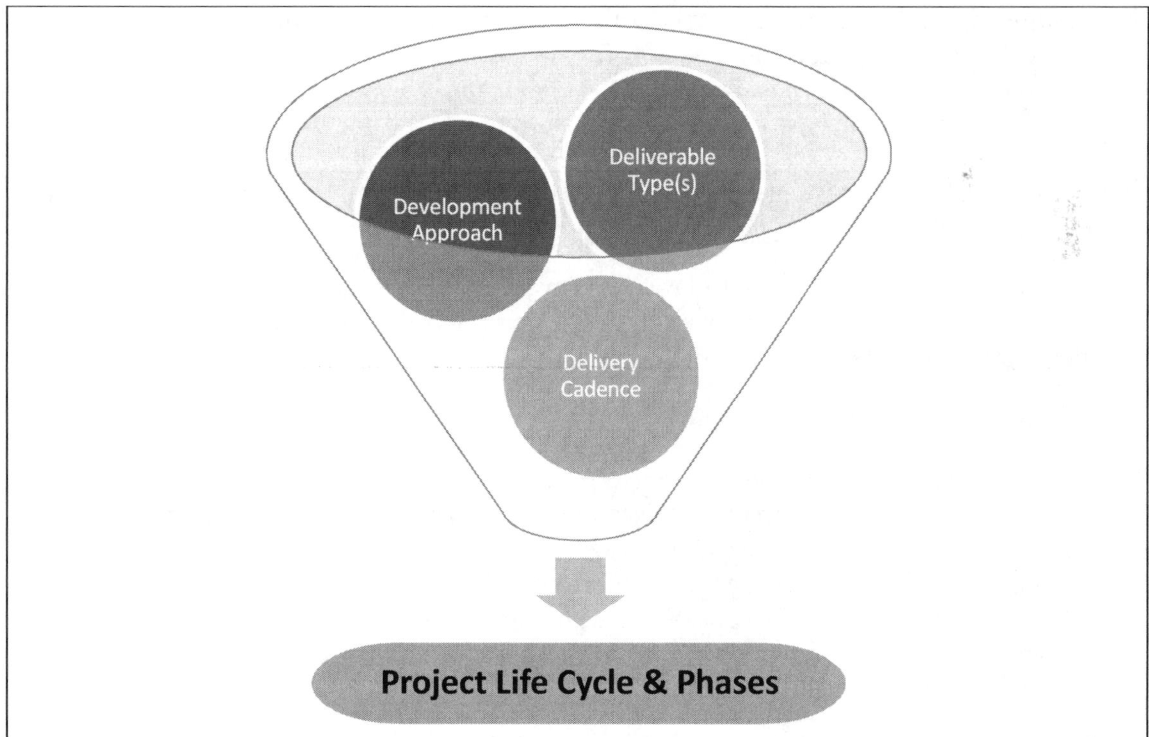

These crucial decisions are made with the objective of utilizing the approaches and methodologies that best deliver value and optimize project outcomes.

Development Approaches

Effective project managers and their teams assess the needs, complexity, and magnitude of the work, along with the expectations of stakeholders, in order to choose an approach that best suits the project. Common development approaches used to create the project deliverables include predictive, adaptive, and hybrid approaches.

Predictive

Predictive approaches require more planning up front than other approaches and tend to work best when the project needs, requirements, constraints, and scope are well understood early on. As a result, the plans that are developed at the start of the project drive the work forward throughout the remainder of the life cycle. Predictive approaches tend to favor process and control over agility. Changes are still permitted, but usually follow a predetermined approval process before plans are revised and the change is officially implemented.

Adaptive

On the other end of the spectrum, adaptive approaches work best in situations where uncertainty of the scope of the deliverables is high, or when a sponsor is unsure of what he or she wants. The adaptive approach is also best when the project manager anticipates many changes to the project scope, its requirements, and other variables throughout the project. A vision for the project is established early on, followed by continual refinement of project requirements as the work evolves into the desired outcomes for customers. Teams utilizing adaptive approaches favor flexibility and collaboration over rigid processes and regularly incorporate input through iterative or incremental methods.

An *incremental* approach uses a series of repetitive cycles (or "chunks" of productivity) to progressively develop the end deliverable. In software development, an incremental approach might be used when building a video game or ERP application. The minimum viable product (MVP) is created and released as the base module quickly—often to begin generating profit. Then, new modules or "expansion packs" are developed and released in subsequent increments. Features and functions are influenced by customer feedback until the final cycle, which ultimately delivers the completed deliverable.

An *iterative* approach also uses a series of repeated cycles, usually to add continuous improvement in features and functionality to one deliverable. Iterations are used to clarify requirements and explore new options that deliver value to the customer.

To highlight the difference in these adaptive approaches:

- The incremental development approach releases a fully functional base component and adds more standalone components with minor fixes later. (Example: Build and open the hospital first, then build the parking garage.)
- The iterative development approach waits longer for the initial deliverable release and spends the remainder of the contracted term improving it. (Example: Release the new Android operating system to the public now, then continue to fix the bugs and deliver security patches via pushed consumer updates as issues occur.)

Hybrid

Hybrid approaches incorporate components from both predictive and adaptive approaches. Project teams may utilize a hybrid approach on their project when a particular phase or deliverable is best produced using a predictive approach, and another phase or deliverable is better suited for a more adaptive approach. For example, if a technology company wanted to develop a new robot to direct intersection traffic during peak transit times, the company might elect to complete the physical design and construction predictively and in a logical sequence, while the software team would utilize an Agile approach to developing the operating firmware and interface. While the robot structure team(s) design and build the structure, create the shell, and test the mechanical function, the software developers have time to code, test, tweak, and retest. In this way, project teams use a combination of predictive and adaptive approaches to deliver value to the customer via a thoroughly tested and developed product on a shortened delivery schedule.

Delivery Cadence

The selected development approach plays a role in when value is delivered on the project in accordance with the selected *delivery cadence*, or when and how often project deliverables are completed. For example:

- A project using a predictive approach, such as the construction of a new building, may have a *single delivery* at the end of the project in the form of the completed building.
- A project to transition a company's timekeeping system from one application to another may have *multiple deliveries* at different points in the project, such as purchasing the new application, completing testing of the new application, and developing a training and implementation plan. Projects with multiple deliveries may produce deliverables in a sequential or nonsequential manner, depending on the project work and requirements.
- A software development project using an iterative development approach may have *periodic deliveries*, which are multiple deliveries on a set schedule. For example, each iteration could last three weeks and deliver a new version of the product on a monthly delivery schedule.

Project Life Cycle and Phases

According to PMI, a project phase is a collection of logically related activities that culminates in the completion of one or more deliverables. These phases make up the project's life cycle as it moves from start to finish. Multiple related phases may also be grouped into project "milestones." While the phases that make up a life cycle may vary from project to project, the project life cycle is directly influenced by the deliverables, development approach, and delivery cadence selected by the project team.

A project in which one phase does not begin until the preceding phase has ended, such as a kitchen remodel, might best be developed using a predictive approach, with detailed plans created during early planning phases that guide the work for the remainder of the project life cycle. (Example: The cabinets must be installed before the wall oven can be delivered.) However, what if the sponsor wants to change the lighting layout or cabinet design mid-project? That same project could also utilize a more adaptive approach, such as an incremental approach. In this scenario, the end customer would provide feedback at the end of each iteration, and the project team would progressively add features to the new kitchen based on that feedback until the completed deliverable was produced (i.e., single delivery). Alternatively, a hybrid development of the kitchen design could utilize 3D tools and an incremental or iterative approach to incorporate end user feedback until the desired design is created, while the physical work associated with the kitchen remodel could follow a more predictive approach (i.e., hybrid).

Delivering Value Through the Development Approach and Delivery Cadence

The selected phases of the project facilitate the delivery cadence and development approach necessary for producing the project deliverables. Ultimately, these phases produce business and stakeholder value throughout the project life cycle.

Selecting the right approach for a particular project depends on many factors. As previously discussed, the nature of the deliverables and other project factors play a significant role in this decision. Deliverables that entail a high level of risk, oversight, or safety requirements may be best developed using a predictive approach. For example, a government project utilizing heavy machinery and subject to detailed regulations or procedures, such as the construction of a new submarine or aircraft carrier, may be best suited for a predictive approach. The production of these types of deliverables may also entail significant investment up front and have a fixed budget, driving the need for detailed planning early in the project. The development of new software or even delivery of a marketing service, however, may have uncertain requirements during the startup phase and require the ability to adapt to changing customer needs. These types of projects may also have a need to deliver a minimum viable product (MVP) early in the project, and therefore would call for an adaptive approach to deliver value to project stakeholders. Project teams should also consider factors such as organizational culture, project team size and location, and other variables that may impact the way in which deliverables can be effectively developed.

Summary

Project managers facilitate the process of making a vision become a reality. They help the customer, sponsor, project team, and other stakeholders realize value through the effective delivery of project deliverables. Deciding on the best development approach, delivery cadence, and life cycle phases are key decisions made in support of these objectives. This will be covered in greater detail in the "Tailoring" section of this guide. Understanding and balancing the characteristics of project deliverables with stakeholder needs and the environment in which the project exists will help determine project success. This performance domain, perhaps more than any other, requires the application of all 12 of the Principles of Project Management identified in the PMBOK Guide in order to optimize project outcomes.

Planning

The Planning performance domain addresses activities and functions associated with the initial, ongoing, and evolving organization and coordination necessary for delivering project deliverables and outcomes; scheduling and estimating are key components. Planning is the way in which project teams prepare to create the project deliverables and ensure project outcomes are achieved. A project manager must also plan early for how to change the plan mid-project as change requests occur and risk responses are required. According to PMI, effective execution of this performance domain results in the following desired outcomes:

- The project progresses in an organized, coordinated, and deliberate manner.
- There is a holistic approach to delivering the project outcomes.
- Evolving information is elaborated to produce the deliverables and outcomes to which the project was undertaken.
- Time spent planning is appropriate for the situation.
- Planning information is sufficient to manage stakeholder expectations.
- There is a process for the adaptation of plans throughout the project based on emerging and changing needs or conditions.

Not all projects require the same amount of time, level of detail, or style of planning to be successful. The most suitable planning techniques for a given project are influenced by several factors, including the nature of the project's deliverables, the selected development approach for the project, organizational and/or regulatory requirements, and even conditions within a market for a product.

Projects utilizing a predictive approach tend to perform detailed planning at the start of the project that guides the work throughout the remainder of the project life cycle. After gaining an understanding of the business case and stakeholder requirements, the project team decomposes the project (or product) scope into lower levels of detail in order to properly plan the means and methods for accomplishing the work. Other variables, such as organizational and/or regulatory requirements, may influence the amount of planning documentation generated by the project team.

When work is unique and uncertainty is high, such as in the development of new software or another innovative product, project teams may perform the work utilizing adaptive approaches (e.g., iterative or incremental). In these instances, project teams conduct some high-level planning up front but save further planning until the "last responsible moment"—i.e., until the cost of further delay would exceed the benefit. This tactic enables the project team to evaluate multiple options and avoid wasted time developing plans that are likely to change or will not be needed. High-level planning may be accomplished in the form of an iteration plan before the start of a new sprint. An adaptive approach to planning may also support a faster time to market for a product when necessary.

Estimating

Estimation is a vital tool to many of the PMI knowledge areas—specifically durations, costs, and resources needed. Plans require estimates, or approximate calculations of the likely outcome of project variables such as the amount of work effort required, the time required to complete certain tasks, and project costs. These estimates play a critical role in developing the schedule, budget, and other plans communicated to project stakeholders. It is likely that project estimates, and the plans informed by them, will change as the project evolves and more information becomes known. For example, the range is likely to be larger—and therefore the level of accuracy lower—for an estimate of the time and level of effort required to build a feature into a new software application during the first iteration of the project, when information is still being gathered, than in later iterations. As experience is gained, either via similar project work or as the project progresses, the level of confidence in an estimate may increase, as well as the degree of precision. While the project team may have originally estimated the build phase of a new software feature to last 2–4 weeks, experience may inform the team later in the project that the creation of a similar feature will take about 10 days to build. For Agile projects, relying on a newly formed team, versus an experienced team that has already worked together, will affect accurate estimations of the delivery cadence, or the rate at which the team can produce deliverables at its peak performance; it takes an average of three to four sprint cycles for a new team to reach full productivity.

The development of the project schedule, the resources required to complete the work, and the order in which the work can and should be completed, also rely upon estimates generated in the Planning performance domain. Once the project scope statement—which clearly defines the deliverables—is developed, the project manager and the planning team will create the work breakdown structure (WBS) to break all of the work required to produce the deliverables into work packages matched to a control account for financial purposes. Project schedule management takes the work packages from the WBS. A project to build a new house may utilize a predictive approach, decomposing the WBS into activities that are then listed, defined, and sequenced to begin forming the project schedule prior to any physical work occurring. Estimates must be developed for the duration of activities, along with the effort and number of human and physical resources required to complete them.

SCHEDULING

Consider the following example of managing complexities of schedule estimation and dependencies. After construction begins on a new house, a project manager realizes that their point estimate of exactly three days to frame the first-floor exterior of the house was too optimistic. Instead of just using the three workers originally identified to conduct the framing, the project manager identifies two additional workers with availability and the skillset required to assist with the work. With the five workers, the framing is complete within four days, and a significant delay to the project schedule is avoided. This technique of "crashing" the schedule attempts to shorten durations for the least incremental cost, which in this case was accomplished by adding people to project activities. Another schedule compression method, called "fast tracking," may be needed later in the project to conduct portions of activities in parallel by starting a successor activity prior to a predecessor finishing (i.e., "lead") or by modifying a successor activity to finish a certain amount of time after the end of its predecessor (i.e., "lag").

Note that the type of dependency present between activities will determine whether or not the schedule can be compressed. Internal dependencies, such as a finish-to-start relationship between project activities, and discretionary dependencies, which could be sequenced based on best practices or preferences of the project team, may be modifiable. In contrast, a mandatory dependency, such as a contractual requirement to conduct a site inspection with the customer prior to breaking ground, or some other type of external dependency that relies upon non-project activities, is likely not modifiable.

Estimates are not exact, and therefore must be adjusted for the risk and uncertainty associated with them. The project's risk management plan should detail planned risk responses and provide information about whether or not there are contingency reserve funds earmarked for these uncertainties. For example, the project team may have identified a risk of encountering contaminated soil during excavation, and may have therefore factored in contingency reserve funds for the planned remediation of the contaminated soil, commensurate with the estimated probability of occurrence. These contingency reserve funds are controlled by the project manager and are separate from management reserve funds. The project manager must appeal to the organization for the management reserve funds, which are typically reserved for unexpected activities not identified in the risk management plan (i.e., "unknown unknowns"). The agreed-upon project work cost estimates plus the project manager's contingency reserve funds form the cost baseline for the project. The cost baseline plus any management reserve funds allocated to the project form the project budget.

SUMMARY

Planning is not limited to the project schedule and budget, but encompasses all organization and coordination associated with the project. This includes communication and stakeholder engagement planning, planning for the project team and logistical details, managing changes to previously established plans, measuring variance to baselines, and more. Planning is a proactive approach that prepares the project team to create the project deliverables and deliver value throughout the project to ensure intended outcomes are achieved.

Project Work

The Project Work performance domain addresses activities and functions associated with establishing project processes, managing physical resources, and fostering a learning environment. According to PMI, effective execution of this performance domain results in the following desired outcomes:

- Efficient and effective project performance.
- Project processes are appropriate for the project and the environment.
- Appropriate communication with stakeholders.
- Efficient management of physical resources.
- Effective management of procurements.
- Improved team capability due to continuous learning and process improvement.

As with all project management activities, processes should be tailored to the unique characteristics of the project environment and project team. Not all projects will have the same number of steps or level of rigor in their processes but should have just enough to ensure the efficient and effective completion of the work while still meeting governance requirements. For example, a large project to construct a new design of a naval submarine would likely have many processes with rigorous checks and balances to meet customer requirements. In contrast, a smaller, more routine project, such as the construction of a shed, may have fewer processes and required compliance steps. Both projects, using processes appropriate for the project and the environment, can be delivered efficiently and to quality requirements through process tailoring.

As the part of the Project Work performance domain, the project manager must also balance various competing constraints, such as fixed delivery dates, budget limitations, or quality requirements, to name a few. Throughout the project, project managers must balance shifting priorities and constraints while maintaining stakeholder satisfaction. During the construction of a new house with a fixed budget, a request for an additional room that would add to the home's footprint may require trade-offs to be made. The additional cost required for the newly added room may require the elimination of a feature that was previously in scope. The additional time required to complete the request may also require the modification of project delivery dates. In these instances, the project manager should meet with the stakeholders to present options, review implications, and come to an agreement on how to proceed.

Quality Assessment and Control

Processes should be evaluated periodically, via prescribed performance metrics, to assess compliance with established project processes enumerated in the quality management plan (for predictive projects) or similar project documentation (for Agile approaches). In looking for ways to optimize processes, some teams may employ Lean production tools and techniques that focus on eliminating waste in a process. Agile teams may utilize retrospective meetings and/or the collection of lessons learned to suggest ways to improve a process and make it more efficient. However, it should be noted that too much time spent tracking conformance to processes can result in non-value-added work. Since time spent on these activities takes time away from the team's work to deliver project outcomes, process evaluation should occur only to the point at which the benefits delivered from reviews outweigh the costs and impacts of not performing them.

Change

The development approach used to deliver the project will also have an impact on how new work and changes are managed on the project. On projects using an adaptive approach, such as the creation of a new software application, there is a general expectation that work will evolve and changes will occur. Change management is an integral component of Agile approaches. In these instances, the project team incorporates stakeholder feedback during each iteration, and the product backlog is continually reprioritized in order to deliver the highest-priority items first. In contrast, predictive projects utilize thorough planning at the beginning of the project to minimize the number of changes needed once the project work ensues. The project manager assesses proposed changes as a result of stakeholder requests or in response to a defect repair need or risk trigger. The project manager works diligently to avoid unnecessary changes, then utilizes the integrated change control process indicated in the integrated change management plan if the need for the change persists. Most change requests will require approval from a change control board before being implemented by the project team.

Communication and Stakeholder Engagement

The project manager also holds the primary responsibility for any project-related communication and engagement. This includes maintaining the focus of the project team and clearly communicating with stakeholders about project status. Communication with stakeholders outside of the project team is executed in accordance with the project's communication management plan; this relies on utilization of the stakeholder register and the stakeholder engagement plan. The needs and communication preferences of project stakeholders affect the distribution of information, as discussed further in the section on the Stakeholder performance domain. Remember that not all stakeholders will require the same frequency or level of detail in communications about project status. However, meeting the information requirements of project stakeholders, particularly those with high levels of influence, can be critical to project success.

Regular interactions with the project team, both formal and informal, help the project manager assess progress toward delivery goals as well as overall team health. This may help to identify team members who are overallocated or provide early indications of potential issues on the project. When the project manager can foster a collaborative team environment by valuing servant leadership, information flows freely among team members. Knowledge is shared, a culture of learning is adopted, and the team's production capability is maximized.

Knowledge Management

Project teams and the organizations they work for can both benefit when learning occurs and knowledge is shared. Without the documentation of lessons learned throughout the project, or a sprint retrospective to evaluate what the team could improve upon in the future, knowledge is lost when the project concludes. Lessons learned work best for capturing explicit knowledge, which can be communicated through words, pictures, or numbers. Documentation of explicit knowledge, such as the steps taken in order to achieve a particular result within an experiment, can benefit future project team members who review the information. Tacit knowledge is more personal in nature and difficult to convey since it is often gained through experience. Skills associated with leadership, intuition, and even innovation are often associated with this type of knowledge. Sharing tacit knowledge requires interactions with those who have the knowledge, such as through a mentorship or job shadowing.

Resources and Procurement

The review of lessons learned documentation from past projects may also shed light on best practices when it comes to managing physical resources or working with procurements. The planning, acquiring, storing, and management of materials and other physical resources from suppliers requires the project manager's attention within the Project Work performance domain. For example, a project to construct a new bridge would require estimates for the type of material needed, its anticipated cost, and expected usage of the material in relation to the overall project schedule. It would also require alignment from suppliers regarding the quantities of material that will be delivered to the job site, as well as when and where they will be delivered. These plans are then integrated into the master project schedule and included as part of the cost baseline. Effective management of physical resources reduces required wait times for material that would hold up other project activities; it also reduces cost by limiting the amount of material stored on-site, and it minimizes the amount of material that goes unused (i.e., waste).

Procurement of materials, products, and services from third-party vendors to be utilized on a project must be conducted via the approved procurement process of the organization unless otherwise stated in the project documentation. Is the resource to be utilized and licensed to the project manager/team? Or will the materials, product warranty, and licensing be held under the ownership of the organization? In many organizations, the project team may need to navigate organizational policies and procedures for the procurement of external goods and services; the organization's project management office (PMO) may already have a defined procedure for procurement or a list of preapproved or preferred vendors. The organization may need to authorize a special control account for the project versus utilizing a functional department account.

Consider a project to construct a new bridge. Funding for the project may come from a state or local government, which then competitively bids the work to one or multiple contractors. The government entity may develop bid documents, such as a request for information (RFI) to identify a set of potential vendors, followed by a request for a quote (RFQ) bid, or a request for proposal (RFP) in which potential vendors provide their proposed solution(s) and the associated cost for performing the work. Regardless of the vendor supplying the material or the policy utilized to procure the goods, a clear statement of work and/or summary of goods provided, licensing, maintenance, and warranty information should be included in all contracts and agreements with third-party vendors.

SUMMARY

Efficient and effective project performance occurs when project processes are appropriately tailored, adequate communication and engagement occurs with project stakeholders, and knowledge is captured for the benefit of current and future projects. These outcomes also help to facilitate the efficient management of physical resources, effective management of procurements, and effective change management practices—all of which result in the effective execution of the Project Work performance domain.

Delivery

The Delivery performance domain addresses activities and functions associated with delivering the scope and quality that the project was undertaken to achieve. According to PMI, effective execution of this performance domain results in the following desired outcomes:

- Projects contribute to business objectives and advancement of strategy.
- Projects realize the outcomes they were initiated to deliver.
- Project benefits are realized in the time frame in which they were planned.
- The project team has a clear understanding of requirements.
- Stakeholders accept and are satisfied with project deliverables.

Projects deliver business value and support the advancement of business objectives, such as the development of a new product or the solution to a longstanding problem. Value is derived from the project's desired outcomes, which are enabled through the creation of project deliverables—the unique and verifiable outputs produced by the project team to complete a process, phase, or project (e.g., a product, a result, a capability to perform a service). They are shaped by the project scope, the stakeholder requirements, and the level of quality upheld by the project team.

The expected value delivery from a proposed project is often noted in a business case document. The business case also provides justification for the expenditure of organizational resources and should demonstrate how anticipated project outcomes align with business objectives. The timing and frequency of value delivery will differ from project to project based on the selected development approach and delivery cadence. A project utilizing a predictive approach may release one or multiple deliverables at the end of the project life cycle (i.e., single delivery) and therefore only generate value for the business after initial deployment. Projects using an iterative approach with multiple deliveries throughout the project life cycle can deliver value earlier and before project completion. Consider the development of a new software application by an Agile team that releases the minimum viable product (MVP) at the end of an early iteration. The MVP delivers value to the business quickly, while subsequent iterations are used to incorporate user feedback and continuously improve the product with new features. This continuous delivery of value may also support varying needs and desired outcomes of project stakeholders.

Projects in which the scope is relatively stable and well-defined (i.e., predictive approach), such as the construction of a house, determine and document requirements early in the project life cycle. Collecting requirements from project stakeholders can occur through a variety of methods, including customer interviews or focus groups, data analysis, or even general observation. But the collection of requirements should not occur in a vacuum. Effective requirements elicitation implies that requirements are documented with stakeholder agreement. Additionally, PMI states that each documented requirement should meet the following criteria:

Criterion	Definition
Clear	Each requirement should have a single, easily identifiable interpretation.
Concise	The requirement should be stated in as few words as possible while still accurately conveying its description.
Verifiable	Each requirement should have proper metrics for establishing whether it has been met effectively.
Consistent	A requirement should not contradict any other requirements.
Complete	The set of requirements should fulfill all identified project and product needs.
Traceable	Each requirement should have a unique identifier.

The identification of requirements and alignment with project stakeholders helps to define the project scope. In the example of a project to construct a new house utilizing a predictive development approach, the project scope and requirements are defined during early planning stages. A work breakdown structure (WBS) may be used to decompose the project scope. Higher levels of the WBS may outline work related to the design, structure, utilities, and finishings for the home, with each level in the hierarchy representing greater levels of detail about the end deliverable. Acceptance criteria for the end deliverable(s) can be documented in a scope statement and referenced before final acceptance of the project.

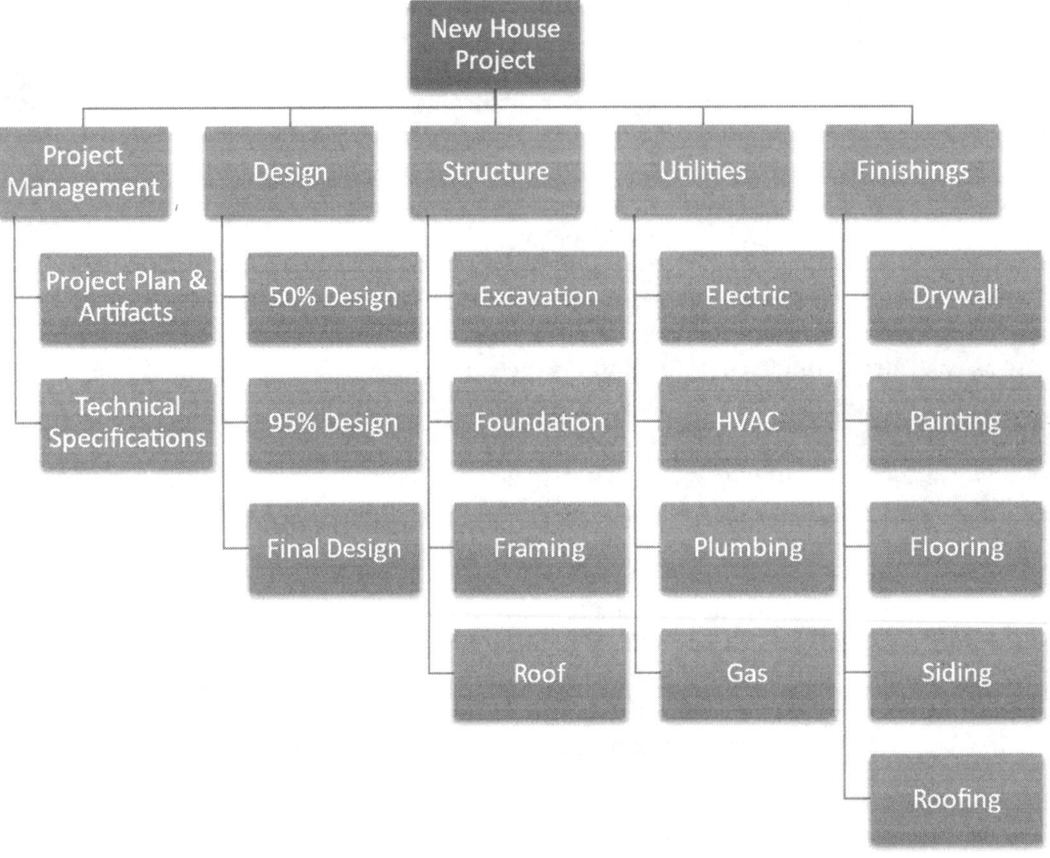

Inevitably, proposed changes will be encountered as construction of the house progresses. To avoid "scope creep," or the addition of new scope or requirements without adjustments to the previously agreed-upon project budget, schedule, and/or resources, predictive projects manage change requests through an established change control system. Change requests are evaluated for the potential value they can bring to the project. That value is compared with the estimated costs associated with realizing the potential value, and is only incorporated into the project plan after navigating an established approval process.

Project teams often utilize a more adaptive development approach when the scope and requirements are likely to evolve over time and/or are subject to a high rate of change. In these cases, a high-level understanding of requirements is documented at the start of the project. Iterations and stakeholder feedback help to evolve the requirements and the project scope as the project progresses. The evolution of the project scope may even lead to the discovery of new requirements during completion of the project work.

Rather than a WBS, adaptive project teams may instead identify "themes" of customer value in a charter or roadmap before developing "epics." Epics organize related work within a hierarchy of requirements, which can then be decomposed further into "features." Features represent related requirements or specific behaviors of a product and are associated with multiple "user stories," which represent an outcome for a specific user.

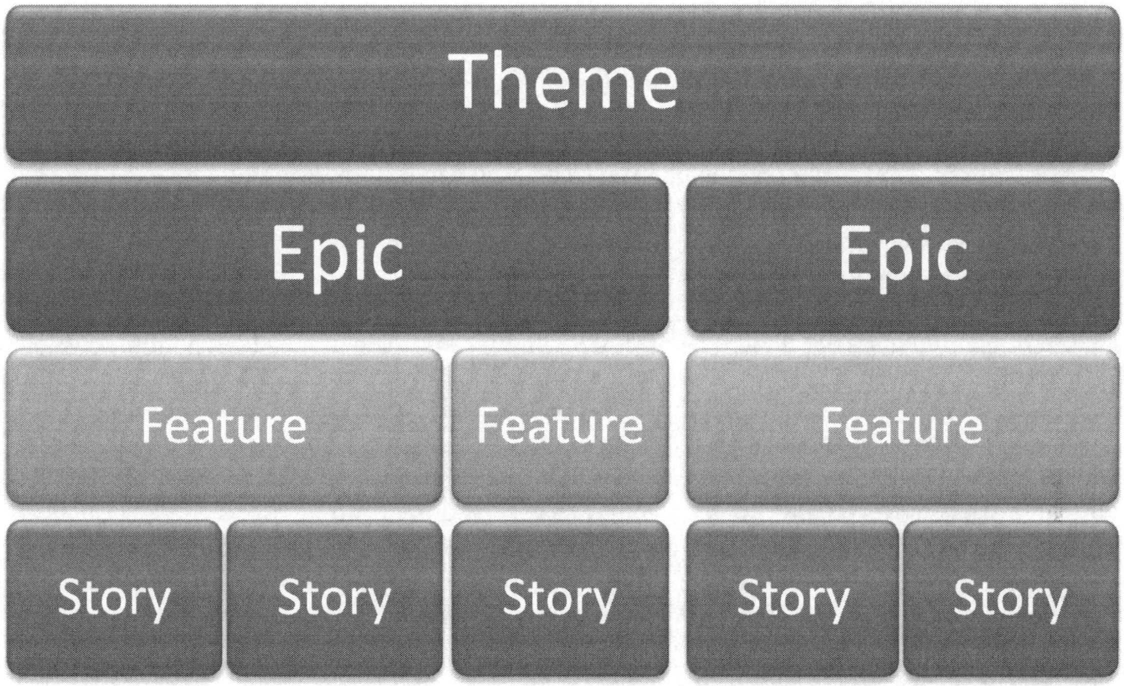

Teams using adaptive approaches conduct high-level planning early in the project and wait until the "last responsible moment" to define the details of user stories. This type of planning helps to avoid wasted time developing plans that are likely to change or will not be needed. Through the collection of requirements from project stakeholders and the decomposition of project scope, a "definition of done" checklist can be created with all the criteria that must be met before a deliverable is ready for customer use.

While projects using a predictive approach need to be aware of potential scope creep, adaptive projects may be subject to "done drift." "Done drift" can occur when the rapidly changing project environment continually modifies the definition of "done." The addition of new requirements pushes the completion date for a deliverable to the right (i.e., delays the completion date), thereby lengthening the project schedule. Eventually, a decision must be made to either release the deliverable without all the latest features incorporated, or to continue to push the completion date to the right and delay value delivery.

Not only must project teams ensure the scope and associated requirements represent the entirety of project needs, but they must also deliver the work to required performance levels. Quality requirements—performance metrics, completion criteria, and a clear statement of work or "definition of done"—should be included in the requirements documents in predictive projects, or in contracts and service level agreements (SLAs) for adaptive projects. The acceptance criteria for deliverables should reflect organizational goals and standards in order to deliver optimal business value. However, there is no one-size-fits-all solution to quality. Project teams must balance the quality requirements of organizational processes and procedures with the costs associated with meeting those needs, also known as the cost of quality (COQ).

While the overall objective of quality activities is to ensure stakeholder requirements are met, the intention is to do so while minimizing wasted resources. The COQ methodology is used to tailor the investment in quality activities to the appropriate level for the project. Project teams must consider the costs associated with compliance and noncompliance with quality requirements.

Quality assurance activities, the development of quality plans or product specifications, and training programs are examples of prevention costs. Prevention costs are planned and incurred before deliverable completion in an attempt to avoid quality issues by preemptively eliminating defects and failures. Appraisal costs include the costs associated with verifying deliverables against specifications, quality audits, and even the assessment of suppliers. These costs are incurred to evaluate the degree of conformance to quality requirements. Appraisal costs and prevention costs are considered as a cost of compliance to quality requirements.

The cost of noncompliance to quality requirements includes internal and external failure costs. When the work fails to meet quality standards, scrap is generated and/or rework occurs. Waste may exist in project processes, and a failure analysis may need to be conducted to identify root causes. These activities represent internal failure costs and must be endured to find and correct defects before the finished product is received by the customer. External failure costs are incurred when defects are discovered after the customer has received the product. Repairing products, processing returns and warranty claims, and handling service complaints are costs incurred by organizations in an attempt to rectify the situation. But some external failure costs are harder to quantify, such as the damaged reputation of a company as a result of defects.

External failure costs are even more detrimental to an organization because of the many costs already sustained to complete deliverables before defects are found. Boehm's Cost of Change Curve depicts the exponential costs associated with defects as the life cycle progresses. Not only are more stakeholders impacted later in the life cycle, but identifying a defect that previous design and development work was based upon can result in significant rework.

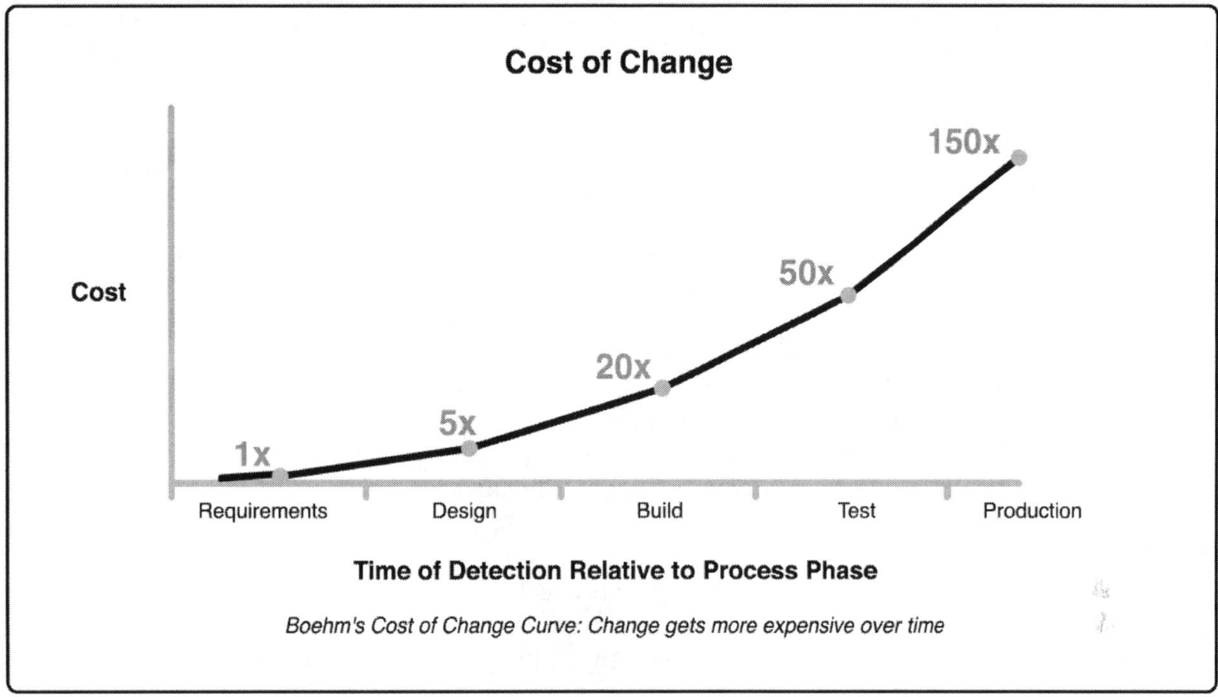

Boehm's Cost of Change Curve: Change gets more expensive over time

Uncertainty and the potential for suboptimal outcomes exist on every project. However, effective project management can help to minimize negative outcomes. The later a defect is found, the more expensive it is to correct, so project teams build quality activities into project processes. Taking a proactive approach to quality can help to avoid the costs associated with change later in the project life cycle while maximizing the probability of attaining the desired outcome.

SUMMARY

The Delivery performance domain is the culmination of the work done in the Planning performance domain. It is influenced by the selected development approach and associated delivery cadence throughout the project life cycle and is enabled by the project processes established in the Project Work performance domain. Through a clear understanding of the project scope and requirements and the production of deliverables to desired quality levels, project teams can deliver value to the organization and project stakeholders.

Measurement

The Measurement performance domain addresses activities and functions associated with assessing project performance and taking appropriate actions to maintain acceptable performance. According to PMI, effective execution of this performance domain results in the following desired outcomes:

- A reliable understanding of the status of the project.
- Actionable data to facilitate decision-making.
- Timely and appropriate actions to keep project performance on track.
- Achieving targets and generating business value by making informed and timely decisions based on reliable forecasts and evaluations.

Measurement helps to evaluate project performance according to the project planning. It demonstrates accountability, communicates project status to stakeholders, and identifies (or even predicts) changes and trends associated with the project. In the Measurement performance domain, project teams utilize the metrics identified in the Planning performance domain to assess the performance of the work being done in the Delivery performance domain.

Measures

Establishing effective measures requires collaboration with the project team and key stakeholders. The type and quantity of measures should be tailored to meet the needs of the project and deliver value to those consuming the information. According to PMI, effective metrics typically meet the SMART criteria:

- They are ***specific*** in what they will measure.
- They are ***meaningful*** to the project and its stakeholders. There should be a connection to the project's business case, project requirements, and/or any project baselines.
- The measures are ***achievable*** by the project team.
- The measures are ***relevant*** and provide value.
- The information is ***timely*** and forward-looking.

Quantifiable measures—also known as key performance indicators (KPIs)—that meet the SMART criteria typically fall into one of two categories: leading indicators or lagging indicators. Leading indicators, such as the number of tasks outstanding or a forecasted resource shortage, help to predict changes or trends. Lagging indicators provide measurements of project deliverables or events that have already occurred, such as measuring performance to the project baseline (e.g., schedule or cost variance).

KPIs should not only be tracked for the sake of data collection, however. In addition to assessing project performance, the Measurement performance domain also requires the analysis of measurable data so that the project team can implement appropriate responses to maintain optimal performance. Leading indicators can be particularly useful for the project team when a negative change or trend is predicted. For example, a project forecasting a budget shortfall in a future month can take action to reverse the forecasted result after identifying the root cause. Lagging indicators are measurement values derived after the deliverable or event is finished, to evaluate performance metrics according to the project requirements. Lagging indicators can also assist the project team in identifying root causes, but they may not always be timely since they rely on data collected after the fact from past events in the project. For example, a software development project with an increasing backlog and a decrease in sprint velocity (i.e., productivity rate) for multiple iterations in a row may need to evaluate the size and complexity of its user stories and break them down into smaller increments.

Baselines established in the Planning performance domain are used as a basis for comparison to actual results during project delivery, particularly with cost and schedule. Comparing planned versus actual start and finish dates can provide both leading and lagging indicators to the project team. Multiple late start or finish dates can signify a trend worth investigating, and if these are on the project's critical path, it could also forecast future delays in the project. Adaptive teams can assess the rate of feature acceptance during iterations to measure progress and use that information to estimate completion dates in future iterations. Regardless of the development approach employed, measuring planned versus actual results can provide insight on project performance and aid in future estimating efforts. Project teams can also measure planned versus actual effort and duration of project activities for the benefit of future resource estimates. The same can be said for measuring planned versus actual costs on the project.

Measurement For Cost Management

Earned value management (EVM) is an established methodology that compares actual to baseline performance and uses those measures to forecast future project performance. Key terms related to EVM include:

- *Planned value (PV)*—the authorized budget for scheduled work as of a given date.
- *Actual cost (AC)*—the cost incurred to date.
- *Budget at completion (BAC)*—the total allotted budget for all planned work.
- *Earned value (EV)*—the measure of the work performed to date, calculated by multiplying the BAC by the project's percent complete.
- *Cost variance (CV) = EV – AC*
- *Schedule variance (SV) = EV – PV*
- *Cost performance index (CPI) = EV / AC*
- *Schedule performance index (SPI) = EV / PV*

For the PMP exam, a variance is a "difference" or subtraction problem. An index will be a division problem.

Using EVM, a kitchen remodel project with a BAC of $20,000 that is 50 percent complete (PV of $10,000) but an AC to date of $12,000 would calculate as shown in the following table.

Measure	Formula	Result	Notes
EV = BAC × % Complete	$20,000 × 50%	EV = $10,000	This is the monetary worth of the work completed to date.
CV = EV – AC	$10,000 – $12,000	CV = –$2,000	A positive number is the goal. This project has cost much more than the value it has earned to date.
SV = EV – PV	$10,000 – $10,000	SV = $0	0 or higher is the goal to be on or ahead of schedule. This project is right on schedule.
CPI = EV / AC	$10,000 / $12,000	CPI = 0.83	1.0 or higher is the goal. 0.83 means the project has achieved 17% less value than expected given the costs incurred.
SPI = EV / PV	$10,000 / $10,000	SPI = 1.0	1 or higher is the goal to be on target.

CPI and SPI are measures used to indicate schedule and cost efficiency on the project. A value of 1.0 indicates that the project is performing to plan, much like a value of $0 for SV or CV indicates. In this case, the measures indicate that the project is performing to schedule (SV = $0, SPI = 1.0) but is currently over budget (CV = –$2,000, CPI = 0.83). If the past were indicative of the future performance on this project, the following quantitative forecasts could also be generated using EVM:

Measure	Definition	Formula	Result
Estimate to complete (ETC)	The expected cost to finish the remaining work.	(BAC – EV)/CPI	ETC = $12,000
Estimate at completion (EAC)	The expected cost of completing all work. (Use this for "forecast" questions on the PMP Exam.)	BAC / CPI	EAC = $24,000
Variance at completion (VAC)	The anticipated budget deficit or surplus upon project completion	BAC – EAC	VAC = ($4,000)
To-complete performance index (TCPI)	The estimated cost performance required to meet a goal	(BAC – EV) / (BAC – AC)	TCPI = 1.25

By evaluating these quantitative forecasts, the project team may be able to make adjustments to avoid the $4,000 budget deficit forecasted by the end of the project (VAC). The team would also know that a CPI of 1.25 would be required for the remainder of the project—workers would need to apply 25% more work effort—in order to finish within the predetermined budget.

Other ways to forecast project performance quantitatively include regression and throughput analysis. Regression analysis uses a mathematical or statistical relationship between input variables and corresponding results to predict future performance. Throughput analysis is used to evaluate system performance by measuring the number of items completed in a particular timeframe. If an adaptive project team has 100 story points in the queue (i.e., backlog), and the batch size—the estimated work to be completed in an iteration—is 20 story points, then it can be reasoned that at least five sprints will be needed to complete the project work. If only 18 story points are completed during the first two sprints, the project team may need to consider adjusting its forecasts for future sprints.

Measurements such as cycle time and lead time can also be indicative of project performance. Consistent cycle times, or the amount of time required for the team to complete a task, can be helpful in predicting the batch size of future iterations. Lead time represents the total time elapsed from work entering the backlog until its release. Long lead times could be a result of too many items being worked on at one time by the project team (i.e., "work in progress"), and/or they could be representative of process inefficiency. Lean systems measure process efficiency by the ratio of tasks in development or verification (i.e., value-adding time) versus tasks that are waiting to be worked on (i.e., non-value-adding time). Information on the number of errors or defects can also provide insight into the effectiveness of project processes.

The number of defects and other external failure costs attributed to the project can directly affect stakeholder satisfaction. A Net Promoter Score (NPS) is one way to quantitatively measure customer—or other stakeholder—satisfaction and willingness to recommend a given product or service to others. Stakeholders are polled on their willingness to recommend a product or service on a scale of 0 to 10, with 10 representing those who are "extremely likely" to recommend. Those who respond with a 6 or below are considered "detractors," while those responding with a 9 or a 10 are labeled "promoters." To calculate NPS, subtract the percentage of respondents labeled "detractors" from the percentage of respondents that are "promoters." Scores range from –100 to 100, with higher scores indicating greater customer loyalty.

Projects are undertaken by an organization to deliver value and support the advancement of business objectives. As stated in the Delivery performance domain, the business case documents detail the expected value delivery from the project and serve as a point of comparison for actual benefits delivered. Organizations may also utilize metrics that measure financial business value such as return on investment (ROI) to measure the amount of financial return versus the cost to complete a project. ROI may be utilized as part of the decision to undertake a project. It can also be measured throughout the project life cycle to ensure satisfactory performance and to ensure that the continued expenditure of organizational resources is worthwhile. The same can be said for net present value (NPV), which measures the difference between the present value of cash inflows and the present value of cash outflows over a period of time. Other organizations may utilize a cost-benefit ratio to determine whether the costs of undertaking the project are greater than its expected benefits. A general rule of thumb is that projects with a cost-benefit ratio greater than 1.0 (i.e., the costs outweigh the benefits) should not be undertaken unless there is a compelling reason to do so, such as for regulatory or social good.

Presenting and Utilizing the Information

Useful information collected in the Measurement performance domain is timely, accessible, and easily digestible by necessary stakeholders. Information radiators and dashboards can be helpful mediums to meet these goals and communicate necessary information to stakeholders. Dashboards are often displayed electronically and show large quantities of collected information through charts and other visuals to communicate the status of important items on the project. Some dashboards may combine colored indicators (e.g., red/yellow/green) with charts, using text where necessary for any required explanation if measures exceed the bounds of established thresholds.

In these scenarios, it is important that thresholds are established early in the project. Aligning with stakeholders on acceptable thresholds for project performance, and the appropriate responses by the project team should those thresholds be crossed (i.e., "exception plans"), enables the project team to be proactive if variances outside the acceptable thresholds are forecasted. It also allows the project team to act quickly if and when a threshold is breached.

Information radiators, also known as Big Visible Charts, are intended to be physically visible to a large audience. In contrast to the complex and electronic nature of dashboards, information radiators are often updated manually and frequently. Sometimes called "visual controls" in Lean environments, information radiators can include task boards that communicate the status of project tasks. A Kanban board may be used to view the number of tasks in each stage of work and to help the project team limit the number of work-in-progress items. Burnup or burndown charts can track the amount of work completed versus the amount of work remaining or the productivity rate of the team (i.e., velocity).

The collection of data and establishment of appropriate metrics is only as useful as the project team's ability to communicate and act on the information. Data is collected and put on display to facilitate action and enable learning by the project team. Ultimately, measurements should help the project team optimize project performance for the successful delivery of project outcomes.

When measurements are used incorrectly, however, they can negatively impact the direction of the project. For example, working on lower-priority tasks out of sequence to improve KPIs, or making decisions that benefit short-term measures at the expense of long-term success on the project, is an example of misusing metrics. The Hawthorne Effect describes the influence on behavior caused by the act of measuring something. This can contribute to unreliable data, either due to specific measures being selected and/or because of the level of importance placed on certain measures by key stakeholders. False interpretations of the data can occur when stakeholders confuse the correlation of two variables because of a particular measurement. Vanity metrics are presented to highlight positive performance to the exclusion of the negative performance indicators and are similar to confirmation bias, where tests are designed to prove a preexisting view or belief. Finally, project leaders should also be wary of goals set by the project team or stakeholders that are not realistically achievable. Setting unachievable goals can be counterproductive because they can contribute to decreased team morale when these unrealistic targets are continually missed.

Summary

The use of measures can help project leaders and other key stakeholders analyze project performance and gain an understanding of the project's status. Measures can also demonstrate accountability and contribute to the development of more effective project plans in the future. Remember that the value of measurements is not rooted solely in the collection of data, but rather in how that data is utilized in order to take appropriate action to optimize project performance and deliver value.

Uncertainty

The Uncertainty performance domain addresses activities and functions associated with risk and uncertainty. Specifically, uncertainty pertains to project risks—both negative threats and positive opportunities—and their correlating responses. According to PMI, effective execution of this performance domain results in the following desired outcomes:

- An awareness of the environment in which projects occur, including, but not limited to, the technical, social, political, market, and economic environments.
- Proactively exploring and responding to uncertainty.
- An awareness of the interdependence of multiple variables on the project.
- The capacity to anticipate threats and opportunities and understand the consequences of issues.
- Project delivery with little or no negative impact from unforeseen events or conditions.
- Opportunities are realized to improve project performance and outcomes.
- Cost and schedule reserves are utilized effectively to maintain alignment with project objectives.

Uncertainty

Projects are inherently uncertain because each is a unique undertaking. Project managers must navigate the varying levels of uncertainty, ambiguity, complexity, and volatility associated with their project. In doing so, they can proactively solve problems, lean on prior planning to make good decisions in complex situations, and successfully deliver project outcomes.

According to PMI, the term "uncertainty" refers to a lack of understanding and awareness of issues, events, paths to follow, or solutions to pursue. At the start of a project, uncertainty is generally high, as the project team seeks to understand the necessary requirements. Project teams may utilize adaptive approaches in order to manage requirements with a high level of uncertainty and progressively elaborate until the final deliverable is produced. But the Uncertainty performance domain also includes accounting for other variables that may affect the environment in which the project is operating. For example, a construction project may need to account for the physical environment and uncertainty related to weather, safety, or working conditions. It also may face volatile prices in the acquisition of materials or uncertain profit margins due to inflation over a multi-year project. A pharmaceutical research project may need to navigate uncertainty in the form of political influences, legal or legislative constraints or requirements, and technical considerations for new or emerging technologies.

Some project teams may seek to reduce the level of uncertainty through information-gathering by conducting further research or engaging with subject matter experts. When there are a finite number of possible outcomes from an uncertain situation, preparing for multiple outcomes may best suit the project environment. Other project teams may develop multiple designs early in the project to analyze alternatives. In some environments, building in resilience to project or organizational processes—so that the project team has the ability to adapt and respond quickly to unplanned changes—may be the preferred method.

Ambiguity, Complexity, and Volatility

Ambiguity refers to a state of uncertainty, which may include difficulty in identifying the cause of events or choosing from multiple options. This can occur in the project environment when there is a lack of effective understanding, known as conceptual ambiguity, or when more than one outcome is possible, known as situational ambiguity. Conceptual ambiguity occurs when similar terms or arguments are used in different ways. For example, a key project stakeholder who was just briefed on a significant project issue is confused when the project manager reports the project as "green" during a status report. A lack of common rules or definitions for key terms may lead to conceptual ambiguity regarding the true health of the project. In attempting to solve that significant project issue, the project manager may be faced with situational ambiguity as they evaluate multiple options that would solve the problem. To find the best solution for the project, the team may attempt to identify causes or relationships between variables using experiments or prototypes. Progressive elaboration is another technique often used by adaptive project teams to iteratively explore new options, develop more accurate estimates, and refine customer requirements.

Complexity exists when outcomes are unpredictable due to dynamic systems and relationships. Human behavior, system behavior, and ambiguity can all contribute to difficulty in managing characteristics of the project or its environment. Much like with situational ambiguity, process-based techniques such as building iteratively or incrementally can be used in complex situations. Project teams may also build in opportunities to engage with stakeholders as part of their process, or even build in a safety redundancy in the form of a "fail-safe" to prevent catastrophic failures. When dealing with complex systems, simulations or decoupling can be used on components of the system. Simulation is used to identify common characteristics of similar, though unrelated, scenarios. Decoupling helps to determine how a piece of the system works on its own by breaking the system down and reducing the number of variables. Other ways of working with complexity include "reframing" techniques. Viewing the system from diverse perspectives or balancing the type of data used are examples of reframing. For example, the project manager may bring the team together for a brainstorming session to get a new perspective on solving a lingering issue. In another example, the project manager may decide to "balance the data" by looking back at past reports to identify trends or help solve a problem, rather than only referencing project forecasts.

Another element of uncertainty, volatility, exists in rapidly changing and unpredictable environments. Volatility in the price of raw materials may impact the cost and schedule of a project to construct a new office building. Similarly, if other economic or social factors are contributing to a limited pool of available resources, such as tradespeople, this could also significantly delay the work on the office building. Combating volatility may require an alternatives analysis by the project team. By looking at different ways to sequence the work or acquire the needed materials, the project team may be able to identify a feasible solution to deliver the project on time and within budget. If an alternative solution is not viable, project teams may be able to utilize cost or schedule reserves set aside to account for uncertain conditions.

Risk and Risk Management

Project teams can navigate uncertainty through risk management techniques. A "risk" refers to an uncertain event or condition that will have a positive or negative effect on project objectives, should it occur. Potential outcomes that would benefit the project objectives are known as "opportunities," while those that would negatively affect the project are known as "threats." Project managers work with their teams and key stakeholders to proactively identify threats and opportunities throughout the project and plan for possible responses, should the risks come to fruition.

The approach to risk management employed by the project team should be tailored to the project, the key stakeholders, and the environment in which the project operates. Risk responses are influenced by the organization and key stakeholders' risk appetite, or the degree of uncertainty a stakeholder is willing to accept. Risk thresholds should be defined and documented early in the project to make clear the level of risk exposure acceptable at any given point in time. For example, a startup company developing a first-of-its-kind software application, but in a race to be the first to market with competitors, may be willing to take on more risk to meet the project objectives than a project managed by a local government using taxpayer dollars to construct a new park. The stakes are different, as is the environment of each project. If the startup company is not the first to market, it risks losing significant market share to a competitor. If the local government project rushes the schedule at the expense of quality, it could put the general public at risk once the park opens. The startup company may opt for speed, while the local government may favor further safety checks at the expense of the project schedule.

Along with risk identification, criteria should be established that will aid in the prioritization of risks. A probability and impact matrix is one way by which the severity of risks can be measured. The project team should tailor the probability (likelihood of risk occurrence) and impact (extent of the impact should the risk materialize) definitions to reflect the risk appetite of key stakeholders on the project.

Term	Probability	Schedule Impact	Quality Impact	Cost Impact
Low	0–33%	+/- 1 week	Negligible	<3% of budget
Med	34–66%	+/- 2–4 weeks	Noticeable impact to project deliverables and/or customer.	3–10% of budget
High	>67%	>1 month	Project does not deliver identified objectives or exceeds the expectations of customer.	>10% of budget

Using these definitions created by the project team, risks are logged in a risk register and assigned an estimated probability and impact. A probability and impact matrix, such as the example below, can help calculate the severity of each risk. The matrix should also be tailored to align with the risk appetite of the organization and key stakeholders.

		Impact		
		Low	*Medium*	*High*
Probability	*Unlikely*	Low	Low	Med
	Possible	Low	Med	High
	Likely	Med	Med	High

Project teams identify risks, assign an estimated risk severity, and develop strategies for dealing with risks. Strategies for dealing with threats often include those listed in the following table.

Threat Response	Definition
Avoid	The project team acts to eliminate the threat.
Escalate	Include higher levels of the organization in the risk response when the threat is outside the scope of the project, or when the response would exceed the project manager's authority.
Transfer	The risk owner is shifted to a third party.
Mitigate	The project team takes action to either reduce the probability of occurrence or reduce the impact of a realized threat.
Accept	No action is planned, but the existence of the threat is acknowledged.

Strategies for helping to realize opportunities include those listed in the following table.

Opportunity Response	Definition
Exploit	The project team acts to ensure the opportunity occurs.
Escalate	Include higher levels of the organization in the risk response when the opportunity is outside the scope of the project, or when the response would exceed the project manager's authority.
Share	The risk owner is shared with a third party who is best able to capture the benefit of the opportunity.
Enhance	The project team takes action to increase the probability of occurrence or impact of the opportunity.
Accept	No action is planned, but the existence of the opportunity is acknowledged.

Risk responses should be reviewed to evaluate whether any planned responses may result in additional risks to the project. It is also important for risks to be consistently reviewed and updated in order to proactively plan risk responses as the project progresses. Contingency reserve may be set aside to address those risks identified by the project team in the form of cost and/or schedule contingencies. In some organizations, management reserve may be available for "unknown unknowns"—events that are unplanned, but still within the scope of work.

Overall Project Risk

Overall project risk describes the effect of uncertainty on the project as a whole. This includes identified risks and the complexity, ambiguity, and volatility of the project and its environment. If the aggregated risk exposure is too much for the risk appetite of the organization, the organization will either implement risk strategies until the risk is compatible with the organization's appetite or decide to not pursue the project altogether.

Summary

All projects will contain elements of uncertainty and will encounter bumps in the road throughout the project life cycle. Much of the work needed to reduce uncertainty on a project should be accomplished via thorough preparation during the Planning phase. Gather input and information from stakeholders and SMEs to identify potential risks. Then, conduct a proper impact analysis of both the likelihood of the risk occurrence and the magnitude of impact. This will provide the insight necessary to develop effective risk responses for a multitude of outcomes. This will foster resilience in the project since you will be able to respond quickly and decisively should a risk trigger occur. Remember that the overall objective is not necessarily to eliminate all uncertainty, but to tailor risk planning and responses to best deliver the project with little or no negative impact from unforeseen events or conditions.

Tailoring

What Is Tailoring?

PMI defines tailoring as the "deliberate adaptation of the project management approach, governance, and processes to make them more suitable for the given environment and the work at hand." Put simply, tailoring is choosing the right people; processes; and inputs, tools, techniques, and outputs (ITTOs) to fit the customer organization's needs for the project. Effective tailoring leads to a smoother project process, a reduction in overall risk, and, ultimately, greater value for the customer.

While project integration management is the overarching hard skill the project manager deploys to complete the project, tailoring is the corresponding soft skill that ensures the customer will derive the maximum benefits in the end. Just as project managers coordinate consultation, planning, execution, monitoring, and controlling efforts for each of the Knowledge Areas, they must give equal and holistic attention to tailoring, or the *process* of managing these individual processes collectively.

The project manager ultimately performs the tailoring under the governance of the customer's organization operating policies, values, and culture, while upholding the standards of the related industry. (For example: Tom Landry managing for the Dallas Cowboys organization within the National Football League. Or, for international football fans, Johan Cruyff adjusting strategies for Barcelona in La Liga Santander versus the Copa del Rey.)

No two projects, deliverables, or organizations are alike. A 150-story high-rise project in Dubai will have considerably different logistical, structural, and development challenges than the same construction project in Manhattan. In Agile software development, projects typically follow an industry-standard software development life cycle (SDLC), but the features, user-story functionalities, tools, and **delivery cadence** are unique to each software application.

Thus, even when developing similar projects for repeat customers, and with the backing and resources of well-established project management offices (PMOs), existing project management templates and past **lessons learned** documents should only be used as guidelines. The project manager will need to develop new planning documentation created specifically for each unique project. For the PMP exam, you must be committed to the concept of tailoring every project.

Why Tailoring?

If you have ever worked with a group of colleagues tasked with forming a list of requirements to help create a **request for proposal (RFP)**, you know that achieving a group consensus is difficult. It is incumbent upon project managers to find and tailor group discussion techniques to lead productive sessions. Then, project managers must guide key decision-makers to adopt the most appropriate project solutions to optimize value for the organization. Demonstrating a deft approach to communication and engagement with stakeholders, plus a keen attention to detail and a genuine interest in representing the core interests of the organization, lies at the core of a project manager's excellent customer relationship management (CRM). Tailoring the project management process to the organization's unique identity is an expected element of good business CRM and ensures a quality review for the project manager at the end.

Tailoring also maximizes stakeholder engagement via the active and timely solicitation of stakeholder **feedback**. Project managers will have fewer obstacles during project deployment if they do the following:

- Utilize approaches and tools that are familiar to the organization.
- Include input from low-level end users.
- Reflect core organization principles.
- Affirm company culture.
- Comply with related policies and regulations.

Tailoring the project approach, processes, people, and tools is also key to effective risk management. It allows the project manager to identify potential problems sooner, as well as mitigate or avoid a negative project impact. Is there pending local or national legislation that might impact the project requirements? Is a regional skirmish in a foreign country threatening the supply of a vital project resource? The project manager can first anticipate a threat, then analyze the risk and formulate a response before documenting the concern in the project risk register. Tailoring is also essential for establishing a transparent and shared vision in the form of a comprehensive project scope statement and **work breakdown structure (WBS)**. This further reduces project risk by ensuring that all funded work and acquired resources will be fully utilized and dedicated toward the production of project deliverables instead of wasted on avoidable rework.

Tailoring a "Successful" Project

PMI concurs with long-standing industry research findings that a project is more likely to be successful when the form, function, and quality requirements of the deliverables are tailored within the bounds dictated by the organizational structure, culture, and goals. The project manager must tailor the project thoroughly and continually to ensure it achieves the PMP definition of "success."

The primary goal of tailoring is to ensure a "successful" project. This means that it meets the scope—meets *only* the scope without **scope creep** or **gold plating** with risky extras—and does so on schedule and on budget. If a project achieves scope and finishes within the designated timeframe and budget, once the customer formally accepts the deliverables and the Close Project process concludes, it is a "successful" project for the purposes of the exam, even if stakeholders are unhappy with the outcome. Projects that do *more* than scope without official change requests, even if they come in under budget and under schedule and receive rave reviews from all stakeholders, are *not* successful for the purposes of the exam, since they exposed the project to more potential risks without official approval. (Expect three or more questions on this concept for the exam. Scope creep is bad. Gold plating is bad. Exposing the project to *unapproved* risk—even if the outcomes are good—is bad.)

You must know the Knowledge Area / process phase matrix, corresponding ITTOs, and document descriptions from PMBOK Guide 6th edition to discern answers quickly for the exam. You will rarely be asked to identify the correct document, technique, or phase directly. Instead, you will need a synthesized understanding from two to three Knowledge Areas to arrive at the suitable answer to "What would PMBOK do?" The majority of questions on the PMP exam will be based on a scenario wherein you will need to identify the type of project methodology, the specific process or phase (the When) depicted within the scenario, and then determine the *best* response. Often, additional misleading or unnecessary information will be written into the scenarios to help separate knowledgeable examinees from "lucky guessers." Answer choices will usually be full-sentence and riddled with tricky logic setups. Imagine question phrasing along the lines of "All of the following answers are rarely false except which two?"

For all questions, first determine the type of project (traditional, hybrid, or type of Agile). Then determine the *when*. (Do a **root-cause analysis** to determine the process phase where the problem or situation first originated.) When faced with a mental coin flip to decide between two answer choices, determining *when* or the related project phase will help you identify the correct tool, output, or strategy-based answer consistently.

Only a small number of exam questions will test your knowledge of a specific PMBOK term with a single-word answer choice. *Tailoring* is important enough to be one of those few. Consider this easy example:

While collecting requirements, a consultation with the organization's purchasing manager has revealed recent difficulties in acquiring a potential key project resource due to ongoing tariff disputes between two of the countries in the supply chain. The project manager raises the issue with the project owner. Ultimately, the decision is made to use another supplier for the resource, and the project budget is adjusted for the cost increase. This is an example of:

A. Accommodating
B. Customizing
C. Tailoring
D. Facilitating
E. Adapting

The correct answer is "Tailoring." Based on language and logic, one could make arguments for A, B, D, and E. They are synonymous, and they are term descriptors related to official PMBOK definitions in other project phases and processes. This question scenario necessitates the deliberate and referential approach to avoiding risk that originated during a planning process—the *when*. The PMBOK Guide 7th edition devotes an entire chapter to tailoring and its planning steps. Therefore, choose C on the exam.

When Does Tailoring Occur?

The PMBOK Guide 6th edition included three tailoring phases. The PMBOK 7th edition divided the tailoring process into four steps instead. The following table provides a high-level view of what should be considered—and *when*—regarding tailoring a project, for the sake of the exam questions. For practical on-the-job applications, however, a more exhaustive and prescriptive list of tailoring considerations for each step of the tailoring process can be found via independent research online and, specifically, on the PMI website.

4 Steps to Tailoring

Tailoring Step	Overall Goal	Participants	Considerations
1. Select project development approach. During Initiation phase while formulating business use case and project charter.	Choose the best development approach for the project.	Project manager and project customer/ owner.	• Predictive (traditional or waterfall?) • Adaptive (iterative or incremental?) • Hybrid (Which components will be Agile?) • Teach customer and top-level organizational stakeholders the approach process and confirm they understand why and how the approach is best for the project.
2. Tailor for the organization. During Early Planning phase while developing project management plan and while developing the scope statement.	Adapt the approach for the specific needs and requirements of the organization.	Project manager with project customer/ owner and top-level organizational stakeholders.	• Organization governance structure • Organization culture / mission statement • Industry standards and regulations • OPAs, EEFs, policies, tools • SMEs within the organization • PMO or project maturity/experience, current or past project lessons learned, and other documentation • Quality assurance and risk tolerance • Organizational constraints and assumptions
3. Tailor for the project. Most tailoring should be included while developing the official project management plan, multiple Knowledge Process Area Management Plans, and key project documents; it should also be baselined in the scope statement.	Adapt the specific project planning for the complexity, type, size, and duration of the project. Be proactive and preemptive to minimize changes later.	Project manager, top-level organizational stakeholders, and all stakeholders of relevance for comprehensive planning documents in all Knowledge Process Areas.	• Adding or removing deliverables or features of deliverables. • Modifying deliverables. • Ensuring quality requirements have been expressed by the organization and included in requirements documents. • Being thorough when developing all project process management plans. • Paying particular attention to the risk register, stakeholder register, and communication management plans.

Tailoring Step	Overall Goal	Participants	Considerations
4. Tailor for ongoing improvement. Additional tailoring here once the scope statement has been baselined requires an **official change request.** Do everything possible to minimize change requests. Agile project changes will differ based on whether it's a sprint-related change or an overall project-governance change.	Adapt based on continuous monitoring and controlling efforts. Be reactive to dynamic events, work performance reports, stakeholder needs, changes in environmental factors, etc.	Project manager and stakeholders as needed. Maintain constant communication and engagement with stakeholders as outlined in the communication management and stakeholder engagement plans.	• Follow official project processes and management plans. • Monitor pending legislation. • Consider and adjust for stakeholder needs (especially as new stakeholders are onboarded) while limiting official change requests. • Utilize feedback loops for a range of stakeholders throughout the project and adjust at key phase gates. • Watch for alternatives for improved process efficiency. • Monitor supply chain issues. • Identify new positive or negative risks. • Adjust for sprint retrospectives and lessons learned.

Strategic tailoring should be completed before and during project planning (Steps 1, 2, and 3) to ensure:

- The most appropriate approach has been chosen for the size, complexity, and type of project.
- The organization needs are matched for structure, project maturity, culture, compliance, and use case.
- The project requirements are clearly defined to minimize risk and avoid buyer's remorse and costly reworks.
- Tools, people, and process choices have been optimized and will be available throughout the project.

Tailor in Steps 1, 2, and 3 to Limit Change in Step 4

Most of the project tailoring occurs before project work begins. This applies to traditional, hybrid, and Agile project methodologies. All projects should be tailored during Steps 1, 2, and 3 to the degree that once project work begins, the need for official change requests is kept to a minimum.

Though both processes result in a project adjustment, tailoring is not "change." Tailoring is proactive and preventative. Change is reactive and often more costly in terms of time or funding. Performing an integrated change request as part of project change management is required after an unanticipated issue occurs, and some official changes are unavoidable. Exceptions might be made for a reduction in scope to keep a project on schedule, a change in scope to update for compliance, or a change in material choices or approach if a new opportunity for cost savings presents itself.

Often, however, tailoring early in the planning can help prevent unnecessary changes. Are unhappy stakeholders with low-level project influence insisting on changes? Have activists established a daily vigil at the site of your high-rise project? For the exam, the "do first" answer is always *review the appropriate documentation* to make sure the plan has been followed. Look for the root cause of the problem. The "do next" answer is *meet with them*—colocation face-to-face is always best. Discuss to understand the nature of the problem. Find the appropriate method to resolve misunderstandings, clarify the project plan and processes, or smooth stakeholder feathers. For the purposes of the exam, the project manager should tailor interactions to do everything possible (short of canceling the project) to limit formal change requests once project work begins, unless an official change would yield a net benefit to the project or avoid a significant risk. (Expect four or more exam questions related to the project change management process and effective tailoring strategies to limit formal change requests.)

Agile Projects and Hybrid Elements Need Early Tailoring Too

Agile emerged from the software industry, where products are pushed out as soon as possible, often when as little as 80% "done," and are continuously improved once released. This generates a "minimum viable product" quickly so organizations may begin integrating the product into their functional operations and returning value in the form of new productivity or resale profit as soon as possible. Deliverables are then tweaked for performance improvement or added features based on testing and feedback from actual users.

Change requests for Agile product design elements, functionalities, and development priority are simple and require very little documentation. They are requested and prioritized by the project owner or customer based on input from organization stakeholders as part of the two- to four-week iterative work period or "sprint." (To an organization transitioning from traditional or waterfall projects, where the change request process is formal and time-consuming, the ease and frequency of change in Agile methodologies will require considerable adjustment. Project managers will need to dedicate additional time to helping the transitioning organization decision-makers understand how to navigate the differences in the types and timing of change requests for Agile, as well as delivery cadence, "continuous improvement" versus a final product, and the payment process for Agile development.)

Recall that project **requirements** are the features, design elements, and functional and quality specifications of the project deliverables. For Agile projects, the "welcome changing requirements" principle applies to the 4th step of the tailoring procedure—during the iterative and ongoing tailoring needed once the project work starts. The project owner or customer is expected to meet with the Agile development team regularly to prioritize the project backlog and provide continuous feedback.

As with traditional projects, the Agile project manager must still complete the prerequisite tailoring process Steps 1, 2, and 3 to optimize success and minimize risk for the entirety of the project before the actual project work begins. The stakeholder register will still need to be as comprehensive as possible at the outset, with a **RACI chart** for accountability transparency and a **stakeholder cube** or **salience model** for effective stakeholder engagement and communication. Requirements—or, in the case of XP Agile, user stories—will need to be clearly defined to identify the broadest list of product features and functionalities before it can be narrowed, honed, and prioritized by the project owner in the project backlog. The specific Agile approach will need to be chosen based on the operational and cultural norms, **organizational process assets (OPAs), and enterprise environment factors (EEFs)** of the customer's organization. The project team will need to identify and commit to the best-for-the-circumstances tools and operational development modalities before the first sprint as well. Will the team need to use a Scrum, Kanban, or Scrumban board for the duration or for a particular sprint? What principles will be included in the team charter? Which development project coordination applications will need to be added to the **project management information system (PMIS)**?

Budgeting and contracting for Agile teams for iterative components of Agile and hybrid projects will also require skillful tailoring at the outset. Many non-technology companies are accustomed to providing final payment for projects upon official closure once the scope has been achieved and deliverables have been formally accepted. Iterative and incremental Agile components require ongoing funding since the scope is always changing. (Hiring an Agile development team is similar to keeping an attorney on retainer. The minimum viable product is released with the understanding that the development team will continue improving it in stages. The Agile project is "done" when the project sponsor and the project team conclude there is no more value to be added to the product—when the project owner declares, "It's good enough.") Thus, Agile projects require as much project tailoring as a traditional or waterfall approach. Project managers will need to provide additional training for organizations who are new to Agile or who are embarking on a hybrid project. When it comes to Agile project deliverables, project owner input is required, change is welcome, deadlines are guidelines, payment is ongoing, and the project may never seem "done."

Tailoring Step 1—Select the Appropriate Approach

As part of the development of the high-level project charter during the Initiation phase, the project manager consults with the project sponsor/owner and the top-level stakeholders for the organization.

What is the life cycle of the project? How can the project be broken into milestones or phases for testing, review, and feedback? What approach is best for the deliverables? If the project has multiple deliverables, consider a different approach (hybrid) for each. Will the organization assign a functional manager to serve as a project coordinator to each deliverable while the project manager oversees the entire program of projects? (How will the project manager tailor project planning to minimize conflicts among project leaders?) When considering an Agile (adaptive) approach, how familiar and comfortable is the organization with the development and delivery cadence and operational tasks such as procurement and accounting?

Agile Suitability Filter Tool

PMI suggests the application of a **suitability filter tool** during consultations with the customer. This "diagnostic visual" helps teams evaluate key high-level factors related to successful project management, then indicates the best initial approach for a project or one of its deliverables. (You can visit suitabilityfilter.com to experiment with a live version of the tool developed specifically for PMI.) The tool provides excellent insight on how variations in key considerations affect the appropriateness of the overall project or individual deliverable development approach.

Tailoring Step 2—Tailor for the Organization

In this step, the project manager collaborates with the project sponsor and top-level organizational stakeholders to refine the **business documents** and use case while drafting the project charter. This collaboration includes the initial brainstorming, mapping, and list generation activities related to the early stages of development for the Knowledge Area project plans.

Many larger organizations will already have a formal project management office (PMO), or **value delivery office (VDO)** for Agile-oriented businesses. The project manager can use organization project planning templates, or in the absence of templates, planning documents from previous projects as a springboard for initial project planning. (Remember, even templates will need to be tailored, since no two projects are alike.) The PMO and VDO divisions will be documenting your project efforts as part of their responsibility to develop and measure repeatable processes and continuous improvement strategies for future projects. Therefore, the project manager will need to ensure that the approach to development and related tools that the project team(s) use to complete the project deliverables are in line with the organization's ongoing project management strategies. Additionally, the project manager should be sure to consider and include the following to maintain conformity with organizational processes:

- OPAs (organization process assets)—Have they completed other projects? Do they have an existing PMO with project management documentation templates, knowledge databases, and lessons learned documents from previous projects? The tailoring efforts must always align with the organization's policies and procedures. On-premise safety procedures, security protocols, and digital tool use policies will be in effect for project teams and direct-hire workers and subcontracted work teams throughout the project.
- EEFs (enterprise environmental factors)—What industry regulations, local laws, and national legislation govern the organization's activities? The organization's culture and mission statement will guide project choices. (An organization that promotes "green" or environmental awareness will be particular about the choice of materials, or even countries of origin for key supplies if those countries stand in violation of the mission statement.) What is the risk appetite of the company? (Is the company slogan "Go big or go home," or "One molecule at a time"?) This information should be collected at this tailoring stage to guide. The results will be included in the risk management plan and used to conduct risk assessments during later stages.
- Is the organizational structure such that departments are self-managed, and employees are given considerable autonomy in how they accomplish their work? Or are the organizational managers prone to micromanaging their employees? (For example: Major hospital systems commission projects to improve processes and tools utilized by medical staff, yet the organizations are managed by non-health care administrators from the areas of business and finance. This also occurs on projects for major university systems wherein each college has its specialized area of expertise yet is administered largely by managers with MBAs.) The organizational structure and its proclivity toward interdepartmental collaboration will considerably influence the planning and execution of project work and its corresponding reporting, monitoring, and controlling efforts. The quality management plan will need to be tailored, as well, to include enough opportunities for process reviews and audits to satisfy organizational oversight requirements, while still allowing project teams to work autonomously. The stakeholder engagement plan should also be tailored to include prescriptive events and feedback loop constructs to facilitate ongoing input and engagement.

The Law Trumps All

Never break the law for the organization. The Project Management Institute specifically states that project managers are in violation of the PMI code of ethics if they knowingly or unwittingly allow or encourage clients to violate the law. Also, contracts become void if they involve activities that break the law. For the exam, if a functional manager is pressuring the project manager to do something that violates company regulations or a local or national law, then do the following: First, check the related plan and other related documents (e.g., risk register, assumption log, issue log), including those related to the policy or regulation in question. Next, discuss the regulation with the functional manager. If the manager persists in requesting that you violate the regulation, then discuss the concern with the project sponsor or other relevant stakeholder up the chain of command.

Illegal activity must be reported. Always begin with discussion to give the stakeholder the opportunity to amend his mindset first, then escalate up the chain of command. Always follow up to make sure the issue has been reported to the proper authorities. You might alienate the functional manager and irritate the higher-level stakeholders for what, to them, may seem a petty infraction. You may even lose your job. However, you are protecting the project and organization by avoiding the risk of noncompliance (e.g., casualties, lawsuits, fines, prison, business closure).

Also, if during the foundation work on your high-rise project, your excavation team discovers an oil deposit, buried treasure, toxic waste, a fossilized Viking ship, human remains, alien artifacts, damage to nearby buildings, a vent in the Earth's crust, or other finds of significance other than dirt and bedrock, you will need to *stop that portion of the project work temporarily* for investigation and review with the sponsor and organization. Then contact the proper authorities. Do not cancel the project, however; continue with other work activities that fall outside of the affected location until a "full stop" is issued by either the organization or authorities. For the exam, even if the organization tells you to keep digging, you are required by law to report the find to the relevant higher regulatory authority. Respect the law and your professional integrity by following the PMI principles.

Tailoring Step 3—Tailor for the Project

The goal for this tailoring step is to complete the initial project planning in a manner that reflects all organizational considerations from Step 2 drilled down to the specific project level.

Much of this tailoring step is completed as part of the planning phase for all Knowledge Areas. The project charter is complete, and the stakeholder register has been established to identify and classify the roles, influence, and interest levels in the project. By the time you complete the Knowledge Area management plans and PMBOK process documents, you will have tailored the project within both the governance of the organization and the standards set by the industry.

The planning phase is a multi-tiered process. As individual process plans are developed, other plans will need to be updated to reflect the corresponding impacts on the other Knowledge Area plans as part of the project integration management process. (For example: As more deliverable requirements and their correlated quality requirements are added during the "collect requirements" step of the requirements planning process, the quality management plan and scope baseline in development will also need to be adjusted.) There are teams of people involved in the planning—a combination of SMEs, organization representatives, vendors, etc. Your stakeholder engagement plan and communication management plan will be established during this tailoring step and planning process phase as well. However, your stakeholder register will be a fluid document that will be tailored throughout the project to reflect additions and movement of stakeholders in and out of categorized groups or stakeholder **networks** reflected in your communication management plan. Your communication management plan will depict the standard method, form, and frequency of communication based on a stakeholder's network or status outlined within the stakeholder register. Additional tailoring will be required for exceptions to the stakeholder's assigned category. (For example: A regional manager for X company, though grouped with the monthly report recipients, may need additional customized communication because he is also part of the project vendor network.)

Assumptions are inputs to the project planning that originate with the organization or pending legislation and are often related to specific hardware, tools, personnel preferences, and schedule milestones. (For example: The digital transformation project will utilize the existing server racks since they were already updated within the last calendar year; only 10 new racks will need to be procured and installed. Or, in addition to the project sponsor, Stewart from the finance department and Hannah from the IT department will be on call throughout the project to liaise directly with the project team.)

Obtain a comprehensive inventory of all organization assets that will be allocated for and required to be utilized on the project *before cost baselining and scheduling begins*. Find out what they've got, what and who they expect you to utilize, and how they expect you and your team(s) to operate now, so you can document the details during the project planning and contracting. Your initial cost baseline and resource management plan will be configured based on these inclusions. The documented exclusions can be reconsidered later as part of risk management strategy or a **resource smoothing** endeavor. To the organization, you will be demonstrating your excellent CRM and your commitment to giving the business the best possible value for the project. You'll help the organization save money on the project by leveraging their existing processes, expertise, and other tangible assets. You will also eliminate surprise interruptions to the work schedule later when the project sponsor starts throwing wrenches at your resource management efforts. ("*Here's my nephew, Jack. He's just out of college. I'd appreciate it if you'd let him sit in on the rest of the project with you so he can gain some experience.*") You don't want to cause hurt feelings, or worse, stop and backtrack on work progress later because the organization leaders are disappointed that you ignored their largesse. ("*We already had one of those just sitting in a storage warehouse. Why didn't you ask?*")

Discussion, prioritization, and clear documentation of project **constraints** should be conducted when tailoring for the project as well. You will be monitoring several interdependent project components wherein a delay in one will risk a delay in the overall **critical path** of the project timeline. (Remember, for project success on the exam, the scope constraint is king and drives all others.) Scope, time, or cost? Quality, risk, resources? Which is most important to the organization? When in conflict, which of the constraints will the organization be most flexible about? If the project starts running significantly behind schedule, will the organization consider decreasing the scope or increasing the budget (a.k.a. **"crashing"** the project) to finish on time? Or will the organization prefer to extend the schedule to maintain the existing scope and control additional costs? The quality management plan, resource management plan, and risk management plan should include statements in the overview about the organization's appetite and expectations in these areas. This will guide decisions later, when constraints conflict with each other throughout the project.

The PMIS Is Vital to Project Operability and Communication

The **project management information system** is a collection of software licenses, applications, knowledge databases, and repositories necessary for stakeholders to communicate, complete work, and view reports. Tailor the components of the PMIS based on familiarity with the organization's existing software—the more familiar the tool, the more likely the stakeholders will be to use it. Also, it saves the organization money by adding users to existing licenses versus investing in new software products for a short-term endeavor. (A savvy tax attorney could "expense" the additional seats to existing organizational software assets as part of ongoing operations versus a project-specific cost too.) Which stakeholder groups will receive access to each PMIS component? Who will administer user permissions for each application? What are the bounds of the organization's digital security and use policies?

An agreement will need to be reached regarding official approaches to common productivity and communication tasks, including:

- Official documentation software (Microsoft Office? Google Workspace?)
- Email format (Outlook? Gmail?)
- Knowledge repository location and access type (local server, Dropbox, shared Google Drive)
- Access type (push versus pull system)
- Project management software (Jira, MS Project, Primavera P6)
- Project collaboration software (Asana, Monday)
- Project wikis or dashboards (Confluence, Trello, Smartsheet, project website)

Tailoring for Agile Projects for the PMP Exam vs. the ACP

For the PMP exam, Agile projects will undergo a similar documented planning process for overall management of the project. If you are also preparing for the PMI-ACP for Agile, or if your experience has been as an Agile project manager and you are now adding the PMP certification, do not overthink *project* planning answers for Agile project questions. The PMP exam will only be testing general awareness of change processes, team operations, common Agile approaches, and the SDLC processes of Agile. Assume a more traditional approach to the overall project planning processes; all process phases, all Knowledge Areas, and most documents will still apply. As a traditional project manager transitioning to managing hybrid and agile projects, you will need to know the specifics of the sprint life cycles and the differences in terminology, such as XP, Scrum, Kanban, Lean, and Kaizen. You will be expected to select the correct conflict management or sprint-appropriate response, using these terms as decision cues and using the methodology as the perspective.

Tailoring Step 4—Throughout the Project

Fortunately, adherence to the PMBOK way for project management means there's a plan for everything. These detailed plans offer transparency to the stakeholders and efficiency for project teams. They set clear, bright lines for project procedures and productivity standards before work on the project begins. Develop the Knowledge Area plans in conjunction with and tailored for the organization during tailoring Steps 1, 2, and 3. Thorough attention to tailoring prior to the start of project work will minimize the number of formal change requests needed once work is underway. For Agile project components, once the project development work begins, changes should be welcome but limited to the priority of project feature development or design elements that are discussed before each sprint and during sprint reviews.

Much of the tailoring completed throughout the project will be related to ongoing process improvement and quality assurance, conflict management among teams, communication and engagement with stakeholders, risk management, and responses to environmental influences like changes in regulations, internal organizational upheavals, or natural disasters.

The PMBOK Guide 7th Edition includes a considerable list of many, but not all, considerations regarding ongoing tailoring. The following are generalized "best approach" considerations for answer choices on the exam. Keep these in mind when answering task-specific questions by domain.

Tailoring for the People (Stakeholders) Domain

- Consider all stakeholders who will be impacted by the project development and implementation, including organization decision-makers, team members, end users, vendors, and lobbyists.

- Be aware of the type and variety of networks in which individual stakeholders and stakeholder groups participate. (For example: A stakeholder can also be an end user employed within the organization, a lobbyist, a local voter, and a taxpayer.) The more networks that stakeholders interact with, the more likely that they may receive misinformation. Therefore, ongoing and correct categorization of stakeholders, coupled with good stakeholder engagement management strategies and a clear communication management plan, will require constant monitoring and tailoring. Will your project knowledge repository be available to all stakeholders, or will certain stakeholder groups receive only periodic updates? Based on the level of influence on the project, which groups of stakeholders will be invited to participate in two-way communication versus a one-way push of information? (For the exam, keep stakeholders who are highly interested in the project "in the loop." They might not have a high level of direct influence, but they can bolster support or dissent for your project based on their networks of association.)
- When choosing tools and methods of communication with project people, include considerations for accessibility and special needs.
- How many locations and time zones are involved? (For the exam, PMI loves colocation—same-place and face-to-face communication as "best" answer choices—even when it is not practical in the real world.)
- Have you actively included appeals to diversity, cultural differences, and age differences?
- Is pre-project training and coaching needed? (Do the top-level organization stakeholders need a brief training course on Agile project methodology? Does the project development team need professional development training on a particular tool, cooperative methods, or DEI?)

Tailoring for the Business (Organization) Domain

- Always inventory all possible organization contributions (or expectations for utilization) of inputs (people, tools, methods, software) for the project and document their inclusion or exclusion in the plan documents.
- Does the organization have budgeting, procurement, preferred or exclusive vendors, cost-estimation, governance, or other guidelines that will influence the project?
- How are RFIs, RFPs, and contracts handled by the organization?
- How does the organization audit its own processes, and what impact will that have on the project's oversight?

Tailoring for the Processes (Work) Domain

- How will knowledge be managed throughout the project to promote the most collaborative work environment? Is there a formal repository for use during development (e.g., Dropbox, Google Drive link, or a Confluence wiki)? Do all users have the required access permissions? Who will manage the permissions?
- Does the organization have control and quality-related policies or existing validation methods, or will you need to collaborate with the organization to develop new methods and templates for the project? If you develop templates, who owns them? Can you use them on other projects with new clients?
- Does the organizational culture (or influential stakeholder groups) enforce one or more aspects of sustainability? (For example: Labor policies and human rights principles, fair contractual practices, community responsiveness, or environmental responsibility.)

- Regarding **uncertainty** or risk, are the project deliverables novel to the industry, or is the project approach new to the organization? Are the selected tools and methods new to the team? How will these considerations impact the risk assessment and tolerance for the project?
- When conducting **measurement** activities, such as determining financial and nonfinancial value for the business or capturing and analyzing work performance data, how will the measurement be performed and reported?
- How will **feedback** be collected, documented, and utilized throughout the project? From whom will the feedback be collected, and how frequently? When you look at phase reviews, sprint reviews and retrospectives, issue logs, and lessons learned updates, do these suggest areas in need of further tailoring to reduce or respond to risks or improve processes?

Big City Museum Improvement—A Practical Example of Tailoring a Multi-Deliverable Program

Let's look at an example of a hybrid program of projects and how a project manager might tailor a project. Tailoring, planning, excellent CRM, and conflict management throughout the project will maintain interest, curtail risk, and ensure not only a successful project by PMI standards, but a favorable project status designation from the organization. Therefore, the most vital information is obtained by consulting directly with and for the organization at the *beginning* of the project when *interest and risk are both at their highest* points. The following is a simple draft of information collected via an initial consultation with the organization project sponsor and top stakeholders. The information collected will be compiled with all existing project plans, design documents, contracts and service-level agreements, the tentative business use case (why they're sponsoring the project and how they expect to benefit), as well as an initial list of key stakeholders that will be used as part of the overall framework for tailoring for the approach, organization, and project.

The information will be key input when drafting the **project charter** and when developing the stakeholder register during the Initiation process. This initial information will also provide the organization-mandated perspective necessary to tailor for the project—the Knowledge Area planning processes. Once the Knowledge Area plans have been completed, the heavy lifting is done. The project manager will have organization-approved and value-oriented plans for reference in order to manage ongoing tailoring (Execution, Monitoring and Controlling, Closure processes) once the project work has officially started. As you read, think about the many risks you can spot. How would you prevent the risk from occurring? Who is accountable, and how will you document that in the official plans? When and how will you conduct stakeholder reviews to collect feedback? What type of industry-mandated quality control standards can you already anticipate? (For the exam, for question scenarios involving stakeholders who are unhappy with project deliverables or the quality, the root cause is a poor "collect requirements" process during early project planning.)

Project Scenario: Big City has decided to stimulate economic growth in its downtown area by revitalizing its Science and History Museum. Big City wants to rebrand itself as a destination city to increase local and external tourism within the downtown area. The project consists of a tight 18-month window for completion, with a budget of $200 million. Big City has already acquired blueprints and the necessary structural building permits. Big City has also commissioned several lead contractors and designers who will coordinate with the project manager. The program has seven sub-projects with distinct deliverables. (These are underlined for reference.)

Project—Annex Structure: Convert one-half of existing Museum Parking Lot B to a four-story state-of-the-art museum display annex. Three floors will be utilized for museum exhibits, while the fourth floor will be developed as a formal event venue.

- Assumptions: Big City will provide a dedicated building contractor for the annex structure.
- Constraints: All construction deliveries and staging must be completed using no more than one-half of the existing parking lot B. No part of Museum Parking Lot A may be used.

Project—Annex Display Stations: Develop 15 uniquely themed and interactive exhibit stations featuring hands-on sensory input via a variety of technology-based manipulation points.

- Assumptions: Big City will also provide a lead interior display theme designer to create the exhibits and liaise with software developers.
- Constraints: Display station design, light and sound integration, and software application integration must be completed within 30 working days prior to the project schedule end to allow for Museum-wide enterprise resource planning (ERP) integration and technology infrastructure update.

Project—Annex Station 15 Apps: Develop 15 software programs with sensory-input APIs to integrate and operate sound, light, video, animatronic, and game outputs at each display station.

- Assumptions: Big City will provide an AV engineer to liaise with software developers.
- Constraints: Software must be compatible with new ERP facilities management software. All apps must be 100% integrated, operational, and bug-free within 30 working days prior to project completion to allow for Museum-wide ERP integration and technology infrastructure update.

Project—Annex Event Venue: Develop a fourth-floor formal event venue with a full commercial kitchen, seating, and ballroom space for 1,200 occupants.

- Assumptions: Big City will provide a dedicated venue designer to plan the space and commercial kitchen design specifications.
- Constraints: The kitchen must have a dedicated delivery zone and freight elevator for uninterrupted employee usage from the parking level to all floors.

Project—Garage: Convert the non-Annex half of Museum Parking Lot B to a four-story parking garage to provide additional parking for the entire downtown entertainment district.

- Assumptions: Big City will provide a building contractor for the garage facility. This appointed contractor will also oversee the construction concerns of the Entrance Update project (below).
- Constraints: All construction deliveries and staging must be completed using this one-half of the existing parking lot. No part of Museum Parking Lot A may be used.

Project—Museum Entrance Update: The current museum will have its front elevation entrance and interior ticketing foyer redesigned to modernize purchasing kiosks and guest queues. (The big T-Rex will be getting a holographic facelift.) Exterior design elements will need to be altered to coordinate with the facades of the new annex and parking garage additions.

- Assumptions: Big City will use the same appointed contractor from the Garage project.
- Constraints: The entrance and lobby will remain operational until the final five-week shutdown. Temporary walls and ongoing dust removal will be required to keep the guest areas safe and clean. Project scheduling efforts should minimize guest inconveniences, potential power shutdowns, and noise pollution.

Project—Technology Command Center Update: The museum operations will need to be conducted through a digital command center that features an on-premise server room, integrated lighting, HVAC, communications, and security technology throughout all three facilities. The update will also include a comprehensive operations ERP suite.

- Assumptions: Big City will hire a dedicated CTO as a full-time project liaison and future Museum Technology Director. Whether newly designed or adopted from an existing vendor, the ERP must integrate its CRM, ticketing and booking, point-of-sale (POS) operations, facilities reservation management, donation outreach, personnel, and financial management. Five weeks (30 workdays) will be allocated once all annex displays are complete to update and install technology infrastructure wiring, hardware, and the ERP integration.
- Constraints: The Museum prefers to maintain all data, software, and hardware on-site; utilization of cloud storage or services should be limited.

Overall Program: This is included in the perspective needed to tailor for the organization, project, and all ongoing processes throughout the project.

- **Assumptions:** The existing museum will be open daily to guests throughout the project(s). The facility will only plan to close for a five-week period (30 working days) at the end of the project window to allow time for technology infrastructure installations and ERP testing.
- **Constraints:** All subcontractors and work teams will sign and abide by a prescriptive list of safety, security, and conditional working terms established by Big City and in compliance with local, state, and national regulations as well as related occupational, tourism, constructional, and technology industry standards. All exterior project work must be completed between 8:00 AM and 8:00 PM to comply with Big City noise ordinances.
- **Tolerances:** Big City has a low tolerance and low appetite for risk. Safety for guests and workers is the top priority, with positive guest relations as the secondary consideration. Precautions should be taken to ensure a safe and secure worksite without interfering with or interacting with guests. The budget for the program of projects is firm; contractors and the program manager will be expected to coordinate resources accordingly. Time allocated for the project is 18 months. If pressed on scope and time, the event venue is Big City's lowest priority—at a minimum, the structural shell, electrical, plumbing, HVAC, and elevator access should be roughed in. If needed, an additional eight weeks will be allocated to finish the commercial kitchen installation and final completion of the trim and furnishment.

(This is a general wish list with known conditions for now. Part of the project charter development process will be to determine if all deliverables are truly needed by the organization and whether the initial budget and schedule limitations are appropriate.)

TAILORING THE APPROACH

Big City wants two new physical structures and a partial structure remodel. Construction projects are predictive, since the scope is usually set at the beginning. Though they can include multiple work activities operating in parallel, they tend to be linear in nature—obtain designs and permits to start, do the work, inspect the work, rework, reinspect the work, finish the work. However, the project manager also needs to arrange for the development of 15 attraction applications. A new ERP solution needs to be researched and either developed as part of the project or procured from a third-party vendor. Then the ERP must be implemented and tested. These software-related deliverables would require iterative development where frequent testing, feedback, and improvement can occur. Unlike many Agile software development projects, where products are iterative, incremental, or both, the software applications here need to be 100% ready for deployment—including development, testing, feedback, improvement, more testing, and final approval—at least 30 working days prior to the end of the project schedule. When considering the project's **critical path**, the start or completion of subsequent activities will be dependent on an early or on-time "finish" of the software applications. (For the exam, these quality requirements for the deliverables will need to be specified within the official project *requirements documents*—not the quality management plan. Also, for work that is part of the critical path, a delay in that work activity will delay the overall project schedule. Expect a few exam questions about timing changes for activities on **network diagrams** and the impact on the project schedule.)

For this program of projects, a hybrid approach is best, wherein the physical structures are managed traditionally and software components are completed and tested via Agile. The project manager will need to first guide the organization committee and the project sponsor to this hybrid approach conclusion. Next, the project manager should make certain the key organization decision-makers understand the differences in hybrid versus traditional project completion. Scheduling and payment for the various work activities will be significantly impacted.

While still in the pre-stages or early stages of planning, there will be brainstorming, idea mapping, voting, and multi-criteria decision analysis (e.g., a matrix or table), plus a variety of planning, estimation, and team-building games involved. These activities stimulate awareness and engagement in the project and its approach, and they help refine and prioritize project scope requirements and risk assessments. The project manager then uses the information and insight from these activities to draft project plans. The Initial Work Breakdown Activity chart below is a very rudimentary blocking activity that should be completed with a group as a card-moving, sticky-note, or whiteboarding activity. The figure is a quick digest while drafting the project charter or during planning stages for the scope WBS, preliminary scheduling, and procurement steps. The white blocks below are big-picture activities that show the initial scheduling dependencies plus high-level information needed to begin the project planning process. The project manager and SME stakeholders can see where potential areas of risk will occur related to scheduling and develop risk responses accordingly. The current lack of clarity and urgency regarding the ERP solution is clear from the chart as well; whether building or buying it, research and development or procurement needs to begin early in the project schedule. The chart also highlights where the organization has already assigned contractors and designers with whom the project manager will collaborate directly. What about subcontractors who will complete the work? Will they be procured by the project manager or by the organization subcontractors?

The project manager should utilize visual organizers during group planning sessions. For our museum example, we've used a chart because it fits in the study guide. The project management industry, and particularly Agile methodologies, often rely on "cards" of information (e.g., actual sticky notes and index cards or virtual equivalents) that can be easily compiled and rearranged—

especially on a whiteboard. "Whiteboarding" is likely to be the correct answer choice to at least one of your exam questions. It's the epitome of an inclusion tool that is hands-on or "high touch" and of low-level technology so everyone can see and participate. Digital whiteboards are a popular alternative for remote teams, but these applications are neither "low tech" nor engaging—one person types on a digital post-it while the others observe remotely. Whether the whiteboard is physical or virtual, the information obtained during pre-project planning will likely end up on a Kanban or Scrum board as formal project issues, tasks, or user stories.

Initial Work Breakdown Activity for 18-Month Schedule

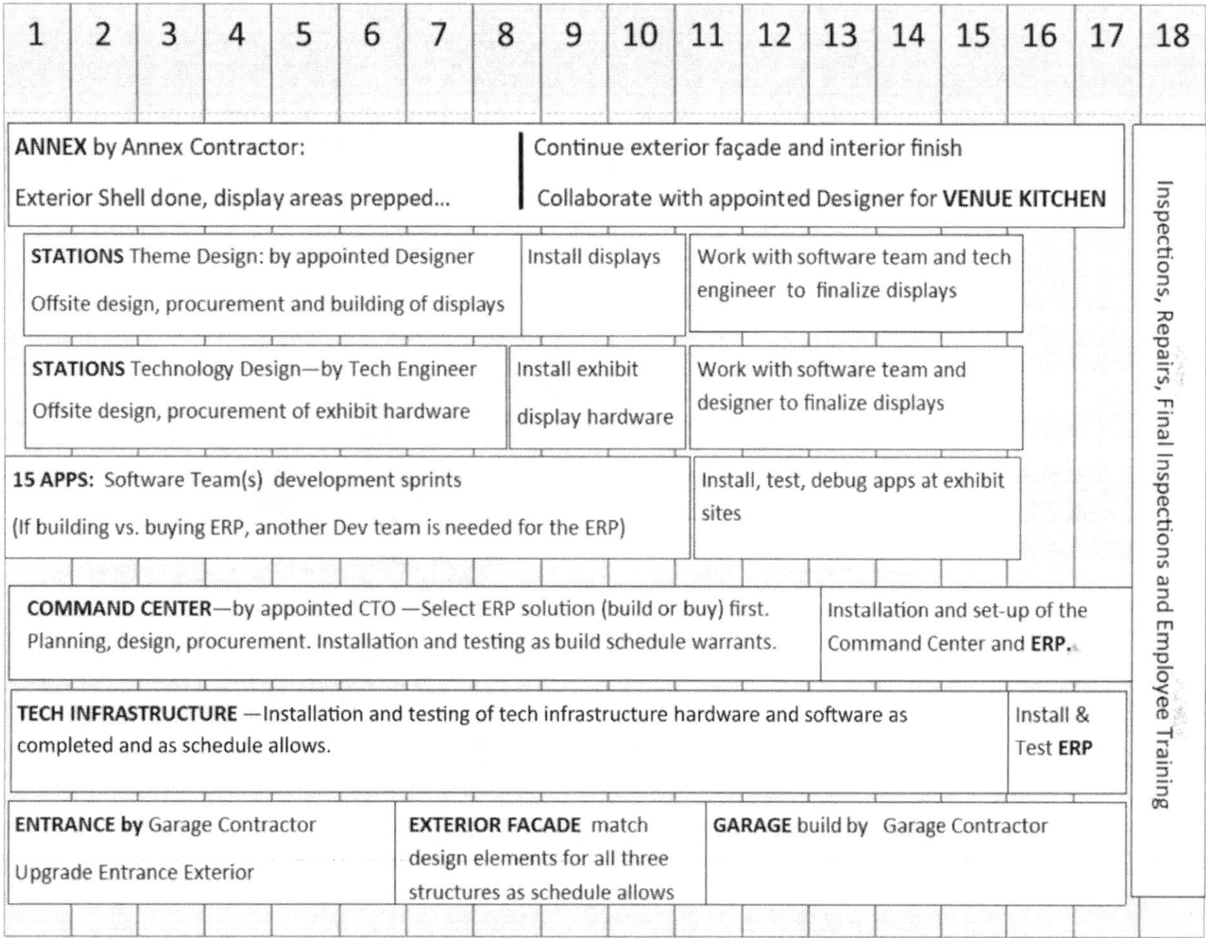

More targeted discussion and planning will occur as the project manager and key stakeholders begin planning the project itself via the Knowledge Area plans and related project documents.

Summary

Tailoring is the deliberate and "considered adaptation of approach, governance, and processes" to make them suitable for the organizational environment and the successful completion of the project. It requires analysis and strategic choices for effective utilization of the project people, processes, and project tools. The four steps to tailoring are: selecting the initial project approach, tailoring for the organization, tailoring for the project, and providing ongoing assessment and improvement throughout the project. The project manager guides the tailoring process with input and assistance from project stakeholders and within the boundaries governed by the organization.

This organization governance helps the project manager integrate all project facets and influences to ensure maximum value from the project for the business.

Models, Methods, and Artifacts

Project managers have an array of models, methods, and artifacts available to them to help carry out project activities across all project performance domains. According to PMI, a **model** is a way of explaining, conceptualizing, or diagramming a process, framework, or phenomenon. Models offer a scaled-down and simplified perspective of a situation and can help a team to analyze problems and make decisions—such as with a Monte Carlo quantitative risk analysis that identifies the probabilities and effects of risks. Based on the application of the model, a project team can determine the most likely outcome of a scenario and make decisions accordingly. A **method** is a means for accomplishing a project deliverable or outcome. For example, the precedence diagramming method (PDM) lays out the dependencies of predecessor and successor project activities. It is a sequencing method used to determine the necessary order of operations for a project. Finally, an **artifact** is something that is created for the project, such as a template, document, or output. An example in an Agile environment could be the product backlog or the sprint backlog.

The use of models, methods, and artifacts in a project environment should be guided by the principles of project management and tailored to the situation. The organization, customers, and environment will all have an impact on the selection of tools. Project managers in organizations with a directive or controlling project management office (PMO) may be required to produce certain artifacts, such as reports or business documents, or to follow a particular development approach. On the other hand, a simple/organic organizational structure or a strong matrix might provide more leeway. In either case, project managers should avoid duplication of effort and unnecessary work that takes time and resources but does not offer value to the project. Project teams should use a "just enough" approach, selecting enough techniques to be effective and efficient while eliminating work that does not add value to the project. This lean, lightweight approach is especially important when following an Agile methodology; one of the principles is simplicity—"the art of maximizing the amount of work not done." The effectiveness and applicability of models, methods, and artifacts should be evaluated throughout the project to ensure they are still appropriate.

Commonly Used Models

Situational Leadership Models

Situational leadership models can be used by project managers to guide their team members toward motivation and growth in a manner appropriate to the circumstances. These models provide a framework for how to use leadership skills and influence toward desired outcomes, whether utilized by authority figures or by team members through emergent leadership. They can be used to support team performance, thereby developing a sense of shared ownership of the project, its vision, and objectives. In alignment with the principle of leadership, effective leaders tailor their approach depending on the situation and the people involved to support both individuals and the team. By tailoring their approach and applying models with empathy and emotional intelligence, leaders can develop high-performing teams that are transparent, collaborative, empowered, and resilient. Below are some situational leadership models useful in a project management environment.

First, **Ken Blanchard's Situational Leadership II** model describes the development of team members in terms of competence and commitment. Leaders adapt their style according to team members' abilities, knowledge, skills (competence), and motivation (commitment) along a continuum, moving from directing to coaching, then supporting, and finally delegating. This model is useful to help leaders tailor their approach to supporting individual team members and inspiring them to grow. Different team members will need individualized approaches at different points in time. A more directive style might be needed in the beginning of a project to establish clarity and confidence, while more collaboration and delegation are appropriate as the team member feels empowered and engaged over time. Junior team members could need coaching for a while, whereas experienced senior members may be ready for delegation at the start of the project. Competence can be grown through one-on-one mentoring, group training, peer support, self-directed learning, or other methods, which can be tailored to the team size and needs.

Next, the **OSCAR** model of mentoring, created by Karen Whittleworth and Andrew Gilbert, is useful for supporting team members in their personal development and cultivating a high-performing team. It is a framework for coaching sessions between a mentor and mentee. Leaders can appraise team members' performance and develop personalized development goals with team members that will support team and individual performance. Mentoring and support are an important part of servant leadership, especially in Agile environments, as leaders remove impediments and obstacles to team members' work and encourage them to develop professionally. Each letter in "OSCAR" stands for a step in the mentoring process, which can be revisited iteratively throughout the mentoring relationship.

- **Outcome**: The outcome is the end goal of coaching. What long-term result is the individual seeking to achieve? What is the desired outcome of each conversation with the mentor?
- **Situation**: The situation is the team member's current knowledge and the way their level impacts relationships and performance. What are their baseline skills and abilities? Why are they at that level? Self-awareness of current capabilities is important for planning a path forward and assessing progress over time.
- **Choices/consequences**: Choices and consequences refer to the options and attendant outcomes of each option that the individual has for achieving results. The leader and team member discuss possible choices to help the individual choose the path for achieving their desired outcome.
- **Actions**: An action is a specific activity the individual can work on to progress toward their goal. The action should be specific, measurable, achievable, relevant, and time-bound (SMART) to be most effective. The team member is committed to accomplishing this action step.
- **Review**: The individual and leader meet regularly to stay on track and maintain motivation. Team member growth can be measured against key performance indicators to track progress toward the goal.

Communication Models

While situational leadership models help project managers apply leadership skills in certain scenarios, **communication models** are more broadly applicable, as communication is critical for project success and is woven into all phases and components of a project. It is a key factor in developing productive working relationships with internal and external stakeholders that maximize positive outcomes. Communication models can be used to demonstrate sender and recipient perspectives, highlight potential pitfalls or challenges of communication methods, and improve effectiveness. This is especially important in multicultural or dispersed situations where the potential for miscommunication may be higher. Communication models are useful for planning and managing communication channels and frequency with both external stakeholders and internal team members.

Useful for evaluating and selecting communication methods, Alistair Cockburn's model of **effectiveness of communication channels** describes effectiveness as a function of richness. The richer the channel or medium, the more effective it is in conveying complex, nuanced information. **Media richness** refers to the amount of information a particular medium can convey. Rich media is characterized by the ability to allow quick feedback, personal focus on the recipient, use of natural language to enhance understanding, and processing several cues at the same time. Some situations call for richer communication channels, when complex or complicated information must be conveyed, while more straightforward or factual content can effectively be communicated through less rich means. An example of rich communication is face-to-face interaction, for example an in-person meeting to kick off a project and establish alignment of values. Agile environments in particular prioritize face-to-face communication, per principle six of the Agile Manifesto. On the other hand, a note or a text message would be a less rich communication channel suited for a quick, direct, and informal exchange among team members. With distributed teams where in-person communication is not possible or is infrequent, strategies for rich communication include having at least one in-person meeting, using audio and video technology when possible, including time for team-building activities, and ensuring access to all necessary information online in an intranet or team website.

Another helpful communication model is the **gulf of execution and evaluation**, a concept developed by Donald Norman, which describes differences between expectation and reality. The **gulf of execution** is the degree to which there is a mismatch between a user's expectations of an item's functionality and what it actually allows them to do. For example, a website page would have a gulf of execution if a user clicked a "Purchase" button expecting to be taken to a payment page but was actually taken elsewhere. The **gulf of evaluation** describes the gap in how well an artifact helps the user figure out or interpret how to use it effectively. An ecommerce website would have a gulf of evaluation if it advertised a sale and invited the user to take advantage of it, but the user could not easily determine how to purchase the discounted item through the website. The gulfs of execution and evaluation are useful for analyzing the effectiveness of project communications. There may be misalignment between what the project manager thinks they are communicating and what stakeholders understand. This model can also be beneficial to keep in mind when determining project scope and objectives to ensure everyone is on the same page for the core deliverables of a minimum viable product.

Finally, the model of **cross-cultural communication**, described by Browaeys and Price, explains how a person's knowledge, experience, language, stereotypes, relationships, and communication style will impact communication. The model is based on the premise that communication does not exist in a void but is influenced by cultural and environmental factors. These may be different local subcultures that team members identify with, or international backgrounds of stakeholders. The model states that the message sender's background influences the message content and transmission, while the receiver's context impacts their interpretation of the message. For example, perhaps a team leader welcomes verbal feedback during a team meeting, but a team member's culture makes them uncomfortable voicing criticism in a public setting. Team members and leaders should be aware of differing expectations and biases, whether conscious or unconscious. They can then adapt communication appropriately, confirming communication is understood and feedback is taken. As an example, a project manager working in another country must learn cultural norms for introductions, interactions, and gestures to ensure their communication is well-received. Actively supporting diversity and inclusion is more important than ever for present-day project teams, cultivating a team culture of respect and support. With awareness of cultural differences and communication styles, team diversity can provide a competitive advantage.

Project Team Development Models

Project teams change and develop over time, and many models have been designed to chart these stages. **Project team development models** help project managers understand their team's dynamics and identify what stage of team development they occupy. This knowledge, in turn, informs decisions on how best to remove impediments, foster a shared vision, and inspire the team to achieve their optimal performance.

Tuckman's Ladder, described by Bruce Tuckman, is a common model used to describe sequences or stages of team development from the first meeting to the eventual disbanding. While every team will likely move through each stage at least once, this is not a guarantee, as it is not uncommon for teams to fail to achieve norming or performing status. Additionally, teams can frequently progress and regress through the middle stages.

- **Forming** is when the team first meets, likely at a kickoff meeting. Team members and their role on the team are introduced. High-level information is shared.
- **Storming** follows, as team members find their positions and may vie for power. Personalities may clash as strengths and weaknesses appear, and it may be a struggle to work together. Some teams are stuck in storming for a long time with elevated hostility, while others move through more easily.
- **Norming** is the stage where the team functions cohesively and begins to act more effectively. Team members are used to interacting with each other, knowing their places, and relying on each other, and they can resolve conflicts.
- **Performing** comes next, where the team is in a mature stage of development and performs with high efficiency and output. The team is characterized by synergy, ownership, trust, adaptability, empowerment, and collaboration.
- **Adjourning** is the final stage, when the project is completed and the team members are reassigned. It may come with a sense of loss if the team had strong bonds.

Similar to the Tuckman Ladder, the **Drexler/Sibbet Team Performance Model** describes the stages of team growth, this time with seven steps. Teams may not progress linearly through all the steps. The first four stages occur during team creation and answer the questions of "why, who, what, and how":

- **Step 1: Orientation**: the *why*. Why am I here? The mission and vision of the project are shared with the team through meetings and/or artifacts such as the business case, project charter, project vision statement, or other strategic documentation. The team orients around the project intentions.
- **Step 2: Trust building**: the *who*. Who are we working with? The project team—and potentially stakeholders—are introduced. Team members begin to get to know each other and their abilities.
- **Step 3: Goal clarification**: the *what*. What is the group doing? Project background information is shared, such as stakeholder expectations, project requirements, assumptions, constraints, high-level goals, and deliverable acceptance criteria.
- **Step 4: Commitment**: the *how*. How are we going to work together? The team plans at a high level how to achieve the project's stated goals and may produce artifacts such as milestone lists, release plans, resources, and budgets.
- The next steps describe team performance and sustainability once it is established.

- **Step 5: Implementation**: the *who, what, when, where.* Plans are decomposed into a backlog or more detailed work breakdown structure, and the team begins to work on output. Teams may be tempted to begin at this step, but the previous creation stages are important for success.
- **Step 6: High performance**: also known as the *Wow!* As the team gets more time and experience, they work together effectively and supportively with little need for direction, aligned with the project goals. This stage is analogous to Performing in Tuckman's Ladder.
- **Step 7: Renewal**: the *why continue?* As circumstances change, the team must reevaluate their dynamics and see if past practice is still working. Changes in deliverables, stakeholders, team membership, or other aspects trigger a review of behavior and protocols, and the team adapts as needed.

Motivation Models

Motivation models are useful for encouraging team members and stakeholders towards effective engagement. Motivation factors can include finances, autonomy, advancement, making a difference in the world, and recognition. Many considerations in the project environment influence what kind of rewards are available—project budget, development methodology, company policies, autonomy of the project manager, and more. Motivation varies from individual to individual and can change over time, both across a team member's career and over the span of a single project. These models can be used to tailor motivators to individual team members and the project context, and they can even help effectively engage stakeholders as follow-up to the stakeholder engagement matrix. Motivation models help plan strategies, develop the team, and execute project work in alignment with project goals.

The model of **hygiene and motivational factors** describes motivators and demotivators that influence job satisfaction in a work setting. **Motivational factors** have to do with the work being performed and include growth and accomplishment. For example, a project team member could be motivated by the chance to develop and practice new skills, by being recognized for achieving a professional goal through the project, or by advancing to a new role. People are satisfied when there are sufficient motivational factors in their work, and dissatisfied when there are not enough. **Hygiene factors** are the conditions of the work context making up the employee/employer relationship. They include policies, benefits, salaries, and the physical setting. Hygiene factors are a necessary foundation for job satisfaction and cause dissatisfaction when lacking, but they are not sufficient in and of themselves to elicit satisfaction. Team members would be unhappy if salaries were low and their work environment was not conducive to quality work, whereas addressing these issues in combination with considering motivational factors would set up the team for efficient, high-quality deliverables. This model encourages leaders to consider motivational and hygiene factors separately and to remember that hygiene factors are necessary but not sufficient for a highly motivated team.

Another model is Daniel Pink's **intrinsic vs. extrinsic motivation**. **Intrinsic motivation** originates inside an individual or has to do with enjoying the content or nature of the work itself. **Extrinsic motivation** is an external reward, such as financial compensation. Pink observed that extrinsic motivators only work to a certain point, similar to how hygiene factors are not fully sufficient for job satisfaction. Once an employee feels they are being paid fairly for their work, intrinsic motivators are more effective. They are also better incentives for complex or challenging tasks. Pink described three categories of intrinsic motivators:

- **Autonomy**: self-determination or self-direction. Autonomous work allows individuals to decide the "where, when, and how" of their work. Remote work, flexible hours, and self-organizing teams are examples.
- **Mastery**: achieving excellence, hitting goals, and continuous learning. Mastering a new code library during the project is an example.
- **Purpose**: wanting to make a difference. Understanding how work contributes to the project vision. Knowing that the project will make a tangible difference in end users' lives is an example.

Another way of categorizing motivations is David McClelland's **Theory of Needs**. McClelland identified the needs of achievement, power, and affiliation as key reasons for performing work. An individual's culture, background, and experiences influence which need is most prominent, and they can change over time.

- **Achievement**: Someone inspired by achievement wants to excel and do work that is both challenging and doable.
- **Power**: Someone motivated by power gravitates to leadership tasks, organizing roles, and more responsibility.
- **Affiliation**: Someone driven by affiliation wants to feel a sense of belonging. They want to be accepted by the team.

Finally, **Theory X, Theory Y, and Theory Z** describe a spectrum of motivation; and, more prescriptively than the other models, these theories identify the accompanying management style that is most appropriate. These models can help project managers tailor their leadership approach to individuals.

- **Theory X**: One end of the spectrum has individuals who are motivated by financial gain, with little ambition or desire for growth. These employees are best managed in a top-down, involved, directive style, which is frequently used in organizations with high levels of bureaucracy or labor-intensive work such as factories.
- **Theory Y**: The other end of the spectrum represents individuals who are intrinsically motivated by their work and calls for coaching and supporting strategies that encourage creativity and innovation. This is more frequently found in creative or knowledge production fields.
- **Theory Z**: Two versions of Theory Z were developed. Abraham Maslow's theory identified transcendent motivators—self-actualization, deeper meaning, and insights. Workers with these motivations are best managed in an approach that fosters such values and growth. Meanwhile, William Ouchi's interpretation focuses on a lifelong job at a company that values employee and family well-being, boosting morale and satisfaction. It derives from a Japanese management style that cultivates a familial, participatory organizational culture.

Change Models

Projects inherently drive change as they aim to deliver value in an organization, moving from the current state to a desired state. This future desired state might be creating a new product or service, modifying an existing system, improving efficiency, or moving the needle on organizational culture. Change management is an integral part of project management, and change models offer a structured approach to helping individuals, groups, and institutions adapt. When the models are tailored to the project situation, they can foster empathy, help avoid individual or organizational change fatigue (too much change in too little time), and support stakeholders through the transformation from current to desired state. When project managers adeptly handle change, they foster adaptability and resiliency, leading to project outcomes that are sustainable and integrated into the fabric of the organization.

The framework laid out in the PMI guideline *Managing Change in Organizations: A Practice Guide* draws from a number of change models to create an overarching approach for **managing change in organizations**. The model is meant to be used iteratively, with feedback gathered at every stage and steps revisited as needed.

- **Formulate change**: Establish the reason(s) for change. Leaders cultivate understanding and buy-in, letting people know the benefits of the transition. A shared vision of the future state is one of the most important elements of managing change.
- **Plan change**: Delineate the actions needed to effect change, including methodology, stakeholder engagement, and sustainability. Set participant expectations for what will happen.
- **Implement change**: Cyclical activities of functionality demonstration, checking the effectiveness and results, and adapting as needed. This iterative element is similar to a continuous improvement approach and reflects the Plan, Do, Check, Act (PDCA) method of problem-solving.
- **Manage transition**: As the future state is reached, project managers monitor the impacts and respond to needs, concerns, or problems that arise during the transition. Outputs are incorporated into everyday operations, and adoption rate and other results are measured.
- **Sustain change**: Closing out the change process, the project manager plans for and establishes continuity of the project results. They continue communication and measure benefits realization to quantify the impact of the change. If the project outcomes replace previous behaviors or processes, they ensure that those activities stop and are succeeded by the new state.

Another model addressing organizational change is John Kotter's **8-Step Process for Leading Change**. This framework focuses on scenarios where the change is conceptualized and implemented in a top-down, directive manner, which is most common in organizations with many levels of management.

- **Step 1: Create Urgency**. Identify the need for change by communicating the opportunities and threats motivating it. This could be pulled from a SWOT (strengths, weaknesses, opportunities, threats) analysis or other risk analysis exercise.
- **Step 2: Form a powerful coalition.** The next step is to identify and engage "change leaders." These people may or may not be leaders according to the organizational chart; they have influence in the organization and have diverse roles, knowledge bases, and political or social capital. This team will be vital for successfully guiding and implementing change.
- **Step 3: Create a vision for change**. The transition is more likely to succeed if the values and mission are clear. At this stage, the leader creates a vision statement and a strategic plan for implementing it.
- **Step 4: Communicate the vision**. This step is revisited throughout the entire process, as frequent and tailored communication is key to project success. The coalition maintains consistent messaging around the urgency, benefits, and vision developed earlier. The vision is shared with and applied to the entire organization as appropriate.

- **Step 5: Remove obstacles**. This step is also iterated as needed. Barriers to change must be dealt with through problem-solving and risk management techniques. Examples of impediments include organizational structure that hinders positive change, outmoded workflows, and individual resistance to change.
- **Step 6: Create short-term wins**. The leader wants to create quick and easy wins to grow buy-in and support. Tangible, visible accomplishments in the change process will keep momentum going throughout the organization. An example is gaining measurable efficiencies from using a new process or improving customer satisfaction.
- **Step 7: Build on the change**. Turning to longer-term goals after the short-term wins, the organization and leadership must sustain the change.
- **Step 8: Anchor the changes in corporate culture**. The changes must integrate into corporate culture to be successful in the long term. Leaders should continue to cultivate the coalition, ensure the vision and its outcomes are communicated to employees, and recognize or award individuals for their contribution or alignment. If the change becomes institutionalized, it will be an integral part of the organization going forward.

A similar paradigm is the **ADKAR Model**, a series of five steps elaborated by Jeff Hiatt. Rather than addressing organizational change, this model represents an individual's experience of change. Project managers can use the model to effectively engage internal and external stakeholders and coach them through their change experience.

- **Step 1: Awareness.** A person becomes aware of the impending change and the rationale behind it. For example, this could be a formal announcement, an informational session, or a kickoff meeting.
- **Step 2: Desire**. For change to be successful, the participants must desire to support the change and its intended outcomes. The project's value, benefits, and deliverables are emphasized.
- **Step 3: Knowledge**. Individuals are equipped with knowledge about implementation. They learn new workflows, systems, and responsibilities the project is bringing. This could be group training and dissemination of documentation on how to use a new operating system or software.
- **Step 4: Ability**. This step moves from theory to practice as people begin to live out the change. People begin practicing with new ways of working and have access to support as needed.
- **Step 5: Reinforcement**. The final step addresses the longevity of the change. Offering rewards and recognition, gathering feedback, and measuring success factors such as adoption rate or efficiency gains help solidify the change and integrate it into usual practice.

The **Virginia Satir Change Model** also describes how people tend to deal with change. This six-step model tracks the feelings, perspectives, and performance of individuals progressing through change stages. It is helpful for team leaders managing change and can also assist team members in self-awareness and effectively coping with change.

- **Late status quo.** The first stage of change is also known as "business as usual." The work environment is familiar and expected. Depending on the individual, this may be perceived as boring and rote, while others enjoy the predictability. Change leaders must have solid communication channels at this stage to begin communicating the change.

- **The foreign element.** An element of change is introduced, such as workflows or processes. This phase can include resistance, minimization, or avoidance towards the change and will likely include an accompanying decline in productivity. Project managers can use empathy to connect with how team members are feeling.
- **Chaos.** As the change takes effect, a level of unpredictability ensues as people respond differently to the discomfort of transition. Normal feelings and actions include anxiety, withdrawal, and anticipation. People may experiment with new ways of working to see what works best and foster creativity.
- **The transforming idea.** The individual is able to make sense of and organize their experience with a unifying or transforming idea. They begin to improve work performance with new ways of coping and moving through the change.
- **Practice and integration.** As new behaviors are adopted, productivity improves and likely exceeds previous levels. This stage may iterate through some trial and error as people determine the best approach, and employees will still need support to navigate it.
- **New status quo.** Similar to Kotter's final step, the change is integrated into everyday life. The newfound stability becomes the new normal.

Finally, the **Transition Model** developed by William Bridges delineates the psychological process individuals go through during organizational change. Unlike previously discussed models, this one presents change and transition as two distinct concepts with separate definitions. According to PMI, change is external to the individual and happens regardless of how they adapt, as with the introduction of a new strategy or process, or an alteration in leadership. Transition, on the other hand, is the psychological process of accepting and adapting to the new situation. The phases of the Bridges Transition Model are as follows:

- **Ending, losing, and letting go**. When faced with change, individuals frequently experience a range of emotions including fear, denial, anger, uncertainty, or resistance. They realize what they will lose and need to leave behind with the transition.
- **The neutral zone**. As the organization undergoes change, feelings may shift to frustration, resentment, or confusion. This stage may also elicit creativity and innovation as coping mechanisms, fostering new ideas. This stage is associated with lower productivity as employees adjust. They have left behind the old situation but not fully integrated into the new.
- **The new beginning**. Finally, as people master new ways of working, the change is accepted and celebrated. Individuals welcome the growth, development, and excitement that accompany change.

Complexity Models

Projects operate in a system of interdependent domains and circumstances, with multiple moving parts both internal and external to the project. Interactions and inputs come from individuals, organizations, technologies, and other factors. While the previous change models are useful for helping teams successfully plan, execute, and integrate change, complexity models help project managers handle the inevitable changes that were not planned or cannot be planned. These models provide a framework for dealing with uncertainty and managing risk. They can help facilitate Agile decisions and may impact the development approach, planning, work execution, and delivery.

The **Cynefin framework** was developed by Dave Snowden to characterize situations by cause-and-effect relationships and to guide decision-making processes. Snowden described five problem contexts that may be encountered:

- **Cause-and-effect**: These events have a clear cause/effect relationship. When the cause of an incident is obvious, best practices should be followed for making decisions.
- **Complicated relationships**: If there are "known unknowns" or a spectrum of possible right answers, decision-makers should gather facts, analyze the situation, and use good practices to inform their responses. These steps are also known as sense, analyze, and respond.
- **Complex relationships**: Where there are "unknown unknowns," no obvious cause/effect, and no clear correct answers, the Cynefin framework offers an approach of probing, sensing, and responding. These steps should be repeated as the environment changes.
- **Chaotic environments**: Cause and effects are unknown, and time does not allow for long information-gathering. Crisis management is the first priority. Decision-makers should act to stabilize the situation, sense the effectiveness, and respond iteratively to manage the situation down to a complex environment.
- **Disordered relationships**: These situations are so complicated that they must be decomposed into smaller pieces that can be labeled as one of the previous categories.

The **Stacey Matrix** takes similar themes and maps out the complexity of a project along two dimensions. On one axis is the uncertainty of requirements, and along the other is the uncertainty of technology used to complete the deliverables. Projects may be categorized as simple, complicated, complex, or chaotic. A project's complexity is an important factor in selecting the development approach and other tailoring considerations.

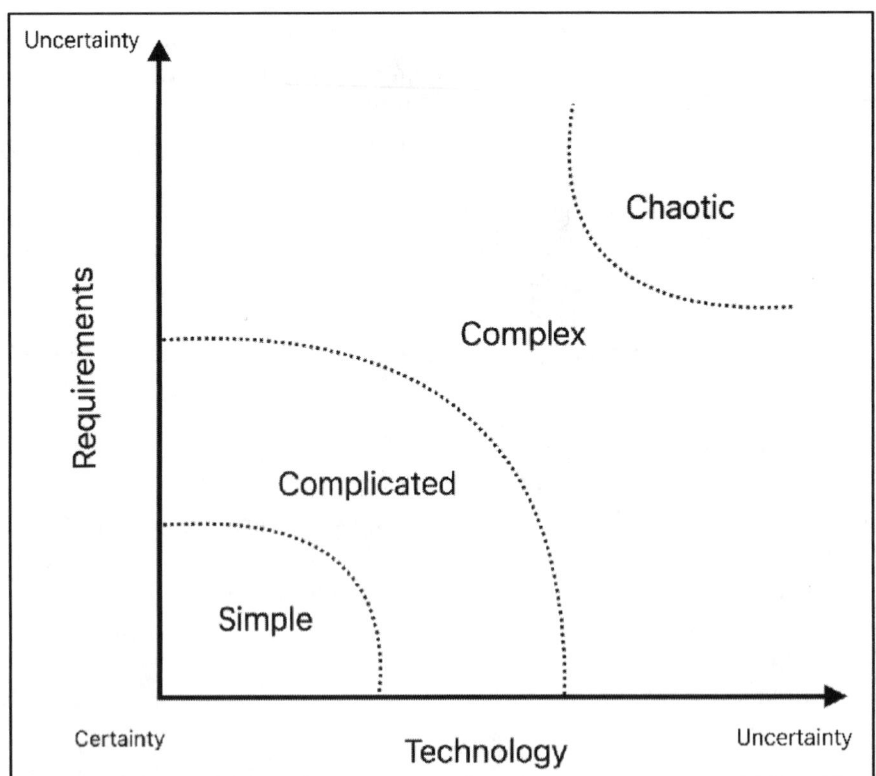

Other Models

These additional models are useful for a range of the project performance domains, covering people skills such as conflict management, negotiation, and stakeholder salience, as well as planning and process groups.

The skill of conflict resolution is extremely important for project success. Conflict is frequently encountered on projects and is not inherently negative; if handled well, it can result in increased trust and commitment among team members. A free flow of ideas without fear of negative conflict fosters innovative solutions. But when conflict is handled poorly, it leads to diminished trust, satisfaction, and morale. The conflict model developed by Ken Thomas and Ralph Kilmann identifies six ways of resolving conflict. The approaches differ in the balance of power among the people involved and in the need to keep a good relationship.

- **Confronting/problem-solving**. This approach views the conflict as a problem to solve—the team members are against the problem rather than against each other. Confronting is used when maintaining relationships is a high priority and when the parties trust in each other's problem-solving skills. A project team may take this approach when a conflict of opinions comes up, working together to address the issue.
- **Collaborating**. Collaborating focuses on learning and understanding the various perspectives on the disagreement. This approach may take some time but is worth it when the people involved trust each other. A project manager may serve as facilitator in a team disagreement to ensure that everyone's point of view is heard and a consensus is reached.
- **Compromising**. When there is no way for all participants to get what they want, compromise is the best approach for resolution. This involves everyone giving something up while getting some of what they want. It is frequently used when participants have the same amount of power. For example, a project manager may work with another project manager to find compromise when a conflict arises over limited organizational resources.
- **Smoothing/accommodating**. This technique is helpful when preserving the relationship and prioritizing the project goals are paramount. It is frequently used when there is a power differential between parties. As an example, in a dispute with the project sponsor, the project manager will likely accommodate the sponsor's wishes to preserve goodwill and keep their support. The conflict is downplayed and smoothed over.
- **Forcing**. Sometimes, in the interest of time, a less-than-optimal approach to resolving conflict is necessary. The person with more authority is able to force their choice on the team. For example, this style may be necessary when a critical deadline is approaching that risks derailing the project, or a health and safety violation has occurred.
- **Withdrawal/avoiding**. Sometimes a problem does not need to be directly addressed—it will resolve on its own, or it is not worth confronting. Other times, if a conflict is too intense, the parties involved need a chance to cool off. In any of these cases, withdrawing or yielding may be the best route. For example, in the case of regulatory bodies or government requirements, compliance is the best option.

Another important interpersonal skill for project management is negotiation. Stephen Covey identified the principle of "Think Win-Win," describing the possible outcomes of a negotiation:

- **Win-win**. The best outcome for negotiation, when each side is happy with the results.
- **Win-lose/lose-win**. The negotiation is more of a competition, and a win for one person is a loss for the other. It includes the case when someone gives up their position and lets the other win.
- **Lose-lose**. The worst possible outcome, everyone loses in the negotiation. This may be caused by a zero-sum mentality and overly competitive outlook.

Covey further described three characteristics that often lead to a win-win situation: **character**, or the maturity of the participants and willingness to see abundance rather than scarcity; **trust**, or accountability between parties; and **approach**, or ability and willingness to empathize with another perspective. Similar to the problem-solving and collaborating of conflict resolution, the negotiating individuals find options that are acceptable to all and meet their ultimate objectives.

The **Salience Model** is used to identify and describe project stakeholders based on three variables: **power** or influence, **legitimacy** of the stakeholder's claim to the project, and **urgency** of their role in the project. This model is helpful in stakeholder analysis and engagement, and in identifying the most salient, or prominent, stakeholders to engage during the project. The stakeholders who are high in all three areas are the most critical, while the model's rank of other individuals will determine their relative importance. The model was created by Ronald K. Mitchell, Bradley R. Agle, and Donna J. Wood.

Other models are applicable to planning and project administration. A helpful model in planning for risk management is that developed by **Barry Boehm**, describing the effort and time to plan. While up-front planning can reduce uncertainty, unanticipated events, or duplicate work, the planning is not without a cost. Too much planning can delay the project, push back the return on investment, lose market share, or fail to address changes that have happened in the interim. At some point, additional planning produces diminishing returns or can even be detrimental to the project. The "**sweet spot**" or optimal planning varies by the project and its context, so planning must be tailored to the specific project.

Finally, the **process groups** are a way of conceptualizing the processes that go into project management. Each group contains similar inputs, outputs, tools, and techniques, and the output of one process can often serve as the input for another. The five groups are general enough to apply regardless of development approach, industry, or functional area of the organization. It should be noted that the process groups are *not* project phases. Rather, they can be used and iterated as needed in each project phase as tailored to the project. According to PMI, the process groups are as follows:

- **Initiating**. These processes kick off a new project or phase when the project manager is permitted to do so.
- **Planning**. The planning processes define the project scope and objectives and plan how to meet project requirements.
- **Executing**. These processes carry out the work that has been planned.
- **Monitoring and Controlling**. These processes track, analyze, and respond to project performance. As the project progresses, metrics are used to determine and manage if changes are required to stay on target.
- **Closing**. The closing processes formally finish out a project, phase, or contract.

Models Applied Across Performance Domains

The following table suggests which methods are particularly useful for each performance domain. The appropriate methods should be determined by the project manager and team based on the delivery approach, project deliverables, organizational requirements, and application domain.

Method	Performance Domain							
	Team	Stake holde	Dev Appr	Plann ing	Proje ct	Deliv ery	Meas urem	Unce rtaint
Situational Leadership Models:								
Situational Leadership II	X				X			
OSCAR	X				X			
Communication Models:								
Cross-cultural communication	X	X		X	X			
Effectiveness of comm. channels	X	X		X	X			
Gulf of execution and evaluation		X				X		
Motivation Models:								
Hygiene and motivation factors	X			X	X			
Intrinsic vs extrinsic motivation	X			X	X			
Theory of needs	X			X	X			
Theories X, Y, and Z	X			X	X			
Change Models:								
Managing change in organizations		X		X	X			
ADKAR		X		X	X			
8-step process for leading change		X		X	X			
Transition		X		X	X			
Complexity Models:								
Cynefin framework			X	X	X	X		X
Stacey matrix			X	X	X	X		X
Project Team Development Models:								
Tuckman ladder	X				X			
Drexler/Sibbet team performance	X				X			
Other Models:								
Conflict	X	X			X			
Negotiation		X		X	X	X		
Planning			X	X	X			
Process groups				X	X	X	X	
Salience		X		X	X			

Commonly Used Methods

According to PMI, a method is a means for achieving an outcome, output, or deliverable. While models previously discussed help conceptualize a scenario, methods provide ways of getting project work done. These brief descriptions of commonly used methods are non-exhaustive and exclude methods that are either so general as to apply across many disciplines, or specific to certain industries.

Data Gathering and Analysis

This category of methods is used to gather and evaluate information. The results may be used as input for various artifacts and are often used to aid decision-making.

Alternatives analysis. This method identifies and assesses the options available in a given situation. It can be used when deciding an approach to take, as when determining project scope or responding to a quality control issue. By identifying the likely results, pros, and cons, one can select the best alternative.

Assumption and constraint analysis. Assumption and constraint analysis clearly lays out the parameters a project is working within to ensure they are consistently applied in planning and documented in something like an assumptions log. PMI defines an assumption as a factor considered to be true, real, or certain without proof or demonstration, while a constraint is a limiting factor impacting the execution of a process, project, program, or portfolio. This kind of analysis is especially useful in the beginning stages of the project, when making time and resource estimates or creating schedules and work breakdown structures.

Benchmarking. Benchmarking compares an organization's processes or products against those of similar organizations to see how they measure up. A project manager might also benchmark one project against another. Benchmarking can be used to gather best practices, generate baselines, and plan for improving current practices or starting new ones. It is especially useful at the outset for project planning and setting expectations.

Business justification analysis methods. These methods provide the rationale for authorizing projects or choices. They are frequently incorporated into the business case and other documents for proposing a project to the sponsor and initiating a project. They are also valuable for tracking project finances and ensuring the project is performing as expected. According to PMI, the definitions are as follows:

Payback period. This is the time needed to recover an investment, often measured in months or years.

Internal rate of return (IRR). The IRR is a project investment's predicted annual yield. The formula includes initial and ongoing costs to forecast the percentage growth rate. The higher a project's IRR, the more value it returns, and the more desirable it is to undertake.

Return on investment (ROI). This is the percent return on an investment. It is calculated by dividing the expected average of net benefits by the initial cost of the investment.

Net present value (NPV). The NPV is the future value of anticipated benefits, in terms of their value at the time of investment. The formula includes current costs, future costs, benefits, and inflation. It can account for a project with multiple returns, for example incremental deliveries. A positive NPV (over zero) is desirable.

Cost-benefit analysis. This kind of analysis compares the financial benefits of a project to the costs.

Check sheet. Also known as a tally sheet, a check sheet is used to gather and categorize data. The results are input for graphs that summarize the data. Check sheets can be used for documenting the steps of producing deliverables or for performing quality control on newly created items.

Cost of quality. These are all the costs accumulated over a product's lifespan to ensure quality: preventing nonconformance to requirements (for example, quality assurance, training, proper materials and equipment), appraising or testing for conformance (time and work for quality control), and the cost of nonconformance (rework, loss of sales or reputation).

Decision tree analysis. A decision tree visualizes multiple combinations of options that can be taken. It is especially useful when combined with expected monetary value analysis to estimate the financial implications of outcomes. In this example chart, the square represents a decision, the circles represent chance (i.e., the percent chance an outcome will happen), and the triangles represent the final result of the path.

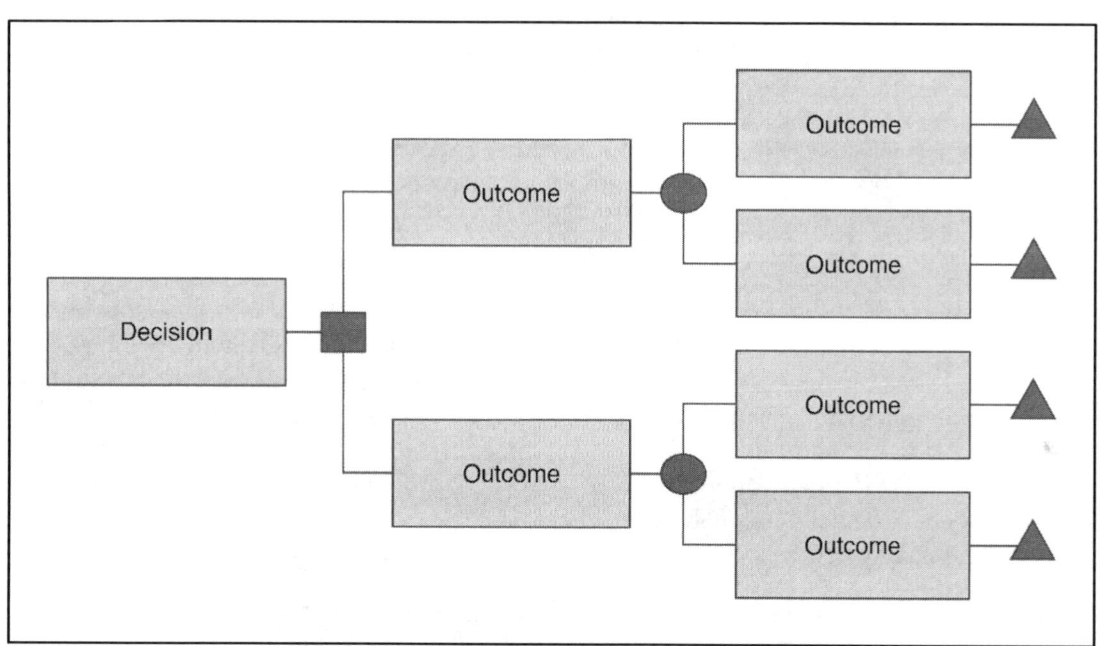

Earned value analysis. Earned value analysis is part of earned value management, which uses a set of formulas to measure project performance based on cost, schedule, and scope. It can be used to evaluate current performance and predict future trends. The **earned value** is the current progress achieved on the project, or what the project is worth. The **planned value** is where the project should be in terms of cost and schedule. The earned value analysis formulas compute indices for cost performance, schedule performance, and to-complete performance (likelihood of coming in at budget) based on variances between the actual performance and the baseline. An index value of 1 or above means the project is at or better than expected performance. For example, a cost performance index (CPI) is calculated by dividing the earned value by the actual cost; a CPI of 1 means the project is on track. But a schedule performance index (SPI) of less than 1, found by dividing the earned value by the planned value, would mean the project is behind schedule. Earned value analysis is extremely useful for catching potential problems early and determining where to course-correct.

Expected monetary value (EMV). Expected monetary value expresses the financial value of an outcome when it is impacted by uncertainty—useful for comparing two very different options or assessing risk. It is computed by multiplying the probability of an event by the economic effect it would have. For example, if a risk such as a storm has an 80% chance of happening and would cost $10,000 in damages to a construction project, the EMV is $8,000. This information is a useful factor for determining whether the budget reserve is sufficient and which risks pose the most financial threat.

Forecast. Forecasts predict an event or outcome in the future based on current information. They may be qualitative, based on opinion and best judgment, or they may be quantitative, using models and past data. Econometric (causal) forecasting uses past relationships among variables to predict future impacts. Forecasts can help a project manager determine whether the project is performing according to schedule or whether some kind of changes in spending, speed or scope of work, etc., need to be made.

Influence diagram. An influence diagram represents a situation's causes, risks, alternatives, and outcomes while depicting the time ordering of events and connections between the variables. It is especially useful for managing risk and planning responses.

Life cycle assessment. This assessment tracks the environmental impact of a service, product, or system by examining all aspects of its production, beginning with the origin of raw materials, moving to processing, transportation, usage, and finally disposal. This type of assessment is particularly important as customer, organizational, and cultural awareness of environmental responsibility rises.

Make-or-buy analysis. This technique compares the costs and benefits of creating a product internally to the price of purchasing it. Make-or-buy analysis begins by identifying product requirements and considers cost, in-house skills, control of the project, and the end result. If the up-front cost of building internally is more expensive than buying from a vendor, but the monthly ongoing costs are less, one can calculate a point at which it would be more economical to make it, or vice versa. This point is found by dividing the difference in up-front costs by the difference in monthly costs. It could be used for evaluating whether to create a custom software program or buy from a vendor, for example.

Probability and impact matrix. A probability and impact matrix displays the probability and potential impact of identified risks on project objectives. It is used for qualitative risk analysis and often utilizes a numerical score or a labeled scale such as RAG (red, amber, green) to rank or group the risks.

Process analysis. Process analysis systematically analyzes and reviews processes, steps, and procedures to identify gaps and areas for improvement. A flowchart or other visual mapping can be used. For example, it could aid a project manager in finding where a breakdown in communication occurred or how to hand off project work between team members more efficiently.

Regression analysis. Regression analysis is a form of econometric forecasting that takes input variables, examines their outputs, and forms mathematical or statistical relationships between them. This technique can identify the most important variables from past data and inform predictions of future performance. It can be useful for making cost estimates and determining which variables may be contributing to outcomes in the project, whether desirable or undesirable.

Reserve analysis. Reserve analysis calculates the amount of risk on a project and whether the schedule and budget reserve (or extra built in) are at an acceptable level. As reserve is utilized for risks during a project, a sufficient amount must be retained for future risk exposure. The sooner reserves are depleted in a project schedule, the higher the danger that it will go off track.

Root cause analysis. This method determines the underlying cause of a variance, defect, or risk. A single root cause may be at the base of multiple issues. When monitoring a project, addressing the root cause and not just the symptoms is key.

Sensitivity analysis. Sensitivity analysis attempts to determine the most impactful project risks or uncertainties. This quantitative risk and financial analysis technique links variations in project outcomes (such as net present value or internal rate of return) to risk variables. A potential output of sensitivity analysis might be a tornado diagram identifying the most impactful risks to the project, helping the project manager decide what to address first.

Simulations. Simulations use models to play out the possible effects of various uncertainties and risk events, often using software tools. For example, Monte Carlo simulations repeat a scenario with variations to create a probability distribution of a range of results and find the most likely outcome.

Stakeholder analysis. This method pulls together quantitative and qualitative data about project stakeholders—whether in a decision-making, management, or customer role—with the goal of identifying which stakeholders should be the most important and influential.

SWOT analysis. This method identifies strengths, weaknesses, opportunities, and threats and can be used to assess organizations, projects, or options.

Trend analysis. Trend analysis uses time series data to identify relationships and predict future results with mathematical models. It assumes that the historical trends will continue into the future and does not identify the causes of the trends. Trend analysis may use lagging indicators, which correlate measures with past experiences (e.g., number of deliverables produced, number of sales) or leading indicators, which indicate likely future behavior (e.g., social media engagement leading to a sale).

Value stream mapping. A lean enterprise technique, value stream mapping diagrams the flow of all information and materials used to create and deliver a product or service. It is a tool for increasing efficiency and eliminating waste.

Variance analysis. This technique identifies the amount of difference between a project's baseline and actual performance and seeks to identify the causes. It may be used as a part of earned value management. Cost variance is the difference between earned value and actual cost, while schedule variance is found by subtracting the planned value from earned value.

What-if scenario analysis. What-if scenario analysis compares predicted outcomes of different scenarios to determine their impact on the project.

ESTIMATING

Estimating methods allow a project manager to approximate the amount of work, time, or cost needed for a project, deliverable, or process. Different methods are appropriate for different situations, including the type of method (quantitative, relative, or qualitative), the development approach, and the level of accuracy required. Estimates may be made during the initial project planning and iteratively revised.

Affinity grouping. This method groups items into categories or classifications based on perceived similarities. Some common techniques are T-shirt sizing (grouping by XS, S, M, L, XL) and Fibonacci numbers. The size/number assigned could stand in for effort, time, or another measure.

Analogous estimating. Analogous estimating bases approximations of cost or time on past data for similar activities. If there is pertinent historical data available, this technique can be valuable, but for projects with high levels of uncertainty and innovation—such as those suited to an adaptive approach—other approaches are more appropriate.

Function point. Often used in software development, this is a unit of measurement for the business functionality of an information system. One point is assigned to a discrete function offered to the user, for example an input screen, prompt, or report. Calculating a functional size measurement (FSM) of a software system can help plan the project work at a high level.

Multipoint estimating. Also known as three-point estimating, this method can be used to combine estimates when there is a high level of uncertainty. A triangular distribution takes the average of optimistic, most likely, and pessimistic estimates, formulated as $E = \frac{(O+ML+P)}{3}$ where E=estimate, O=optimistic, ML=most likely, and P=pessimistic. The Program Evaluation and Review Technique (PERT) uses a weighted distribution prioritizing the most likely value, with the formula of $E = \frac{(O+4ML+P)}{6}$.

Parametric estimating. Parametric estimating makes use of past data and project parameters as input for software algorithms to generate estimates. This technique may produce deterministic or probabilistic results. It is accurate and reliable but requires a large amount of historical data. Parametric estimating is especially useful in industries with well-documented precedents and information and measurements that scale easily, such as construction.

Relative estimating. Relative estimating is based on comparisons rather than absolute units such as dollars or hours. Comparisons may be with similar work in other projects or a previous phase of the same project. Relative estimating is frequently used in change-driven or adaptive approaches. It is easy and often collaborative to implement, but it is not appropriate for highly complex tasks or estimates requiring a high level of detail.

Single-point estimating. This technique uses past information to generate a best-guess number. Single-point estimating is contrasted to methods that produce an approximate range.

Story point estimating. Frequently used in adaptive environments, story points represent the level of effort and can be used to estimate work needed to complete a user story, or work that can be done in a sprint or cycle. For example, a team might know they can complete 25 points per sprint and take on stories totaling that number. Story points take the complexity and uncertainty of a task into account.

Wideband Delphi. Wideband Delphi is a technique to achieve an estimation consensus. Subject matter experts come up with estimates individually, then discuss them together with the project team. The individuals who created the highest and lowest estimates explain why, then everyone redoes their estimate. The process is repeated until the group reaches a consensus. A well-known variation of Wideband Delphi is called planning poker.

MEETINGS AND EVENTS

The following are different kinds of meetings that are important for project management. Some are most commonly used in adaptive environments, while others are more generic. Meetings are vital for project communications and for engaging team members and stakeholders.

Backlog refinement. At this meeting, the product owner works with the team to prioritize or reprioritize and refine items for the upcoming iteration. Backlog refinement is an example of progressive elaboration, or incrementally planning from high-level to more specific as information becomes available.

Bidder conference. Also known as a contractor conference, vendor conference, or pre-bid conference, this involves meeting with prospective vendors to share details of a procurement prior to their submitting a proposal. This kind of meeting is important for project procurement.

Change control board. The stakeholders who are responsible for approving changes to the project meet to review change requests and approve, delay, or deny them. Decisions are documented in a change log and shared with the appropriate people.

Daily standup. In this meeting, also known as a daily scrum, the project team briefly answers three questions round-robin: What did I complete since the last standup? What am I planning to complete before the next one? What are my impediments or obstacles?

Iteration planning. An iteration planning or sprint planning meeting involves discussing the details of user stories (backlog items) and acceptance criteria (definition of done) to be used for an upcoming iteration.

Iteration review. At the end of an iteration, the project team and product owner meet with stakeholders to review what has been completed at the iteration or sprint review. The customer can see any demos and request changes for the next iteration/sprint.

Kickoff. A kickoff meeting brings together the project team and key stakeholders to begin a project, phase, or iteration. It involves setting expectations and establishing a common understanding of the project goals.

Lessons learned meeting. This type of meeting takes place at the end of a project, phase, or iteration to discuss knowledge learned and find ways to improve. Team members and stakeholders discuss what went well to incorporate into best practices, as well as what could be done better next time. The information might be included in an organizational knowledge repository if available.

Planning meeting. A planning meeting takes place to create or revisit project plans and ensure commitment from stakeholders. A planning meeting can be used for any component of the project, for example planning risk management or product releases.

Project closeout. At the project closeout meeting, the project sponsor or product owner gives their final acceptance of the deliverables, finalizing the product delivery.

Project review. At the end of a phase, a review meeting discusses what has been completed, as well as any variances, and decides whether to move to the next phase or redo the phase, perhaps with modifications. At the end of a project, the review meeting determines if the project is ready to transition to operations.

Release planning. At a release planning meeting, the project team decides the initial roadmap for release and determines the schedule for releasing increments of value, a deliverable, or the full product.

Retrospective. A kind of lessons learned meeting used especially in Agile environments, the retrospective encourages participants to explore the results of an iteration to find ways of improving processes and deliverables.

Risk review. Risk review meetings are held regularly to assess existing known risks, identifying if they are still active or if their probability, urgency, or expected impact have changed. The planned risk responses are reviewed for effectiveness. New risks are also analyzed and documented.

Status meeting. At regularly scheduled intervals, the project team meets to share information about project performance. The frequency of status meetings is usually determined in the communications management plan.

Steering committee. At a steering committee meeting, top-level stakeholders meet to ensure the project is moving in the right direction and make any decisions that are beyond the project team's authority to make.

Other Methods

These methods do not belong to a particular category but are useful for planning, completing work, and measuring results.

Impact mapping. Frequently used during product development in Agile environments, impact mapping visualizes product strategy and is a way to analyze the impact of decisions and features on the product roadmap and on customers. It is most effective when applied early on in planning.

Modeling. Models are simplified depictions of a system or deliverable and are helpful for identifying gaps and potential problems. Examples include prototypes and diagrams. They might be used for designing a physical product or for tracking user journeys through a software application.

Net Promoter Score (NPS). Net Promoter Score is a means of measuring customer satisfaction and loyalty. It is measured as an index from −100 to 100 based on how likely a customer is to recommend a product or service. By measuring before and after, the results might tell a project team if a change to a product achieved the outcome of improved customer satisfaction.

Prioritization schema. Prioritization schemas are useful for ranking and prioritizing a variety of project elements such as requirements, risks, features, or other project components. There are many schemas available; some common ones include multicriteria analysis, the MoSCoW method (must have, should have, could have, won't have), and the Kano model. The Kano model graphs implementation priority (must-have/basics, performance enhancements, and delighters) against customer satisfaction.

Timebox. A timebox is a short, set time period within which to work. Examples include a two-week or month-long sprint, spending 8 hours to plan for a month-long sprint, or 15 minutes for the daily scrum.

Methods Applied Across Performance Domains

The following tables suggest which methods are particularly useful for each performance domain. The appropriate methods should be determined by the project manager and team based on the delivery approach, project deliverables, organizational requirements, and application domain.

Method	Performance Domain							
	Team	Stake holde	Dev Appr	Plann ing	Proje ct	Deliv ery	Meas urem	Unce rtaint
Data Gathering and Analysis Methods:								
Alternatives analysis				X	X	X		X
Assumptions and constraints analysis				X		X		X
Benchmarking						X	X	
Business justification analysis				X			X	
Payback period			X	X			X	
Internal rate of return				X			X	
Return on investment				X			X	
Net present value			X	X		X	X	
Cost-benefit ratio				X			X	
Check sheet						X	X	
Cost of quality				X		X	X	
Decision tree analysis				X				
Earned value analysis				X			X	
Expected monetary value				X				
Forecasting							X	
Influence diagram				X				
Life cycle assessment				X				
Make-or-buy analysis				X	X			
Probability and impact matrix				X				X
Process analysis				X	X	X	X	
Regression analysis				X			X	
Root cause analysis					X	X		
Sensitivity analysis				X	X	X		
Simulation				X			X	
Stakeholder analysis		X		X	X			
SWOT analysis				X				X
Trend analysis							X	
Value stream mapping				X	X	X		
Variance analysis							X	
What-if scenario analysis				X				X

Method	Performance Domain							
	Team	Stakeholde	Dev Approach	Planning	Project	Delivery	Measurem	Uncertaint
Estimating Methods:								
Affinity grouping				X				
Analogous estimating				X				
Function points				X				
Multipoint estimating				X				
Parametric estimating				X				
Relative estimating				X				
Single-point estimating				X				
Story point estimating				X				
Wideband Delphi				X				
Meeting and Event Methods:								
Backlog refinement		X		X	X	X		
Bidder conference		X		X	X			
Change control board					X	X		
Daily standup				X	X			
Iteration review		X			X	X		
Iteration planning		X		X	X	X		
Kickoff	X	X			X			
Lessons learned		X		X	X	X		
Planning				X				
Project closeout	X	X			X			
Project review		X			X	X	X	
Release planning		X		X				
Retrospective	X			X				
Risk review					X			X
Status					X		X	
Steering committee		X			X			
Other Methods:								
Impact mapping	X	X		X		X	X	
Modeling						X		
Net Promoter Score®		X					X	
Prioritization schema		X			X			
Timebox			X	X	X	X	X	

Commonly Used Artifacts

PMI defines an artifact as a template, document, output, or project deliverable. The artifacts described below are frequently used in different domains of project management; the list excludes artifacts that are very generic or overly specific, and those that result from specific methods described previously, such as cost estimates. These artifacts should always be tailored to the development approach and project environment.

Strategy Artifacts

These documents contain strategic and business-related information about a project and are usually high-level. They are used to convey project purpose, direction, and benefits and are frequently useful to stakeholders and sponsor(s). Strategy artifacts are created at the beginning of the project and usually do not change. They can help make the case for a project to be sponsored by the organization and guide project planning.

Business case. The business case lays out the value proposition of a project, or the value that it will deliver to customers or other stakeholders. It describes the financial benefits as well as other tangible and intangible outcomes should the project be approved.

Business model canvas. Frequently used in lean start-ups, a business model canvas is a concise document (often one page) that summarizes the project's value proposition, users, infrastructure resources, and finances. It often uses visualizations to convey information.

Project brief. Similar to the business model canvas, a project brief describes the project's goals, processes, and expected deliverables. It can be used to make the case for the project.

Project charter. A project charter authorizes a project and gives the project manager official authority to use the organization's resources for the project. It is issued by the project sponsor.

Project vision statement. The project vision statement concisely conveys the project's purpose and provides inspiration and direction for the project team. It can be used to evaluate periodically that the team is aligned with project goals.

Roadmap. The roadmap is a document that gives a bird's-eye view of the project, including milestones, reviews, decision points (also known as phase gates), and other important events.

Logs and Registers

While strategy artifacts are usually static, logs are updated continuously as circumstances in and surrounding the project change. Also known as registers, logs dynamically document and track specific aspects of a project.

Assumption log. PMI defines an assumption as a factor considered to be true, real, or certain, without proof or demonstration, while a constraint limits the options for managing projects, programs, portfolios, or processes. An assumption log records assumptions and constraints in the project, for example those that underlie estimates or decisions, and is updated as information emerges or factors change.

Backlog. A backlog is a list of the work to be done in the project, ordered by priority. A backlog may be created for a product, requirements, impediments, or other components. In projects that use Scrum or other Agile frameworks, the product backlog is composed of user stories and is pulled from to plan work for the next iteration.

Change log. The change log lists all the change requests submitted and their status (e.g., accepted, rejected, delayed, needs modifications). Any change to deliverables, project management plans, or other documentation must be requested through a formal process and recorded in the log.

Issue log. An issue log documents any situation that could impact the completion of project objectives. In contrast to risk, an issue is a situation or event that has actually happened. The log identifies and tracks issues and lists the person responsible for monitoring and resolving them.

Lessons learned register. This document is updated with knowledge acquired over the course of the project or phase in order to share knowledge with the team and organization. Lessons learned can be applied to improve work performance for the duration of the project and for future projects, especially if added to the organizational process assets (OPA).

Risk-adjusted backlog. This version of a backlog includes activities that address risks to the project, whether threats (negative risk) or opportunities (positive risk). For example, there might be a task for coding a module as a backup if a suitable external library is not found. The backlog might also include risk-based spikes, or a short, intensive activity to investigate and mitigate a risk.

Risk register. The results of risk management activities and processes are documented in the risk register. The log includes the risk probability, impact, scores, and planned response, as well as the party responsible for managing it. The risk register documents risks that individually or cumulatively could impact the project.

Stakeholder register. A stakeholder register lists the project stakeholders, the results of stakeholder assessment, and any other relevant information. The stakeholder register could document current and desired attitudes toward the project and planned steps to garner support.

Plans

As project teams or the project manager decide how to accomplish project objectives, they formalize these plans in documents that address various components of the project. These plans may be combined into a comprehensive project management plan. A plan may be a written document or a visualization and is often available online in a central location.

Change control plan. The change control plan identifies members of the change control board, delineates the board's authority, and lays out the change control process to ensure changes to the project plan go through the authorized means. Changes to any part of the project management plan must go through the formal process.

Communications management plan. This plan defines what information to share with whom, what method to use, who is responsible, and when. A communications management plan can be applied at the project, program, or portfolio level. It can apply to internal and external communications, as well as documenting how communications are archived and accessed.

Cost management plan. The cost management plan describes the planning, estimation, structure, and control of costs of a project or program. It delineates the acceptable level of precision and control thresholds, or at what amount of variance action is warranted.

Iteration plan. These are the goals and plan for the current sprint or iteration, developed in a timebox at the start of each sprint.

Procurement management plan. This plan details how products or services will be purchased outside the organization for use in a project or program, including reporting, scheduling, metrics, and vendor selection.

Project management plan. The project management plan describes how all aspects of the project will be administered, including execution, monitoring, controlling, and closing.

Quality management plan. The quality management plan describes how product quality will be monitored and controlled, how methodologies and metrics will be used, and how the applicable policies will be administered in a project or program.

Release plan. A release plan describes the features or results that will be produced over multiple iterations and the expected timeline. This is commonly used in software development projects.

Requirements management plan. This plan delineates how project or program requirements will be evaluated, documented, prioritized, measured, and managed. Requirements management is handled differently in a waterfall/traditional approach, where requirements are generally fixed, versus in an Agile environment, where requirements may be variable.

Resource management plan. The resource management plan describes how the project's resources—whether human or physical—are acquired and managed. It may address the types of contracts to be used, roles and responsibilities, and resource calendars.

Risk management plan. This plan identifies how risk management activities will be carried out, including how risks are identified, analyzed, and addressed. For some projects, these activities largely fall under integrated risk management at the program or portfolio level and are determined by senior management.

Scope management plan. The scope management plan defines how project scope is developed, monitored (as compared to the baseline), controlled, and validated or formally accepted.

Schedule management plan. This plan describes how project or program schedules are developed, monitored, and controlled. It defines the units of measurement, level of accuracy, metrics, and control thresholds.

Stakeholder engagement plan. This plan delineates activities and approaches to cultivate positive and productive stakeholder involvement throughout the project.

Test plan. The test plan describes any tests that will be applied to deliverables, such as unit testing, so that formal and verifiable testing procedures are documented.

Hierarchy Charts

Hierarchy charts are visual representations illustrating the relationships and ranks among different levels or layers of data. The most general topics are presented at the top, providing increasingly specific details as the chart descends. These charts are regularly updated and expanded upon as the project progresses and more information becomes available.

Organizational breakdown structure. Similar to a traditional organizational chart, this chart represents the organizational units involved in a project and the activities (work packages) they are responsible for, including execution and approvals.

Product breakdown structure. The product breakdown structure represents the components of a product, their function, and deliverables.

Resource breakdown structure. This chart depicts resources needed in a project by category and type and is useful for identifying constraints and gaps in planning.

Risk breakdown structure. The risk breakdown structure represents possible risks to the project. It can be organized by project phase or goal and is used to categorize risks.

Work breakdown structure (WBS). This chart decomposes the scope of work into work packages to visualize the scope and help create the scope baseline. It is accompanied by a WBS dictionary to identify and define terms.

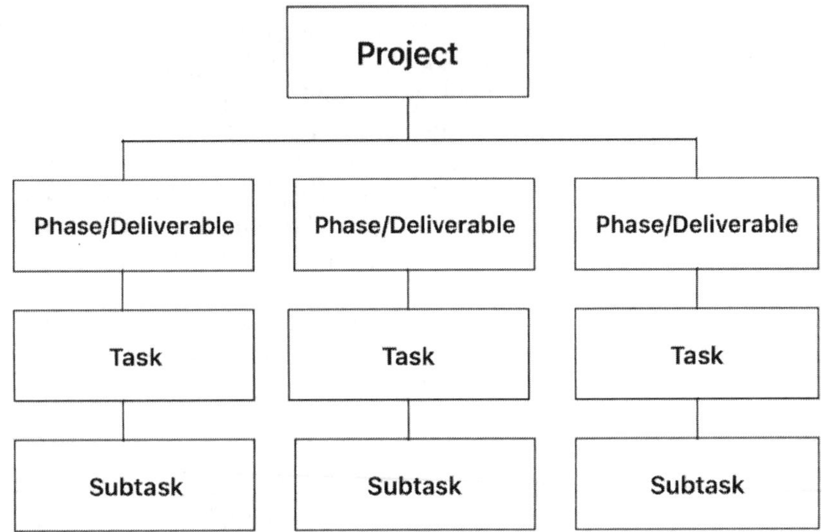

Baselines

PMI defines a baseline as the approved version of a work product or plan. Once an item is baselined, change control is required to update it. Baselines provide the basis from which to compare planned vs. actual performance and expose variances that need to be addressed.

Budget. The budget is an official estimated cost for a full project or a component.

Milestone schedule. A milestone schedule lists important project events and their anticipated dates.

Performance measurement baseline. This baseline integrates scope, schedule, and cost baselines to manage and analyze project activities. Earned value analysis uses this baseline to measure variance and make predictions about performance.

Project schedule. The project schedule models planned activities, dates, and durations, and can include milestones and required resources. The schedule is input for network diagrams to visualize project work.

Scope baseline. This baseline incorporates the approved scope statement, work breakdown structure (WBS), and WBS dictionary, and is the baseline from which to compare performance.

Visual Data and Information

Visualization artifacts condense and present data that has been collected and analyzed in a way that is easier to digest and interpret as meaningful, actionable information. These artifacts may be included in reports and communications and are input for decision-making. Examples include graphs, charts, matrices, and diagrams.

Affinity diagram. Frequently used in brainstorming and solution generation, an affinity diagram groups many ideas into clusters to review and analyze them.

Burndown/burnup chart. Often used in Agile projects, these artifacts chart either the work remaining or the work completed in an iteration or on a deliverable.

A burndown chart graphs work (measured in units such as story points or effort) versus time.

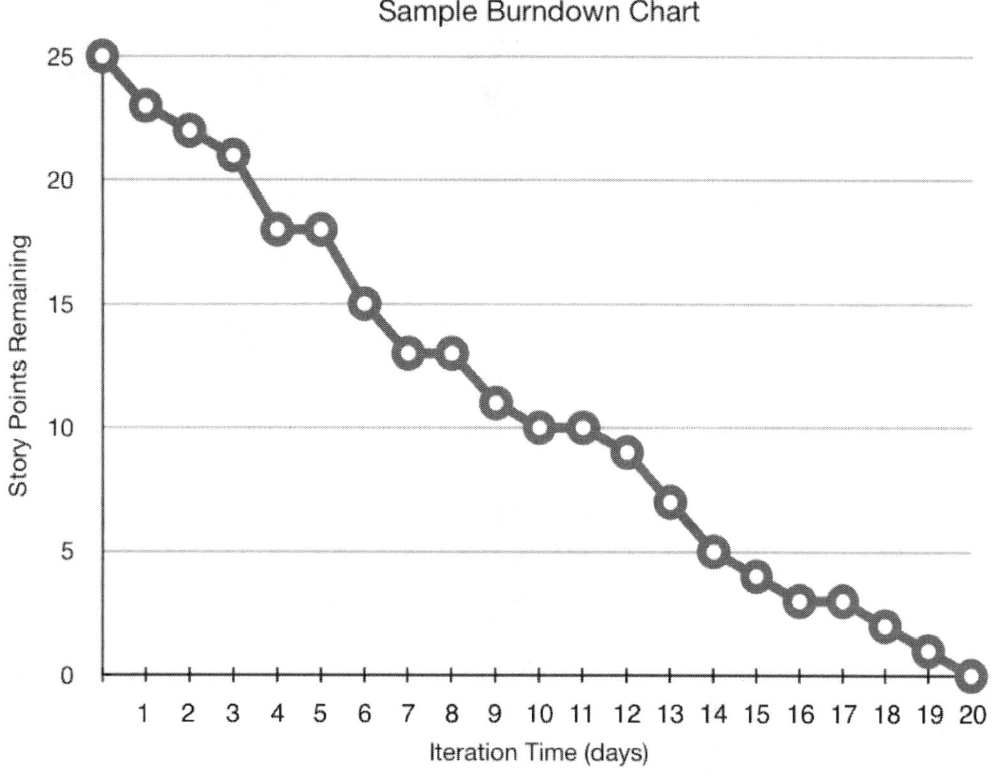

A burnup chart graphs the work completed against time, and often includes the total work planned, which may change over the course of the project via approved change requests.

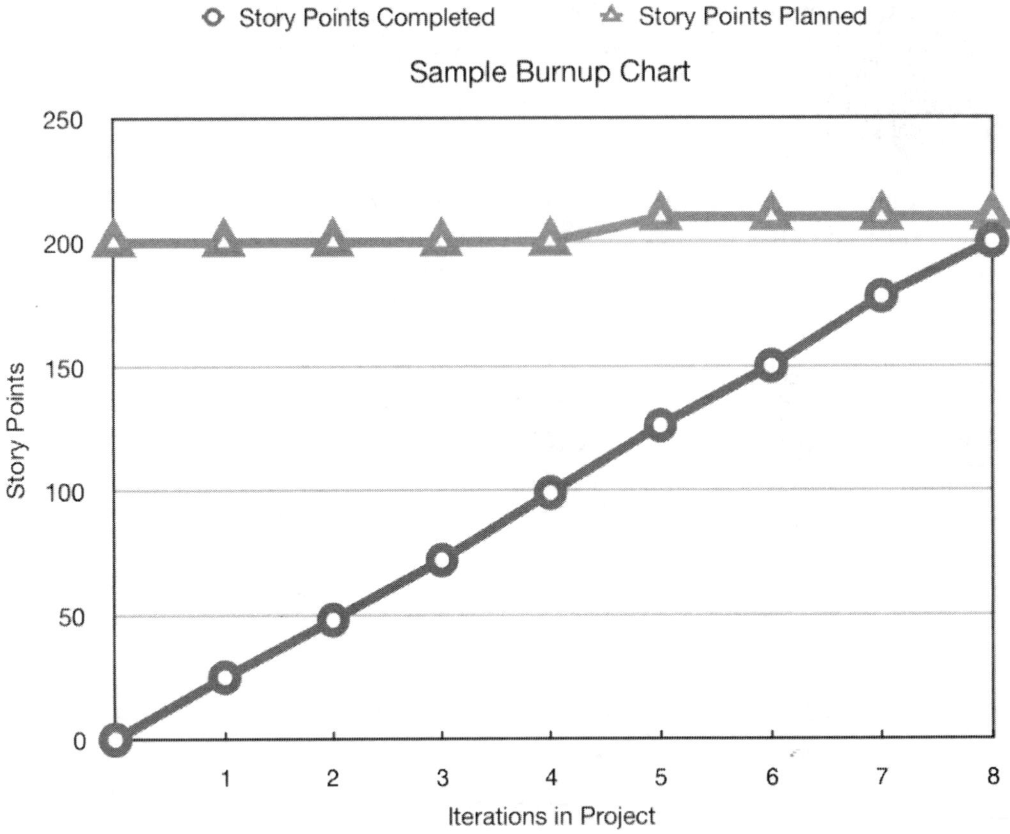

Cause-and-effect diagram. This kind of diagram is used to find the root cause of issues in the project.

Cumulative flow diagram (CFD). This diagram tracks features in various workflow states over time and can show throughput, cycle time, and bottlenecks. At a minimum, the diagram charts tasks completed, in development, and in the backlog; some charts also include more work-in-progress states like design, quality assurance, and testing. In the example below, the lines represent the backlog, tasks in development, tasks in testing, and tasks completed.

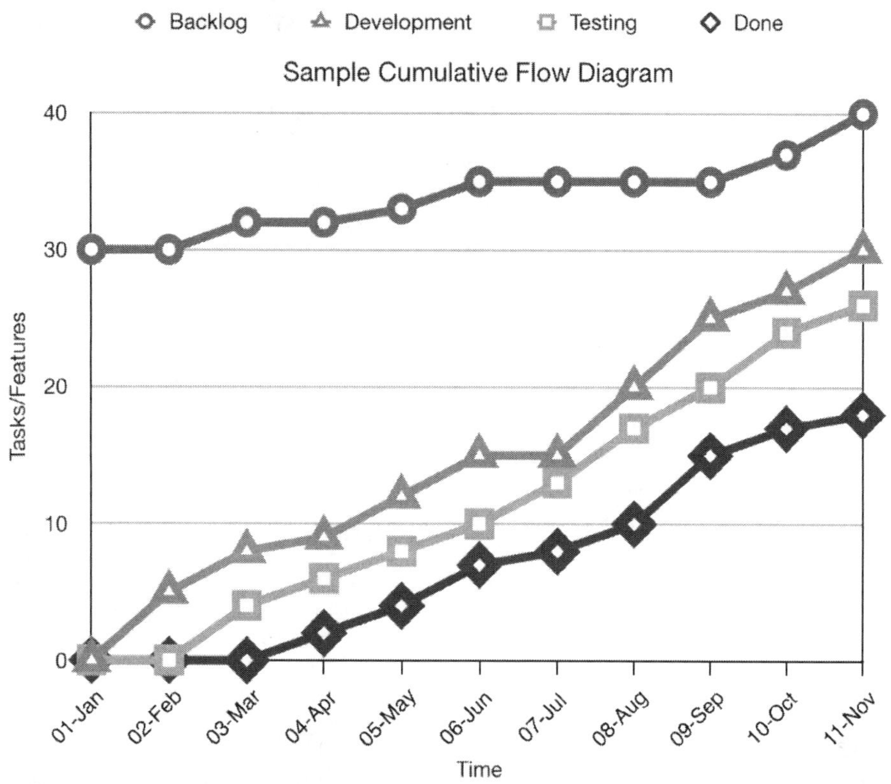

Cycle time chart. A cycle time chart displays the average time it takes to complete a task or produce an item over time, usually as a bar chart or scatter graph.

Dashboards. A dashboard provides real-time or regularly updated information about various measures of progress on the project to gauge performance overall or in specific areas.

Flowchart. Flowcharts diagram system and/or workflow processes, mapping the journey from input, through the various activities within the process, to the final output.

Gantt chart. Used for visualizing schedules, this chart graphs project activities on the *y*-axis against dates on the *x*-axis. Activity durations are depicted as bars on the graph.

Histogram. A histogram is a type of bar chart depicting the frequency of numerical data.

Information radiator. Similar to dashboards, information radiators are visual displays of project progress such as features delivered, responsibility assignment, threats, and current iteration information. They are commonly tactile in nature, made with physical material rather than digital, and easily accessible for organizational information-sharing.

Lead time chart. This chart depicts the time as a bar chart or scatter graph from the order of a product through shipping, including production.

Prioritization matrix. Useful for grouping items by importance, this matrix shows effort on the *x*-axis and value on the *y*-axis.

Project schedule network diagram. This visualization of project workflows shows the relationships among work activities. Activities are represented in boxes or nodes and connected to related items, most commonly using the precedence diagramming method, which shows dependencies (predecessors and successors). This example shows the critical path, or the longest path of activities, and the amount of float or time the activity can be delayed. All numbers represent days of the project.

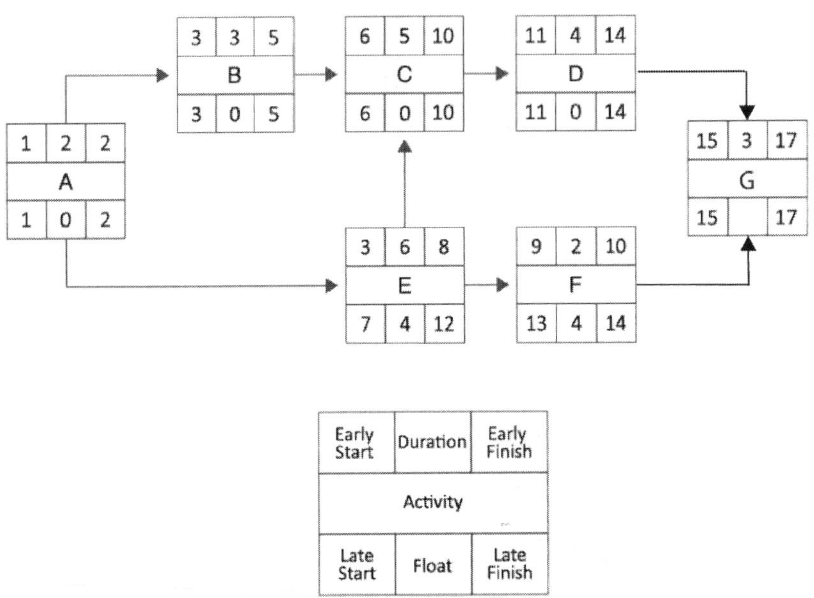

Requirements traceability matrix. This artifact tracks the origin and implementation of requirements throughout the entirety of the project. Each requirement should be linked with a deliverable to ensure that all requirements and project objectives are addressed.

Responsibility assignment matrix (RAM). This matrix displays the resources associated with each work package; an example is a RACI chart, which shows which role(s) are responsible, accountable, consulted, or informed of project activities or outcomes.

Scatter diagram. A scatter diagram graphs the relationship between variables to determine correlation, typically with the independent variable on the horizontal axis and the dependent variable on the vertical axis.

S-curve. This graph shows the progress of the project, usually as cumulative costs, over time. Costs are expected to accelerate towards the middle of the project and level off near closing; the graph can help identify issues if it does not match the expected curve.

Stakeholder engagement assessment matrix. A tool for stakeholder engagement, this matrix displays the actual and desired involvement, with statuses such as unaware, resistant, neutral, supportive, and leading.

Story map. A story map visualizes the full functionality of the product under development, providing a high-level view of the product and how the features fit together.

Throughput chart. Shown as a scatter diagram or a bar chart, this graph shows accepted deliverables over time and can reveal trends in the flow of work completion.

Use case. A use case describes or shows how a user interacts with a system and what they can achieve.

Value stream map. A lean enterprise technique, a value stream map demonstrates the flow of all information and materials used to create and deliver a product or service. It is a tool for increasing efficiency and eliminating waste.

Velocity chart. Frequently used in Agile projects, this chart shows the speed at which the team can move deliverables through production, validation, and acceptance, often measured in story points. Teams aim for a steady, sustainable velocity and can calculate the expected completion time when velocity is known.

Reports

Condensing data into meaningful information, reports communicate important project information like status and summaries to stakeholders such as sponsors, business owners, leadership, and PMOs. Reports may be archived as part of information management processes.

Quality report. A quality report includes quality management issues, analyses of quality management activities such as audits, and recommendations for corrective actions and process or product improvements.

Risk report. Updated periodically throughout the project, risk reports document the status of identified risks and overall project risk exposure.

Status report. Status reports document the current state in areas such as cost, schedule, and deliverables, what has been completed since the last report, and performance forecasts.

Agreements and Contracts

Agreements are documented communications that specify the intended obligations and actions for participants in the agreement. Project agreements are often formalized as contracts, which legally bind the seller to provide the identified product or service and the buyer to pay for it. Contracts may be signed by someone with higher authority in the organization if the project manager is not authorized to do so. Having contracts in place is a means of managing risk, as there is legal recourse should the terms and conditions be breached. Some of the most common types of contracts are described below.

Fixed-price contracts. These contracts set a fixed price for a well-specified result. In these contracts, the seller, rather than the buyer, carries the risk of overruns. Common variations include firm fixed price (FFP); fixed-price incentive fee (FPIF), which includes an incentive for performance; and fixed price with economic price adjustment (FP-EPA), which adjusts for inflation or cost changes over a long period of time.

Cost-reimbursable contracts. Under these contracts, the seller is paid the cost of work plus a fee. They are used when the scope is variable or not clearly defined up front. The buyer risks paying overruns. Kinds include cost plus fixed fee (CPFF), cost plus award fee (CPAF) based on buyer satisfaction, and cost plus incentive fee (CPIF) based on performance.

Time and materials (T&M). This contract sets a fixed rate (such as an hourly fee) plus materials, not to exceed a certain amount. The statement of work is not specified in the contract, making it useful for temporarily adding staff or subject matter expertise to the project.

Indefinite delivery indefinite quantity (IDIQ). This contract offers an undefined amount of goods or services within set limits, in a set period of time. It can be used in engineering, architectural, or IT projects, for example.

Other agreements. Some additional types of agreements common in project management are the memorandum of understanding (MOU), memorandum of agreement (MOA), service-level agreement (SLA), and basic ordering agreement (BOA).

Other Artifacts

These miscellaneous artifacts address other project purposes that are not covered in previous categories.

Activity list. The activity list breaks down scheduled activities and provides a description, scope of work, and unique identifier. It may include relationships to other parts of the project, lead and/or lag time, resources, and constraints. The purpose is to give the project team a good understanding of the work to be performed.

Bid documents. These documents solicit proposals from prospective vendors for project resources. While the bid documents vary based on the goods or services, industry, and organizational requirements, the following are typical documents sent from buyer to seller:

Request for information (RFI)—request for preliminary or further information

Request for proposal (RFP)—request for a proposed solution

Request for quote (RFQ)—request for a detailed specification and price quote

Metrics. Metrics are attributes that can be quantified and measured to track process performance. For example: rate of task completion, projected finish date, number of defects, or projected final cost.

Project calendar. The project calendar lists working days and shifts during which project activities may take place.

Requirements documentation. This document contains product requirements and other details about them, such as priority, acceptance criteria, category, and other information.

Project team charter. The charter is a social contract that documents team values, working agreements, ground rules, team norms, and other expectations. It fosters team cohesion and communication.

User story. According to PMI, this is a brief description of an outcome for a specific user, which is a promise of conversation to clarify details. It describes the ideal functionality from the customer perspective, answering the "who" and "why" with details discussed in person. User stories are often formulated as follows: "As a (role), I want (functionality) so that (business benefit)," or "Given (the scenario), when (the action), then (the result)." Effective user stories are independent, negotiable, valuable, estimable, small, and testable (abbreviated with the acronym INVEST).

ARTIFACTS APPLIED ACROSS PERFORMANCE DOMAINS

The following tables suggests which artifacts are particularly useful in each performance domain. The appropriate artifacts vary from project to project and should be determined by the project manager and team based on the delivery approach, deliverables, organizational requirements, and application domain or industry.

Artifact	Performance Domain							
	Team	**Stake holde**	**Dev Appr**	**Plann ing**	**Proje ct**	**Deliv ery**	**Meas urem**	**Unce rtaint**
Strategy Artifacts:								
Business case		X		X				
Project brief		X		X				
Project charter		X		X				
Project vision statement		X		X				
Roadmap		X	X	X				
Log and Register Artifacts:								
Assumption log				X	X	X		X
Backlog				X	X	X		
Change log					X	X		
Issue log					X			
Lessons learned register					X			
Risk-adjusted backlog				X				X
Risk register				X	X	X		X
Stakeholder register		X		X				
Plan Artifacts:								
Change control plan				X	X	X		
Communications management plan		X		X	X			
Cost management plan				X				
Iteration plan				X				
Procurement management plan				X	X			
Project management plan		X		X	X			
Quality management plan				X	X	X		
Release plan				X		X		
Requirements management plan				X		X		
Resource management plan				X	X			
Risk management plan				X	X			X
Scope management plan				X		X		
Schedule management plan				X	X	X		
Stakeholder management plan		X		X				
Test plan				X	X	X	X	

Artifact	Performance Domain							
	Team	Stake holde	Dev Appr	Plann ing	Proje ct	Deliv ery	Meas urem	Unce rtaint
Hierarchy Chart Artifacts:								
Organizational breakdown structure	X	X		X				
Product breakdown structure				X		X		
Resource breakdown structure	X			X	X		X	
Risk breakdown structure					X			X
Work breakdown structure				X		X	X	
Baseline Artifacts:								
Budget				X	X		X	
Milestone schedule			X	X	X		X	
Performance measurement baseline				X	X	X	X	
Project schedule				X	X		X	
Scope baseline				X	X	X	X	
Visual Data and Info Artifacts:								
Affinity diagram				X	X			
Burn chart				X		X	X	
Cause-and-effect diagram					X	X		X
Cycle time chart						X	X	
Cumulative flow diagram						X	X	
Dashboard					X		X	
Flow chart				X	X	X		
Gantt chart				X	X		X	
Histogram							X	
Information radiator					X		X	
Lead time chart						X	X	
Prioritization matrix		X			X	X		
Project schedule network diagram				X	X			
Requirements traceability matrix				X		X	X	
Responsibility assignment matrix				X	X			
Scatter diagram					X	X	X	
S-curve				X			X	
Stakeholder engagement assessment		X		X	X			
Story map				X		X		
Throughput chart						X	X	
Use case				X		X		
Value stream map					X	X	X	
Velocity chart						X	X	

Artifact	Performance Domain							
	Team	Stake holde	Dev Appr	Plann ing	Proje ct	Deliv ery	Meas urem	Unce rtaint
Report Artifacts:								
Quality report					X	X	X	
Risk report					X			X
Status report					X			
Agreements and Contracts:								

Artifact	Performance Domain							
	Team	Stake holde	Dev Appr	Plann ing	Proje ct	Deliv ery	Meas urem	Unce rtaint
Fixed-price		X		X	X	X	X	X
Cost-reimbursable		X		X	X	X	X	X
Time and materials		X		X	X	X	X	X
Indefinite time, indefinite quantity		X		X	X	X	X	X
Other agreements		X		X	X	X	X	X
Other Artifacts:								
Activity list	X	X		X	X			
Bid documents		X		X	X			
Metrics				X		X	X	
Project calendars	X			X	X			
Requirements documentation		X		X		X	X	
Project team charter	X				X			
User story		X		X		X		

PMP Exam Tips

Many of your questions will consist of a multi-sentence scenario that will provide some clues, but not all, related to a project—the agent of action, the type of project approach (predictive, hybrid, or Agile), and indicators of a project status or problem. Sometimes additional information will be included that has no bearing on the question. The question will almost always reside in the last sentence of the scenario paragraph.

The exam is long, with little time to spare for even the strongest of readers. For each question, we urge you to **look at the actual question first by reading just the last sentence in the scenario. Then scan the answer choices *before* you read the scenario from the beginning**. Knowing the question and category of answer you're looking for will trigger the appropriate schema in your brain before you begin reading. You will read more efficiently by focusing on the appropriate scenario clues. This will also reduce the number of times you will need to read the scenario, reduce overall brain and eye fatigue, and help you maintain mental stamina for the duration of the exam.

A handful of questions will ask you to recall a single term or theory. The majority of questions will ask you to select the best PMI-sanctioned answer out of at least three reasonable answer choices that are commonly utilized in the real world.

Common question formats:

- All of these are true about managing (*X stakeholders*) except which answer?
- Which of these statements about the (*X process*) is not false?
- Which of these are principles of the (*X theory*) of project management? (Select THREE.)
- What is the correct sequence of actions the project manager should take during this process?
- The stakeholder is demonstrating which effect of the (*X theory*) of development?
- Why did the stakeholder act in this manner?
- Which response is the stakeholder least likely to make?

Understand the "When"

Most of the simple term-recall answer choices for the PMP exam will be associated with Agile projects. The predictive and hybrid project questions, nearly 80% of the exam, will ask you to select the best course of action or list of attributes from among a series of subjective answer choices. Each answer choice could be arguably "correct." Save yourself the headache of having to do a mental coin toss among two to three sound answer choices on 180 questions by **understanding "when" you are in the question scenario process**. A thorough understanding of the Knowledge Area ITTOs (inputs, tools, techniques, and outputs), as well as the 5 project phases and 4 project tailoring steps, will help you find the PMI-preferred answer quickly.

Some questions will simply ask which process the project manager is currently in, or which output is being created in the scenario based on key inputs and techniques specific to one Knowledge Area. For example, if the project manager is conducting a final review of a product to affirm that all of the product features and quality requirements have been achieved based on the scope, this indicates the Control Quality process. However, if the project manager is presenting a verified product to the project sponsor so the organization representative can confirm that scope has been met for the product, this indicates the Validate Scope process. You would need to differentiate between the two processes based on the inputs, tools, techniques, and outputs as "when" cues. More often than not, however, the question scenario will challenge the test-taker's higher-level thinking skills by including only obscure allusions to a Knowledge Area or process in the question scenario. You will need to utilize inferencing to determine "when" the related activity is taking place, "why" a problem has occurred, "what" tools, plans, or techniques are involved, and "how" to apply or determine the correct, PMI-approved resolution.

Another common question scenario will include complaints from stakeholders—they didn't receive a report, they feel they have been misinformed, they are unsatisfied with the product, or they are concerned because their suggestions aren't appearing in the project prototypes. They are disrupting your project schedule via calling, emailing, or verbally protesting; on the surface, it appears to be a communication problem. However, you must conduct a root cause analysis to find out what caused the issues the stakeholders are complaining about. **How could you have avoided the complaint to begin with? *When* during the project did the problem originate?** If the exam question does not directly ask which specific process was ill-performed, the question will ask what the project manager "should do," "should have done," "should do *first*," or "should do *next*."

What should the project manager **do first**? Or what would you **do next**? These are very common question setups on the exam. PMI is testing your process sequence knowledge here. Look for answer choices similar to the following—and always in this order—when you encounter a "do first" or a "do next" question. Always:

- Review plan and project documents to confirm, verify, or understand before anything else.
- Conduct a root cause analysis to understand the source of the problem.
- Meet with the scenario stakeholder, preferably face-to-face, to discuss and try to understand the problem.

Another variation of this frequent type of question is, "What **should** the project manager **do**?" (Note, there's no "first" or "next" on this "should do" question.) This is a "best approach" versus a procedural question. Therefore, consider the order of events already included in the scenario, whether explicitly stated or implied by nature of the "when" of the related process and procedural step, then determine the answer choice based on "What would PMBOK do?"

Save valuable time on the test:

- Even if you are unsure on a question, mark an answer—any answer—and flag the question for review, then move to the next question. **DO NOT leave questions blank with the intention of coming back to them later; you may run out of time.** Wrong answers won't hurt you, but answers left blank—when time runs out, or because of a technical glitch—are wasted opportunities for accruing points. When you have no idea and are pressed for time, eliminating one or two wrong answers, then making a quick pick of the remaining choices, will improve your lucky-guess odds considerably. Also, the exam is divided into three distinct sections. **You will not be able to go back and review the questions in a section once you move on to the next, so make sure all questions are answered before that one-third of the overall time runs out.** Try to make an answer choice within one minute for each question; time moves faster than you think on the exam, and you may need more seconds on the most challenging questions.

- At the end of the first one-third of the test, and again at the end of the two-thirds mark, you'll be offered an opportunity to take a break. You will have a full 1-minute countdown to decide whether to take a break or keep going before the test clock starts rolling again. Take at least 45 seconds to relax your brain *before* clicking the "take a break" button. Take advantage of that free time to rest. And take a break whether you think you need it or not; the fatigue will compound with interest by the end of the test if you don't give your eyes and brain a break.
- Earned value management (EVM) formulas: Some questions will narrow the calculation or project status decision you'll need to make by focusing on just one EVM formula; these take little time to calculate. However, there will be very few questions on the exam that will require you to **manually** calculate the full range of EVM formulas. That takes considerable time for very little score gain. If manual calculations are not your strong suit, it may be better to make an educated guess based on the clues in the scenario and answer choices. **Mark an answer,** "flag" it for follow-up if time allows at the end of the section, and move on to the next question. The time you will save on three questions will probably allow you to double the correct-answer credits when applied to other questions in the interim.

Things to Keep in Mind When Answering Questions

- It is preferred to choose tools and communication opportunities that are inclusive, face-to-face, and hands-on.
- During meetings, use "low-tech and high-touch" prototypes and information radiators like whiteboards and sticky notes.
- For Agile projects, remove productivity blockers at the administrative level, but let the team solve the problem. Empower the team, allow them time to build skills, find them focused training if needed, and follow up. Do not do the training yourself.
- For Agile projects, Kanban boards are excellent solutions for limiting work in progress when there is too much work to do; for visualizing and resolving confusion during a process; or for addressing bottlenecks in productivity.
- For Agile and hybrid projects, the project manager should train the organization stakeholders on Agile processes. When they resist their Agile project obligations, continue to train, and—if necessary—train again.
- The **product owner prioritizes the backlog—*never*** the team or the project manager. If the product owner refuses to prioritize the backlog, the project manager should continue to educate the product owner on Agile.
- Transparency in project development builds trust. The project manager should endeavor to prevent conflict and rework that can occur due to misunderstandings.
- For answer choices, make sure the **solution addresses the problem** and is always for the **best benefit of the project**. Always follow up afterward.
- For disagreements and misunderstandings, find the **root cause** and come up with a **shared, clear consensus** for a solution.
- Be certain to create opportunities to engage stakeholders in product reviews. **Utilize feedback loops** where the team builds, stakeholders test and review, and then the team improves the build based on stakeholder input.
- For predictive projects, **never allow a change to the plan without an approved change request** according to the PMI integrated change control process (or via the change management plan tailored specifically for the project.) Do your best to **limit the number of changes** needed.
- Aim for win-win scenarios in conflict management and develop contracts that are fair to both parties.

- Emotional intelligence is key to effective communication. 90% of a project manager's job is communication. More than half of what you communicate to others is done nonverbally (including tone of voice).
- Always collaborate to get the issue resolved—don't solve it yourself. Always consult the plan.
- Ensure compliance. The law trumps all. Contracts are void if they include activities that break the law.
- Always **formally close phases and projects**—even if they are cancelled for any reason.
- Update the lessons learned register, the stakeholder register, and the risk register throughout the project.
- Stakeholders are the best people to inform you about their roles and interests. The project team represents the best people to break down work estimates and select tools—they're the subject matter experts.
- The project manager should never make rash decisions. Always review the plan, investigate root causes, discuss problems, and hold stakeholders accountable. Don't immediately go over a stakeholder's head to supervisors and upper-level management without persistent efforts to understand and address the problem one-on-one first. However, for an ethics violation, PMI insists the project manager should ensure laws and policies are never broken, and PMI's core values and principles are never misrepresented.

PMP Practice Test #1

Want to take this practice test in an online interactive format?
Check out the bonus page, which includes interactive practice questions and much more: **mometrix.com/bonus948/pmp**

1. During a product walk-through at the end of a project phase, the customer asks for another color option to be added for future items produced. What steps should the project manager take next?

a. Reference the work breakdown structure for the feature and formally close out the project phase.
b. Check the project scope statement and acceptance criteria for whether these changes are in scope and submit a change request to the change control board.
c. Submit a change request to amend the business case to include the change.
d. Update the assumptions log and the project schedule to reflect the requested change.

2. You have negotiated a cost-plus fixed fee (CPFF) contract on behalf of the organization to procure and install plumbing fixtures in all 350 of the bathrooms in your golf resort project. How can you ensure your seller is not making additional profit in addition to the terms of the agreement?

a. Arrange to pay once all work is complete instead of quarterly installments.
b. Verify the seller is not reducing the scope.
c. Refuse to authorize cost overruns.
d. Monitor all invoices to make sure you are not being charged for extra items.

3. You have been hired to manage the new emergency room addition project for Big City Hospital. The project will double the hospital's current ER capabilities and feature its own on-site laboratory and imaging center. You are currently expanding the stakeholder register to ensure you have identified all currently known stakeholders, including their roles within the organization as well as the ER expansion project. You also need to know their responsibilities on the campus as well as their level of interest or awareness in the project. Who should be considered the BEST source of information for these stakeholder register details?

a. The project sponsor
b. The stakeholders
c. The organization's functional managers
d. The organization's senior management

4. A project team member is particularly outspoken in meetings and does not usually listen to the opinions or feedback of others. What should the project manager do first?

a. Communicate the issue to HR and request to set up a meeting with the team member.
b. Bring up the problem in a status meeting.
c. Request that the team member be replaced with another employee who has the same skill set.
d. Set up a private meeting with the team member to review the team charter, which includes the team values and ground rules set up for team communication.

5. While planning project communication, you are attempting to determine what to communicate to stakeholders and the best method of communication, as well as the proper format, timing, and frequency. Which of these tools or techniques will yield the appropriate output for the Plan Communication process?

a. Communication requirements analysis
b. Stakeholder salience cube
c. Communication preference survey
d. The PMIS

6. While the project manager was managing a new high-rise project, one of the senior contractors notified the project manager of a significant problem with the vertical supports. The project manager utilized a fishbone diagram to discover the root cause of the problem. He then worked with the contractor and structural experts to identify a solution before implementing the solution. Two months later, the contractor notified the project manager that the problem with the vertical supports was still occurring. Which step did the project manager forget to do?

a. He didn't seek sponsor input for the correct solution.
b. He should have used a Pareto chart to identify the problem instead.
c. He should have solicited solution advice from city inspectors prior to implementation.
d. He didn't follow up to confirm that the solution actually solved the problem.

7. Which of the following is an output of formally closing a project?

a. Updates to the assumptions log
b. Updates to the lessons learned register
c. A risk report
d. A quality report

8. A software development team has accumulated technical debt, or reduced code quality, that needs to be cleaned up and standardized through refactoring. Which of the following is a possible cause?

a. The team lacks a clear definition of "done," or the criteria for a deliverable to be considered ready to be used by a customer.
b. The team has too much documentation that is obtuse and difficult to navigate.
c. The defect cycle time—the time between defect discovery and correction—is too long.
d. The project team needs to focus on addressing risk during backlog grooming to develop a risk-adjusted backlog.

9. The project manager is calculating the expected monetary value (EMV) of risks on the risk register to update the probability impact matrix. Which risk has the HIGHEST EMV?

Risk	Probability	Economic Impact	EMV
A	10%	$100,000.00	
B	50%	$50,000.00	
C	20%	$80,000.00	
D	25%	$40,000.00	

a. Risk A
b. Risk B
c. Risk C
d. Risk D

10. A project manager has worked with procurement representatives to prepare a request for proposal (RFP) and host a bidder conference. Now they must analyze and select a seller. The project team evaluates proposals on their technical quality, then invites the selected seller to negotiate the cost of the project. What selection method did the project manager use?

a. Quality-based/highest technical proposal score
b. Fixed budget
c. Sole source
d. Least cost

11. A team leader realizes there is a supply chain issue for some important components that may delay the project. He brings together the team to have a brainstorming session for solutions, welcoming any and all ideas. What factors of high-performing project teams does this situation exemplify? CHOOSE TWO

a. Recognize and reward team members for their work.
b. Encourage open communication.
c. Foster shared ownership.
d. Build shared understanding of project benefits.
e. Mentor team members in cross-functional work to expand their skills.

12. Which of the following is NOT part of the core values of Agile?

a. Customer collaboration
b. Responding to change
c. Contract negotiation
d. Individuals and interactions

13. In an Agile project, the __________________ represents the project requirements from the organization, while the __________________ represents the work to be done during the next cycle of up to four weeks.

a. project scope; product backlog
b. project backlog; sprint backlog
c. sprint backlog; project scope
d. product backlog; sprint backlog

14. All of the following statements related to the WBS are true EXCEPT:

a. The WBS breaks project work down into packages for easier scheduling and cost estimating.
b. The WBS itemizes the project activities to be sequenced and scheduled.
c. All of the required project work is represented in the WBS.
d. The WBS dictionary provides specific details about work package scheduling requirements, staffing, budgeting, and other information.

15. A project team has prototyped a new retail product, but the prototype does not meet the specifications listed in the project requirements. What should be the next step for the project manager?

a. Request that the PMO assign new resources to the project to ensure the next prototype is more successful.
b. Hold a stakeholder meeting to demonstrate the prototype and analyze the root causes of the issues.
c. Inform the project sponsor of both the good and bad project updates in the next status report and record information in the lessons learned register.
d. Meet with the project sponsor to determine whether the product is viable and if changes to the requirements are needed.

16. A project manager is leading a team composed of personnel from various functions across a weak matrix organization. The team has met with frequent delays due to their other assignments and siloed knowledge in business units. What can the project manager do to improve team efficiency and coordination?

a. Coordinate a knowledge share for team members to learn about each other's business units and build cohesion.
b. Meet with the project sponsor and request their assistance in influencing the functional managers.
c. Work with the functional managers to share the project vision and see if they can prioritize the team members' project work.
d. Perform integrated change control and compress the project schedule to adapt to team members' other responsibilities while meeting the project deadline.

17. As the project manager on the Big City Museum project, you are the organization's buyer, entering into an agreement with a vendor to procure lighting installation services. The project sponsor has asked you to push for a contract that is most favorable to the organization. The sponsor wants to make sure the seller will accept responsibility for all errors and damages related to the installation, while also controlling cost over the 18-month period of construction. Which contract type is best for the buyer in this situation?

a. Cost plus fixed price
b. Fixed price
c. Cost plus incentive
d. Time and materials

18. New members of a distributed team are struggling to learn workflows for the project, as different versions of documentation are located in various places. What can the project manager do to support the team?

a. Perform the project integration process to update the communications management plan and the lessons learned register.
b. Consult the OPA for knowledge management templates that can be used.
c. Set up a central online location for project information that the project team can securely access.
d. Plan a virtual knowledge cafe for the project team to share information more effectively.

19. As a project manager, you want to be certain you are minimizing risk and change requests while integrating all project processes to produce required deliverables efficiently. To do so, you are currently conducting a variance analysis as part of aggregating work performance information. You are also initiating change requests for defect repairs. Which process are you in?

a. Control Scope
b. Control Quality
c. Monitor Risks
d. Validate Scope

20. A company is developing an app to make some in-house work more user friendly and is contracting out the creation of the user interface. The vendor has repeatedly produced defective code, and the project manager believes they are in breach of contract. What should the project manager do next?

a. Work with the procurement office and legal counsel to determine whether to pursue legal action against the vendor or what steps to take next.
b. Withhold payment to the vendor until they have corrected issues to the customer's satisfaction.
c. Close out the contract and reissue the request for proposal (RFP) to select a new vendor.
d. Review the procurement documentation to determine the consequences of breach of contract and discuss with the vendor to find a solution.

21. A company is undertaking an Agile project with an experimental—but frequently updated—technology that brings high uncertainty and risk of failure to the project. What is an approach they can take to monitor and manage the risk?

a. Perform a Kano analysis to identify the most impactful threats to the project.
b. Fast-track the project schedule in order to gain float time that can be used if risk events should occur.
c. Perform and update a decision tree analysis as the new technology evolves so that risk response plans are up to date.
d. Groom the backlog to address high-value, high-risk items early and include time to address risks.

22. While working on a project to install maple flooring in the entrance of the new Super Bowling Center in town, you have been given a budget of $5,000. You have completed $1,500 worth of work, and you have spent $3,000. Based on this progress, what do you forecast as the total cost of the project?

a. $7,500
b. $8,000
c. $10,000
d. $12,000

23. A project manager is managing a small theme park project. He is overseeing the process to solicit development ideas and proposals from sellers for uniquely themed conveyance vehicles to transfer patrons to and from the parking lot to the park entrance ticketing center. The project sponsor is unsure what he and the organization are looking for yet, but the organization prides itself on innovation and welcomes a breadth of ideas from potential sellers. The conveyance vehicle designs must enhance the theme of the park and must transport up to 25,000 visitors per day efficiently and in an environmentally conscious manner. The project budget is capped at 3 million dollars. How should the project manager disseminate the requirements information to potential contractors to ensure that no seller receives preferential treatment in this search for creative solutions?

a. Publish source selection criteria and requests for information via relevant trade websites and publications.
b. Host a bidder conference to publish selection criteria and call for requests for information.
c. List a call for requests for information on the organization's website.
d. Push the source selection criteria and a request for information to related engineering and technical departments at all nearby colleges and universities.

24. As a project manager, you agree that dependable employment with opportunities for employee growth will foster better worker productivity, more positive employee morale, and increased company loyalty. You follow which theory?

a. Expectancy Theory
b. Theory X and Y
c. Two-Factor Theory
d. Theory Z

25. While managing a golf resort project, the project manager needs input from stakeholders representing the client member group regarding preferred features for the clubhouse. The project manager decides to use an anonymous survey to seek unbiased and genuine input from client member stakeholders representing a range of levels of membership. The manager is using which tool?

a. A SWOT analysis
b. A Monte Carlo simulation
c. A Delphi technique
d. A stakeholder salience cube

26. A project team is tasked with creating a new variation of a popular retail product. The team plans to create a prototype, then incorporate stakeholder feedback and requested changes into successive versions. What steps can the team take to manage the process?

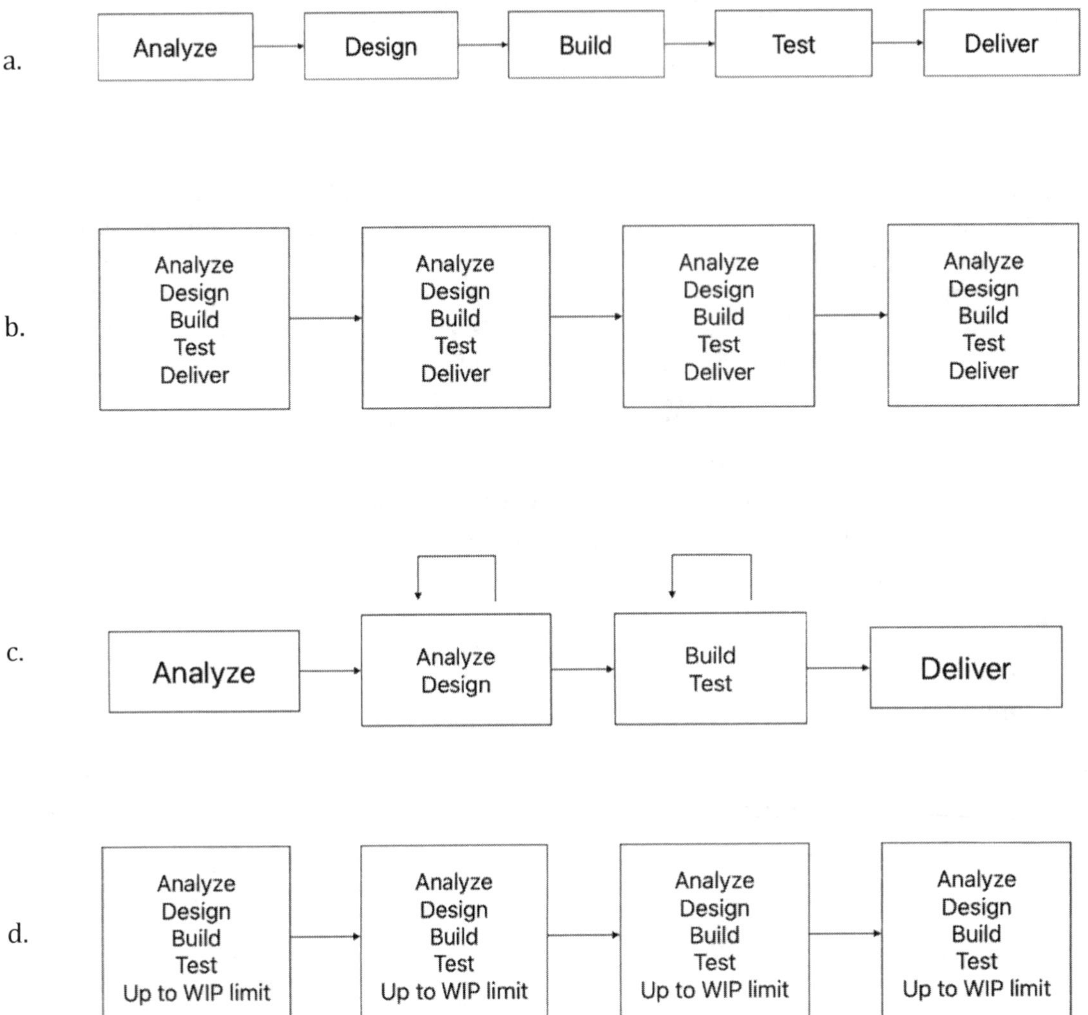

27. W. Edwards Deming advocated quality improvement via which approaches? Select TWO:

a. SWOT analysis
b. Plan-Do-Check-Act
c. Tornado diagrams
d. Attribute sampling
e. TQM

28. An adaptive project has had negative feedback from many users on several successive iteration demos, despite trying to incorporate feedback into the next iteration. The team is gathering input through the monthly demos and the test user surveys in between. What approach can they use to reduce negative feedback and satisfy the customer?

a. Have customers and developers interact more frequently, daily if possible.
b. Identify a champion to promote the product and influence users to a positive perspective.
c. Implement retrospectives more frequently so the team can identify ways of becoming more effective.
d. Ask team members to work overtime in the next iteration to ensure an acceptable deliverable.

29. A colleague is managing a video game project for a start-up company and is in the planning process for quality management. She asks you for advice about the depth and frequency of testing during sprints. Though you are not very familiar with the software development life cycle, you encourage your colleague to investigate and consider testing practices from more established companies in the industry before finalizing the testing processes and frequencies for her own project. You are encouraging her to engage in:

a. Cost-benefit analysis
b. SWOT analysis
c. Benchmark analysis
d. Affinity analysis

30. Where would you find a detailed list of deliverables for a project?

a. Requirements documentation
b. Project charter
c. Scope statement
d. The WBS

31. While working with multiple sponsors and stakeholders on a software project, it is vital to ensure that everyone is evaluating, working with, and discussing the correct version of the software in development, as well as any related software library tools at the same time. Where will you specify the process for tracking and selecting the correct version of the software when needed?

a. The PMIS
b. The configuration management plan
c. The scope management plan
d. The communication management plan

32. A project-based software company is chartering a project sponsored by an external organization. The project will use experimental new technology. What information will be in the project charter? CHOOSE TWO

a. A contract between the seller and buyer defining the terms of agreement
b. Who benefits from the project and how
c. A detailed description of the project scope
d. The acceptance/release criteria for the project
e. How the project requirements will be defined

33. All of the following are outputs of the plan procurement process EXCEPT:

a. Procurement agreements
b. Statement of work
c. Procurement strategy
d. Procurement management plan

34. A project team is working with the product owner to develop user stories for the upcoming iteration. The team has had trouble in the past with stories being significantly more or less effort than they originally estimated. What technique can they use to obtain better estimates of the work needed for each user story?

a. T-shirt sizing (affinity grouping)
b. Parametric estimating
c. Functional size measurement (function points)
d. Sensitivity analysis

35. A company has been growing quickly over the last several years, which has introduced complexity into the projects being undertaken. Some staff members are struggling to keep up with assignments on multiple projects, and a procurement audit has revealed subscriptions to several similar tools by different project managers. What can the company do to successfully adapt to its recent growth?

a. Establish standard decision-making criteria to evaluate new purchases that must be approved by the purchasing department.
b. Set up a project management office (PMO) to centralize and standardize systems, assignments, documentation, and work methodology.
c. Hire more staff so that team members are not multitasking and can focus on a single project at a time.
d. Increase the decision-making authority and discretionary spending budget of project managers to properly resource their projects.

36. During the initialization phase of the Big City Museum Update program, a project manager has helped the sponsor and clients develop business cases for several projects to be considered for inclusion in the overall program. Two projects have emerged as semifinalists. The landscape project will cost $75,000 and will improve the aesthetic appeal of the museum campus, while the holographic T-Rex project will cost $60,000 and create a huge visual impact for visitors. What is the opportunity cost for selecting the landscape project over the T-Rex hologram?

a. $75,000
b. $60,000
c. -$15,000
d. $15,000

37. A Scrum team planned to complete 30 story points in the upcoming iteration. What is a likely interpretation of the burndown chart below?

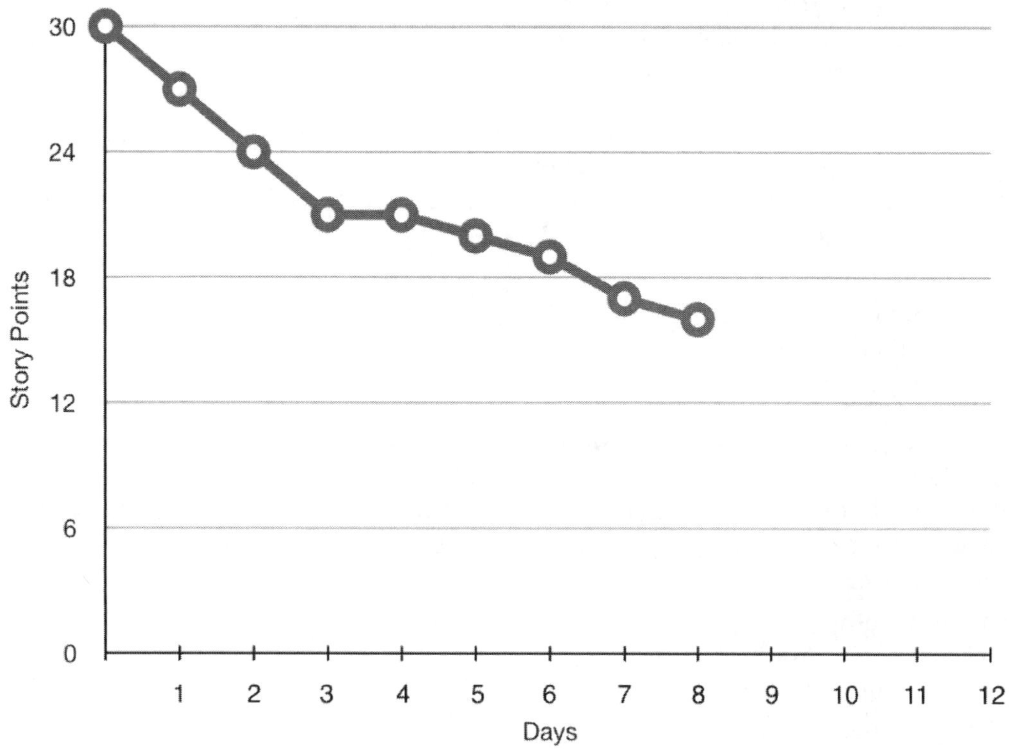

a. The team has entered the performing phase of team development and is on target.
b. After a demo, the customer made some requests, and more features have been added to the backlog.
c. A team member became ill a few days in, and the team has fallen behind.
d. The team's cycle time is getting shorter.

38. The Big City Museum Update is a hybrid project requiring two new structures and an update to an existing structure, as well as a technology infrastructure integration and several software applications.

While monitoring the schedule on the Big City Museum project, the project manager observes that all activities have been scheduled in a logical sequence to be completed within the project parameters. However, the software development projects started five days earlier than originally scheduled; the software development team needed time to complete the application designs before they could begin the actual work of coding. How would you accurately describe the relationship between the start of the coding work and the completion of the design work?

a. Start-to-finish with a five-day lag
b. Start-to-finish with a five-day lead
c. Finish-to-start with a five-day lag
d. Finish-to-start with a five-day lead

39. Your earned value report calculations for your golf resort project yield a CPI of 1.1 and an SPI of 0.8. Which of these statements is true regarding the project?

a. It is under budget and ahead of schedule.
b. It is over budget and ahead of schedule.
c. It is under budget and behind schedule.
d. It is over budget and behind schedule.

40. The project manager has been filled in on the project objectives and vision, has been assigned a project team, and has begun their first iteration. At the end of the iteration, several user stories are incomplete, and some quality defects have been identified. What might the project manager have neglected to do?

a. Risk identification
b. Team assessments
c. Requirements gathering
d. Daily standups

41. A project manager is reviewing the project resource calendar and schedules, and he realizes that a few team members are double-booked on simultaneous activities. He adjusts the activity start and finish dates so that all team members are doing their usual eight hours of work each day and extends the project deadline by two days. What technique did the project manager use?

a. Resource smoothing
b. Resource optimization
c. Resource assignment
d. Resource leveling

42. The market research department at Company A found a niche for a children's toy not widely available on the market. The company chartered a project to design and produce the new product. What strategy can they follow to get a successful product quickly to market?

a. Check the organizational process assets (OPA) repository for the project plans of previously successful products.
b. Perform unit tests on project components to ensure quality on the assembly line.
c. Create a prototype to receive quick feedback from a subset of customers, then work to develop a minimum viable product (MVP).
d. Perform a life-cycle assessment on the product to discern the environmental impact of the process.

43. The organization is undertaking a new project to implement a new digital asset management system and wants to bring on a subject matter expert to advise on system configuration. What kind of contract should the organization use?

a. Time and materials (T&M)
b. Indefinite delivery indefinite quantity (IDIQ)
c. Service-level agreement (SLA)
d. Firm fixed price (FFP)

44. The city of Anytown commissioned a construction project for a new library. The project manager received a phone call from the neighboring town's mayor expressing concerns about the architectural sketches she saw in the newspaper, saying they did not adequately capture the character and culture of the region. The project manager reviewed the stakeholder register and verified that Anytown city council had approved the designs. What steps should he take next?

a. Draft a memorandum of understanding (MOU) between the mayor and the city council.
b. Hold a town hall for residents of the area to provide feedback on the library designs.
c. Update the stakeholder register and stakeholder analysis to include this important stakeholder in future decision-making.
d. Thank the mayor for her opinion, then document and monitor the situation but make no changes to the project plans.

45. An Agile team makes use of acceptance test-driven development by creating acceptance tests before writing the code, ensuring the code is efficient and meets the criteria. What is another practice the team can use to build in quality?

a. Perform continuous integration by frequently incorporating completed work into the whole and retesting.
b. Use impact mapping with the team and product owner to clarify expectations and requirements.
c. Implement a Kanban board to visualize the project workflow and identify where defects are occurring.
d. Incorporate data from the burnup chart to understand team velocity and areas for improvement.

46. An organization is beginning to adopt more Agile project management practices, and the project management office is using the Virginia Satir change model to understand how the organization is experiencing the changes. They have identified the need for more adaptive processes and introduced the use of daily standups and regular retrospectives. Some employees are interested and excited about these practices, but some are anxious about the change, and their overall performance is decreasing. According to the change model, what can the organization expect the next step to be?

a. People will implement and practice the new behaviors using trial and error, and performance will exceed previous levels from before the change was introduced.
b. Employees will stabilize and find a new status quo.
c. The foreign element that disrupts the status quo will be introduced, which will lead to some resistance.
d. Workers will have a transforming idea, a way to understand and appreciate the new reality, and begin to improve productivity.

47. Which of the following statements is NOT true regarding issues and risks?

a. The issues are documented in the issue log, while risks are documented in the risk register.
b. Issues and risks are identified at the beginning of the project, during the planning phase.
c. Issues require a solution and a follow-up confirmation that the problem has been solved.
d. The project owner should assign one owner to each issue reported during the project.

48. A project manager is using earned value management (EVM) formulas to forecast the project's performance if current trends continue for the second half of the project. The planned value (PV) is $10,000, the earned value (EV) is $9,000, and the actual costs (AC) are $12,000. What is the cost performance index (CPI)?

a. CPI = 0.75
b. CPI = 1.33
c. CPI = 0.83
d. CPI = 0.9

49. While sequencing activities on a golf resort development with the project team, you explore a variety of scenarios to help anticipate the risk of delays or inefficiencies in resource allocation. ***Can you build the parking garage at the same time as the resort welcome center? What if you laid the concrete roadways before beginning construction of the primary buildings? What would happen if you delayed the start of the pool construction to utilize those workers for the hospitality cabana?*** **This activity sequencing method would be known as:**

a. Monte Carlo simulation
b. Resource leveling method
c. Critical path method
d. Precedence diagramming method

50. The Tiny Home Haven Community has repeatedly denounced the golf resort project you are managing because the single entry to the resort requires commercial traffic to pass directly through their neighborhood. The community is threatening to sue since the peace and quiet of their neighborhood will be disturbed by traffic to and from the resort. You meet with the project sponsor and key stakeholders. The organization decides to purchase additional vacant property on another access highway. The project manager then submits a formal change request and receives change control board approval to officially add the entrance to the opposite side of the resort instead. The project will no longer require access traffic through Tiny Home Haven. This is an example of:

a. Creating a workaround
b. Avoiding the risk
c. Mitigating the risk
d. Transferring the risk

51. A programmer working on an adaptive project has come across an issue, and despite implementing several common tactics, he is unable to solve the problem. He asks a teammate for their input, and soon several team members are coordinating together on individual tasks to get the user story completed. What technique is the team demonstrating?

a. Swarming
b. Mobbing
c. Pairing
d. Exploiting

52. While managing the Museum Update project for Big City, the sponsor-appointed designer informs you she is running behind and will need an additional 4 days to complete her installation activity. Your review of the network diagram shows the activity has an early start on day 7, an early finish on day 12, a late start on day 16, and a late finish on day 21. Which of the following statements is true?

a. The installation activity is on the critical path.
b. The successor activity will be delayed.
c. The installation will delay the project.
d. The installation will not delay the project.

53. During a product backlog refinement meeting with the product owner, a team discovers they are unsure of the technical dependencies of a particular user story. What approach could they take?

a. Dedicate a small group of team members to perform test-driven development (TDD) for the user story.
b. Plan a research spike for the next iteration to investigate the dependencies.
c. Decompose the user story into smaller components to understand the dependencies.
d. Escalate the obstacle to the project sponsor to determine if the user story aligns with the product vision.

54. A new project has been chartered with scope defined and requirements gathered. The project manager is now planning resource management and determining roles and responsibilities. Which artifact would be a possible output of this process?

a. RACI chart
b. Resource breakdown structure
c. Prioritization matrix
d. Stakeholder engagement assessment matrix

55. An organization is piloting a hybrid project management approach, and some stakeholders are clearly uncomfortable with the change. What are some ways the project manager and change leaders can ease the transition? CHOOSE TWO

a. Remove old documentation and tools so that staff cannot fall back on business as usual.
b. Send out regular emails with reminders of the CEO and senior leadership's emphasis on the changes and the consequences of noncompliance.
c. Set up check-in meetings and anonymous surveys to gather information and feedback.
d. Continue to introduce new techniques regularly and trust that staff will adapt with time.
e. Motivate the staff to try new techniques with some easy, fun challenges that involve giveaways and prizes.

56. Your teams are implementing corrective security patches, defect repairs, and approved changes to several of the application programming interfaces (APIs) and hardware integrations for several of the Big City Museum Annex project displays. Which process group are you performing?

a. Initiating
b. Planning
c. Executing
d. Monitoring and Controlling

57. Hybrid projects require opportunities for stakeholders to review the project deliverables. Which of these allow for open evaluation of the products by the stakeholders? Choose TWO:

a. Manage quality
b. Control scope
c. Validate scope
d. Sprint review meetings
e. Sprint planning meetings

58. You have finished working with the sponsor and a planning team to develop the requirements documents. Select the correct sequence of planning processes that need to be performed before you can develop the project schedule.

a. Create a network diagram, create a detailed activity list, create a WBS, estimate activity durations.
b. Create a network diagram, create a WBS, create a detailed activity list, estimate activity durations.
c. Create a WBS, create a detailed activity list, create a network diagram, estimate activity durations.
d. Create a detailed activity list, create a network diagram, estimate activity durations, create a WBS.

59. What are some of the characteristics of an Agile team? CHOOSE TWO

a. At least ten members
b. Co-located if possible
c. Maximize work in progress
d. Thrive with servant leadership
e. Prioritize multitasking

60. You recently inherited the role of project manager in the middle of a remodel project for Big City Apartments. There is currently a stack of aging change requests coming from a variety of stakeholder networks. You are unsure how to process the multitude of change requests and are worried about the impact the changes will have on the scope, schedule, and budget for the project. Which of the following provides the best option for guidance?

a. The requirements documents
b. The previous project manager
c. The project management plan
d. The change management plan

61. A project has been started to assess the feasibility of a new product. At the end of the first phase, a review of the prototype is held. The product has met quality standards and received positive feedback, and per-unit production is higher than predicted. What should the project team do next?

a. Continue to the next phase as planned because the feedback was positive.
b. Repeat the phase with cheaper materials and see if quality and positive responses can be maintained.
c. End the project because the return on investment would not be sufficient to justify the project.
d. Remain in the project phase to see if internal or external factors lead to a change in the results.

62. The theory that states that change should be initiated by any organization member at any time on the path toward continuous improvement is referred to as:

a. The Gulf of Evaluation
b. Parkinson's Law
c. Kaizen theory
d. Shu-Ha-Ri

63. You've been appointed by Big City Hospital to make improvements to waiting room space designs with the goal of improving satisfaction scores on patient and visitor surveys. You are expected to coordinate the resources, activities, and information. You have limited authority over project decisions. You also must coordinate with the functional facilities manager to get the required funding and staffing resources. Which kind of organizational structure are you working with?

a. Strong matrix
b. Weak matrix
c. Balanced matrix
d. Functional matrix

64. A company plans to overhaul and update all its software systems. In order to do this, they are using a scaled adaptive framework that involves multiple teams coordinating their work. Representatives of each team conduct standups twice a week to discuss completed work, planned work, current obstacles, and upcoming impediments that might affect other teams. What scaling framework is the company using?

a. Scaled Agile Framework (SAFe)
b. Scrum of Scrums (SoS)
c. Disciplined Agile (DA)
d. Scrumban

65. A project has passed its final phase gate, and the project manager is preparing to do closing activities. Which actions would the project manager take to formally close out the project? CHOOSE TWO

a. Transfer knowledge to operations to continue production.
b. Obtain acceptance of deliverables.
c. Submit lessons learned to the PMO repository.
d. Remedy identified defects and log them in the quality report.
e. Check with the PMO for organizational project management governance standards to comply with.

66. The level of authority the project manager has on a given project is determined by ________ and documented in ____________.

a. the interview and negotiation skills of the project manager; the project management plan
b. the organizational structure; the team charter
c. the industry and technical knowledge of the project manager; the project charter
d. the organizational structure; the project charter

67. A project manager is creating the project management plan for a newly charted project and wants to be mindful of external influences, factors, and challenges when planning scope and monitoring risks. What is an example of factoring in the external environment?

a. The project manager incorporates information about facilities access guidelines when creating the project calendar.
b. The project manager consults a commercial database to find standardized cost-estimating information.
c. The project manager incorporates portfolio-specific requirements for data security in the information management plan.
d. The project manager uses an approved template for external communications.

68. A Scrum master is planning stakeholder engagement for the software development project they are leading. Which of the following is the best way to keep the customer involved?

a. Perform user acceptance testing with the customer for each feature to validate that it meets requirements.
b. Invite the customer to the retrospective every two weeks to show progress.
c. Engage in pair programming with the customer to uncover user experience problems.
d. Periodically email the customer with project updates to keep them apprised of progress on their own time frame.

69. The deliberate choice of the project management approach, methodologies, governance, tools, and processes to make them more suitable for the needs of the organization and the goals of the project is referred to as:

a. Accommodating
b. Customizing
c. Tailoring
d. Adapting

70. All of these are true regarding integration management EXCEPT:

a. Project integration management is a collective set of processes implemented to identify, define, and coordinate all components of a project successfully.
b. The project team is responsible for conducting project integration.
c. The project management plan is the primary output of integration management planning.
d. Communication is the primary process related to successful project integration management.

71. You are managing a project to develop an automated scoring system for the new Super Bowling Center project. After the project has already completed three of the required seven project modules, the project sponsor informs you they have decided to go with an existing software suite that is more cost-effective and already includes a scoring system. Therefore, the sponsor is canceling your component of the project. Which should you do NEXT?

a. Close the project.
b. Stop all project work and release the project team.
c. Work with the team to document the lessons learned.
d. Temporarily stop work on the project to allow time to renegotiate with the sponsor.

72. A project team has recently transitioned to using a hybrid approach to project management. They are struggling with configuration management and version control of project documentation, as requirements and priorities change frequently. What is the best technique the project manager can use to better manage the project artifacts?

a. Produce status reports that are sent out to the project team weekly to keep everyone on the same page.
b. Set up visual controls such as a task board and burn charts that are updated daily and easily visible to everyone.
c. Establish change control procedures for documentation to avoid the Hawthorne effect.
d. Update the scope baseline and the WBS in the project management information system (PMIS) for the team members to reference.

73. A Pareto diagram illustrates the common 80/20 principle or conclusion that 80% of problems occur due to 20% of the causes. The Pareto diagram is an example of:

a. A cause-and-effect graph
b. A histogram
c. A scatter diagram
d. A control chart

74. A consumer technology company is working on an iterative project developing a new software product when multiple academic and market research publications indicate that the demand, as well as the competition, may be higher than they originally anticipated. What might the company do to respond to the external change?

a. Include incremental development in their approach so that increments of value can be released to capture market share as soon as possible.
b. Add a predictive component to the project so that it can be completed faster and released as soon as possible.
c. Continue prototyping so that the highest-quality product is released to consumers when it is finished.
d. Crash and compress the schedule so that the project is completed more quickly.

75. While analyzing risk on your beachfront golf resort, you have utilized a matrix to analyze likelihood and potential impact of the risk of hurricanes of varying intensity. You have utilized which approach to prioritize project risks?

a. Earned value analysis
b. Sensitivity analysis
c. Quantitative analysis
d. Qualitative analysis

76. An Agile team leader has tracked the coding errors found in the testing phase, and consolidated data into a histogram of the average number of daily errors in each iteration. The team leader has been trying various techniques to improve code quality. What is a possible interpretation of the data visualization?

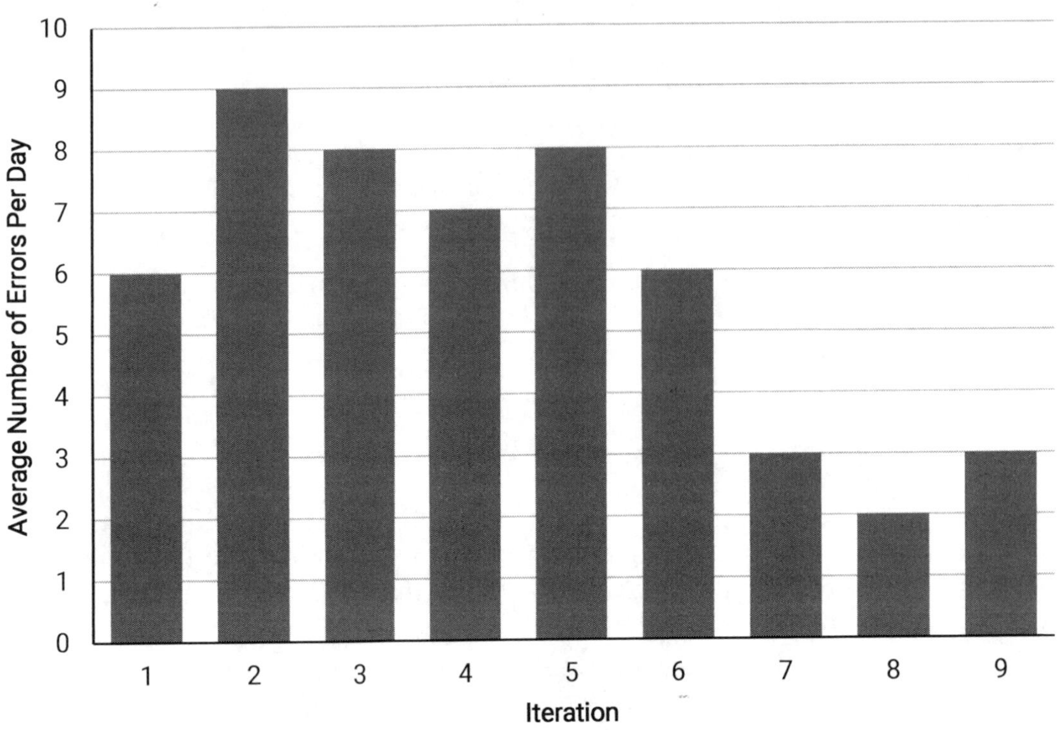

a. In iteration seven, the team began practicing pair programming.
b. In iteration five, the team started using the fist-to-five method for backlog refinement.
c. In iteration three, the team implemented test-driven development.
d. In iteration six, the team used a Kanban board to track work in progress.

77. A sponsor hired you to manage an API enhancement feature for a website landing page. It includes an animated character that issues the user a reward that differs based on which menu option the user selects. The project design is simple with very few features. At the end of the project, the sponsor accepts the deliverable since all requirements have been met. Which statement best describes this project?

a. The project is of low grade and high quality.
b. The project is of high grade and high quality.
c. The project is of low grade and low quality.
d. The project is of high grade and low quality.

78. During the Plan Risk Management process of the Big City Museum Update project, which of these will NOT be included in the risk management plan?

a. The categories or potential causes of risks, including environmental, technological, supply-chain, and staff-related factors
b. The identified roles and responsibilities of key project risk management stakeholders
c. The list of identified risks on the project
d. The methodologies, data sources, tools, and risk assessment approaches used

79. A project stakeholder has fallen behind several times on administrative paperwork for the project, increasing the risk of falling behind schedule. The project manager is upset about the situation, and furthermore, a few team members have voiced concerns that the stakeholder is intentionally delaying the project. How can the project manager best respond?

a. Speak with the stakeholder while practicing awareness of their own reactions and emotions, withholding assumptions about motivation.
b. Ask the team members if they have evidence the stakeholder is purposely slowing down the project.
c. Meet with the stakeholder's functional manager to voice concern about the behavior.
d. Elevate the issue to the project sponsor for feedback on how to proceed.

80. A project manager who is inexperienced has made several mistakes on a project. However, the team continues to be supportive due to the manager's charisma and self-effacing sense of humor. Which form of power is the project manager exhibiting?

a. Reward power
b. Expert power
c. Formal power
d. Referent power

81. Big City has hired you to manage its museum update project. You have been provided with a generous project budget. Big City has already hired and appointed several key designers with whom you must coordinate throughout the project. Big City has stipulated that all project work must be completed between 7:00 AM and 6:00 PM each day and that only parking lot B may be utilized for project deliveries and staging. You also have only 18 months to finish the project. These stipulations by the organization are referred to as:

a. Constraints
b. Assumptions
c. Conditions
d. Tenets

82. Which of the following would NOT be part of a user story?

a. Risk statement
b. Justification
c. User type
d. Goal

83. A potential project sponsor representing the Big City Convention Center has heard about the Big City Museum Update project in the works and is excited about the possibility of adding more parking adjacent to the convention center. Since you are the project manager for the museum project, the convention center client calls you one morning and asks for a quick estimate for a parking garage structure to replace the convention's single-tiered parking lot. He asks you to send it before lunch today. What type of estimation would you perform for this request?

a. Heuristic estimation
b. Analogous estimation
c. Bottom-up estimation
d. Three-point estimation

84. The Big City Museum project is scheduled to be finished in 30 days. The venue designer has proposed several late-project changes to the new banquet facility that will be certain to please the Big City donors at the Grand Opening Gala. Meanwhile, the head contractor for the parking garage structure has just resigned suddenly. Protestors have set up camp again in the delivery lot and are blocking vehicle access to the worksite in response to excessive construction dust in the area. Additionally, you've just received a call from the city inspector's office—three building code violations have been discovered. Which is the MOST important concern you should address first?

a. Hire police to clear and guard the worksite entrance so work may continue.
b. Address the code violations to ensure compliance with regulations.
c. Initiate a change request for the modifications to the venue to complete them on time.
d. Find or promote a replacement for the head contractor that resigned so work may continue.

85. A project manager at a start-up organization is putting together a team for an Agile project. How might they go about doing so?

a. Speak with the PMO about who is available for the project.
b. Identify the employees who are experts in the applicable subject areas.
c. Plan training and shadowing to bring team members up to speed on the required skills.
d. Seek staff members who have specializations as well as more generalizable skills.

86. In order to get the best talent for the job, an Agile team is engaging some programmers from multiple time zones, some in another country. What are some ways that the project manager can support virtual team cohesion? CHOOSE TWO

a. Periodically send team members in person to do pair programming with team members they do not usually work with.
b. Offer bonuses to the team in the geographic location of the top performer.
c. Implement 360-degree feedback assessments to gather information from team members on effectiveness and areas of improvement.
d. Plan an in-person kickoff meeting with virtual attendance options for everyone who can join.
e. Use messaging and texting to maintain communication among team members asynchronously.

87. A project has an estimated cost of $100,000 and an estimated duration of 10 months. You are currently at the end of month 5, the project is 40% completed, and your actual cost at this point is $60,000. Based on your SPI, what is the status of the project?

a. The project is on schedule.
b. The project is behind schedule.
c. The project is ahead of schedule.
d. There is not enough information to calculate the SPI.

88. When reviewing RFPs submitted by three vendors for the new ERP system, which of these should the project manager be MOST concerned about?

a. The technical background of the vendor
b. The ease of use for the end users in the organization
c. The financial solvency and support capabilities of the vendor
d. The proprietary data security of the organization

89. An adaptive project team has gathered information from retrospectives and sprint demos and has found that the feedback is in line with the product vision but adds some large changes to the product roadmap. What can the team do to incorporate and integrate the customer requests?

a. Submit a change request to update the work breakdown structure and scope statement so that the baseline includes these changes.
b. Update the plans for future releases to include the new features and plan them in more detail later on in iteration planning.
c. Stop the current iteration and begin working on the requested changes.
d. Write detailed user stories and plan out the next several iterations—including the updates to the product roadmap.

90. A project manager who prefers to lead the team via offering incentives versus increasing quotas chooses to exhibit __________ over __________.

a. reward power; referent power
b. referent power; formal power
c. coercive power; expert power
d. reward power; coercive power

91. A project to implement a new payroll system is nearly complete. According to the project schedule, the new system must go live and be in working condition before the old system can be shut down. What kind of precedence diagramming method relationship is being described?

a. Finish-to-start (FS)
b. Finish-to-finish (FF)
c. Start-to-start (SS)
d. Start-to-finish (SF)

92. The project team cannot agree on the final design of their product. They have discussed options and still disagree, and if the conflict continues, they will miss a milestone. What is the next step to take?

a. Hold a problem-solving workshop to find a solution.
b. Avoid the conflict for now and work on other work packages.
c. Send out a poll to all project stakeholders to take a vote.
d. Bring in the project sponsor to force a resolution so the project stays on schedule.

93. The program manager is currently managing several projects related to the Big City Museum update. During the project work, the display designer appointed by Big City convinced one of the software teams to make changes to the application specifications. It didn't require any additional time to make the changes and required no additional funding. Therefore, the software developers made the changes without notifying the program manager. During the final testing, the Big City project sponsors are surprised to discover a considerable difference in the content and layout of the display versus the scripting and design represented by the earlier prototype. The Big City sponsors express their displeasure with the program manager and require the display to be redesigned. Which of these led to the negative response by the sponsors?

a. A failure to follow the communication plan
b. Ineffective prototype design
c. Poor development of the quality management plan
d. Lack of adherence to the change control process

94. Which TWO of the following are NOT utilized during the Determine Budget planning process?

a. Cost management plan
b. Project schedule
c. Work performance data
d. Activity cost estimates
e. Procurement management plan

95. While you were managing the Big City Museum Update project, the project sponsor denied a change request for three new display centers to be added to the fifteen centers already included in the project scope. Though the project sponsor agreed the new display ideas would improve museum guest experiences, the budget and timeline for the project could not be altered to include the additions. Therefore, the project sponsor emphatically declined the change request. Three months later, a group of project stakeholders approach the project manager with a request to add the three new display centers to the project. How should the project manager deal with this situation?

a. Inform the project sponsor of the new request and ask how to proceed.
b. Consider the effect of the changes on the time, cost, schedule, risk, quality, resources, and other constraints.
c. Issue a change request to have the change control board reconsider.
d. Tell the stakeholders the additions cannot be made during this project.

96. All of these are true about assumptions EXCEPT:

a. Project managers should include assumptions to minimize project risk.
b. Assumptions are understood to be real or certain and not based on demonstrable data.
c. Assumptions are collected for planning purposes from a variety of stakeholders.
d. Assumptions are nonnegotiable and absolute.

97. A large adaptive team is using Crystal methodology for a project to overhaul some critical software for a hospital system. What method should the project team use?

a. Crystal Orange
b. Crystal Clear
c. Crystal Red
d. Crystal Yellow

98. A project manager is working with stakeholders to document requirements for a newly chartered project in a highly regulated environment. At the first few planning meetings, several stakeholders identify new features that they believe would make the product more successful and debate the scope statement. What should the project manager do next?

a. Use an adaptive approach and assign a product owner to gather user stories from the stakeholders.
b. Use a predictive approach and create a requirements traceability matrix and work breakdown structure that can then be approved by the stakeholders.
c. Use a hybrid approach and focus on creating prototypes or mock-ups to clarify the requirements.
d. Use a balanced matrix approach and hold workshops with stakeholders to progressively elaborate the requirements.

99. You are managing a project with the goal of designing a new high-tech widget. The results from the latest use of a control chart to monitor your project's process reveal that one side of the mean has seven data points grouped together. Which of the following statements is true?

a. This is normal, and some irregularities should be expected.
b. This is a concern that requires further investigation.
c. The process is still within control limits.
d. The variations are due to random causes.

100. While monitoring risk on a project, the project manager tracks identified risks, continually analyzes existing risks, watches for risk trigger events, and is constantly monitoring for the emergence of new risks. The project manager is also implementing risk responses and evaluating their effectiveness. The outputs of this process include all of the following EXCEPT:

a. Project management plan updates
b. Change requests
c. Work performance information
d. Variance and trend analysis

101. You have just been hired as the replacement project manager for the Super Bowling Center project, which is currently reported to be 70% complete. During project walkthroughs, you discover that several of the deliverables that were reported as finished are still not complete. While the project sponsor believes the project is nearly finished, the actual status of the project reveals it is less than 50% complete. What should you do?

a. Decline the position; you were hired under false pretenses.
b. Crash the project to get the project on schedule.
c. Hold an immediate meeting with key stakeholders to solicit their input to get the project on schedule.
d. Research and develop an accurate status of the project and notify the sponsor immediately.

102. After completing the project technology hardware and software updates, the project manager, the project team, and three of the four key stakeholders assigned to review the work believe the updates are complete. One of the important stakeholders disagrees, however, and is claiming the work does not meet the requirements. How should the project manager handle this concern?

a. Since only one of the four disagrees, declare the work finished and proceed with the closing process.
b. Launch a claims process against the dissenting stakeholder for breach of contract.
c. Meet with the team member responsible for the work and review the WBS and requirements documentation to ensure all work was completed.
d. Issue a change order to address needed changes.

103. Your project currently has 8 stakeholders plus yourself. The sponsor has just asked you to add 5 new stakeholders effective next month. How many more communication channels will you have added to your project by the end of next month?

a. 36
b. 55
c. 72
d. 91

104. The project manager is pulling together information to plan the project budget. One phase contains experimental work using new techniques, so lessons learned from past projects are of limited value in this instance. She consults with expert stakeholders to get cost estimates for the phase and receives a most likely total of $55,000, an optimistic total of $30,000, and a pessimistic total of $65,000. Using simple three-point estimating, what should the budget be set at?

a. $55,000
b. $52,500
c. $50,000
d. $60,000

105. A project manager overseeing a golf resort development project is concerned about the constant conflicts between the project subcontractors, as well as within some of the development teams. Statistically, which of the following contributors is the LEAST likely to cause conflict among team members?

a. The schedule
b. Project priorities
c. Personality differences
d. Resource allocations

106. You've just been designated as the project manager in the Big City Museum Expansion project charter. What should you do first?

a. Create the WBS.
b. Develop the team charter.
c. Develop the project schedule.
d. Classify the stakeholders for the project.

107. You are managing the Big City Museum expansion project. The project planning team has developed the WBS dictionary and has delivered the project activity duration estimates. What should you do next?

a. Create an activities list.
b. Create a RACI chart.
c. Develop the project schedule.
d. Sequence the activities.

108. A project manager is overseeing the Big City Museum Update project, which includes a technology infrastructure update and a new ERP system to include modules for HR, scheduling, ticketing, and accounting. The project manager contracts with an ERP vendor who will customize an existing ERP solution and integrate it with the new museum technology infrastructure. The contract stipulates that the ERP vendor must conduct a review with the organization's IT team prior to installing each module of the ERP. However, the ERP vendor has already installed and pushed out three of the four modules without review or approval from the IT team. What should the project manager do regarding the vendor?

a. Issue a stop payment order with accounting.
b. Cancel the contract and find another vendor.
c. Issue a default letter to the vendor.
d. Have the IT team inspect the installed ERPs immediately.

109. All of these are true regarding project change management in a predictive project EXCEPT:

a. The project manager should implement change requests as soon as possible to keep the stakeholders satisfied.
b. Changes should be used for preventative actions, corrective actions, or defect repairs.
c. The project manager should make every effort to avoid unnecessary changes to the project.
d. The project manager should consider the impact of change requests on the scope, cost, time, quality, risk, and all other factors of the project before submitting a change request.

110. For a regularly scheduled review, a project manager provides suggestions via email to a team member about how he can improve his time management. The project manager believes that direct, straightforward communication is best and wants the team member to have her feedback in writing. However, the next day, the team member approaches her and is very upset, believing he is in trouble. What is a likely explanation for this situation?

a. The project manager did not follow the communications management plan.
b. The team member wished for a more formal written report to be given.
c. The project manager was adopting a forcing style of conflict resolution, when the team member preferred a more collaborative approach.
d. The team member had a different communication style and would have preferred to receive the feedback in person.

111. You have been assigned by your PMO to a project in a foreign. At the end of the first sprint, the product owner expresses his satisfaction with the first phase of the project and awards each of the team members a weekend vacation on his private yacht. How should you respond to this offer?

a. Accept the gift as one of the benefits of your position.
b. Accept the gift, but inform your manager in case of a future challenge of your ethics.
c. Decline the gift because it would be considered taxable income in your country.
d. Decline the gift since it would be considered a conflict of interest with your company.

112. The sponsor of an Agile project is very enthusiastic about the project and would like frequent updates on how it is progressing. They have not worked with an Agile development approach before. How can the project manager share this information?

a. Encourage the sponsor to engage with the team and hear their perspective on the project.
b. Invite the project sponsor to come check the information radiator as often as they like.
c. Include the project sponsor in the daily standup meetings and retrospectives to learn more.
d. Create a custom report to send regularly to the sponsor via email.

113. A staffing company is deciding whether to make a software program in-house or purchase one from a vendor. Building the program themselves would have an up-front cost of $100,000 and $5,000 in monthly maintenance. A vendor would cost $75,000 at the beginning and $10,000 monthly for support. At what point would it be cheaper to build in-house if the product will continue to be used well into the future?

a. After 25 months
b. After 10 months
c. After 2 months
d. After 5 months

114. An organization is seeking to analyze the business value of its project management processes and eliminate unnecessary work. What technique could they use?

a. Business justification analysis
b. Value stream mapping
c. SWOT analysis
d. Crystal methodologies

115. An adaptive team is planning how to deliver benefits to the customer. What document would identify the value of the project to the customer?

a. Iteration plan
b. Agile manifesto
c. Benefits management plan
d. Agile charter

116. The project team is working together with the product owner on the product roadmap and identifying key items for the next release. The Scrum master wants to get the input of all team members while avoiding groupthink. Which method could the project team use?

a. Wideband Delphi
b. Dot voting/multi-voting
c. Kaizen
d. Shu-Ha-Ri

117. The project manager is mentoring an entry-level team member on a telecommunications project. Together they have identified the desired outcomes, assessed the mentee's current situation, and analyzed potential choices to reach the goals and the consequences. What are the other steps of the OSCAR coaching and mentoring model?

a. Have accountability for one's choices and measure the results.
b. Commit to specific actions in a given time frame and meet regularly to review.
c. Cultivate a positive attitude and take ownership of the results of one's actions.
d. Identify the action steps needed to achieve outcomes and periodically renew one's commitment to the goals.

118. A high-profile construction project is going according to plan until a grassroots community group begins protesting on social media. What would be an appropriate next step for the project manager?

a. Update the communications management plan with a new strategy for influencing the community group towards a more positive attitude towards the project.
b. Submit a change request to add this negative publicity to the risk register and plan a risk response.
c. Review the communications management and stakeholder engagement plans, then perform stakeholder analysis on the group and update the stakeholder register.
d. Send a memo to the project sponsor about this new potential blockage to the project.

119. A manufacturing project needs to compress the schedule due to some unforeseen shipping delays. They are obligated to ship some component parts to a vendor for assembly by the end of the calendar year. Industry practices recommend a particular kind of paint that takes a long time to cure, but another paint that dries faster is acceptable. What kinds of dependencies that impact the schedule compression are being described?

a. Shipping parts to the vendor is a mandatory dependency, and the recommended paint is a discretionary dependency.
b. Shipping parts to the vendor is an external dependency, and the recommended paint is an internal dependency.
c. Shipping parts to the vendor is an internal dependency, and the recommended paint is a discretionary dependency.
d. Shipping parts to the vendor is a mandatory dependency, and the recommended paint is an internal dependency.

120. An important stakeholder for Project B is the finance department, as the project relies on procurements being processed in a timely manner. On the stakeholder engagement matrix, the project manager has evaluated the department head as neutral and would like to influence them to be supportive. What can the project manager do next?

a. Plan to have an in-person meeting for the next project communication, with feedback and active listening.
b. Engage the project champion to encourage the finance department towards a more favorable position.
c. Prioritize pull communication for project communications with the finance department.
d. Analyze what noise or barriers might be interfering in the communication channels with the finance department.

121. While conducting team assessments, an adaptive team leader finds that the team members have siloed skillsets and would benefit from knowledge sharing. What practice can the team leader implement or enhance to best facilitate this?

a. Require team members to be dedicated to one project.
b. Ask the team to produce functional increments frequently.
c. Limit the team's work in progress.
d. Co-locate team members as much as possible.

122. The project manager is monitoring project risks and discovers there is an opportunity to present on the project at a new conference on the topic, potentially increasing publicity and interested users. The project manager is not sure their proposal to present will be accepted, but they crash the project schedule to have more of it completed by the conference and submit a proposal. What positive risk response is the project manager using?

a. Accepting
b. Sharing
c. Escalating
d. Enhancing

123. As the project manager for the Big City Museum Update project, you are continuously referring to the communication management plan and stakeholder management plan to meet stakeholder expectations. You frequently communicate with them to address their concerns, request feedback for project deliverables, resolve their issues, and process their change requests. These actions correspond to which process?

a. Plan Stakeholder Engagement
b. Identify Stakeholders
c. Manage Stakeholder Engagement
d. Monitor Stakeholder Engagement

124. A project manager has noted that the team's output has improved considerably over the past few iterations, from both senior and junior members. What might be a good way to recognize the improvement?

a. Reallocate the project's extra funds as a bonus for the team member that completed the most story points.
b. Consider each team member's motivators and plan a team celebration as well as individualized appreciation for the team members.
c. Find ways for all team members to take on more responsibility in upcoming phases.
d. Plan an off-site retreat for team-building activities.

125. This project schedule network diagram displays the duration of each activity. Which option is the critical path?

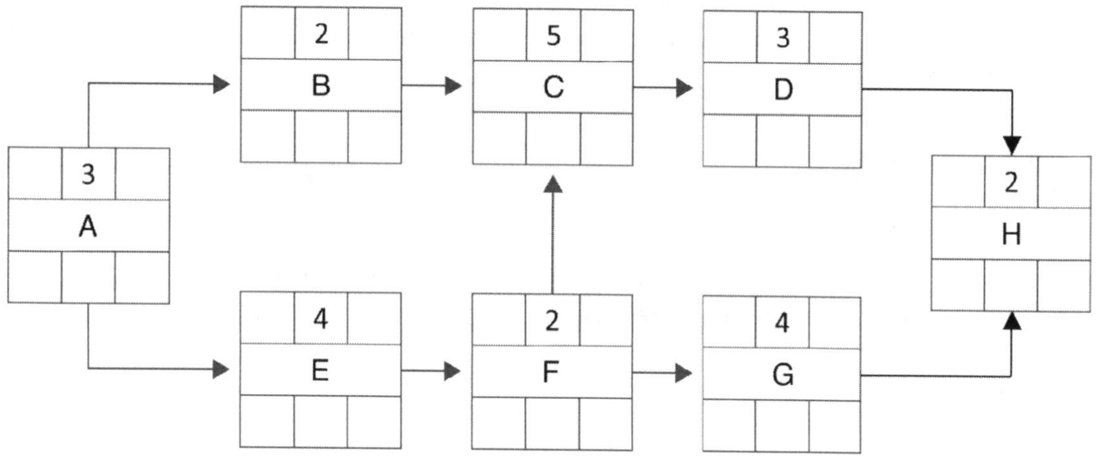

a. ABCDH
b. AEFCDH
c. ABCFGH
d. AEFGH

126. Rather than having a detailed project schedule, a team uses a flow-based approach of pulling tasks through the workflow as resources are available, limiting the work in progress, and displaying the tasks and their statuses on a large, visible board. What method is the team likely using?

a. Kanban
b. Dynamic Systems Development Method (DSDM)
c. Agile Unified Process (AgileUP)
d. Scrum

127. While managing the Big City Museum Update project, the project manager is examining one of the new interactive thematic displays to see if all of the lights and sound effects deploy at the appropriate time when the correct API conditions are triggered. The project manager is conducting:

a. An inspection
b. An audit
c. A process review
d. A SWOT analysis

128. Which of the following demonstrates effective servant leadership?

a. Selecting the most effective and familiar tools for the team to use
b. Prescribing the conflict resolution processes the team should use to resolve differences
c. Holding team members accountable for productivity issues
d. Continuously communicating the project vision

129. While analyzing the technology infrastructure update for the Big City Museum project, the project team and the sponsor are concerned that the IT staff will not have the time or capability to monitor its volumes of data adequately as originally planned. Instead, you and the team explore options via third-party cloud providers to offload some of the duties. This would be an example of:

a. Accepting the risk
b. Avoiding the risk
c. Mitigating the risk
d. Transferring the risk

130. A multi-year construction project is negotiating a contract for building supplies with a new vendor with whom the organization has not worked previously. What kind of contract should the organization use?

a. Cost plus fixed fee contract (CPFF)
b. Fixed price incentive fee contract (FPIF)
c. Fixed price with economic price adjustment contract (FP-EPA)
d. Cost plus award fee contract (CPAF)

131. While you are managing an ERP software development project, your newly formed team is struggling to balance personal opinions and individual preferences for work styles. There are frequent disagreements during daily standup meetings, and two of the team members refuse to speak with each other. The team is currently in which stage of Tuckman's theory of team development?

a. Forming
b. Storming
c. Norming
d. Performing

132. A project manager overhears a disparaging comment from one of his team members that criticizes his choice of management style. He believes it is important to supervise every detail of his team's work; if he doesn't closely monitor the team, they will get lazy, slow productivity, and risk delaying the project. Which theory of management categorizes the project manager?

a. Theory X
b. Theory Y
c. Theory Z
d. Two-Factor Theory

133. Each of the following statements is true regarding nonverbal communication EXCEPT:

a. It includes tone of voice.
b. It can include gestures, facial expressions, body language, and manner of dress.
c. It requires careful word selection to maximize the effective listening of the audience.
d. It represents more than 50% of what we say when communicating.

134. Which of the following are examples of servant leadership on an Agile team? CHOOSE TWO

a. Identifying a potential bottleneck in paperwork required by the finance department and working with the department to streamline the process so it does not impede the project team's work
b. Arranging professional development activities to nurture team members and grow their competencies, even if it means they grow beyond their current role
c. Focusing on rewarding the top-performing team members and disincentivizing poor performance
d. Having a hands-off approach and letting the team members determine their own goals and decisions
e. Directing project work to ensure team members understand and align with the processes and tools in place

135. A project manager has set specifications for incoming materials, trained team members, created workflows for verification and quality control, and built into the budget an amount for scrap and rework. What aspect of the cost of quality (COQ) has the project manager NOT yet addressed?

a. External failure
b. Internal failure
c. Appraisal
d. Prevention

136. Two of the outputs of the Identify Risks process are the risk register and the risk report. Which statement most accurately describes the difference between the two documents?

a. The risk report describes general risks for the overall project, while the risk register identifies specific individual risks.
b. The risk register describes general risks for the overall project, while the risk report identifies specific individual risks.
c. The risk report gets an immediate update when a new risk is identified.
d. The risk register gets an immediate update when a new risk is identified.

137. A project manager at a large organization is leading a hybrid project that will first develop new software modules in an Agile manner, followed by predictive phases for implementation and training. The project team members are highly regarded and skilled in their work, but as the project begins, the project manager does not understand why the work breakdown structure is not being followed and the team pushes back on documentation they are directed to produce regularly. What might be the reason?

a. The team is operating with an Agile mindset, while the project manager is using a Waterfall approach.
b. The project manager has not performed a stakeholder analysis to understand the team members and their motivations.
c. The work breakdown structure has not been decomposed into work packages of sufficient detail.
d. The project manager has not facilitated team-building activities to move the team past the storming stage.

138. While you are investigating options for procurement of light fixtures for your golf resort project, your organization requires you to seek three independent bids from a list of approved vendors. These requirements would be classified as which type of procurement process inputs?

a. Organizational process assets
b. Source selection criteria
c. Agreements
d. Requests for proposals

139. You are managing Big City's Museum Annex construction project, and you are ready to authorize and initiate work in the correct sequence at the appropriate time in accordance with the organization's enterprise environmental factors. Which tool, technique, or document drives this process?

a. The work authorization system
b. The PMIS
c. The WBS
d. The project schedule

140. All of the following are true regarding the project resource calendar EXCEPT:

a. It shows the availability of resources throughout the project.
b. It is utilized to determine opportunities for leveling and smoothing.
c. It shows the work shifts available by date.
d. It is created during the schedule activities.

141. A project manager is planning an exhibit at Museum Z, and some artifacts that were supposed to be on display are evaluated as too fragile. The project manager does not have the authority to decide whether to use other items or alter that part of the exhibit, so he brings the issue to the museum director. What risk response strategy is the project manager using?

a. Transfer
b. Mitigate
c. Escalate
d. Accept

142. A project manager works in a small organization and functions fairly autonomously. When planning a project, in what areas is the project manager most likely to rely on organizational governance and policies? CHOOSE TWO

a. Procurement
b. Value delivery
c. Schedule management
d. Stakeholder engagement
e. Risk management

143. During the planning phase of the Big City Museum Update project, the project manager will create multiple software development teams from a mix of preassigned and independently hired developers. All of the following statements are true regarding this process EXCEPT:

a. Team member availability should be documented in the resource calendar.
b. This is part of the Acquire Resources process.
c. The team charter will be an output of this process to document the expectations for team interactions and productivity.
d. Rewards, recognition, and training should be included in the planning documentation.

144. A project manager under a PMO is gathering resources for a new project and discovers that another project manager needs to engage several of the graphic designers at the same time. What can the project manager do to solve this situation?

a. Look at the project calendar to see if there is enough float to delay the graphic designers' activities.
b. Check the requirements management plan to determine whether requirements can be met without these activities.
c. See if the PMO has templates for contracting out the work.
d. Consult the schedule and see if activities can be rearranged for when the graphic designers are available.

145. A project has unexpectedly had to move up the delivery date by several weeks. The project manager wants to hire some additional workers in order to meet the deadline. What are some risks to be aware of? CHOOSE TWO

a. The scope of the project should be adjusted to accommodate additional workers.
b. At some point, adding resources leads to increased cost for diminishing returns.
c. The acceptance criteria need to be updated for the project.
d. The project manager must work with the project sponsor to rebuild the business case.
e. There needs to be time built in for knowledge transfer and learning as resources are added late in the project.

146. During a sprint retrospective, team members identified a bottleneck in which back-end developers were waiting for the front-end developer to complete tasks. What approach should the Scrum master take to clear this obstacle?

a. Hire additional developers with a time and materials contract.
b. Plan cross-training so that more developers can take on front-end tasks.
c. Bring in a subject matter expert in front-end development.
d. Work with the product owner to reprioritize the backlog to avoid the bottleneck.

147. An adaptive project team has created a wireframe of a website that has undergone extensive testing by the team. It is robust and streamlined, has a powerful backend, and is visually appealing. However, at the iteration demo, the client complains that the most common customer journeys take too many clicks to navigate. What dimension of quality has the team neglected?

a. Resilience
b. Reliability
c. Satisfaction
d. Uniformity

148. You are in the middle of managing a project to build a new rocket ship in order to shuttle astronauts to the International Space Station. It is part of a contest hosted by the government wherein the organization who completes the first successful rocket will win the exclusive government shuttle contract for the next 20 years. You have managed the project for your organization during months of project planning, research, and development. Now, a rival company has managed to develop a sufficient rocket ahead of your own organization's project and has secured the prize of the long-term contract. Your sponsor knew the project would be a financial gamble at the outset, but the organization accepted the risk because of the excellent long-term opportunity. Now your sponsor's organization is left without a viable rocket and has also lost the cost of the materials, labor, patents, permits, and other expenses. The costs incurred as part of the gamble the organization made are referred to as:

a. Opportunity costs
b. Depreciation costs
c. Absorbed costs
d. Sunk costs

149. A Scrum team is conducting a retrospective after a release to find ways to improve. What is an outcome of a retrospective?

a. The team identifies a few action items to improve in the next work period and a way to measure outcomes.
b. Each team member is assigned as many ways to improve as possible before the next retrospective.
c. The team focuses solely on ways to improve quantitative measures.
d. The team identifies the individual responsible for each of the failures or mistakes in the previous work period.

150. After three months of working for your organization's PMO, one of your colleagues confides in you that he doesn't really have his PMP certification—he just listed it on his resume. What should you do?

a. Ignore the confession for the sake of maintaining a positive team environment.
b. Report the confession to the PMO manager.
c. Report the confession to PMI.
d. Convince him of the merits of the PMP process and oblige him to achieve the certification.

151. An Agile team has established a velocity of 50 story points per two-week sprint, and there are an estimated 300 story points left in the project. How soon can the team expect the project to be completed?

a. 6 weeks
b. 12 weeks
c. 15 weeks
d. 8 weeks

Refer to the following for questions 152 - 154:

Use the table to create a network diagram

Activity	Preceding Activity	Durations (# days)
Start		0
A	Start	4
B	A	5
C	A	3
D	A	4
E	B, C, D	5
F	E	4
G	E	2
H	F, G	4
Finish	H	0

152. Based on the network diagram for these activities, what is the critical path?

a. ABEFH
b. ABEGH
c. ACEGH
d. ADEGH

153. What is the late finish on Activity E?

a. 14
b. 15
c. 16
d. 18

154. What will happen to the project schedule if Activity B gets delayed by 6 days?

a. There will be no change to the schedule since C and D can be run in parallel.
b. Activity H can be compressed to recapture the lost time.
c. There is enough float at Activity E to decrease the delay to only 3 days.
d. The overall schedule will increase by 6 days.

155. Which of these are outputs of Plan Quality Management and inputs for both Manage Quality and Control Quality?

a. Control points
b. Statistical samples
c. Audit reports
d. Quality metrics

156. Two project team members cannot figure out how to get along, and it is impacting team morale and the quality of their work. What can the project manager do?

a. Use their positional power to encourage the team members to resolve their conflict.
b. Ask the more junior team member to concede to the more senior team member, as they have more experience.
c. Call a team meeting to problem-solve using the Plan, Do, Check, Act (PDCA) method.
d. Have a private meeting with the two team members to discuss their differences and figure out how to collaborate.

157. While managing the Big City Museum Update project, you have encountered constant disruptions from inner-city dwellers who object to the noise, dust, and traffic congestion associated with the project. Community activists have frequently protested on-site, putting jobsite safety at risk, and they have also blocked the single-entry point for jobsite traffic and deliveries. At the conclusion of the third town hall meeting with the stakeholders, you convince the sponsor and the organization decision-makers to issue free museum entrance tickets to each family in exchange for keeping the project worksite entrance clear and refraining from additional protesting on the property. The community organizers agree reluctantly before the meeting is adjourned. This is an example of which conflict resolution technique?

a. Collaborating
b. Smoothing
c. Forcing
d. Compromising

158. A project manager has been asked to explore how their organization can adopt more Agile mindsets and practices. Which of the following are NOT ways of using Agile approaches? CHOOSE TWO

a. Plan regular intervals for teams to reflect on how to become more effective.
b. Place team members on multiple projects to diversify their skillsets.
c. Look for ways that projects can be restructured to deliver incremental value.
d. Ask division leaders to identify ways they can reduce local inefficiencies.
e. Provide spaces for teams to do their work together face-to-face (a commons).

159. A new project manager has realized that a large amount of the senior team members' knowledge of tasks and troubleshooting is tacit and difficult to express, gained from years of experience in the field. She would like to facilitate knowledge transfer to more junior members. What technique can she use with the project team?

a. Ask the senior members to document their experiences in a database to share with other team members.
b. Plan job shadowing between junior and senior team members.
c. Set up a knowledge fair so junior team members can meet briefly with each senior member.
d. Host a training event to ensure all team members have the same knowledge base.

160. A project team is using Scrum methodology to develop a new app for a fitness brand. Which of these artifacts is the team most likely to use?

a. Activity list
b. User guide
c. Sprint backlog
d. Schedule network diagram

161. When an Agile project team consults with the project sponsor and organization stakeholders to continually test and refine, and then finalize, the product scope over a series of iterations, this is referred to as:

a. Shared vision
b. Requirements gathering
c. Progressive elaboration
d. Collaborative processing

162. A project team working on a marketing project has had issues with print samples coming back from a vendor that are not to their specifications. What could the project manager do to ameliorate the situation?

a. Consult the procurement management plan and work with procurement to select another vendor that will meet project specifications.
b. Conduct a make-or-buy analysis to see if the products can be manufactured in-house to better control the work.
c. Perform a root cause analysis to determine the source of the problem.
d. Use a Monte Carlo analysis to forecast the probable outcome of this risk.

163. When a project manager conducts an EMV analysis, all of the following are true EXCEPT:

a. EMV analysis helps determine the earned value of a project by comparing the projected cost and schedule versus the current status of the project.
b. EMV analysis often uses a decision tree analysis to determine whether to make or buy a portion of the project.
c. EMV analysis helps assign a dollar value to a risk to weigh its impact on the project.
d. To calculate the total projected cost of a decision or risk, multiply the percent of probability by the risk cost to determine the EMV. Then, add the result to the initial decision cost for a total potential cost of a decision.

164. A project manager is working on a multi-module video game that includes a base game module during the project's initial release. Additional expansion modules are planned for an incremental release every three months. However, after the release of the third expansion module, several stakeholders are now claiming the base game module did not meet their requirements. How should the project manager have prevented stakeholder dissatisfaction with the project?

a. Include the stakeholders during the Validate Scope process.
b. Include the stakeholders during the development of the project management plan.
c. Include the stakeholders in the development of the quality management plan.
d. Include the stakeholders in the Collect Requirements process.

165. An adaptive project team needs to contract with outside specialists for some of the project work. What is a strategy they can follow to reduce risk and make the contract work in a flexible environment?

a. Include a request for information (RFI) in the contract that can be adapted as needed.
b. Use a fixed price incentive fee contract (FPIF) so that changes to the requirements are covered by the incentive fee.
c. Use a terms of reference (TOR) for each user story as it is pulled into work in progress.
d. Use a master agreement for the overall contract and include the scope of work in an appendix.

166. Project X is about halfway through completion when the company's strategic plan is updated, placing higher priority on other projects. Funding for project X is reduced, and it will need to be completed in a shorter timeline. The project is following an Agile life cycle. How should the project team respond to these changes?

a. Host a retrospective to collaboratively determine what work to complete in the remaining project timeline.
b. Prioritize the backlog so that the easiest features are at the top, so the team can complete the highest number of user stories in the given time.
c. Submit a change request to the change control board to reflect the requirement changes and update the change log.
d. Prioritize the backlog so that the most valuable features are at the top, and complete a minimum viable product.

167. A project manager notices that the team members seem unmotivated and uninterested in their work. The project manager meets with the team to re-establish the project mission and remind them of the professional growth they will achieve. An individual indicates that the team's primary issues are that they feel underpaid and unable to use the tools they want due to restrictive company policy. This scenario is an example of which model?

a. Norman's model of gulfs of execution and evaluation
b. McClelland's theory of needs
c. ADKAR model
d. Herzberg's model of hygiene and motivational factors

168. After the fourth sprint of an Agile software project, the product owner asks the project manager for an updated completion timeline for all twelve of the modules in the project backlog. What is the project manager's best source for determining the average production capability of the project team?

a. The burnup chart
b. The burndown chart
c. The velocity chart
d. The Kanban board

169. The project manager has come to the end of the project and has performed a final inspection of the deliverables prior to the hand-off to the sponsor. Select the correct order of closing process tasks:

a. Finalize the lessons learned, release the team, obtain formal acceptance, close the contract.
b. Obtain formal acceptance, finalize the lessons learned, release the team, close the contract.
c. Release the team, obtain formal acceptance, close the contract, finalize the lessons learned.
d. Obtain formal acceptance, release the team, close the contract, finalize the lessons learned.

170. An organization is commissioning a custom-built software program to handle one of their business functions. The company has a general idea of what need the software will fill but does not have a very detailed set of requirements yet. However, they want to see a return on their investment as soon as possible and are willing to use discrete modules when completed. What development approach would be a good fit?

a. Predictive
b. Hybrid
c. Iterative
d. Incremental

171. While estimating the activity resources for the Big City Museum Update program of projects, the project manager will be engaged in all of the following EXCEPT:

a. Hiring the development team and construction workers
b. Providing a basis of estimates
c. Listing the resource requirements
d. Creating a resource breakdown structure

172. All of the following are true about communication EXCEPT:

a. Most of what we communicate in person is transmitted nonverbally.
b. Receiving feedback means the intended recipient received and agreed with the message.
c. Noise can interfere with active and effective listening.
d. Email can be a method of both encoding and decoding information.

173. You are managing a golf resort development project and have just finished the third month of a 14-month project. Your EV = $126,000, while your AC = $110,000. One of your crew supervisors informs you that several defects have been discovered in the foundation work, and a portion of it will probably have to be reworked. There may be a significant risk of cost overrun. What should you do first?

a. Contact the project sponsor to let them know there may be a problem requiring a request for their contingency reserves.
b. Ask the crew supervisor to replace the crew responsible for the defects.
c. Confirm the amount of your management reserves to defray the cost of the rework.
d. Evaluate the cause of the defects and the cost of the rework.

174. The project manager for a grant-funded project to remodel a community center is planning communication with stakeholders. He needs to share project updates with the local community and achieve as wide a reach as possible. The funding organization is a formal, well-respected organization that requires detailed documentation of stakeholder engagement. Which of the following modes of communication would be the best choice?

a. Start a social media account and use trending hashtags to boost views.
b. Hold a town hall meeting to present the project and gather feedback.
c. Create a project website for pull communication that can be visited by anyone who is interested.
d. Start a focus group of influential community members and share updates with them to pass on to the community.

175. The project manager has been distributing reports and summaries about the project as planned. He has received several requests from functional managers for information that is not in the regular reports they receive. What should the project manager do next?

a. Check the communications management plan, analyze stakeholder needs, and submit a change request to update the plan.
b. Reference the communications management plan and let the stakeholders know they need to refer to the reports they receive.
c. Check the stakeholder engagement plan and add the functional managers' requests to the lessons learned register.
d. Analyze stakeholder needs and begin sending the stakeholders the information they requested.

176. All of the following are true regarding the role of a PMO EXCEPT:

a. It helps monitor compliance with organizational project management policies, procedures, and processes.
b. It is key to early project decision-making guidance by prioritizing projects, making recommendations for stakeholders, and offering a selection of pre-approved vendors.
c. It develops templates, research, and advice to facilitate best practices for project management.
d. It performs a role similar to a VDO in Agile-centric organizations.

177. Partway through a manufacturing project, new governmental regulations restrict the use of some materials the project is utilizing due to their environmental impact. What would be the best way for the project manager and the organization to respond?

a. Continue the project as is to avoid rework and scrap of work already done, since the regulations are new, and no best practice has been established yet.
b. Calculate the cost of noncompliance and take a calculated risk of partial compliance to avoid stakeholders losing their investment.
c. Plan to redo part of the project to comply with regulations and use the opportunity to create a sustainability report highlighting the company's environmental responsibility.
d. Pause the project and take a conservative approach, waiting to see what other organizations will do to respond to the regulations.

178. At the close of a project, the project manager is archiving project documents as organizational process assets (OPA) for reference for future projects. What artifact would most likely be included?

a. Prioritization schema
b. To-Complete Performance Index (TCPI)
c. Test plan
d. Work performance data

179. An Agile team leader is analyzing the cumulative flow diagram to measure cycle time and identify potential blockers that need to be addressed. In which workflow step does the team appear to have an issue?

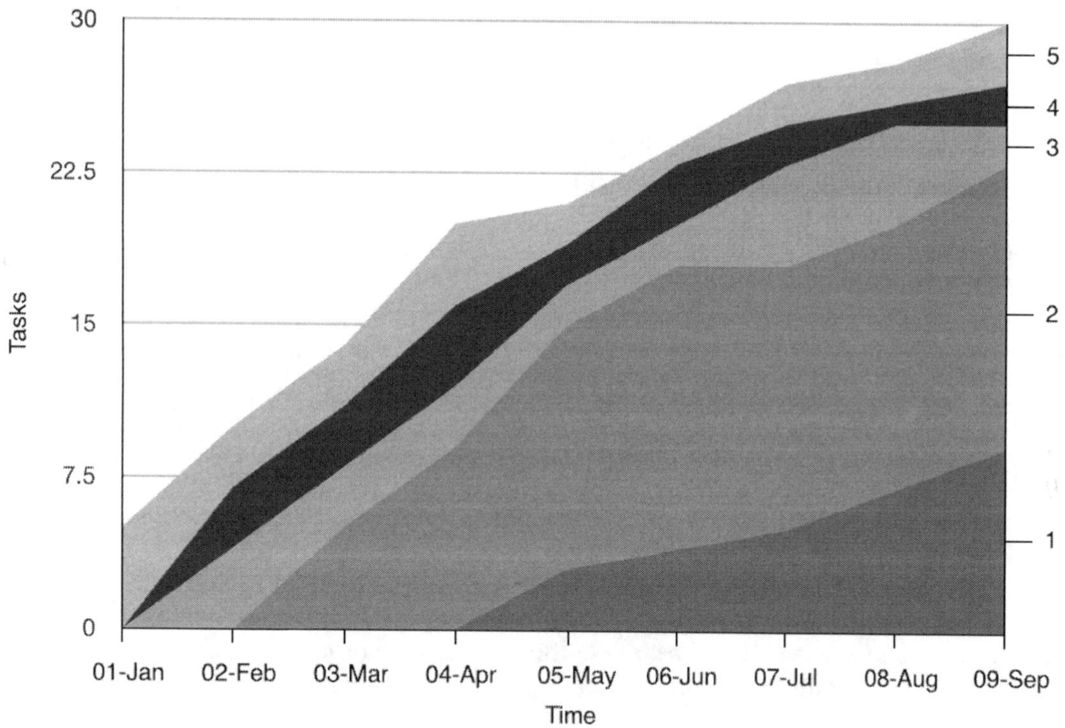

a. Backlog
b. Development
c. Analysis
d. Testing

180. A project manager is working with the sponsor, technical lead, and impacted business groups to select a development approach using an Agile suitability filter model that assesses factors related to culture, the team, and the project. The organization has historically not delegated decision-making to project teams. The team will include approximately 50 people, the deliverables must be delivered as a finished whole, and the project is in a very regulated industry. What development approach would be best for this project?

a. Iterative
b. Predictive
c. Incremental
d. Hybrid

Answer Key and Explanations for Test #1

1. B: The project manager should ensure that the changes do not constitute some scope creep (work outside of the planned scope) and, if not, they should submit a formal change request. The project phase should not be closed yet, as the deliverables have not been accepted by the customer. The business case does not need to be amended when requirements change, and the schedule should not be changed without formal approval.

2. D: The project manager needs to conduct close auditing of the invoices to watch for items that are not associated with the project. Since the seller is billing for parts and labor as an ongoing part of the work, CPFF agreements are usually paid in continuous installments to ensure the seller has the means to sustain the work. Occasional cost overruns will occur as supply chain or scheduling disruptions emerge, as they are a common component of project work; however, they should still be watched closely. The seller would make less money with fewer fixture installs, so there is no financial advantage for the seller to reduce the scope. Auditing the invoices ensures the project manager has done all he or she can to keep an eye on unexpected financial fluctuations with a particular vendor. The vendor will also be less likely to make deliberate invoicing "mistakes" when he or she knows the project manager intends to correct them.

3. B: Project stakeholders include everyone who will be impacted by the implementation of the project. The greater a project manager's understanding of the roles, influence, interest, and awareness levels of each stakeholder group regarding the project, the better ability they will have to engage and communicate with stakeholders effectively, as well as identify potential risks throughout the project. The project sponsor, functional managers, and senior managers might not have frequent interactions with all of the stakeholders within the organization. Therefore, the best depth of information will come from surveys, meetings, job shadowing, and other interactions with each of the stakeholders directly.

4. D: The project manager can remind the team member of the team charter and the values to which the team has agreed, such as respect and listening. Addressing the issue in front of the whole team at a status meeting would likely be embarrassing and unproductive. The project manager may need to involve HR and/or find a replacement if the issue becomes too severe, but those actions are not warranted as first steps.

5. A: Communication requirements analysis provides a procedural approach to ensure the needs of all stakeholders are taken into consideration. It is designated as the principal tool for this phase of communication planning. The other answer choices contribute to the communication management plan, yet they lack comprehensive insight for the appropriate needs, occasions, and methodologies for project communication. A survey might be distributed to stakeholders, but rarely does the sender receive a 100% rate of response. The stakeholder salience cube is used during the Plan Stakeholder Engagement process to determine and rate stakeholder influence, impact, and interest in the project; the information can be included in the stakeholder register. The stakeholder register will then be utilized as an input to the Plan Communication Process. The PMIS is the collection of software and knowledge repositories for the project, which will include the means and the methods of communication for the project.

6. D: According to PMI, the project manager should always follow up to make sure the solution was effective. In the scenario, the project manager already involved several experts. Answer A can be ignored since the sponsor will probably know less than the experts already consulted. Answer B refers to the 80-20 diagram that graphs a series of problems versus the probable attributed causes—the Pareto principle hypothesizes that 80% of problems are the result of only 20% of possible causes. In this scenario, the fishbone diagram was the best choice to identify the root cause of a single problem. Answer C is a possibility, but the project manager did consult experts. Answer D is the best choice, however. It is a glaring omission from the PMBOK guidelines for procedural problem and conflict management. For exam scenarios, whether making a change, implementing solutions, de-escalating conflicts among stakeholders, or sending team members for training, the project manager must always follow up to verify the implemented measures have worked.

7. B: For a project to be formally closed, exit criteria must be met, such as the customer accepting deliverables, reassigning personnel and resources, ensuring all costs are charged to the project, and creating final reports. The lessons learned register is updated and archived for future use. The assumptions log should be updated throughout the project, but once the project is closed, no more assumptions are updated. Likewise, risk reports and quality reports share the status and forecasts throughout the project but are no longer needed at the close of the project. Summaries of risk and quality information may be included in the final report.

8. A: Technical debt, or degraded code quality due to lack of maintenance and refactoring, can be caused by pressure to rush, insufficient documentation, and poor definition, among other things. A common and clear definition of done (DoD) is part of the Scrum pillar of transparency and contributes to efficient, effective code. The defect cycle time and risk-adjusted backlog do not directly relate to technical debt.

9. B: The expected monetary value (EMV) is calculated by multiplying the probability by the economic impact. The EMVs are $10,000, $25,000, $16,000, and $10,000 respectively, so Risk B has the highest financial impact.

10. A: This method takes the highest-ranked technical proposal and selects it if the financial aspect can be satisfactorily negotiated. The fixed-budget method involves disclosing the available budget to sellers in the RFP and selecting the best technical proposal within budget limits. Sole source involves a proposal from one specific seller, and least cost evaluates purely on cost when the contract is routine or has well-defined outcomes.

11. B and C: Some key characteristics of high-performing project teams include open communication, which allows for open and safe dialogue that builds trust and collaboration, and shared ownership of project outcomes. The other options are also characteristics of high-performing teams but are not part of the situation described.

12. C: Agile in its pure form values customer collaboration over contract negotiation. Agile emphasizes individuals and interactions over processes and tools, working software over comprehensive documentation, and responding to change over following a plan. Agile was developed for the software industry but is quickly migrating into more traditional project planning.

13. D: The product backlog is the list of requirements for the project; the overall project can be broken down into multiple product deliverables, with each having their own product backlog. This product backlog is regularly prioritized by the product owner prior to each sprint planning meeting to incorporate changing feature and function ideas, as well as to adjust to reflect product urgency. The product owner updates the order of the product backlog before the project team decides how many points of work from the product backlog can or should be accomplished during the next 2- to 4-week sprint. The narrowed choice of work is referred to as the sprint backlog. For the exam, remember the product owner prioritizes the product backlog, while the team manages the sprint backlog.

14. B: Though the WBS provides the foundation for planning, the project activities are generated as an activities list during the Plan Schedule process.

15. C: Project managers model integrity and transparency, including honesty to stakeholders. While the prototype failed, the team was allowed to experiment and learn from the failure. Future project teams will benefit from the knowledge gained.

16. C: Project managers use their influence to remove obstacles and impediments. They use emotional intelligence and interpersonal skills to build working relationships and clear the way for the project team. Overcoming silos can be difficult in organizations where project managers have little formal power, but forming positive relationships is the first step.

17. B: The fixed price is the best option for the buyer since the seller assumes all risks once the price is set. Conversely, a time-and-materials agreement represents the worst option for the buyer, since the buyer has very little control over the production schedule or cost overruns. Select time and materials only when the scope is high level (very vague) and the production schedule is very short. The cost-plus options are fair to both parties, since both allow the seller some flexibility on cost while the buyer (project sponsor) uses the fixed price or incentives to motivate the seller to get the job done based on a buyer-specified target (e.g., under budget, or within X number of months). For the exam, know which types of agreements favor the buyer versus seller with regard to the potential risk outlined in the question scenario. If a scenario does not indicate a favorability preference for one negotiating party over the other, choose the answer that is most fair to both parties. PMBOK promotes win-win choices during negotiations and conflict management situations.

18. C: Distributed teams especially rely on technology for communication, and a central information system will reduce miscommunication, duplication, and out-of-sync information. The communications management plan and lessons learned register may need to be updated, but this option does not directly answer the question. The organizational process assets (OPA) may have templates, but they may not be tailored to a virtual team. A knowledge cafe could help onboard the new team members but will not help keep the documentation uniform.

19. A: Variance analysis, work performance information, and change requests are tools and outputs from the Control Scope process. Control Scope is performed via frequent inspections and walkthroughs as the work is being completed, with the goal of avoiding the need for change requests due to defects, as well as avoiding scope creep. Answer D, Validate Scope, occurs at the end of the product development as a final test of the product to make sure it meets all requirements before submitting it to the project sponsor for final review and, hopefully, acceptance. Control Quality compares the production and project process to the quality management plan with the goal of improving the processes for both this project and future projects. Monitor Risks is performed throughout all project processes.

20. A: While project managers often work closely with vendors to monitor procurement, there are usually strict policies and procedures in place around procurement, and project managers are not authorized to enter into or alter a contract. The project manager should work with those in authority to determine the procedures to follow when contracts have not been followed. Taking direct actions such as withholding payment, reissuing the RFP, and working with the vendor themselves are not appropriate responses.

21. D: A risk-adjusted backlog factors in tasks that address risk and prioritizes high-value user stories that carry risk early in the project. A Kano analysis measures customer responses to features, and fast-tracking a project schedule carries risks of its own. A decision tree analysis may be useful but is not sufficient on its own as a risk response.

22. C: Questions about "forecasting" refer to the estimate at completion, or EAC.

$$EAC = \frac{BAC}{CPI}$$

From the scenario values, $BAC = \$5{,}000$, $AC = \$3{,}000$, and $EV = \$1{,}500$.

$$CPI = \frac{EV}{AC} = \frac{\$1{,}500}{\$3{,}000} = 0.5$$

Therefore, $EAC = \frac{\$5{,}000}{0.5} = \$10{,}000$.

23. B: A bidder conference is the best method of minimizing preferential treatment of vendors at the outset of the procurement processes. PMI emphasizes the importance of submitting the same message to all potential vendors at once—preferably during a co-located event—to ensure that the message is delivered consistently and all potential vendors have equal access for question-and-response. Answers A and C can be utilized in conjunction with the bidder conference but do not necessarily ensure the uniformity of the message content, delivery, and access. Answer D might promote the organization's "innovation" agenda, but the project is already underway. Professional suppliers will be required to ensure accountability and minimize project risk.

24. D: Theory Z refers to Ouchi's "Zen"-like model of the ideal manager-employee relationship described in the scenario. (Remember "Z" for "Zen" and "zap" for an "ouchi.") Theory X is McGregor's unpopular micromanagement style. (Think "X" for "strikes out" with the workers.) Theory Y is McGregor's belief in the positive power of worker autonomy. (Think "Y" for "Yes," workers can and will be capable and productive with minor supervision when management shows trust.) Expectancy Theory is the belief that people behave based on what they expect as the result of their behavior. If they are paid well and acknowledged, they will work well for the organization. The <u>Two</u>-Factor Theory refers to Herzberg's two-pronged hygiene and motivation theory. It states that worker health, safety, and working conditions, coupled with recognition and advancement opportunities, are necessary to keep workers productive and loyal. (Remember "H" for "<u>H</u>erzberg," and for "<u>h</u>ygiene," which is "<u>h</u>alf" of the Two-Factor Theory.) Theories on the exam may be referred to via the authors, theory names, alternative names, or descriptors.

25. C: A Delphi technique is a survey or questionnaire usually used to protect anonymity or collect information from a range of levels of stakeholder influence. SWOT is a risk analysis tool to assess strengths, weaknesses, opportunities, and threats. Monte Carlo simulations are "what-if" scenarios. Stakeholder salience cubes assess stakeholder interest, need, level of influence, and other project-related attributes for managing stakeholder engagement.

26. C: Because the project includes prototyping with feedback and refinement, an iterative approach is the best way to manage changes. A is a predictive approach, which works well when requirements are stable. B demonstrates an incremental approach, with deliveries of features or value throughout the project, and D is flow-based Agile that may not use time-boxing but limits the work in progress at any given time.

27. B and E: Plan-Do-Check-Act refers to the recurring cycle of process steps; plan the process, implement the process, measure and compare results, then change the process to promote continuous improvement. TQM refers to Deming's theory of total quality management, where every person in the company is responsible for the quality of the product. SWOT analysis is used for risk analysis to measure strengths, weaknesses, opportunities, and threats. Tornado diagrams are used during risk sensitivity analysis. They compare two outcomes of a proposed action and consist of graphics shaped like inverted pyramids. Attribute sampling tests a product for the presence or absence of a characteristic and yields a binary "yes" or "no" output. (Variable sampling is similar, but the characteristic is rated over a range of possible outputs, such as "excellent," "very good," "good," and "bad.")

28. A: One of the guiding principles of an Agile mindset is that business people and developers must work together daily throughout the project. With monthly demos and surveys as the only source of feedback, the team is likely not getting enough input. A champion is helpful for moving resistant or neutral stakeholders to a more positive opinion, but this scenario involves multiple end users who are not satisfied, so that is not the best approach. More frequent retrospectives would not satisfy customer needs. Working prolonged overtime is unsustainable, and it does not guarantee a satisfactory product for the users.

29. C: Benchmarking refers to comparing values and procedures to industry standards as well as historical data from prior projects within the organization. A cost-benefit analysis weighs the cost of an activity versus the expected benefits. A SWOT analysis looks at opportunities and threats related to risk. An affinity diagram is a form of data representation where project-related objects of any sort can be grouped and categorized based on common characteristics (e.g., stakeholders likely to protest the project, or which risks would be related to natural disasters).

30. C: The scope statement is a highly detailed document that describes exactly what will be produced by the project; the deliverables and acceptance criteria (what needs to be done); exclusions (what will *not* be done); assumptions; and constraints. The project charter lists high-level deliverables being commissioned for the project during the initialization phase, but it does not drill down into specific design and functionality features. (Example: "The Big City Museum renovation project will include an update to the existing lobby, a new annex featuring interactive displays and a rooftop event venue, and a parking garage structure.") The requirements documentation enumerates how the project work should be performed and includes product feature requirements and quality requirements, as well as process methodologies and procedures required by the organization. The requirements documentation is then used to create the WBS. The WBS decomposes project work—both directly related to the product and the logistical management of the activities—into work packages. These are further detailed and aligned with specific accounting department codes in a corresponding WBS dictionary. The scope statement is combined with the WBS and the WBS dictionary to form the project scope baseline. (For the exam, remember that the deliverables are in the scope statement, while quality standards are in the requirements documents.)

31. B: The purpose of the configuration management plan is to catalog the description and characteristics of the product or deliverable by phase of completion or iteration. For example, when developing a video game, the development teams will be finishing the required changes to Fight Module B version 2.5 during the sprint. During production, the configuration management plan describes the production goal for each iteration, logistics for development such as tools and storage location, and methods for requests for change. Once the software is developed and ready for release, the configuration management plan gets a final update for the version number. Answer A, the PMIS, would be a logical second guess since it represents the software tools for use during the project versus software developed as a deliverable for the project. However, the scenario is concerned with proper version control—during project development, that falls within the domain of the configuration management plan.

32. B and D: As an innovative software project, this will likely use an Agile approach. Agile project charters are short and lightweight, answering why the project is being done, who benefits and how, what "done" means, and how to work together. A contract is not part of a project charter, and the scope is usually variable in an Agile project. The requirements definition is part of a requirements management plan.

33. A: Procurement agreements are the output of the next sequential process, conduct procurement. The procurement management plan details constraints and assumptions for procurements, the way risk will be managed, and the organization's preferred contract formats specific to different types of work (e.g., construction foundation, software development, or lighting installation). The procurement strategy indicates how the project will be performed—which components will be completed by organization staff, what will be produced by project teams, and what will need to be purchased from third parties. The statement of work is adapted from the project scope baseline for deliverable components that will be procured from third parties. It clearly defines what deliverables need to be produced by a vendor as well as the required performance metrics and reporting formats. Other key outputs of the Plan Procurement process (not included here) are the bid documents such as requests for information (RFIs), invitations for bid (IFBs), or requests for proposals (RFPs). These are the Plan Procurement process documents that will be scrutinized via the procurement selection criteria. They will help form the agreements and contracts that will be output during the next process, Conduct Procurement.

34. A: T-shirt sizing is a form of affinity grouping, a method of categorizing items based on their similarities. The sizes (S, M, L, or whatever is used) are relative to each other. Estimations of effort in Agile projects are often relative, as there may not be much historical project data to base estimates on. Parametric estimating uses an algorithm to estimate based on past data and parameters. Function points calculate business functionality in a software system, and sensitivity analysis assesses the impact of risks on the project.

35. B: An organic or simple organizational structure is typical of small organizations and typically has flexible arrangements. As the company grows, more coordination is needed to overcome silos and inefficiencies. A PMO would provide standardized tools and resources as well as support and coordination for project managers. Standard criteria for purchases and hiring more staff would be useful, but would only address part of the problem. Increasing the authority of project managers would solve the staffing issue but lead to other inefficiencies without coordinating their efforts.

36. B: The opportunity cost is the value of the project not chosen, or the $60,000 of the T-Rex project. There is no calculation involved in determining the opportunity cost. Exam scenarios will often include additional information—some of which may not be necessary. It is a good idea to first read the last sentence of the scenario to discern the actual question, then skim the answer choices before starting at the top of the scenario. This will help you maintain mental endurance during the exam.

37. C: The burndown chart measures how many story points have been completed over time. A few days into the project, the team's momentum slowed down. The loss of a team member is a plausible explanation.

38. D: A lead is a head-start for a successor activity, while a lag is a delay or gap between a predecessor activity and the successor activity. Start-to-finish activities are linear and sequential; do activity A as the predecessor, then do the B successor activity—or successor activity C if activity B is being performed in parallel with activity A. For finish-to-start activities, however, the predecessor activity (final design) must be finished before the successor activity (the coding) can begin.

39. C: A CPI value over 1 is under budget. In this scenario, the project is 10% under budget. The SPI value must be 1 or greater to indicate the project is on or ahead of schedule.

40. B: The project manager should have assessed team members' skills at the outset to determine what kind of training and development was needed for the team, so that deficiencies could be quickly addressed. Risk identification and standup meetings might have uncovered the need for training, but the project manager needs assessments for more data.

41. D: Resource leveling is an optimization technique that adjusts the project schedule to achieve a more even distribution of resources. Unlike resource smoothing, resource leveling can affect the critical path on the schedule network diagram. Resource smoothing uses float to adjust the schedule but maintains the critical path. Both are resource optimization techniques.

42. C: A prototype can be used in an iterative manner to gather feedback for subsequent deliveries. A minimum viable product includes only the essential features a product needs to be useful and aims at eliminating waste and overwork. These approaches give the project team rapid information on customers' opinions, which they can incorporate into a streamlined finished product. The project plans of previous projects may have some useful information, but because this is a novel product, they will not translate directly. Unit tests are used for ensuring code quality, and a life-cycle assessment will not ensure the product goes to market rapidly.

43. A: A time and materials contract sets a fixed rate but not a detailed statement of work. This allows outside support for the project while allowing flexibility for the project needs. An indefinite delivery indefinite quantity contract sets a range of goods or services in a given time period, while a firm fixed price contract is for well-defined goods or services.

44. D: According to the salience model, stakeholders can be categorized based on power, legitimacy, and urgency. The most prominent stakeholders for the project are Anytown residents, so the neighboring mayor does not have a legitimate claim—nor the power—to influence a change to the project. The best course of action is to document and monitor the situation while maintaining a positive relationship.

45. A: Agile teams include quality in their requirements and build in iterative, frequent practices like test-driven development and continuous integration to find errors quickly. Impact mapping helps clarify and decompose requirements but does not necessarily affect quality. A Kanban board manages workflow and efficiency but does not directly impact quality. Finally, the burnup chart shows work completed over time rather than quality.

46. D: The organization has passed through the stages of late status quo (or "business as usual") and the introduction of the foreign element that causes a shift, and they are in the chaos stage, where unfamiliarity leads to some creativity and some anxiety along with low performance. Next, the transforming idea is when people find a way to cope and work performance begins to increase. This is followed by practice and integration, and finally the new status quo.

47. B: Potential known risks to the project are identified during the planning phase, assessed for the likelihood of occurrence and impact on the project, analyzed for possible responses, and documented in the risk register. The process of identifying risk continues throughout the project. Remember, risks can be negative threats or positive opportunities, though they may or may not occur during the project. Issues, however, are always problems that occur unexpectedly during the project that have a negative impact on the project progress (e.g., activists camping on the doorstep or a sudden change in regulations). When issues occur, they are documented in the issue log—not the risk register—and they are assigned a team member as the official "owner" who will be responsible for investigating a solution and monitoring its progress. The project manager must follow up after the issue owner declares the issue solved in order to confirm the solution has resolved the issue. If an issue cannot be solved within a reasonable timeframe or with contingency reserves, the issue will get elevated to the "risk" level and processed in accordance with the risk management plan.

48. A: The CPI is calculated as earned value divided by actual cost, or $CPI = \frac{EV}{AC}$. Calculate $\frac{\$9{,}000}{\$12{,}000} =$ 0.75. A CPI of less than 1 means the project is over budget, 1 is on target, and over 1 means ahead of budget.

49. A: Monte Carlo simulations can be used for scheduling, cost estimation, risk assessment, or a variety of other project processes. They involve problem and solution exploration via hypothetical scenarios. The precedence diagramming method (PDM) would be used to consider the sequencing of activities. The consideration of delaying one activity to use the same work crew for two activities would be a resource leveling method. And the critical path would provide the initial boundary or constraint for all resequencing considerations. However, the question specifically targets the "what if" or Monte Carlo simulation.

50. B: The sponsor changed the route via the new property purchase and integrated change control process to avoid the risk of lawsuit from the Tiny Home community entirely. Answer A, the workaround, is an unplanned, quick response during a work activity to keep the process moving temporarily until a more permanent solution to the issue can be found. PMI does not consider workarounds viable long-term solutions in risk management. Issues must be thoroughly investigated, and appropriate solutions must be implemented and confirmed. Mitigating risk involves utilizing tactics to minimize the negative impact that a triggered risk event may incur. In this scenario, however, there is no other long-term solution other than moving the entrance or buying the Tiny Home community and forcing the owners to move. Transferring risk always involves sharing the risk with a third party; the organization sacrifices preference, control, and additional costs but reduces the likelihood of triggering the risk event and/or shares the cost of the damages that occur if the risk event occurs. A fourth option for risk management is risk acceptance, where the known risk is likely to occur, but the organization is willing to proceed anyway. For example, during the peak of the COVID pandemic, organizations accepted the risks of supply chain disruptions and stakeholder availability due to the unpredictable nature of the pandemic and its impact on the workforce and economy.

51. A: Swarming is when several team members coordinate their work to complete a task. Mobbing is similar, but it involves working simultaneously on the same problem. For example, all of the team members might gather at the same computer to collaborate on fixing the issue. Pairing is working together with one other team member, which works well for troubleshooting coding issues. Exploiting is a response to a positive risk (opportunity) to ensure that it happens.

52. D: To find the float on the activity, calculate $LF - EF = 9$ days. (You can use $LS - ES = 9$ days as well.) The designer only needs 4 additional days, so the extra time will not delay the project. For Answer A, a critical path activity can only have a float value of 0. Therefore, the activity is not on the critical path, and the successor activity will not be delayed.

53. B: A spike is a time-boxed interval used for research or prototyping. An architectural spike tests out a proof of concept, while a risk-based spike investigates risks. Test-driven development is the practice of writing automated tests before creating the product so that mistakes are easily caught, rather than a means of investigating dependencies. There is no indication that the user story is too big and needs to be decomposed. The obstacle may eventually need to be elevated to the sponsor, but the project team needs to gather information first.

54. A: A RACI chart is a type of responsibility assignment matrix (RAM) that shows who is responsible, accountable, consulted, or informed of project activities, decisions, and deliverables. A resource breakdown structure is a hierarchical chart of the resources needed for the project and does not necessarily address roles and responsibilities. A prioritization matrix is a means of categorizing items into quadrants based on effort or impact and importance; it could be used to prioritize risks or features, but not for assigning responsibilities. Finally, the stakeholder engagement assessment matrix delineates stakeholder engagement rather than roles or responsibilities.

55. C and E: Motivational strategies and two-way communication are conducive to adoption and assimilation of change, as well as providing space for concerns to be addressed. The other techniques involve removing scaffolding, force/threats, or providing no support, all of which are likely to backfire or at least prolong the transition.

56. C: Rework for needed repairs that result from change requests issued during the monitoring and controlling process gets sent back through the executing process. The executing and monitor/controlling processes are reciprocal or iterative until all quality requirements are met on the project, and then the products or deliverables are presented to the customer for final review and acceptance.

57. C and D: The Validate Scope process in predictive or traditional projects is the official opportunity for the sponsor to evaluate the product output based on the requirements criteria in the scope. In Agile projects, the official sponsor evaluation of the product progress occurs more frequently—usually monthly—during the sprint review meetings. For choices A and B, the project manager manages quality and controls scope. The purpose of sprint planning meetings (choice E) is to choose which of the work from the prioritized product backlog will be conducted during the upcoming sprint.

58. C: At the end of the Plan Scope Management procedure, you would create the work breakdown structure (WBS) by breaking the project work into categorized work packages. Then, during the Plan Schedule Management process, you would create a detailed activity list of all project work based on the WBS work packages. You would next sequence the activities via a network diagram to show dependencies and determine the critical path of activities. After that, you would estimate the activity durations before you can create the schedule.

59. B and D: While it is not required, Agile teams work best when co-located for collaboration and face-to-face communication. Agile encourages servant leaders to support the team's self-management and growth. Teams should limit the work in progress in order to expedite work overall, they should be 100% dedicated to the project, and they should operate in groups of 3 to 9.

60. C: The project management plan is the umbrella plan developed during the project integration management process. Information about the scope, schedule, and budget are included within its subsidiary plans. The previous project manager may be able to give some guidance, but as the project manager, you are bound by the project management plan as your source for project information.

61. B: Phase gates, or review gates, describe decision points to evaluate project progress and make go/no-go decisions. The product holds promise because it meets quality standards and did well in user testing, but the project team should see if a new prototype would be more cost-effective. Continuing the project as is or remaining in the phase would likely cause the project to go over budget. The project does not need to be ended yet, as it may still be worth the investment given some changes.

62. C: Kaizen theory lies at the core of Lean Agile development. Some of its core principles applied within development processes include collective ownership of a problem and solution, minimization of waste such as waiting and rework, and a focus on continuous improvement. Parkinson's Law declares that workers will utilize all of the time allotted for a task—even when the time is not needed. Therefore, a project manager should limit schedule durations when possible to reduce wasted time and materials during the interim. The Gulf of Evaluation refers to the difference between the presenter's description of a product and the expectations of the stakeholder. A stakeholder's imagination can produce unrealistic expectations for a final product without a prototype or illustrations and clear descriptions of a product's features, functionality, and quality requirements. The project manager for predictive projects should utilize feedback loops—frequent opportunities for stakeholder input and testing—to keep the contracted project requirements versus stakeholder expectations for the deliverables aligned throughout the project. Agile methodologies minimize stakeholder disappointment due to a "surprise ending" upon product delivery since regular reviews are an integral component of Agile development. Shu-Ha-Ri is a project methodology theory adapted from martial arts to depict a path to mastery. *Shu*—obey the rules to keep the status quo, *Ha*—break free from the rules to make opportunity, *Ri*—transcend or go beyond via an original path. Shu-Ha-Ri is the equivalent of "thinking outside the box" for innovation.

63. B: This would be considered a weak matrix since the project manager has a low level of authority. If the scenario specified the project manager's authority as "little to none" and the project manager had to appeal to the functional manager, that would indicate a functional matrix. For the exam, only a strong matrix and project-oriented structures give the project manager full control of the resources. A balanced matrix shares control of resources with the functional manager.

64. B: A Scrum of Scrums involves multiple Scrum teams coordinating their work by having representatives attend standup meetings 2-3 times a week. Scaled Agile Framework focuses on enterprise value streams and detailing roles and practices at portfolio, program, and project levels. Disciplined Agile follows certain Agile principles to avoid being too narrowly focused and too prescriptive. Scrumban is an Agile framework blending of Scrum and Kanban methods.

65. A and C: Knowledge transfer is a key component of closing out projects so that they can be transferred to operations, production, or the customer and produce value. Sharing lessons learned with other project managers and/or future projects is another important step. Obtaining acceptance of the deliverables would be part of a phase gate decision, which has already happened. The defects should have already been addressed before approvals, and PMO and organizational standards should be addressed early on and throughout the project.

66. D: The project manager's authority level—over both project management decisions and control of the resources—is determined by the organization structure (strong matrix, functional, virtual, etc.) and is documented in the project charter. The project charter, created during the initializing process phase, is the first document of the project and provides the authorization for both the project funding and the project manager. Answers A and C factor into the choice of project manager, but PMBOK is most concerned with documentation and the process tailored for the organization framework. The team charter comes later, during the Acquire Resources process.

67. B: Commercial or industry databases are an example of a factor external to the project environment. Company facility policies, data requirements of the business unit, and organizationally approved templates are examples of the internal environment.

68. A: User acceptance testing (UAT) is a means of involving the customer in validating the deliverables against the requirements/desired functionality. The sprint demo, rather than the retrospective, demonstrates progress at the end of each iteration. Pair programming involves two team members checking each other's work. While emails would be helpful, they do not actively engage the customer as well as UAT.

69. C: Tailoring is the official PMI term for the strategic customization of the project from end to end. The other answer choices are synonyms.

70. B: Project integration management is the responsibility of the project manager. (For the exam, remember the RACI (responsible accountable, consulted, informed) chart distinctions. One individual is responsible or "owns" the task. Project teams are usually in the "accountable" column, except when determining the sprint backlog and tools for development on Agile projects—then the teams are "responsible.") Ineffective communication is one of the biggest contributors to project risk.

71. C: The project will need to be closed according to the official sequence of the Close Project process. First, the project manager needs input from the team to document the lessons learned before the team can be released; answer C is "next" before answer A can conclude. For the exam, contracts are void if they break the law, and the sponsor can cancel a project in progress when the organization decides there is a greater net benefit (faster or cheaper) elsewhere or when the project deliverable has become obsolete due to legislation, environmental factors, social or political pressure, or other advancements within the industry. Remember that all projects or product development phases that are interrupted and terminated must close via the closure process.

72. B: In a lean environment, information radiators are also known as visual controls. They are highly visible for everyone to see and can show processes as well as comparisons between actual and expected performance. These kinds of dashboards are common in adaptive environments to display metrics and share information in a timely manner. This technique will establish one source of information that is up to date. Status reports are useful for providing information on work since the last update, but may not be timely enough or have the right information for the project team. The Hawthorne effect states that measuring something may influence the behavior being measured, which is not relevant to the scenario. Given that the requirements are changing frequently, a scope baseline and WBS as used in predictive approaches is not appropriate. Furthermore, asking the project team members to check the PMIS is less efficient than a big visual display.

73. B: A histogram is a bar chart that shows frequency; it can reflect three values at once (e.g., month of year, total amount of expenses, and percentage of change over time). A cause-and-effect graph is a root-cause diagram like the famous Ishikawa fishbone diagram. A scatter diagram shows trends between variables. A control chart is utilized for product testing with a control range established above and below an acceptable mean. Up to six consecutive data point collections falling outside of the control range is still considered "in control." The Rule of Seven dictates that after the seventh consecutive data point that falls out of range, an inspection and adjustment should be made since the product testing is no longer in control.

74. A: Incremental life cycles are optimized for speed of delivery, so that a frequent delivery of smaller deliverables gives value to the customer as soon as possible. If the company can be first to market and then add updates and deliverables, they may capture market share. Adding a predictive component would not necessarily speed up the project, and crashing/compressing the schedule (adding more resources or overlapping activities) are usually predictive techniques for speeding up the project schedule and not often recommended in Agile, as a sprint is not changed once started, nor are these techniques sustainable. Continuing to prototype would likely produce a quality product but risks not being the first to market.

75. D: Qualitative analysis is a high-level approach involving input from historical events and subject matter experts. It looks at the likelihood of a risk occurrence (via a percentage value) and provides a quick estimate of the impact of the risk on the project (e.g., schedule delay, loss of reputation, or increased costs). The project manager can then prioritize risks based on the balance of likelihood versus impact. (An earthquake would have a high-dollar impact on the project but isn't very likely to occur. A hurricane, however, is very likely to occur and has a high-dollar impact. The risk of hurricane and related risk responses would be highly prioritized.) Quantitative analysis takes the high-priority risks and examines them in quantifiable, data-supported detail. Earned value analysis is from the Manage Cost process, while a sensitivity analysis is a tool used within the greater Quantitative Analysis process.

76. A: A common practice in eXtreme Programming (XP), pair programming pairs two team members together to alternate writing and reviewing code, catching mistakes as early as possible. The lower average number of errors indicates the success of the method. Using the fist-to-five method is a means of decision-making, and a Kanban board improves efficiency, but neither technique reduces errors. Test-driven development would also reduce errors, but iteration three still had a high number of errors.

77. A: Products can be categorized as low grade or high grade based on the number of features and the complexity of development. For example, building a child's swing set for the yard is a low-grade project that still requires high quality of development for safety issues. This project is "simple" with "few" features, yet since it has been accepted by the sponsor, it has met the quality requirements. Therefore, it is "high" quality. PMBOK insists that although projects can be of low or high grade, they must all be of high quality.

78. C: The risk register identifies the list of known risks and is a separate project document that will receive frequent updates as the project progresses.

79. A: Emotional intelligence is recognizing one's own emotions and those of others, as well as acting appropriately and with empathy. The project manager practices emotional awareness by managing their feelings and seeking to understand the stakeholder rather than making assumptions. They may need to speak with team members or the functional manager eventually, but the first step is hearing from the stakeholder directly.

80. D: Referent power is based on personality and a manager's likeability; it's a key quality to have for effective negotiation. Reward power is based on the tangible and intangible benefits a manager can offer. Formal power is the legitimate power that comes from the manager's authorized role within the organization. Coercive power refers to a style that manages by threat of punishment.

81. A: "Constraints" is the official PMBOK project term for the hard-line conditions an organization or regulatory body can impose on a project. They are based on facts established by a governing body and may or may not be subject to change during the project. Assumptions differ in their level of flexibility and lack of factual or data support. (Examples: "For now, we will assume that our current servers will suffice and won't need an update. We can reconsider the budget later if that is not the case." Or "Let's assume that new legislation will pass and plan accordingly. If the proposed bill fails, we can look at other options later.")

82. A: User stories do not include risk statements, though the goal of the user story might ultimately help minimize a potential risk. User stories do include a user type (by role or persona), a goal or requirement, and a justification or explanation of value. An example might be: "As the patient admittance clerk, I need a patient lookup tool that locates patients by birthdate, name, or phone number to reduce retrieval time on duplicate names or birthdates." The admittance clerk is the "user," the requirement or goal is a three-value lookup option, and the justification or reason is to increase efficiency when she encounters five Bob Smiths born on July 1.

83. B: Analogous or "top-down" estimation is the highest level of estimation when a quick response is required without any project details or research; it is based on past (or, in this case, current) experience with a project that is similar in size and duration. Heuristic estimation is based on the "rule of thumb" concept by industry experts. It is also high-level but slightly more accurate (e.g., "Typical wiring for an entire hotel floor will run you about $50K"). Though not an answer choice here, parametric estimation involves the manipulation of a value of a parameter to provide a closer estimate (e.g., carpet is $6 per sq. foot for a floor that is roughly 4,000 sq. feet). Three-point estimation utilizes the $TE = \frac{O+4M+P}{6}$ formula (total expected duration, optimal, pessimistic, and most likely). Bottom-up estimation requires the most time since each activity is researched and estimated in detail. Bottom-up is the most time-intensive method, yet it is the most accurate and least risky of the various types of estimation.

84. B: The law (local and state) trumps all. The project manager must comply with regulations and industry standards first. Answer C would be "gold-plating," or extra work not approved for the project; a change request would be needed, but there are more pressing matters with the existing scope at present. Answer A is a quick and temporary solution until a meeting can be scheduled to discuss the protesting stakeholder concerns, but the code violations must be addressed first. Also, finding a replacement, as in Answer D, is going to take more time (while the code violations are addressed).

85. D: Agile teams are generally composed of "T-shaped" people who have generalized skill sets and can supplement other areas, rather than "I-shaped" people who have depth but not necessarily breadth of knowledge. A start-up would likely not have a project management office (PMO), and training may be necessary, but the project manager must adequately assess the team's skills first.

86. D and E: Virtual teams benefit from at least one in-person meeting to get to know team members, if possible. They rely on technology to remain connected across time zones. While virtual pair programming is a good option, sending team members in person would likely be cost-prohibitive and inefficient. Bonuses for the team of the top performer would generate competition rather than cohesion, and 360-degree feedback is an assessment approach rather than a team-building technique.

87. B: Not all cost estimation and earned value management (EVM) formula questions will necessarily require a calculation. For the exam, the ratio of time investment to point value yields a poor return, since completing a full panel of EVM formulas can take minutes. Look for shortcuts to narrow answer choices quickly. In this scenario, at the end of 5 months, the project is exactly halfway to completion and should be 50% complete. Answers A and C can be eliminated immediately. We can verify this by calculating the SPI. Use the formula $SPI = \frac{EV}{PV}$ to calculate $SPI = \frac{\$60{,}000 \times 40\%}{\$60{,}000 \times \frac{5}{10}} = \frac{\$24{,}000}{\$30{,}000} = 0.8$. An SPI of less than 1 means the project is behind schedule.

88. D: PMI's guiding principles of integrity of stewardship, as well as risk awareness and prevention, charge the project manager to respect the law above all, then protect the organization's interests and assets through all project-related decisions and activities. This obligation to protect and promote applies not only to the organization's financial goals, but the organization's enterprise environmental factors (EEFs) as well. Though Answers A, B, and C are all important selection criteria for a vendor, the introduction of a new software system into a company's technology infrastructure presents a tremendous security vulnerability. (In the technology sector, this lack of trust in "black box" software and firmware technologies—where operational procedure is invisible and beyond the control of the organization—is one of the primary reasons companies have been slow to migrate to cloud platforms, blockchain databases, or artificial intelligence (AI) integrations. The potential risk of expensive lawsuits due to security breaches would bankrupt most organizations.) The overall risk of Answer D outweighs any other consideration due to risk.

89. B: Large changes to the project scope can be integrated into the release and iteration plan in an upcoming release. Agile planning is done at the last responsible moment, with details of user stories elaborated in the planning meeting for the upcoming iteration. Agile teams do not use work breakdown structures and scope baselines as predictive approaches do, as the scope is expected to change. Iterations are generally completed once started, with the product owner having authority to stop it.

90. D: The project manager in the scenario rewards workers versus penalizing them for underperformance.

91. D: The precedence diagramming method models a project schedule with activities as nodes connected by relationships that demonstrate the sequence of activities. In start-to-finish relationships, a predecessor activity cannot finish until a successor activity has started. Finish-to-start, the most common, means the successor cannot start until the predecessor has been completed. Finish-to-finish means the successor cannot finish until the predecessor has also finished, while start-to-start indicates the successor cannot start until a predecessor has started.

92. D: The project team has already tried to find a compromise without success. In the interest of time, keeping the project on track, and staying in alignment with the sponsor, a forcing approach is necessary from someone with authority.

93. D: The problem originated when the designer and developers deviated from the approved design without utilizing the change control process. Many software-based projects utilize Agile methodologies wherein the change process is fluid and informal compared to the change control process of predictive or hybrid projects. Agile development requires the direct and regular involvement of the project sponsor throughout the project; due to ongoing feedback, there are no surprises at the end of the project. In this scenario, however, although software is one component, the sponsor has not been regularly updated. For exam purposes, assume this is a traditional project approach with a formal change process required. The change process is requested by any stakeholder, then researched and guided by the project manager. (There will likely be at least one question on the exam regarding disappointed stakeholders. At times the answer may be poor communication, poor collection of requirements, or poor stakeholder engagement. Base your answer selection on the root cause of the problem, or "when" the project diverged from the anticipated path.)

94. C and E: Work performance data is an output of Direct and Manage Project Work. The procurement management plan details which resources will need to be obtained from outside vendors as well as the processes for establishing and maintaining contracts for goods and services. The project schedule, activity cost estimates, and cost management plan are inputs for the Determine Budget process.

95. D: The best answer is to tell the group "No." The proposed changes have already been denied by the project sponsor. Therefore, there is no need to inform the sponsor. If the scenario had asked what the project manager should "do first," all change requests begin with a review of the documents and considerations (as in answer B), followed by C as a "do next." For the exam, the deliberate omission of a "do first" or "do next" in a question should leave you to default to the "best" answer option. Also, once the project manager and project sponsor have validated the scope and have formally accepted the deliverables, major additions, updates, or changes to the product will need to be conducted via a new and separate project. (In this question scenario, a reasonable alternative answer choice might be "Tell them no"—because the sponsor already rejected the changes once—"and propose a separate project after the conclusion of the current project.")

96. D: Assumptions are general understandings or conditions but can be fluid, flexible, and subject to change. (Example: "The technology update assumes the project will utilize the existing on-premises server rooms and equipment; no additional technology will be required for servers 102, 103, and 104.") Operating under the assumption of the availability of existing tools and resources for project use can minimize risk by deploying familiar tools for quicker user adoption or by saving additional expense by utilizing resources already on hand. Taking stock of assets, assumptions, and constraints from a breadth of project stakeholders during the initializing and planning process phases enables the project manager to develop a comprehensive and proactive risk register.

97. C: Crystal methodology recommends more lightweight procedures for smaller and less important projects, and more rigor if the project is larger and more critical. In Crystal recommendations, the number of people involves ranges from 1 to 500, and criticality ranges from comfort, to discretionary money, to essential money, to life. Crystal Red is for teams of up to 100 people and for when defects cause loss of essential money or life.

98. C: Because the requirements are not well-defined, an adaptive approach would be beneficial to elicit requirements over time, and prototypes or demonstrations would help stakeholders concretely understand what they are looking for. However, due to the strict regulations, some parts of the project will likely need to be predictive and follow strict protocols. Therefore, a hybrid approach is most appropriate.

99. B: Seven or more data points grouped on one side of the mean or the other triggers the Rule of Seven, where the process must be investigated. Seven or more indicates a nonrandom element may be affecting production, and the process is not in control.

100. D: The project manager uses variance and trend analysis as the tools during the process—not an output. Much of the variance and trend focus is applied to work performance data in conjunction with the Control Scope and the Manage Quality processes to avoid or mitigate the risk of waste, schedule overrun, rework, or faulty products.

101. D: Whether there is a production delay, project issue, or conflict management concern, always research and investigate the project plan and related data *first* to confirm the project is proceeding according to plan and to understand the source of the problem. Crashing the project will increase the budget for a project that is probably already over budget—you don't know until you obtain an accurate project status via answer D. Holding a meeting with the stakeholders won't be effective because you don't have a full picture yet, and you would need to notify the project sponsor next. As the project manager, you are expected to drive the project decisions in conjunction with accurate data and the awareness of the project sponsor. In this scenario, the rest of the stakeholders can be consulted after the sponsor is updated.

102. C: Review the documents first. Though not an option here, the next step would be to meet with the dissenting stakeholder to show how the project documentation specifications—the functionality, feature, and quality requirements—align with the work output. Next, the project manager should seek the root cause of the misalignment and consider the change request or rework. If all deliverable work has met requirements and a majority of the stakeholders remain in agreement, it will be up to the project sponsor whether to accept the deliverables.

103. B: The base formula for communication channels is $\frac{n(n-1)}{2}$ where n is the number of stakeholders. This scenario was looking for the difference between the original total channel count and the new.

You originally had 9 stakeholders, including yourself. $\frac{9(9-1)}{2} = 36$ original channels.

With the addition of 5 new stakeholders, your base stakeholder count will be 14.

$\frac{14(14-1)}{2} = 91$ channels at the end of next month.

91 channels next month – 36 original channels = 55 additional channels added.

For calculation questions, remember the importance of order of operations with the mnemonic PEMDAS: parentheses, exponents, multiplication, division, addition, subtraction. For communication channels specifically, you need to begin with n, the total count of stakeholders. You must add the new stakeholders to the existing count of stakeholders before completing the channel calculation.

104. C: Three-point estimating takes the average of optimistic, most likely, and pessimistic estimates, or $\frac{O+ML+P}{3}$. The PERT technique weights the most likely estimate using the formula $\frac{O+4ML+P}{6}$.

105. C: With regard to projects, schedule conflicts, project priorities, and resource allocations are the root cause of more than half of all conflicts in project management. (Remember, money and staff are resources too.) Personality differences come into play as a secondary source of conflict via a reaction to one of the other three root causes of project conflict.

106. D: You are still in the initialization process phase. Though the project charter has been developed, the stakeholder register is the second key output of this phase. The key organizational stakeholders will have been named in the project charter, but it is now time to expand the stakeholder register. You will need documentation of who your known stakeholders are, and their level of influence and level of interest in the project, before you can begin planning for answers A, B, and C. (For the exam, remember that the stakeholder register is updated throughout the project as new stakeholders appear and existing stakeholders either leave or change roles. Additionally, the process of updating the stakeholder register does NOT require a formal change request.)

107. D: You must sequence the activities prior to developing the schedule. Answer A, create the activities list, has already been completed in this scenario. A RACI chart is used to categorize stakeholders (responsible, accountable, consulted, informed) by level of influence on the project; a RACI chart has nothing to do with activity scheduling.

108. C: Project managers must ensure vendors are complying with the terms of the contract. Before altering the payment schedule or officially canceling a contract with a vendor, a project manager is required to issue an official default letter to the vendor. Answer D is a reasonable real-world response for a "should do *first*" question; the IT team will need to inspect the vendor's installations soon or risk the possibility of a security breach. However, Answer D does not address the actual question in this scenario of what to do about the vendor. For the exam, be mindful of "do *first*" and "do *next*" questions, which indicate steps in a process, versus the "should do" questions, which usually default to the "best" response option.

109. A: Proper planning and risk assessment should be done prior to the execution process phase as part of tailoring for the organization and the project; this minimizes the need for changes once project work begins. The exam is likely to include several questions regarding change management.

110. D: Communication models demonstrate how senders' and recipients' knowledge, experience, and styles influence communication, and that face-to-face is the most well-rounded communication channel. The two individuals had different approaches that needed to be reconciled, and the project manager should have chosen a different channel based on the individual team member and what was being communicated. There is no indication that the communications management plan was not followed or that the team member wanted a more formal review.

111. B: According to PMI, you should not accept gifts from sponsors since it could tarnish your integrity if perceived as a conflict of interest; the exception reflected in this scenario would be if the giving of the gift is part of the standard business culture in that country. In that case, accept the gift graciously in order to not offend the giver. (Adopt the "When in Rome..." approach, but let your boss know so your integrity is not questioned later.)

112. B: An information radiator is a low-tech, highly visible way of sharing project information in a timely manner. It is preferred in Agile projects as a means of sharing information with the organization without disturbing the team. The project manager is responsible for shielding the team from distractions, and getting updates from the team directly would take them away from their work. The standup meetings and retrospectives are for the project team to plan their work and improve processes, not for updates with stakeholders. The information radiator is more direct, timely, efficient, and personal than an email report.

113. D: A make-or-buy (or build-or-buy) analysis calculates whether it is more economically beneficial to outsource something or build it in-house. A simple method is to divide the difference between the up-front costs by the difference between the monthly costs, or:

$$\frac{Inhouse\ cost - Outsource\ cost}{Inhouse\ monthly - Outsource\ monthly}$$

The result is the number of months until it would be cheaper to build in-house, so if the product is being used for a longer period of time, it will no longer be economical to outsource. Of course, other factors such as skillsets, solution availability, resources, quality, and control impact the decision as well.

114. B: Originating in the lean enterprise approach, value stream mapping investigates the flow of information and materials that create a product or service, with the intent to improve efficiency. Non-value-added steps are eliminated. Business justification analysis methods provide metrics that make the case for a project, while SWOT analysis is a decision-making framework that identifies strengths, weaknesses, opportunities, and threats. Crystal is an Agile project management methodology.

115. D: An Agile charter introduces the themes of the project, including the product vision, who benefits and how, the definition of "done," and the flow of work. An iteration plan elaborates the work for an upcoming iteration, while the Agile manifesto is a set of four key values of the Agile mindset. A benefits management plan does elaborate the benefits of a project and how they will be tracked, but it is associated with a predictive approach.

116. A: This technique uses rounds of anonymous estimates to build a consensus. Dot voting or multi-voting does not avoid the bandwagon effect, as participants can see what others are voting for. Kaizen is a process improvement approach aiming for incremental changes for the better, while Shu-Ha-Ri is a model of skill acquisition progressing from following rules, to choosing how (or whether) to implement rules, to mastery and innovation.

117. B: The OSCAR model, created by Karen Whittleworth and Andrew Gilbert, helps leaders to support the personal development of others. The five components are outcome, situation, choices/consequences, actions, and review.

118. C: The project manager should first refer to the communications management plan and the stakeholder engagement plan to see what has been planned for managing the community group. They should then perform stakeholder analysis and update the stakeholder register with new information. While reaching out and engaging the group according to new communications plans will be vital, it should be preceded by preliminary analysis.

119. A: A mandatory dependency is a relationship between activities that is contractually required or is inherent to the work. The project team is contractually required to deliver parts at a certain time, so this cannot be modified. A discretionary dependency is founded in best practices or project preferences, and it may be modifiable. An external dependency exists between project activities and non-project activities and is usually out of the project manager's control, while an internal dependency is between project activities and might be flexible.

120. A: Face-to-face communication is the most rich and effective method, allowing for both nonverbal cues and more interactive feedback and response. The project champion might help with influencing the finance department, but the project manager should be proactive in managing the situation first. Pull communication relies on the recipient to seek out the information and would not help this scenario. Finally, there is no indication that miscommunication is happening, so it is not necessary at the moment.

121. D: Co-location allows team members to absorb information "through osmosis" and share knowledge effortlessly. Being dedicated to a single project enhances productivity but does not necessarily lead to knowledge sharing. Similarly, delivering increments of value and limiting work in progress (WIP) helps the team to be focused and productive but does not necessarily result in shared information.

122. D: Enhancing an opportunity describes the process of using means to increase the chances of an opportunity occurring to influence an outcome; however, the probability of the opportunity is still not certain. In contrast, exploiting is forcing the opportunity to happen. Accepting is doing nothing to respond to the opportunity. Sharing involves splitting the benefit of the opportunity with a third party, and escalating is bringing it to a higher authority, like the supervisor or program manager.

123. C: You are in the process of executing or "doing" the work of managing stakeholder engagement according to the stakeholder management plan, and as the project manager, you are responsible for its ultimate success or failure. The goal of this process is to keep your stakeholders satisfied via positive relationships, persistent communication, and effective coordination among all stakeholder groups. Answer B, Identify Stakeholders, begins during the initializing phase and continues throughout the project. Plan Stakeholder Engagement occurs during the planning phase and outputs the stakeholder management plan. Monitor Stakeholder Engagement audits the stakeholder management activities for compliance with the stakeholder engagement plan as well as opportunities to improve the engagement processes.

124. B: The project manager should learn what motivates team members as individuals. A single bonus would reward one individual at the expense of others and is a misuse of other funds. While more responsibility and autonomy is a motivator, it may not be received the same way by senior and junior developers. Finally, a retreat with team-building activities is more likely done at the beginning of the project.

125. B: The critical path is the longest path or sequence of activities through the project, where there is usually no flexibility on start dates in order for the project to finish on time. The critical path is calculated by adding up the activity durations along the various paths and determining which one is the longest. Adding up the durations of each consecutive activity in answer B leads to 19 days. Option A is 15 days, option D is 15 days, and option C is not possible according to the diagram (the arrow shows that activity F must precede activity C).

126. A: The Kanban method is derived from lean thinking and is characterized by visualizing workflows, limiting work in progress, and valuing transparency of process. The Kanban board, with columns for workflow states like To Do, In Progress, Testing, Done, or other steps, is the most well-known and utilized part of the approach.

127. A: Inspections generally apply to a product or a work activity to gauge whether or not the work is successful according to the scope. Audits scrutinize the work based on the entirety of the process. (Is the method of output efficient, safe, and proceeding according to the quality management plan?) A process review is part of the audit process. A SWOT analysis evaluates risk during the Plan Risk Management process.

128. D: Above all, the servant leader keeps the team's focus on the project. Answer C is also within the scope of the project manager's duties, but it is not specifically indicative of servant leadership. Answers A and B are not appropriate for Agile teams since the teams self-manage and select their own tools and processes on behalf of the group; the project manager is there to guide and coach. Keep in mind that modern Agile has changed the term "servant leader" to "leader" to give the project manager more assertive authority when needed. For the exam, a servant leader keeps the team focused on the project vision by removing obstacles so the team can manage their own work.

129. D: Rather than assigning staff unfamiliar work that would likely result in costly errors, the company can instead transfer the risk to a third party that specializes in data storage, retrieval, and administration. The organization will incur more long-term operational costs by utilizing the cloud services vendor. However, the organization will reduce the likelihood of triggering the risk event (since data security will be monitored by experts) and will share the financial responsibility of the damages with the cloud services company in the event of a security breach. (Insurance policies are examples of transferred risk as well. A homeowner shares the risk and expense of repairs in the event of natural disasters by incurring an additional cost investment in advance.)

Avoiding the risk entirely would require a complete change of plan—via the integrated change control process—to evade the risk trigger. Accepting the risk involves setting aside significant reserves for when the inevitable anticipated risk occurs; there is enough opportunity to be achieved by continuing the project to offset the additional expenses incurred with the risk. Mitigating the risk involves a slight deviation in the plan to reduce the impact of the risk. A mitigating solution here would be to install additional data backup systems and commit to funding and deploying a mandatory, ongoing training regimen for all of the organization's IT team. From a security standpoint, the organization may not have the protection offered by the cloud services experts, the organization would still be responsible for the cost of infrastructure upkeep and training, the likelihood of the risk trigger occurring would be reduced, and the organization would still be able to assume full control of its data administration procedures.

130. C: This kind of contract includes predetermined financial adjustments that can account for inflation or price fluctuations over time and is ideal for long-term contracts.

131. B: The Tuckman's Ladder theory asserts that it takes some time for a new team to form or get to know each other well enough to establish a team charter and settle into a workflow. Storming occurs when differences of opinion and work styles cause conflicts. Eventually, the team will "norm" by settling down and conceding to each other or by agreeing to disagree. The team then hits their full productive stride in the performing stage. The team completes final reviews and team reflections during the adjourning stage.

132. A: McGregor's Theory X suggests people do not like to work and require micromanaging to keep them on task. McGregor's Theory Y suggests people inherently like to work and find satisfaction in autonomy and work done well. (For the exam, be a Theory Y manager.) Theory Z is from William Ouchi and claims it is an organization's responsibility to take care of its employees; if employees are well treated and well compensated, they will be loyal to the organization and be willing to invest more of their effort. The Two-Factor Theory refers to Herzberg's hygiene and motivation factors that employees need to be productive. Hygiene factors include salary, schedule, and working conditions that physically affect a worker's well-being, while motivation factors such as training, recognition, and upward mobility are equally important.

133. C: Nonverbal communication uses no words. Tone of voice, however, is considered nonverbal. Several communication theorists attribute more than 70% of the messages we send to nonverbal communication. For the exam, 50% or more is a safe response.

134. A and B: Servant leadership responsibilities include removing organizational impediments and providing mentoring, development, and support to team members. The other approaches (transactional, laissez-faire, and charismatic) may be appropriate in other situations. One of the Agile Manifesto tenets is "Individuals and interactions over processes and tools." While there is value in set processes, the human element and flexibility are more highly valued.

135. A: The project manager has not accounted for external failure costs, that is, costs associated with defects that make their way to the customer. Examples include repairs, warranties, returns, and damage to reputation. Internal failure costs are incurred when defects are found and remediated. These are the costs of noncompliance. Appraisal costs are for determining conformance to quality requirements through measuring and monitoring, while prevention includes product/service requirements, quality planning, quality assurance, and training. These are the costs of compliance.

136. A: The risk report is a holistic statement for the overall project, while the risk register is a catalog for known individual risks on the project. An initial risk register is created at the outset of the project, wherein risks are designated by an ID, a risk type, potential cause, and the affected department or area of the project. The risks identified in the risk register are then subjected to the Plan Risk Response process, where a preliminary response is added to the risk register. Once the project work begins, additional risks usually originate as issues in the issue log and progress to formal inclusion to the risk register upon further analysis.

137. A: Agile teams perform best when self-organized and self-managed, as the team owns their work product while the servant leader facilitates and empowers them. Furthermore, working software is prioritized over comprehensive documentation. The project manager is treating the Agile phase as they would a predictive project, rather than adapting their approach.

138. A: Specific policies or procedure constraints for vendor solicitation outlined by the organization are part of the organizational process assets (OPAs) for the project. Requests for proposals, vendor selection based on the source selection criteria, and eventual agreements will follow. However, the process is guided by the mandates of the vendor policy within the organizational process assets.

139. A: The work authorization system utilizes the work breakdown structure (WBS), the work activities list, and the project schedule to deploy the actual work based on the authorization parameters agreed to within project contracts with the organization. The goal of the work authorization system is to ensure that work is conducted in a controlled, predictable manner and only at the right time. A project manager must make sure needed resources are available at the right time and not sitting in storage risking theft or decay. (Remember, "waiting" is one of the seven "wastes" that Lean project managers want to avoid.) Appropriately timed utilization of resources ensures the project manager can monitor and control work effectively as well. The project management information system (PMIS) is a collection of software tools and knowledge banks for conducting the project processes.

140. D: The resource calendar is created during the Acquire Resources process. The project manager must define the project activities during the scheduling phase before the planning and acquiring resources process can begin.

141. C: When a threat is outside the project scope or the response exceeds the project manager's authority, escalation passes the decision to someone with the proper authority. The transfer of risk shifts responsibility to a third party who handles the risk and its impacts. Mitigation is taking early action to reduce the threat's probability or impact, and acceptance offers no proactive action to the risk.

142. A and E: Procurement and contracts are regulated, involve legal obligations, and are usually outside the project manager's authority. Risk management is also related to legal compliance and may be managed by a business unit for the entire organization. Decisions about value delivery, schedule management, and stakeholder engagement are specific to individual projects and are less likely to involve organizational policies (although they still could).

143. D: Rewards, recognition, and training are tools utilized during the develop team process—you can't reward someone for work that has yet to be completed. Remember that "acquiring" is "hiring" the team; have them meet, greet, and establish the team charter. The resource calendar is the "big picture" of team member availability (e.g., Mary will be on maternity leave in December). This does not reflect the day-to-day work schedule for long-term team members.

144. D: The first step would be to see if project activities can be rearranged and have the graphic designers perform the work when they are available. The PMO may have a procedure for contracting with outside vendors, but the project manager would need to see if it is in the budget. The schedule network diagram shows float, not the project calendar, while the requirements management plan describes how requirements will be planned, tracked, and reported.

145. B and E: The law of diminishing returns means that at some point, the project will hit a limiting factor and increasing resources will yield less value. For example, adding additional labor to a manufacturing project will cease being effective if there is no room in the warehouse for them to work. Second, a learning curve is expected when new personnel must learn and practice the work. In this scenario, the scope, acceptance criteria, and business case do not need to be adjusted, only the cost and resources.

146. B: Agile teams are empowered to work collectively and self-organize. Learning new skills and being able to share the work allows for flexibility, skill growth, collaboration, and team ownership of the work. The team could plausibly hire additional developers or bring in an expert, but these options would be more costly, disrupt the team cohesion, and be more directive and less of a servant leader style. The team works collaboratively with the product owner, but the product owner must prioritize features that are valuable to the customers over features that are easier for the development team.

147. C: Satisfaction means a positive experience for customers, including usability. The website was of high technical quality but did not pay enough attention to what would satisfy the customer. Resilience refers to dealing with unforeseen circumstances, reliability is being able to deliver consistent results, and uniformity is parity or equality with other deliverables.

148. D: Sunk costs occur when the project has ended with no viable deliverable and no additional compensation to cover the expense. Costs lost to unrealized deliverables can also be considered sunk when a project makes an abrupt change in course. The money invested in the development of abandoned prototypes is considered lost. Fortunately, creative corporate accounting can often yield tax deductions to offset the lost investment. Opportunity costs are the cost of the alternatives not taken or the projects not chosen in lieu of the preferred choice. For example, when considering the purchase of storage shed A at $8,000 versus storage shed B at $12,000, if you decide to purchase shed A, your opportunity cost would be $12,000—the cost of the shed option not chosen. Absorbed costs refer to gray-area costs for which there may not have been project funds allocated originally. Instead, they are paid from budgets from other departments via creative accounting. For example, if a project manager needs a single-license access to a software program already utilized by the organization, the functional accounting office might agree to fund the single license out of the existing IT department budget and let the IT department absorb the cost. Depreciation costs refer to the reduction in financial value of assets such as machinery, computers, and vehicles over time.

149. A: During retrospectives, the team identifies a limited number of action items they can attack in the next iteration and decides how to validate the success or failure. Trying to change too many things at once will likely lead to none of them being done well. Retrospectives address both the qualitative (feelings, people, relationships) and the quantitative (processes, tools, data) for ways of improvement. Finally, retrospectives are not about assigning blame, but are meant to help the team reflect and make incremental changes for the better.

150. C: According to the PMI code of ethics, you must report all misrepresentations to the PMI office. The other answer choices may seem more appropriate to avoid conflict in a real-world scenario, but for the exam, stick with the "What would PMBOK do?" choice. Also, for question scenarios that create a compromised situation where a lie would make a solution more palatable, always opt for the answer choice that maintains honesty and integrity.

151. B: Velocity is the average story points completed per iteration and can be used to estimate how much longer the project will take. Calculate $300 \div 50 = 6$ two-week sprints, or 12 weeks.

152. A: ABEFH yields the highest value of 22 days. The critical path is always the longest path.

153. A: Refer to the solution notes regarding calculating the late start of a predecessor activity for converging paths on a backwards-pass. Use the lowest late start value going backwards to set the late finish value for E.

154. D: Activity B is on the critical path. Therefore, the entire schedule will be increased by 6 days since there is no float on the critical path.

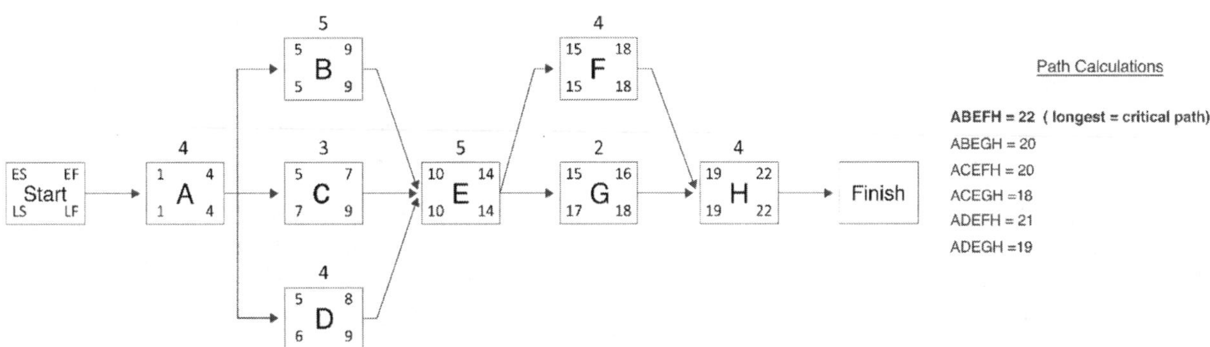

155. D: Quality metrics are the standards of measurement for project quality. Plan Quality Management outputs the quality management plan. The plan includes the processes and approaches the project will utilize to ensure quality (e.g., Lean Six Sigma or ITIL) and states the KPIs for project quality. Manage Quality occurs during the executing phase and uses the quality metrics to test the product or deliverable compared to the requirements in the project scope. Control Quality is part of monitoring and controlling quality for the project processes themselves. There are four processes that are interdependent and easily confused. The project manager performs inspections and walkthroughs frequently to control scope; he or she ensures all of the scope requirements—and only those requirements—are being met to avoid scope creep and gold plating. At the same time, the project manager is also managing quality by comparing product testing data to the quality metrics in the quality management plan. The project manager is also using those same quality metrics to control quality—converting performance data into performance information reports and comparing the project processes with the quality management plan. When the product is finished, the project manager verifies the deliverables have met the scope requirements as an output to the control quality process. He or she then confers with the sponsor to validate the scope.

156. D: The project manager investigates misunderstandings and supports the team through conflict resolution. When the project manager facilitates the conversation and invites the team members' participation, they will have buy-in with the result. A collaborative solution is preferable to forcing a resolution based on authority or seniority. Plan, Do, Check, Act (PDCA) is used for iterative process improvement rather than conflict resolution.

157. D: Compromising occurs when both sides must give up something; neither party walks away completely satisfied. Smoothing involves acknowledging the opposing side's arguments or feelings—and sometimes involves being humbled or chastised—to end a potentially volatile encounter that might make things worse; you smooth ruffled feathers temporarily while making a strategic retreat. Forcing uses power of authority or flexing of status to exert pressure on the opposing party to agree or comply. Collaborating is the only win-win approach—both sides work together to find a solution that satisfies all parties.

158. B and D: The Agile Practice Guide identifies some organizational practices that are roadblocks to organizational agility, including rewarding local efficiencies rather than cross-organizational optimization and pulling employees onto too many projects rather than being dedicated to one at a time.

159. B: Tacit knowledge is more difficult to explain and document than explicit knowledge, as tacit knowledge is more personal, gained from experience, and involves general know-how. Job shadowing would be the best opportunity for newer team members to learn by seeing how senior members do their work and discuss it on the job. Learning by experience rather than from a database is more useful for this kind of information, and while a knowledge fair might increase networking, the information shared would not be in depth. A training event would not address the kind of knowledge and skill that appears through on-the-job shadowing.

160. C: Agile approaches tend to create the minimum responsible documentation, which means creating required artifacts while eliminating waste or excess work. The sprint backlog is a necessary list of user stories the team plans to complete in the given time box. An activity list includes schedule activities, identifiers, descriptions, and scope of work, and is associated with more predictive approaches. A user guide is helpful but likely outside the scope of the project team's planned work. Project schedule network diagrams are associated with predictive approaches when all activities and their dependencies can be mapped.

161. C: Progressive elaboration is encouraged in Agile development since the lack of strict scheduling allows for frequent changes and refinement of the scope from sprint to sprint. It is similar to the requirements gathering process in predictive projects, but the scope is always subject to reinterpretation. Choices A and D are not official PMBOK terms.

162. C: Before taking any further steps, the project manager should gather more information and find out if there has been a miscommunication with the vendor and whether the issues stem from the project team or the vendor. The other options might be useful or viable after gathering more information, but the project manager must know more about the source of the problem to properly troubleshoot.

163. A: Answer A refers to the earned value management, or EVM, formulas used to measure earned cost and schedule performance value for the project. Expected monetary value analysis, or EMV analysis, is part of the quantitative risk analysis process. It looks at the total cost of decisions—the risk cost of action choice 1 versus action choice 2.

164. A: The Validate Scope process occurs at the end of a project phase or milestone and serves as a final test of the deliverable (or its incremental component). The product is evaluated based on performance and quality requirements as itemized in the requirements documents as well as the acceptance criteria from the project scope statement. In this scenario, the stakeholders were already aware of their requirements, so answers B and D can be eliminated. The quality management plan is focused on the appropriateness, efficiency, and efficacy of the project production processes.

165. D: Because adaptive projects involve a high level of change and contracts are fixed, a type of contract that can accommodate flexibility is needed. The elements that do not change are in the master agreement, while the specifics of the work are in a supplement that can be more easily amended. A request for information (RFI) is used to request information on the goods and services that sellers are providing. In fixed price incentive fee (FPIF) contracts, the buyer pays a set amount, and the seller can earn more if they meet additional defined criteria. Terms of reference (TOR) are used when contracting for services and include tasks, quality standards, and schedule.

166. D: Adaptive projects respond to change by updating and refining the backlog accordingly. A way of focusing on delivering value is to create a minimum viable product, which has only the core features needed to be successful. A retrospective identifies ways of improving project work, while features that are easy to complete may not be the most important to the customer. A change control process with a change control board is a predictive change management technique.

167. D: The theory states that if motivational factors like achievement and advancement are lacking, employees are dissatisfied. Furthermore, hygiene factors such as policies, pay, and environment are necessary but not sufficient for satisfaction.

168. C: The velocity chart tracks the productivity points of work completed by the team each sprint; the project manager and team can utilize the data for productivity planning in future sprints. (It takes a few sprints for the team to find its stride, so early sprints on a velocity chart may not be representative of the team's capability.) The burnup chart shows how much work has been completed on the project, while the burndown chart shows how much work is remaining. The Kanban board, like a Scrum board, is an information radiator for work in progress during the current and possibly adjacent sprints.

169. B: Closure begins with the formal acceptance of all deliverables by the sponsor. The team(s) are needed to make minor adjustments and help update the lessons learned before they are officially released to other projects. Closure ends with closing the contract, wherein the accounting office is notified that it is officially time to pay and send invoices per the contract terms. The lessons learned documentation gets filed with the PMO and as a part of the knowledge transfer to the sponsor with the deliverables. (For the exam, if the project is canceled early for any reason, all projects must go through a complete closure process. Project phases may also require a complete or partial closure process as well.)

170. D: Incremental life cycles provide finished deliverables throughout the project that can be used right away, rather than a final delivery at the end. This approach offers speed of delivery and lets the customer receive value from a part of the solution. Incremental development also allows for adaptation and change of scope as the project progresses. Since the project is developing a novel product with a high level of uncertainty, predictive or hybrid approaches are not appropriate. An iterative approach allows for adaptation, but does not necessarily deliver increments of usable deliverables early on.

171. A: Though the project manager commits to a number of teams or team members required during the estimate activity resources phases, the actual recruitment and establishment of worker teams does not begin until the acquire resources process. Estimating activity resources includes as one of its outputs a list of resource requirements to be procured. The resource breakdown structure (RBS) itemizes resources into a hierarchy of resource categories (e.g., people, hardware, firmware, software, materials). A basis of estimates is also included as an output to describe the rationale, range of estimates, and methodologies involved in the resource calculations.

172. B: Feedback is the return acknowledgement that the recipient did receive the message, however, there is no requirement for agreement with the message. Remember that noise and interference (synonymous terms) are things that interrupt active and effective listening. Email is a means to both encode and decode information.

173. D: "Do first" answers should usually require researching and investigating first the documentation, then the root cause. Answer B cannot be considered until the cause of the defects has been determined. Answers A and C are incorrect statements of procedure—the project manager controls the contingency reserves (already included in the project budget), while the organization and project sponsor issue management reserves.

174. C: Stakeholder engagement needs to be tailored to the intended audience and the situation. In this scenario, the funder has asked for well-documented communications to a wide community audience, and a formal tone would best fit their reputation. A project website could be as formal as needed and would be available for anyone in the community to visit. A social media account would be too informal, while town hall meetings and focus groups could be harder to document thoroughly—and, most importantly, would reach a smaller audience.

175. A: The communications management plan includes information about who needs what information and when, and it makes sure that communication is monitored throughout the project. As needs change, the plan is altered through the change management process to adapt to these changes. The stakeholder engagement plan would not have detailed information about communications schedule and distribution, and no changes should be made outside of the change request process.

176. B: The project management office does not provide guidance for specific project-related decisions. These are tailored for the organization and the project by the project manager, with the consultation of the organizational stakeholders.

177. C: Compliance with regulations is extremely important for the project's success and for the organization's reputation. The project manager and the organization must do so even if it means considerable rework, but putting out a report and generating publicity about their environmental stewardship is a way of turning the risk into a positive opportunity to build goodwill and reputation. Avoiding compliance or partial compliance are risks that could impact project success and organizational reputation negatively. Pausing the project is a feasible approach, but it does not take full advantage of the situation.

178. C: The components of the project management plan can be useful for future projects to see how aspects were handled in a similar situation. A prioritization schema is a method for prioritizing requirements or project components. The output might be archived for future use, but not the method itself. The TCPI is the cost performance needed to meet project goals and may be incorporated into project reports, but it is not a standalone artifact. Work performance information and reports that summarize data are more likely to be retained than the raw work performance data.

179. D: The band for testing is thicker than the others, indicating that many tasks have accumulated in this step. The team leader should prioritize removing impediments and improving efficiency of testing.

180. B: Predictive/waterfall development approaches tend to work best for projects in critical or highly regulated industries. The top-down authority approach works fine for predictive projects but contradicts a hallmark of self-managing Agile teams. The large team size is also not suitable for Agile, and it cannot be delivered incrementally, which rules out answer C. None of the characteristics given indicate that an Agile approach is appropriate.

PMP Practice Test #2

To take this additional PMP practice test, visit our bonus page:
mometrix.com/bonus948/pmp

How to Overcome Test Anxiety

Just the thought of taking a test is enough to make most people a little nervous. A test is an important event that can have a long-term impact on your future, so it's important to take it seriously and it's natural to feel anxious about performing well. But just because anxiety is normal, that doesn't mean that it's helpful in test taking, or that you should simply accept it as part of your life. Anxiety can have a variety of effects. These effects can be mild, like making you feel slightly nervous, or severe, like blocking your ability to focus or remember even a simple detail.

If you experience test anxiety—whether severe or mild—it's important to know how to beat it. To discover this, first you need to understand what causes test anxiety.

Causes of Test Anxiety

While we often think of anxiety as an uncontrollable emotional state, it can actually be caused by simple, practical things. One of the most common causes of test anxiety is that a person does not feel adequately prepared for their test. This feeling can be the result of many different issues such as poor study habits or lack of organization, but the most common culprit is time management. Starting to study too late, failing to organize your study time to cover all of the material, or being distracted while you study will mean that you're not well prepared for the test. This may lead to cramming the night before, which will cause you to be physically and mentally exhausted for the test. Poor time management also contributes to feelings of stress, fear, and hopelessness as you realize you are not well prepared but don't know what to do about it.

Other times, test anxiety is not related to your preparation for the test but comes from unresolved fear. This may be a past failure on a test, or poor performance on tests in general. It may come from comparing yourself to others who seem to be performing better or from the stress of living up to expectations. Anxiety may be driven by fears of the future—how failure on this test would affect your educational and career goals. These fears are often completely irrational, but they can still negatively impact your test performance.

Elements of Test Anxiety

As mentioned earlier, test anxiety is considered to be an emotional state, but it has physical and mental components as well. Sometimes you may not even realize that you are suffering from test anxiety until you notice the physical symptoms. These can include trembling hands, rapid heartbeat, sweating, nausea, and tense muscles. Extreme anxiety may lead to fainting or vomiting. Obviously, any of these symptoms can have a negative impact on testing. It is important to recognize them as soon as they begin to occur so that you can address the problem before it damages your performance.

The mental components of test anxiety include trouble focusing and inability to remember learned information. During a test, your mind is on high alert, which can help you recall information and stay focused for an extended period of time. However, anxiety interferes with your mind's natural processes, causing you to blank out, even on the questions you know well. The strain of testing during anxiety makes it difficult to stay focused, especially on a test that may take several hours. Extreme anxiety can take a huge mental toll, making it difficult not only to recall test information but even to understand the test questions or pull your thoughts together.

Effects of Test Anxiety

Test anxiety is like a disease—if left untreated, it will get progressively worse. Anxiety leads to poor performance, and this reinforces the feelings of fear and failure, which in turn lead to poor performances on subsequent tests. It can grow from a mild nervousness to a crippling condition. If allowed to progress, test anxiety can have a big impact on your schooling, and consequently on your future.

Test anxiety can spread to other parts of your life. Anxiety on tests can become anxiety in any stressful situation, and blanking on a test can turn into panicking in a job situation. But fortunately, you don't have to let anxiety rule your testing and determine your grades. There are a number of relatively simple steps you can take to move past anxiety and function normally on a test and in the rest of life.

Physical Steps for Beating Test Anxiety

While test anxiety is a serious problem, the good news is that it can be overcome. It doesn't have to control your ability to think and remember information. While it may take time, you can begin taking steps today to beat anxiety.

Just as your first hint that you may be struggling with anxiety comes from the physical symptoms, the first step to treating it is also physical. Rest is crucial for having a clear, strong mind. If you are tired, it is much easier to give in to anxiety. But if you establish good sleep habits, your body and mind will be ready to perform optimally, without the strain of exhaustion. Additionally, sleeping well helps you to retain information better, so you're more likely to recall the answers when you see the test questions.

Getting good sleep means more than going to bed on time. It's important to allow your brain time to relax. Take study breaks from time to time so it doesn't get overworked, and don't study right before bed. Take time to rest your mind before trying to rest your body, or you may find it difficult to fall asleep.

Along with sleep, other aspects of physical health are important in preparing for a test. Good nutrition is vital for good brain function. Sugary foods and drinks may give a burst of energy but this burst is followed by a crash, both physically and emotionally. Instead, fuel your body with protein and vitamin-rich foods.

Also, drink plenty of water. Dehydration can lead to headaches and exhaustion, especially if your brain is already under stress from the rigors of the test. Particularly if your test is a long one, drink water during the breaks. And if possible, take an energy-boosting snack to eat between sections.

Along with sleep and diet, a third important part of physical health is exercise. Maintaining a steady workout schedule is helpful, but even taking 5-minute study breaks to walk can help get your blood pumping faster and clear your head. Exercise also releases endorphins, which contribute to a positive feeling and can help combat test anxiety.

When you nurture your physical health, you are also contributing to your mental health. If your body is healthy, your mind is much more likely to be healthy as well. So take time to rest, nourish your body with healthy food and water, and get moving as much as possible. Taking these physical steps will make you stronger and more able to take the mental steps necessary to overcome test anxiety.

Mental Steps for Beating Test Anxiety

Working on the mental side of test anxiety can be more challenging, but as with the physical side, there are clear steps you can take to overcome it. As mentioned earlier, test anxiety often stems from lack of preparation, so the obvious solution is to prepare for the test. Effective studying may be the most important weapon you have for beating test anxiety, but you can and should employ several other mental tools to combat fear.

First, boost your confidence by reminding yourself of past success—tests or projects that you aced. If you're putting as much effort into preparing for this test as you did for those, there's no reason you should expect to fail here. Work hard to prepare; then trust your preparation.

Second, surround yourself with encouraging people. It can be helpful to find a study group, but be sure that the people you're around will encourage a positive attitude. If you spend time with others who are anxious or cynical, this will only contribute to your own anxiety. Look for others who are motivated to study hard from a desire to succeed, not from a fear of failure.

Third, reward yourself. A test is physically and mentally tiring, even without anxiety, and it can be helpful to have something to look forward to. Plan an activity following the test, regardless of the outcome, such as going to a movie or getting ice cream.

When you are taking the test, if you find yourself beginning to feel anxious, remind yourself that you know the material. Visualize successfully completing the test. Then take a few deep, relaxing breaths and return to it. Work through the questions carefully but with confidence, knowing that you are capable of succeeding.

Developing a healthy mental approach to test taking will also aid in other areas of life. Test anxiety affects more than just the actual test—it can be damaging to your mental health and even contribute to depression. It's important to beat test anxiety before it becomes a problem for more than testing.

Study Strategy

Being prepared for the test is necessary to combat anxiety, but what does being prepared look like? You may study for hours on end and still not feel prepared. What you need is a strategy for test prep. The next few pages outline our recommended steps to help you plan out and conquer the challenge of preparation.

Step 1: Scope Out the Test

Learn everything you can about the format (multiple choice, essay, etc.) and what will be on the test. Gather any study materials, course outlines, or sample exams that may be available. Not only will this help you to prepare, but knowing what to expect can help to alleviate test anxiety.

Step 2: Map Out the Material

Look through the textbook or study guide and make note of how many chapters or sections it has. Then divide these over the time you have. For example, if a book has 15 chapters and you have five days to study, you need to cover three chapters each day. Even better, if you have the time, leave an extra day at the end for overall review after you have gone through the material in depth.

If time is limited, you may need to prioritize the material. Look through it and make note of which sections you think you already have a good grasp on, and which need review. While you are studying, skim quickly through the familiar sections and take more time on the challenging parts.

Write out your plan so you don't get lost as you go. Having a written plan also helps you feel more in control of the study, so anxiety is less likely to arise from feeling overwhelmed at the amount to cover.

Step 3: Gather Your Tools

Decide what study method works best for you. Do you prefer to highlight in the book as you study and then go back over the highlighted portions? Or do you type out notes of the important information? Or is it helpful to make flashcards that you can carry with you? Assemble the pens, index cards, highlighters, post-it notes, and any other materials you may need so you won't be distracted by getting up to find things while you study.

If you're having a hard time retaining the information or organizing your notes, experiment with different methods. For example, try color-coding by subject with colored pens, highlighters, or post-it notes. If you learn better by hearing, try recording yourself reading your notes so you can listen while in the car, working out, or simply sitting at your desk. Ask a friend to quiz you from your flashcards, or try teaching someone the material to solidify it in your mind.

Step 4: Create Your Environment

It's important to avoid distractions while you study. This includes both the obvious distractions like visitors and the subtle distractions like an uncomfortable chair (or a too-comfortable couch that makes you want to fall asleep). Set up the best study environment possible: good lighting and a comfortable work area. If background music helps you focus, you may want to turn it on, but otherwise keep the room quiet. If you are using a computer to take notes, be sure you don't have any other windows open, especially applications like social media, games, or anything else that could distract you. Silence your phone and turn off notifications. Be sure to keep water close by so you stay hydrated while you study (but avoid unhealthy drinks and snacks).

Also, take into account the best time of day to study. Are you freshest first thing in the morning? Try to set aside some time then to work through the material. Is your mind clearer in the afternoon or evening? Schedule your study session then. Another method is to study at the same time of day that you will take the test, so that your brain gets used to working on the material at that time and will be ready to focus at test time.

Step 5: Study!

Once you have done all the study preparation, it's time to settle into the actual studying. Sit down, take a few moments to settle your mind so you can focus, and begin to follow your study plan. Don't give in to distractions or let yourself procrastinate. This is your time to prepare so you'll be ready to fearlessly approach the test. Make the most of the time and stay focused.

Of course, you don't want to burn out. If you study too long you may find that you're not retaining the information very well. Take regular study breaks. For example, taking five minutes out of every hour to walk briskly, breathing deeply and swinging your arms, can help your mind stay fresh.

As you get to the end of each chapter or section, it's a good idea to do a quick review. Remind yourself of what you learned and work on any difficult parts. When you feel that you've mastered the material, move on to the next part. At the end of your study session, briefly skim through your notes again.

But while review is helpful, cramming last minute is NOT. If at all possible, work ahead so that you won't need to fit all your study into the last day. Cramming overloads your brain with more information than it can process and retain, and your tired mind may struggle to recall even previously learned information when it is overwhelmed with last-minute study. Also, the urgent nature of cramming and the stress placed on your brain contribute to anxiety. You'll be more likely to go to the test feeling unprepared and having trouble thinking clearly.

So don't cram, and don't stay up late before the test, even just to review your notes at a leisurely pace. Your brain needs rest more than it needs to go over the information again. In fact, plan to finish your studies by noon or early afternoon the day before the test. Give your brain the rest of the day to relax or focus on other things, and get a good night's sleep. Then you will be fresh for the test and better able to recall what you've studied.

Step 6: Take a Practice Test

Many courses offer sample tests, either online or in the study materials. This is an excellent resource to check whether you have mastered the material, as well as to prepare for the test format and environment.

Check the test format ahead of time: the number of questions, the type (multiple choice, free response, etc.), and the time limit. Then create a plan for working through them. For example, if you have 30 minutes to take a 60-question test, your limit is 30 seconds per question. Spend less time on the questions you know well so that you can take more time on the difficult ones.

If you have time to take several practice tests, take the first one open book, with no time limit. Work through the questions at your own pace and make sure you fully understand them. Gradually work up to taking a test under test conditions: sit at a desk with all study materials put away and set a timer. Pace yourself to make sure you finish the test with time to spare and go back to check your answers if you have time.

After each test, check your answers. On the questions you missed, be sure you understand why you missed them. Did you misread the question (tests can use tricky wording)? Did you forget the information? Or was it something you hadn't learned? Go back and study any shaky areas that the practice tests reveal.

Taking these tests not only helps with your grade, but also aids in combating test anxiety. If you're already used to the test conditions, you're less likely to worry about it, and working through tests until you're scoring well gives you a confidence boost. Go through the practice tests until you feel comfortable, and then you can go into the test knowing that you're ready for it.

Test Tips

On test day, you should be confident, knowing that you've prepared well and are ready to answer the questions. But aside from preparation, there are several test day strategies you can employ to maximize your performance.

First, as stated before, get a good night's sleep the night before the test (and for several nights before that, if possible). Go into the test with a fresh, alert mind rather than staying up late to study.

Try not to change too much about your normal routine on the day of the test. It's important to eat a nutritious breakfast, but if you normally don't eat breakfast at all, consider eating just a protein bar. If you're a coffee drinker, go ahead and have your normal coffee. Just make sure you time it so that the caffeine doesn't wear off right in the middle of your test. Avoid sugary beverages, and drink enough water to stay hydrated but not so much that you need a restroom break 10 minutes into the test. If your test isn't first thing in the morning, consider going for a walk or doing a light workout before the test to get your blood flowing.

Allow yourself enough time to get ready, and leave for the test with plenty of time to spare so you won't have the anxiety of scrambling to arrive in time. Another reason to be early is to select a good seat. It's helpful to sit away from doors and windows, which can be distracting. Find a good seat, get out your supplies, and settle your mind before the test begins.

When the test begins, start by going over the instructions carefully, even if you already know what to expect. Make sure you avoid any careless mistakes by following the directions.

Then begin working through the questions, pacing yourself as you've practiced. If you're not sure on an answer, don't spend too much time on it, and don't let it shake your confidence. Either skip it and come back later, or eliminate as many wrong answers as possible and guess among the remaining ones. Don't dwell on these questions as you continue—put them out of your mind and focus on what lies ahead.

Be sure to read all of the answer choices, even if you're sure the first one is the right answer. Sometimes you'll find a better one if you keep reading. But don't second-guess yourself if you do immediately know the answer. Your gut instinct is usually right. Don't let test anxiety rob you of the information you know.

If you have time at the end of the test (and if the test format allows), go back and review your answers. Be cautious about changing any, since your first instinct tends to be correct, but make sure you didn't misread any of the questions or accidentally mark the wrong answer choice. Look over any you skipped and make an educated guess.

At the end, leave the test feeling confident. You've done your best, so don't waste time worrying about your performance or wishing you could change anything. Instead, celebrate the successful completion of this test. And finally, use this test to learn how to deal with anxiety even better next time.

Review Video: Test Anxiety
Visit mometrix.com/academy and enter code: 100340

Important Qualification

Not all anxiety is created equal. If your test anxiety is causing major issues in your life beyond the classroom or testing center, or if you are experiencing troubling physical symptoms related to your anxiety, it may be a sign of a serious physiological or psychological condition. If this sounds like your situation, we strongly encourage you to seek professional help.

Additional Bonus Material

Due to our efforts to try to keep this book to a manageable length, we've created a link that will give you access to all of your additional bonus material:

mometrix.com/bonus948/pmp